Michel Remery

Tweeting
with
GOD

Big Bang, prayer, Bible,
sex, Crusades, sin, career ...

IGNATIUS PRESS   SAN FRANCISCO

Download the TwGOD app!

Available on the App Store

Get it on Google play

Find more information about every page in this book using the free #TwGOD app:

- Download the #TwGOD app: www.tweetingwithgod.com.
- Use the app to scan any title illustration **SCAN** (on left pages above the #TwGOD bird, hold your phone above the image).
- Watch videos, follow links, and read more, directly on your smartphone.

For the young people of the JP2 Group and the #TwGOD team

Original edition: *Twitteren met GOD interactief: Oerknal, bidden, Bijbel, seks, kruistochten, zonde, carrière …*
© 2012, 2014 by Michel Remery and JP2 Stichting, Leiden, Netherlands
Cover Photograph © 2009 by Roman Eisele
All rights reserved

Photo editor: Edith Peters
Graphic design: Patrick Jimenez

Imprimatur:
✠ J. van den Hende, Bishop of Rotterdam
July 23, 2012

English translation by Jonathan Price

Scripture quotations have been taken from the Revised Standard Version of the Holy Bible, Second Catholic Edition, © 2006 by the Division of Christian Education of the National Council of the Churches of Christ in the United States of America. All rights reserved.

Excerpts from the *Catechism of the Catholic Church*, Second Edition, © 2000 by Libreria Editrice Vaticana–United States Conference of Catholic Bishops, Washington, D.C. All rights reserved.

Excerpts from the *Compendium of the Catechism of the Catholic Church* © 2006 by Libreria Editrice Vaticana. All rights reserved.

Quotations from the popes and the official documents of the Catholic Church are from the Vatican website: http://w2.vatican.va. Used with permission.

Excerpts from the English translation of *Rite of Baptism for Children* © 1969, International Commission on English in the Liturgy Corporation (ICEL); excerpts from the English translation of *Rite of Marriage* © 1969, ICEL; excerpts from the English translation of *Rite of Confirmation* © 1975, ICEL; excerpts from the English translation of *Rite of Penance* © 1975, ICEL; excerpts from the English translation of *Pastoral Care of the Sick: Rites of Anointing and Viaticum* © 1982, ICEL; excerpts from the English translation of *Rites of Ordination of a Bishop, of Priests, and of Deacons* © 2000, 2002, ICEL; excerpts from the English translation of *The Roman Missal* © 2010, ICEL. All rights reserved. Used with permission.

English translations of *Magnificat, Benedictus, Nunc Dimittis* © 1988 English Language Liturgical Consultation (ELLC). www.englishtexts.org. Used with permission.

Sequences for Easter and Pentecost from the *Lectionary for Mass for Use in the Dioceses of the United States of America*, second typical edition © 2001, 1998, 1997, 1986, 1970 Confraternity of Christian Doctrine, Inc., Washington, DC. All rights reserved.

© 2015 by Michel Remery and JP2 Stichting, Leiden
Published 2015 by Ignatius Press, San Francisco
All rights reserved
ISBN: 978-1-62164-015-8
Library of Congress Control Number 2014959898
Printed in the United States of America ∞

About this book

This book can give you support if you want to grow in your faith and in your relationship with Jesus. The project *Tweeting with GOD* (#TwGOD) provides you with the basics about faith in God based on what the Bible and the Catholic Church teach. See also the website www.tweeting withgod.com and the #TwGOD app. The book can serve as a basis for group discussions or for a deepening of belief after a formal study of the faith. It can also help you to explain your faith to others. St. Peter calls on believers to "always be prepared to make a defense to any one who calls you to account for the hope that is in you" (I Pet. 3:15).

The questions in this book are real questions from young people. For a few years, young people gathered together every other week in the author's church in Leiden, Netherlands, (not far from Amsterdam) to discuss their faith. They called their group the JP2 Group, after Pope John Paul II (see Tweet 2.50). All topics were fair game, and nothing was taboo. So, do not expect a complete catechesis in this book (see Tweet 1.9). The answers are formulated as they would be when talking with young people; they are not scholarly or exhaustive. The questions are grouped in the book around global topics to make them easier to find.

Pope Francis called the project *Tweeting with GOD* very important. While he placed his hand on one of the books to bless the project, he prayed for a few moments for all the people who will read these books in search of the truth in their lives (see Picture). His words are directed also to you: "Today, Jesus is calling each of you to follow him in his Church and to be missionaries. The Lord is calling you today! Not the masses, but you, and you, and you, each one of you. Listen to what he is saying to you in your heart" (Homily, July 27, 2013). (See Tweet 4.3–4.4).

This book deals with the essence of faith, God, the Creation, the Bible, and the ways that God relates to us. It also deals with the origin and history of the Church and how the Church is present in the world. Furthermore the book deals with prayer, how difficult life can be, the role of the church building, and what the liturgy and the sacraments do for us. It also deals with the Christian life and the different choices that you may be confronted with as a believer.

Read more

In the "Read more" boxes you will find references to texts that further explain or develop a particular topic. Most references have paragraph numbers. Texts include the following:

- the Bible (see Appendix 1 for a list of abbreviations),
- the *Catechism of the Catholic Church* (CCC),
- the *Compendium of the Catechism of the Catholic Church* (CCCC), and
- *Youth Catechism of the Catholic Church* (YOUCAT),

Find direct links to these and many more sources via the app or at www.tweetingwithgod.com.

Preface

This book was written for you! There may be all sorts of reasons why you picked it up. Maybe you liked the title. Maybe you are looking for answers. Maybe it was a gift. Maybe people are asking you about your faith. Or perhaps you picked it up because you were bored. Whatever the reason, as you start reading, I would like to suggest four things.

Dare to ask!

You're free to ask questions. Your questions express your thoughts and doubts. They tell you about who you are, what you long for, and what you have to do. Answers help you to move forward. In this book, I'm sure you'll run into lots of your questions (and hopefully some answers).

Dare to think!

Everyone can think. But *really* thinking is something we do not do all that often. Do you ever think about who you are? Where you came from? Where you're going? Or, are you mostly concerned with your daily life? I challenge you to think about the answers in this book.

Dare to listen!

Listening can be quite difficult, especially if deep down you think you already know the answers. Real listening can be quite confrontational. It can teach you about who you are, what you truly think, and what you believe. The Tweets in this book may help you with that.

Dare to have faith!

Having faith in Jesus is not so bizarre or illogical as some people think. Quite the contrary: many questions can be answered only through our faith in Jesus. But we don't believe only with our heads. Perhaps even more importantly, we believe also with our hearts.

My own vocation

When we talk about callings, young people often ask me about my own vocation to become a priest. After my studies at Delft Technical University, I enjoyed my job as an architect, had a wonderful girlfriend, a good salary, excellent career opportunities, and a nice car. Everything was going well, and I did not think about becoming a priest. But at some point something began to gnaw inside me. I was restless, and I did not understand why. I had everything I could desire, didn't I? After a while, I asked a priest to be my spiritual director (SEE TWEET 3.4&4.6).

First I learned to pray. Then I learned to trust God. That was not easy! And to be honest, it is still not always easy. But I noticed that I was becoming less concerned merely about what I wanted and that everything God asked of me seemed good. Eventually there came a day when I knew the answer during prayer: to be truly happy with God I had to be a priest. The decision to do so is still the best decision of my life! Similarly, God has a plan for you. And the great thing is that you will certainly be happy if you cooperate with his plan. For this reason, I challenge you to trust God and to seek your calling (SEE TWEET 4.6).

SCAN

Faith in God is not always easy. When I studied architecture, I used to go to church occasionally, but I saw only old people there. It seemed clear to me that the Church would not continue to exist for much longer. That changed, however, when I attended World Youth Day in Manila and met young Catholics from all over the world. Not only were they my age, but they were full of enthusiasm for Jesus and his Church.

Getting to know Jesus has been a long journey for me, and there are still many things I don't know about him. So, I keep asking questions. But in my heart I am sure that I can rely on him and on the Church. I trust him. That is faith. In my life I have discovered that Jesus wants to be my friend – a friend who cares about me and wishes the best for me. That's why I am happy, even when I have to go through difficulties, and even when I'm sad or in pain – because I'm not alone!

I really hope that this book will help you to discover this for yourself. Jesus wants to be your friend too. He only wants one thing: that you will be happy in this life and the next. That's why he wants to help you to know him better, to talk to him, to pray. He wants to help you to see how much sense it makes to have faith. He wants to answer all your questions.

Father Michel Remery

Table of Contents

Part 1 – Tweets about God: the Beginning & the End

Introduction by Timothy Michael Cardinal Dolan, Archbishop of New York

Part 2 – Tweets about the Church: Origin & Future

Introduction by José H. Gomez, Archbishop of Los Angeles

Part 3 – Tweets about You & God: Prayer & Sacraments

Introduction by James Conley, S.T.L., Bishop of Lincoln, Nebraska

Part 4 - Tweets about Christian Life: Faith & Ethics

Introduction by Salvatore Cordileone, Archbishop of San Francisco

Part 1

Tweets about God: the Beginning & the End

Introduction

Of all the events and appointments on my calendar, I especially look forward to those three or four nights throughout the year when I celebrate Mass for young adults at Saint Patrick's Cathedral in New York City. The cathedral is packed with over 2,000 men and women, working professionals in their 20s and 30s, who are seeking a closer relationship with Jesus through his Church, hungry for the truth and eager for fellowship and support from other faithful Catholics their own age. They come hoping that as their bishop I will be able to help them in their faith journey, and I certainly try to do that for them.

But, they also inspire me to a deeper faith, for if in this city that is the very center of business, communications, culture, and entertainment – called the "capital of the world" by Pope Saint John Paul II – there still exists this yearning for God, then I know that the future of the Church is in very good shape.

I often spend extra time after these Masses, meeting with those present and answering their questions. Some questions are simple and fun, like what kind of music do I enjoy listening to or who would I root for in a Saint Louis Cardinal/New York Yankee World Series. But most reflect the challenges that these young adults experience in living out their faith in today's world, a world that often tells them that their beliefs are foolish, old-fashioned, and out of step with reality.

Tweeting with GOD by Fr. Michel Remery taps into the longing for Jesus, and the desire for a closer relationship with him, that so many young people feel today. He tackles their questions with straightforward answers, all presented in a clear, concise format. Everything is addressed: from is there a God, why did he create us and the universe, and is the Bible true, to who was Jesus, why is Mary so important, what does it mean to have faith, and how can we know our ultimate goal in this life – and the next.

Before someone can love Jesus, he has to get to know him. Jesus himself understood this. Remember what he told his first disciples? "Come, follow me." Spend time with me. Listen to me. It's the same invitation that he extends to you and me today! And what did he tell those Apostles just before he went up to heaven? "Go, therefore, and make disciples of all nations, baptizing them in the name of the Father, and of the Son, and of the Holy Spirit, teaching them to observe all that I have commanded you. And behold, I am with you always, until the end of the age."

This book inspires us to obey that last command! @DonMichelRemery combines the timeless teaching of our faith with the best of modern technology, and #TwGOD is a great way for us to follow our Lord's final instruction!

✠ Timothy Michael Cardinal Dolan
Archbishop of New York
@cardinaldolan

SCAN

1.1 Doesn't the Big Bang rule out faith in God?

For a long time, scientists have been trying to learn more about how the world came into existence. In Europe, for example, an institute for the study of physics, the European Organization for Nuclear Research (CERN), constructed a machine to try to model the Big Bang. That's very interesting, highly technical stuff. However, some people think that the Church is against that sort of thing and only accepts the biblical story of Creation in Genesis (SEE TWEET 1.2) as an explanation for how the universe came into being (often called creationism). But that certainly isn't true. The Church is not at all opposed to science. Quite the opposite!

Catholic wisdom

Throughout the ages, the Church has nurtured many great scientists (SEE BOX). For example, it was a Catholic priest, Fr. Georges Lemaître (†1966), who first suggested the theory of the Big Bang. He was honored by the Church in several ways, which in itself shows that his theory does not contradict the claims of faith.

In fact, whereas Fr. Lemaître's ideas met a lot of resistance from outside the Church, he was supported by Pope Pius XII (†1958). Although the Big Bang theory does not directly prove creation by God, it is certainly compatible with the biblical story of Creation, in which God first said: "Let there be light" (GEN. 1:3). There is nothing to stop us from seeing God as the one who struck the match for this creative firecracker some 14 billion years ago!

Origin of life

Like the Big Bang, the theory of genetics was also first developed by a priest, Gregor Mendel (SEE TWEET 1.3). The picture of the universe and of life presented by such theories includes gradual development over time. This picture is consonant with a Catholic understanding of the world in which God gives his creatures the dignity of contributing to this unfolding development (SEE TWEET 1.3). Indeed the Latin word for unfold, *evolvere*, which was used by St. Augustine in the early fifth century to describe the development of the universe, is the origin of the modern word

Who are the best-known Catholic scientists?

There are a lot of Catholics among the great scientists and scholars of history. The Franciscan Roger Bacon (†1292), for example, was ordered by the pope to write a book about philosophy and natural science. Cardinal Nicolas of Cusa (†1464) developed lenses to help near-sighted people. Catholics were the first to map the world: think of Marco Polo (†1324), Bartholomeu Dias (†1500), and Christopher Columbus (†1506).

The brilliant works of Leonardo da Vinci (†1519) are well known. But don't forget Nicolas Copernicus (†1543), who first brought forward the theory that the earth revolves around the sun. The Jesuit scholar Fr. Matteo Ricci (†1610) was the first to work on a Chinese dictionary. Another Jesuit, Fr. Angelo Secchi (†1878), was the first to classify stars according to their spectra (spectroscopy).

Jean-Baptiste Lamarck (†1884) was the first to formulate a theory of evolution and Gregor Mendel (†1884) is the father of genetics (SEE TWEET 1.3). These learned men were all Catholics, as were Alessandro Volta (†1827) and André-Marie Ampère (†1836), who made great discoveries in the field of electricity.

evolution. In this discussion it is important to understand the limitations of scientific theories about the origins of the universe: they can describe only how things have changed over time. Since the things they describe are not self-causing (they did not create themselves), there remains a need for a first cause (SEE TWEET 1.9). This initial cause of all things we call God. Moreover, Catholic thinkers, along with others, have perceived great order and beauty in the way the universe is put together. Although not a formal proof, this underlying order is conducive to belief that the universe is the work of a creative, divine intellect.

Creation out of nothing

The story of Creation tells us how God has made the world with great care. He made everything out of nothing (*ex nihilo*, in Latin). He made both the vast universe with all its solar systems and the smallest molecule in your body. When you realize this, you experience God's closeness and know he is everywhere, even in deep space; if a space traveller were floating in the darkness between planets, God would be present there (Ps. 139:8–12).

> The Big Bang theory does not rule out faith in God. On the contrary, it can be believed as the way God began his creation of the universe.

Read more

Creation: CCC 282–299; CCCC 54; YOUCAT 43.

SCAN

1.2 But seriously, did all that Adam and Eve business really happen?

The Bible tells us about the creation of Adam and Eve, the first man and woman. The fact that there are two different creation stories, one directly following the other (GEN. 1:26–28; 2:7–8, 18–24), shows us that we cannot take them as literal descriptions of what happened. Nevertheless, they are not nonsense. It's not so much the how of creation that matters here, but the why.

Adam and Eve's story tells us a lot about the relationship between man and God and about the way people relate to each other. For example, it tells us that God created us according to his plan and that "God saw everything that he had made, and behold, it was very good" (GEN 1:31). Because of this, we can be happy with what and who we are. The story also tells us that we are all one family, with Adam and Eve as our common ancestors, and that we all share in the same "genetic disease": our fallen human nature, which leads us to sin (SEE TWEET 1.4).

A responsible task

When God created the world he paid particular attention to the creation of mankind. He made us as creatures in his image, after his likeness (GEN. 1:26). This gave us a unique place in creation (SEE TWEET 1.48). God loves us, and we can love both God and other people. God made us as male and female for the companionship of marriage (GEN. 2:24; SEE TWEET 4.19). We were given responsibility for the world, so much so that we were given the task of naming all living creatures (GEN. 2:19). God said to Adam and Eve: "Be fruitful and multiply, and fill the earth and subdue it; and have dominion over the fish of the sea and over the birds of the air and over every living thing that moves upon the earth" (GEN. 1:28). This responsibility involves respect for creation (CCC 2415; SEE TWEET 4.48). So, caring for the environment is very Catholic!

Was God alone?

"In the beginning God created the heavens and the earth" (GEN. 1:1), says the Bible. But he wasn't alone: "The Spirit of God was moving

Brother against brother

Adam and Eve had children. Their eldest son, Cain, was a farmer; his brother Abel was a shepherd. When both brothers made an offering to God, God accepted only the offering of Abel (GEN. 4:4–5). Cain was furious and killed his brother. When God asked him where Abel was, he said: "I do not know; am I my brother's keeper?" (GEN. 4:9). God said: "What have you done? The voice of your brother's blood is crying to me from the ground" (GEN. 4:10). As punishment, Cain had to leave his land. God told him: "When you till the ground, it shall no longer yield to you its strength; you shall be a fugitive and a wanderer on the earth" (GEN. 4:12). In spite of Cain's horrible deed, God continued to love him and showed it by making sure nobody harmed him.

over the face of the waters" (GEN. 1:2). That is the Holy Spirit. The New Testament says that Jesus – the living Word of God (SEE TWEET 1.29) – was with God at the beginning: "In the beginning was the Word, and the Word was with God, and the Word was God" (JN. 1:1). Whenever we read "God said …" (GEN. 1:3), Jesus was also present. Actually, Jesus is the Word that God spoke! This is a good example of how the New Testament explains the Old Testament (SEE TWEET 1.10). God has always existed in three Persons (SEE TWEET 1.33). For that reason, St. Paul said all things were created through Christ and for Christ (COL. 1:16–17).

Six days?

The story of Creation is a beautiful, poetic tale (GEN. 1–2). But do Catholics have to close their eyes to what science has to say about the beginning of the earth? Certainly not! In the fourth century, for example, St. Augustine wrote that the days mentioned in the Bible are not actual days (sunrise to sunset), because the sun was created only on the fourth day! (DE CIVITATE DEI XI,7). Okay. Not literally six days, then. But why then do we still read the story of Creation? Because it presents us with some very important truths about God, the world, and man. It is not just a story with a moral, but revealed, symbolic history. For example, it tells us that there is only one true God, instead of many gods; that when God created the world he paid particular attention to us, whom he also created; and that his creation was very good before evil came into the world (SEE TWEET 1.36).

> The story of Adam and Eve is not a scientific explanation of the origins of mankind, but it speaks to us about our human condition.

Read more

The creation of man: CCC 343; CCCC 63; YOUCAT 56. *Respect for creation:* CCC 2415–2418, 2450–2451, 2453–2455; CCCC 506–508; YOUCAT 436–437. *The Creator:* CCC 279–292, 315–316; CCCC 51–52; YOUCAT 41, 44. *Creation:* CCC 337–349, 353–354; CCCC 62–65; YOUCAT 46–48.

SCAN

1.3 Evolution or creation?

The theory of evolution, which is taught in schools everywhere, is not in itself contrary to Catholic faith. It was a Catholic priest, Fr. Gregor Mendel (†1884), who developed the theory of genetic heredity, which provides the foundation for the modern understanding of Darwinian evolution. The human body could well have evolved in some way.

Survival of the fittest?

But from knowledge of evolution we should not conclude that people are merely animals or that human actions must be guided by the principles discovered by Charles Darwin (†1882), whereby species flourish when only the strongest survive and evolve (as in the "survival of the fittest"). Such ideas can lead to social injustice and even to terrible violence against the weaker members of society (think of the National Socialism of the Nazis, which championed the survival of the fittest). The theory of evolution can help us to understand the way living organisms develop over time, but it must not be a basis for denying the equal dignity of all human beings, who whether weak or strong have been created by God in his own image. For this reason, we as Christians have a particular concern for the weaker members of society. The social teaching of the Church is based on this (SEE TWEET 4.45).

Human animals?

All animals have a remarkable ability to adapt to their natural habitat, and they have a power to act and a desire to flourish not found in machines. Human beings, however, have capacities far beyond those of animals. To illustrate this difference, the philosopher Ludwig Wittgenstein (†1951) said that a dog knows its master, but not that its master is coming home the day after tomorrow. G. K. Chesterton (†1936) observed that birds build nests, but they do not build nests in the Gothic style (EVERLASTING MAN). Such examples illustrate that animals do not think in terms of time or about any of the abstract ideas that make possible language, art, architecture, ethics, science, philosophy, or theology. We human

What about dinosaurs and aliens?

The existence of dinosaurs has clearly been proven by palaeontologists and other scientists. The earth is many billions of years old and has gone through different geological phases. This does not contradict the Catholic view on the origin of the earth. Pope John Paul II once said: "The truth cannot contradict the truth" (Oct. 22, 1996). Real scientific truths will never be in contradiction with the truth of the faith (SEE TWEET 1.5). Therefore, the Church is not afraid of science.

Once in a while we are surprised by vague photographs that seem to depict a UFO or an extraterrestrial creature. Some say God wanted to practice first before he created human beings, and so he made aliens. But there is no indication at all of this in the Bible or in good science.

Although astronomers can see ever more of the universe, life beyond earth has not been found, although there are planets where that is a theoretical possibility. Even if there is life outside earth, it has been created by God in love. For this reason, we do not have to worry about questions concerning aliens.

beings, on the other hand, are able to think abstractly. Our thoughts and desires can go beyond our instinct to survive in this moment. This supports the idea of human beings having immortal souls. Animals are satisfied to be what they are, but human persons seek ultimate happiness and are discontent with finite, created things alone.

Immortal soul

Our souls make us the persons we are and give us the freedom to make conscious choices. Unlike animals we can make choices based on our sense of what is morally right and wrong. We do so by consulting our conscience, our knowledge of good and evil (SEE TWEET 4.1 AND 4.12). God loves every human being so much that he gave each one a soul that will continue to live after his body dies. God created our souls the very moment that our lives began, at conception (SEE TWEET 4.26). Our souls are the core of our lives; they make us human, giving us minds and wills. Because we have human souls, we are able to love God and one another.

 Evolution and creation are not mutually exclusive. Evolution is evident in nature, but we, with our souls, have been created by God.

Read more

Evolution: CCC 282–289; CCCC 51; YOUCAT 42. *The soul:* CCC 362–368, 382; CCCC 69–70; YOUCAT 62–63.

1.4 What are original sin and the fall of man anyway?

For us Christians, it is essential that God created the world out of love. But what is also crucial is how mankind deals with it. God created everything good (GEN. 1:25). But that is not our only experience of the world! Natural disasters, war, poverty, crime, and disease; if you look around, you see that the world is full of suffering and evil.

A heavy freedom

There is evil in the world because God has given us free choice (SEE TWEET 1.34). We can consciously choose for God or against him. You can love someone only if you are left free to choose whom to love. Naturally, God wants us to choose to love him. That is why he created us! But because we are free, we can also reject God, which is sin and which separates us from God. In our weakness we are tempted to abuse our freedom and to deny God by choosing against him. Even if we do not want to sin, often evil strongly appeals to us. As a consequence of original sin, we are easily tempted (SEE BOX).

The fruit and the snake

The story of Adam and Eve tells about the first, that is, the original, sin (SEE BOX). They were tempted by evil (GEN. 3). They knew very well what God wanted. He was very clear: there was one tree from which they may not eat the fruit, or they would die (GEN. 3:3). Only one forbidden tree in all of paradise, with so many other trees! Yet they listened to an evil voice, which in the Bible is portrayed as a serpent. The voice promised them that they would not die but would become like God, knowing good and evil, if they would only eat the forbidden fruit (GEN. 3:5). The latter at least was true: quickly afterward, they did learn about evil.

After disobeying God's command, Adam and Eve dared not look at God anymore and concealed themselves from him (GEN. 3:8). They were ashamed of their nakedness and clothed themselves in fig leaves (as the couple is often depicted in art) (GEN. 3:7). Thus they kept their distance from the one who had made them and

What is original sin?

You could say that we are born into a history of evil, the series of personal sins committed by those who came before us. Unfortunately, each generation passes on many troubles to the next generation. Original sin is not the same as these personal sins. Original sin is the loss of "original holiness and justice" (CCC 405) through the first sin. This first sin was committed by Adam, or "first man", who freely chose to disobey God (GEN. 3).

Because of original sin human nature is wounded (SEE TWEET 4.10). Humanity is no longer perfect as it was at the Creation because our closeness to God has been disrupted. Our minds are darkened, and our wills are weakened; we are subject to ignorance, deception, and disordered desires. As a result, nobody is without sin and everyone must die at some point.

Yet Baptism washes away both original sin and all our own sins (SEE TWEET 3.36). What remains after Baptism is concupiscence, which is a strong tendency toward pleasure that weakens us and tempts us to go beyond the limits God gives us. Thus, time and again we need God's forgiveness, which he gladly gives to those who honestly ask for it in the Sacrament of Reconciliation (SEE TWEET 3.38).

who really loved them. The first sin is called the Fall because it put distance between God and man. The book of Genesis shows how, with the Fall, man lost his original innocence and as a result his closeness to God, who is the source of life and love.

A divine poem

The Adam and Eve story tells us a lot about God and the human condition in a poetic form. This revealed history communicates in a symbolic way things that truly happened. Mankind's first disobedience, which brought sin into the world, is both a fact and a lesson important for people of every age. The story sheds a lot of light on the situation in which we now find ourselves. It shows us how important it is to choose to follow God and to respect the limits he gives us (CCC 396). The Fall disrupted the beauty of creation. Separated from the source of life, man was destined to die, which was not originally the plan of God. Yet, with the birth of Jesus, God changed that forever (SEE TWEET 1.26).

> The first man & woman fell from God when they chose against him and committed the first, original, sin. We have inherited their fallen condition.

Read more

God's original plan: CCC 374–379, 384; CCCC 72; YOUCAT 66. *The Fall:* CCC 386–390; CCCC 73; YOUCAT 67–68.
Original sin: CCC 396–409, 415–419; CCCC 75–77; YOUCAT 68–69.

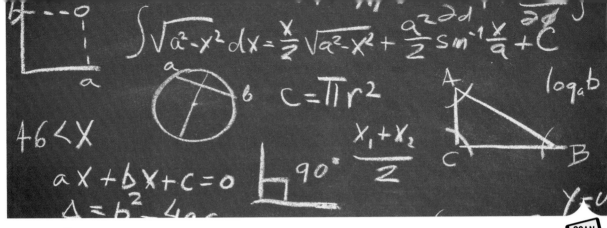

1.5 Do science and faith contradict each other?

Creation or coincidence?

Sometimes it may seem as if faith and science contradict each other. But that really isn't true. Science has never shown that faith in Jesus Christ is unjustified. The Church does not oppose scientific research. Quite the contrary: there have always been plenty of Catholic scientists (SEE TWEET 1.1). Also, there has been a Pontifical Academy of Sciences for centuries. The Church does teach, however, that scientific research must take place within certain moral and ethical limits. For example, research may never deliberately harm human dignity or life. For this reason, research that involves the destruction of human embryos should not be allowed (SEE TWEET 4.34).

Freedom through truth
Some scientists and believers have become stuck in their own ways of looking at the world and are incapable of putting their own ideas up for discussion; they reject anything that seems to contradict them. History has plenty of examples of some heated discussions, for instance, the case of Galileo Galilei (SEE BOX).

We don't have to be afraid of the truths that science can discover. Jesus himself said: "The truth will make you free" (JN. 8:32). That means we can certainly ask questions, investigate, and conduct scientific research. Doing so can help us to grow in our faith, because we can see how beautiful God has made the world. But there's more than just exact science: not everything can be counted or measured. For example, the study of theology tries to find answers to questions about God.

God's work
Speaking of the complex structure of the universe, Pope Benedict XVI, quoting a psalm, said that the starry heavens "proclaim the glory of God" (SEE PS. 19(18):1). And he added that the results of scientific research enable us to praise God, as they improve our understanding of the laws of nature. This way, we are encouraged to "look upon the work of the Lord with gratitude" (ANGELUS, DEC. 21, 2008). At the same time, we should never lose sight of the fact that God is always greater than what science can

Was the Church wrong about Galileo Galilei?

The Italian scholar Galileo Galilei (†1642) is often mentioned as an example of a scientist at odds with the Church. As the story goes, Church leaders silenced Galileo simply because he had said that the heliocentric theory of Copernicus (†1543) was true, that the earth revolved around the sun. This notion met with a lot of opposition, both inside and outside the Church, and lacking sufficient proof, Galileo was forced to withdraw to his villa for the rest of his life. Still, his daughter became a nun.

Later Galileo was proved to be mostly right. However, the Galileo affair is much more complex than often portrayed, with misunderstandings on both sides, and on more matters than the solar system. When the scientific evidence became clear, the Church accepted that the earth revolved around the sun. The contributions of Galileo to science have since been praised by the Church, and his name has been cleared of all blame. Pope Pius XII called him a great scientist (DEC. 3, 1939). Pope John Paul II regretted that Galileo suffered much at the hands of Church leaders (NOV. 10, 1979) and formally asked forgiveness for their treatment of him (MAR. 12, 2000).

discover about his creation. That's why faith in Jesus Christ remains the single most important thing, because only he, as the Son of God, can reveal the full truth about his Father.

Faith and science

The Second Vatican Council, an important gathering of the Church (SEE TWEET 2.48), wrote in 1965 that God "can be known with certainty from created reality by the light of human reason" (DEI VERBUM, 6). By using their reason, that is, by thinking carefully, people can come to the conclusion that God exists (SEE TWEET 1.6).

Faith and science are both very important. Pope John Paul II wrote an encyclical (a papal letter) about the relationship between faith and human reason: "Faith and reason (*fides et ratio*) are like two wings on which the human spirit rises to the contemplation of truth; and God has placed in the human heart a desire to know the truth – in a word, to know himself – so that, by knowing and loving God, men and women may also come to the fullness of truth about themselves" (FIDES ET RATIO, INTRODUCTION).

> The truth, whether it is discovered through science or faith, does not contradict itself. Jesus said: "The truth will make you free."

Read more

Science and creation: CCC 282–289; CCCC 51; YOUCAT 41. *Laws in creation:* CCC 339, 346, 354; CCCC 62, 64; YOUCAT 45.

Creation or coincidence?

1.6 Can I recognize God in nature and in the world?

From time to time, we hear stories in the news about how a journalist has published secret documents on the Internet. Sometimes this information is a real revelation to society. Writers, artists, and musicians also reveal things to us. If you read a text, study a work of art, or listen to a musical composition carefully, you can learn something about the person who created it.

If you look at the natural world and see how beautifully everything fits together, several questions almost automatically present themselves.

Where does it all come from?

You may know the feeling of wonder, of (almost) reverence when you see a newborn baby. Everything that's necessary to become a fully grown man or woman is already present: 10 little fingers, 2 shining eyes, and a tiny mouth that nevertheless produces lots of noise. Or maybe you know the experience when, tired of climbing, you reach the top of

a mountain and, still panting, look around to take in the gorgeous view. At such a time, you may wonder: "Where did all this come from?" In a couple of weeks an entire plant can grow from a small seed. After a seed germinates and pops open, all the principal parts of a plant are already there in miniature. Step-by-step they grow and mature. Nature works so wonderfully well that you may ask how it could have been a coincidence that it came to be this way.

Questions about the beginning

If you would take the time and effort to look carefully, you would start to ask yourself questions about the origin of everything. Could there be someone who made it all so beautiful? Could man be more than an accident of nature?

There are many interesting scientific theories about the origins of the earth and the life upon it, but there isn't a single one that can explain everything (SEE TWEET 1.1). In short, none of these theories is complete without assuming that a

26

God as a gardener

A Catholic who was ridiculed by some atheists because of his belief in God pulled out his mobile telephone and a pocket knife. He opened the back of the phone and laid it on the table between them. "If I were to tell you that all these little electronic components fell into place purely by accident," he said, "then you'd have a big laugh at me. But now look at nature. Wouldn't it be quite a coincidence if it had all developed and ordered itself by accident?" Our awe in observing the complexity and beauty of nature can encourage us to believe in God.

However, creation is not a dead mechanism, and God is not like a computer designer or a watchmaker who sends his creations into the world without any further thought. God is more like a gardener who continuously cares for his garden. Jesus compared his Father to a vinedresser who cares for the vines he has planted, cutting away the branches that have withered or died and tending those that can still survive. In this image, Jesus himself is the vine, and all the people together in him form the branches. Thus he invites everyone to remain united with him (Jn. 15,1).

mind or a creator is behind it all. We call that God. In this way, many great thinkers have come to the conclusion that God must exist and that he created the world.

Nature reveals God

If that is true, then we must also be able to learn something about God by looking at his creation, at nature. St. Paul said: "Ever since the creation of the world his invisible nature, namely, his eternal power and deity, has been clearly perceived in the things that have been made" (Rom. 1:20). Even though there's a lot we don't know about God, he has revealed a number of important things about himself in nature. For example, that he exists and has created the world. That's why we sometimes speak of the natural revelation of God.

Many questions remain, however. Does God continue to care for the world? (See box.) If he is still concerned with the world, why do natural disasters happen? These kinds of questions we will save for later (see Tweet 1.35). For now it's enough to conclude that we can know something about God and his revelation by looking at his creation called nature.

> Just like an artist, God reveals something of himself in his creation. Surely the order and beauty that we see did not come about by accident.

Read more

God in nature: CCC 31–36; CCCC 3; YOUCAT 4.

1.7 Why should I believe in God?

SCAN

Hidden deep inside each person there is a longing for God. But that longing can be quite difficult to identify. Our lives are full of all sorts of stressful activities. It is often only after a profound experience of something really important that we realize that this longing is even there. At that point we learn to listen to the voice of conscience, which tells us the difference between good and evil and which ultimately points to God (SEE TWEET 4.1). There are also signs of God's existence in the world. Just look at the complexity of everything. Did it all simply come into being by chance? Or is God behind it? (SEE TWEET 1.6.)

God longs for you

Whether you believe in him or not, God loves you. Ultimately it was God who, through your parents, gave you life. And God goes further than that: he wants to give you his own life through Jesus (SEE TWEET 1.26). You too can live with God! For that to happen, you need only to accept the plan he has for you and then to cooperate with it (SEE TWEET 4.3). The aim of the plan is to make you happy, both now and forever in heaven (SEE TWEET 1.45). Like a parent who loves his child, God wants only what is best for you (ROM. 8:14). Jesus taught us that we can freely speak to God as our Father. He understands everything and sends us the Holy Spirit, who helps us to believe (SEE TWEET 1.32).

Should I believe because others want me to?

We can answer this in one word: no. No one can believe because he should or must. You can only believe willingly, from your heart. And no one but you is master of your heart. You can begin to believe once you start to know God. Although your parents or friends may or may not like it, the choice is yours alone.

If you can come to the point where you really listen to the part of yourself that wants to know more about God, then you can believe that he exists and that he loves you. Ultimately, faith is a gift from God, but it is a gift we can ask for in prayer. Just like the man whose son was

True or important?

The English author C. S. Lewis once said: "Christianity is a statement which, if false, is of *no* importance, and, if true, of infinite importance. The one thing it cannot be is moderately important" (CHRISTIAN APOLOGETICS). The conclusion is that a person should choose to live as a Christian "to be on the safe side". If God does not exist, when the believer dies he would have led a good life and might merely discover that there is no life after death (or not realize this, since he would be dead). But if God does indeed exist, and a person lived as if he did not, by breaking God's commands without remorse, then he would have a problem when he died: he would have little chance of making right what he had done wrong!

C. S. Lewis (†1963) was an important defender of the Christian faith. He was good friends with fellow author J. R. R. Tolkien (*The Lord of the Rings*). Give his books a try: start with *The Screwtape Letters* and *Mere Christianity*. He also wrote the series The Chronicles of Narnia.

seriously ill, you can say to Jesus: "I believe; help my unbelief!" (MK. 9:24). When you are convinced that God exists, you can overcome any difficulties – not because they don't exist anymore, but because you are no longer facing them alone!

Happiness

We long for complete happiness, which is always just a little out of reach. Many people try to find happiness in the things we commonly associate with success: career, luxuries, power, possessions, and fame (SEE TWEET 3.7). But people who rely solely on these things end up disappointed. Ultimately, complete happiness can be found only in God. As God's creation (GEN. 1:26), we have a natural longing for him (SEE TWEET 4.1). However, in

practice we often seem to run away from God! Sometimes it is only after trying everything else that we find God. God promised the people of Israel a bountiful life in freedom, but they had to suffer for 40 years before they could enter the Promised Land (SEE TWEET 1.24). Our lives are also full of difficulties. Still, a happy end with God is waiting for us, just as the Promised Land awaited the Israelites.

Your ultimate happiness can be found only in God, who made you, knows you, and loves you: Do you need any other reason to believe?

Read more

Longing for God: CCC 27; CCCC 2; YOUCAT 3.

1.8 Could there be only one truth?

"What is truth?" Pilate asked when Jesus said to him: "For this I have come into the world, to bear witness to the truth" (Jn. 18:37). Many people wonder what truth is. It's a very good question.

Feel, think, believe

In the thirteenth century the great thinker St. Thomas Aquinas asked the same question. He said that "truth is the correspondence of thought and the thing" (Summa I.16.1). Sometimes we change our minds or opinions about something. Then it isn't the things in themselves that change, but rather, the way we see them. We must continuously try to make sure that our thoughts about things correspond to the way they really are, because both the way we perceive things and how we consider them can be mistaken!

For this reason St. Thomas said that we can find the truth through the use of our senses (empirical truth), through reflection (philosophical truth), and through our faith as revealed by God (theological truth). By reflecting on our experiences in the world, and by combining this with what Jesus told us, we can come to know the truth about God and ourselves.

My truth or the Truth?

Jesus said: "Every one who is of the truth hears my voice" (Jn. 18:37). He often spoke about the truth and said that only the truth will make us free (Jn. 8:32). God's Word is truth (Jn. 17:17), and Jesus said of himself: "I am the way, and the truth, and the life; no one comes to the Father, but by me" (Jn. 14:6). In the words of St. Thomas, Jesus is the perfect correspondence between God and us. Therefore, Jesus is like a bridge between heaven and earth. Jesus is the Truth. Not everyone agrees with that. Many people think that truth is relative and depends on what a person thinks, feels, or believes (SEE BOX). They think that each person can simultaneously hang on to his own truth, even when each person's truth is different from everyone else's. Since the truth in this case is what a person (or subject) thinks, truth is thought to be *subjective*.

A little fable about truth

An old fable tells of a group of blind men who encountered an elephant for the first time in the palace of the rajah. The blind man who stuck out his hand and touched the elephant's side said that an elephant is as smooth as a wall. But the man who touched its trunk said that an elephant is as round as a snake. The one who took hold of its tusk said that an elephant is as sharp as a spear, and the one who grasped its tail said that an elephant is as thin as a rope.

What's the truth? The rajah said that all the men were correct in a way, but that they could discover the whole truth about the elephant only by putting all the pieces together. This fable is often cited in order to illustrate that no single religion is right, that each one reveals a little bit of God. This conclusion is overly simplistic; just look at how much the different religions directly contradict each other. The funny thing is that the fable is also often used to say that we can never learn the real truth. But the rajah in the fable rightly said that the blind men could know the truth by putting all the pieces together. The elephant does not change because of the way in which it is talked about. Although the men had different, subjective conceptions of the elephant, in reality there was only one elephant in the palace, with objectively determinable characteristics. So there is one truth after all. In the same way there is only one God. We can find pieces of the truth about him in creation (SEE TWEET 1. 6), in the words God has spoken to us (SEE TWEET 1.10), and in the life and death of Jesus (SEE TWEET 1.26).

Actual truth

Jesus speaks of an *objective* truth, his own person, which is valid for everyone, independent of what he believes. Some trees, for instance, seem to be dead in the winter. But that is not the case, since they begin to bloom again each spring. You could say that *for you* the truth is that the trees die and then come back to life again, but that isn't actually *the* truth. In fact, the trees stay alive and only change their appearance. The latter is *objectively* true. The message of the Gospels is also objectively true, whatever other people think, say, or believe (SEE TWEET 1.20). This truth becomes concrete and tangible when you consider that Jesus walked the earth as a man. Through everything he said and did, Jesus proclaimed who God is: our Creator, who loves us and who hopes that we accept his invitation to be happy forever in heaven. This is the most important truth that we could ever discover.

> Truth does not depend on what people think (subjective), but is what actually exists (objective), and thus is true. Jesus is the truth.

Read more

God is truth: CCC 214–217, 231; CCCC 41; YOUCAT 32.

1.9 Is it logical to believe? Can I ask questions?

SCAN

It usually does no harm to ask questions. Quite the opposite, in fact, questions often show that you're thinking about your faith! When Jesus was 12 he was already asking questions of the teachers in the Temple, "and all who heard him were amazed at his understanding and his answers" (Lk. 2:46–7). By asking questions you can delve deeper into the truths of your faith.

Explaining the faith

Pope Benedict XVI said during a meeting with journalists how important it is to "present the reasons for faith" (Nov. 26, 2010). Books like *Tweeting with GOD* can help you to think about what your faith means to you. At the same time it is good to realize that there is something even more important: the fundamental truth that God loves us.

"Whatever is proposed by the pastor, whether it be the exercise of faith, of hope, or of some moral virtue, the love of our Lord should at the same time be so strongly insisted upon as to show clearly that all the works of perfect Christian virtue can have no other origin, no other end than divine love" (ROMAN CATECHISM, INTRODUCTION, 17).

Does God fit into our understanding?

We can get to know God through the use of our minds. Whereas our understanding is limited, God is not. So, we can never completely know or comprehend God. Yet, God has revealed himself in such a way that we learn something about him through each of his actions in history (SEE TWEET 1.6). That's why it is good to ask critical questions, especially when you are really striving for an answer. This often requires continued and persistent searching.

At the same time, there may be questions to which we cannot find the answers. Sometimes God cannot be contained in an answer. In these cases, when God is incomprehensible to us, we can approach the truth by quietly contemplating his greatness and his love.

Is it logical to believe?

Who, in fact, is God? Is he a human invention to answer questions such as "Why am I here?" or "Why must people die?" Does God exist merely in the minds of weak people who find comfort in a fantastic hero? The father of communism, Karl Marx (†1883), called religion "the opium of the people" that keeps them sedated. Is faith an illusion or a placebo? Or is there more to it? Through the centuries many learned scholars have contemplated the existence of God and come to the conclusion that God must exist. Aristotle, a Greek philosopher from the fourth century B.C., and St. Thomas Aquinas, a medieval scholar, spoke of God as the "unmoved mover". Nothing in our world moves of its own accord; everything is moved by something else. So what caused the very first movement? In other words, what is the first cause? (See Tweet 1.1.)

Quite a puzzle! It would have to be something or someone that is "unmoved", having no beginning and no end (since time is a measure of movement). This being we call God. Other great minds have also thought it logical to believe in God. Another scholar from the Middle Ages, St. Anselm of Canterbury, spoke of God as "that than which nothing greater can be thought". The English scientist Isaac Newton (†1726) saw God as that which had determined the laws of nature. Agreeing with Newton, the twentieth-century genius Albert Einstein wrote: "Everyone who is seriously involved in the pursuit of science becomes convinced that a spirit is manifest in the laws of the universe – a spirit vastly superior to that of man."

Where can I read more about the faith?

First of all, we can learn about our faith in the Bible (SEE TWEET 1.10). There are many translations. A good translation is the Catholic RSV (Revised Standard Version). There is a book that describes the most important elements of the Catholic faith: the *Catechism of the Catholic Church* (CCC). It is worth consulting this book regularly. Because it explains all aspects of our faith, it is a rather large book. The *Catechism* is summarized in the *Compendium of the Catechism of the Catholic Church* (CCCC), and for young people in *YOUCAT*. These texts can help you to find answers to questions that ultimately contribute to forming your personal relationship with God.

 Your questions reveal that you think about God. Thus you can understand the logic of faith with your head, and experience God in your heart.

Read more

Seeking God: CCC 28–30; CCCC 2; YOUCAT 3. *Happiness with God:* CCC 30; CCCC 2; YOUCAT 3.

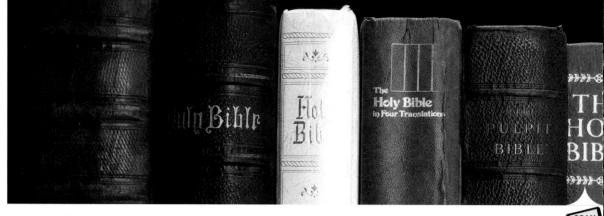

SCAN

 ## 1.10 Why is the Bible so important?

It's very interesting to consider the origins, history, and structure of the Bible. But it's even more important to realize that the Bible is a fantastic treasure, one that can change your life if you let the text speak to you.

Word of God

With good reason the Bible is called Sacred Scripture or the Word of God. The Bible is not only about God, it is also about you! Every text in the Bible has words for you from God. It's not merely a book with words written a long time ago: God wants to speak to you here and now through these ancient texts.

The Bible contains the totality of God's written revelation about himself and his plan of salvation (SEE TWEET 1.27). It is the only book you can never finish reading. You can always discover something new in a Bible verse. The more you read it, the more you discover the ways in which God speaks to his people, and the more you learn to discover the Will of God in your life (SEE TWEET 3.4).

God is love

The most important message that the Bible can give is that God truly loves us. We can read about how he created us, and the whole world, out of love (SEE TWEET 1.2). Out of love he sent prophets to guide his people along the right path. Out of love he cared for his people during their long wanderings and saved them from oppression and other difficulties (SEE TWEET 1.24). Eventually, it was out of love that God became man and Jesus was born. With Jesus, God himself walked on the earth and told us about his love for us. Crucially, it was out of love that Jesus sacrificed his life, died on the cross, and rose from the dead (SEE TWEET 1.26). After his Resurrection, he again walked the earth and preached before ascending into heaven. The Bible gives us the account of many people who witnessed those events and then told others about them. The Resurrection of Jesus is a promise of God that we, too, will rise from the dead and will be able to live forever with him in heaven (SEE TWEET 1.50).

How can I look up a citation from the Bible?

The Bible has been divided into three components:

- books
- chapters
- verses

If we want to refer to the first three verses of the Bible, first we mention the book (Genesis), then the chapter (1), and then the verses (1 to 3). In order to save space, the names of the books are often abbreviated (GEN. 1:1–3). See Appendix 1 in the back for a full list of abbreviations. Some names are present in more than one book in a series, for example, the first and the second books of Kings (I KGS. AND II KGS.).

Old and new

The two parts of the Bible, the Old Testament and the New Testament, form a unity. Together they tell us about God's love for mankind. In the Old Testament we see God preparing a people for the New Testament, which fulfills the Old; thus, "the two shed light on each other; both are true Word of God" (CCC 140). Therefore, we can consider the whole Bible as a source of help and guidance for our life as Christians. We can say to God, with words from Scripture: "Your word is a lamp to my feet and a light to my path" (PS. 119:105). In the New Testament, Jesus explained to his followers that the Old Testament spoke about him: "Beginning with Moses and all the prophets, he interpreted to them in all the Scriptures the things concerning himself" (LK. 24:27). He warned them, as he warns us, that the most important thing is not to conduct a merely intellectual study of the Bible, but to have a personal relationship with him (JN. 5:39–40). The English word *Bible* could be read as an acronym for Basic Instructions before Leaving Earth. Only by approaching Jesus can we truly come to know God and to live forever. That is the ultimate message of both the Old and the New Testaments.

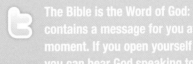

The Bible is the Word of God: it contains a message for you at this moment. If you open yourself to it, you can hear God speaking to you.

Read more

Importance of the Bible: CCC 101–104; CCCC 24; YOUCAT 14. *Importance of the Resurrection:* CCC 638; CCCC 126; YOUCAT 104.

1.11 Does God speak to us only through the Bible? Or does he speak in other ways as well?

We can find traces of God in his creation, and we can know God through our reason (SEE TWEET 1.6). Nevertheless, without further assistance we can know only a little bit about who God really is. Thankfully, he has given us other ways to get to know him. He reveals himself in ways that go beyond his revelation in nature. Surpassing the limits of our reason, *supernatural* revelation enables us not just to know *about* God, but to know him and to love him.

Two ways

This supernatural revelation reaches us in two ways: through Sacred Scripture (the Bible) and through the Sacred Tradition of the Church. St. Paul pointed to the importance of both: "Brethren, stand firm and hold to the traditions which you were taught by us, either by word of mouth or by letter" (II THES. 2:15). God's revelation is complete with Jesus and ends with the death of the last Apostle. Since Jesus' Ascension into heaven, the Holy Spirit has helped the Church to improve her understanding of the completed revelation. The Holy Spirit's assistance to the Church is still going on today (SEE TWEET 2.13).

Only the Bible?

The German Protestant Martin Luther (†1546) rejected the Sacred Tradition of the Church. He taught the doctrine of *sola scriptura* (by Scripture alone) (SEE TWEET 2.36). That's why Protestants try to base their knowledge of God on the Bible alone. However, the Bible itself does not say that God reveals himself only through the Bible. It does say that the Church is the "the pillar and bulwark of the truth" (I TIM. 3:15). Many Bible verses can be understood in different ways, including literally. But it can be misleading to take the literal meaning of verses without regard for their context. For example, throughout history there have been people who quoted from the Bible to call for war: "And when the Lord your God gives them over to you, and you defeat them; then you must utterly destroy them" (DEUT. 7:2). But

Who was St. Paul?

The Apostle Paul was for some time a zealous persecutor of the Christians, that is, before he underwent a dramatic conversion. He said of himself that he used to persecute the Church of God fiercely and tried to eliminate her (Gal 1:13).

Once, when Paul was on the road to Damascus, he saw a great light and heard Jesus ask him: "Why do you persecute me?" (Acts 9:4). From that moment on, Paul became one of the most enthusiastic followers of Jesus. He said he was called by the Will of God to become an Apostle of Jesus (I Cor. 1:1).

About 20 years after Jesus died, St. Paul wrote a number of letters to the various Christian communities where he had preached the good news of salvation. In this way he remained in contact with the young local churches (SEE Tweet 2.18). These letters are part of the New Testament (SEE Tweet 1.18).

One revelation, two ways

During the first century of the Christian Church, texts about Jesus were included in the New Testament. These were written by St. Paul (SEE BOX), the writers of the four Gospels (the Evangelists), and others (SEE Tweet 1.17). These texts were passed on to the next generations together with orally transmitted information about the right way to interpret them. The latter, the content of our faith not in the Bible, is known as Tradition.

Scripture and Tradition form a unified whole that has been entrusted to the Church: "Both of them, flowing from the same divine wellspring, in a certain way merge into a unity and tend toward the same end" (Dei Verbum, 9). The Sacred Tradition about the Word of God that Jesus entrusted to the Apostles has been passed down to their successors. These men, the bishops, in turn have the responsibility of safeguarding and spreading this Word. An excellent example of Tradition is the Profession of Faith said by Catholics and other Christians each Sunday (SEE Tweet 1.31).

other verses have been used to preach peace: "Blessed are the peacemakers, for they shall be called sons of God" (Mt. 5:9) Who is right? In order to decide, it's important to read the Bible in the right way (SEE Tweet 1.19 AND 1.20).

> God speaks to us through Scripture and Tradition. Together they form the complete revelation of God that the Church has always passed on.

Read more

Scripture and revelation: CCC 75–79; CCCC 12–13; YOUCAT 12. *Using your mind:* CCC 36–38, 50; CCCC 3–4, 6; YOUCAT 4–5, 7.

 ## 1.12 Did God write the Bible himself?

When you leaf through the Bible, you find many different forms and styles of writing. There are exciting stories, beautiful poems, inspiring prayers, and challenging letters. There are also monotonous lists of births and deaths. The oldest writings date from almost 1,500 years before the birth of Christ. Before being written down, the information had been passed orally from generation to generation.

The authors of these stories hail from various periods and places (SEE Box). Some of these books were worked on for several generations before they were written down in their current form. For example, biblical scholars think that the book of Isaiah had three different authors, each of whom lived in different historical times. Nevertheless, we can still read Isaiah as one single text.

Inspiration

The various authors of these texts have at least one thing in common: they were all inspired by the Holy Spirit of God when they wrote (II Tim. 3:16). The style they used was partly determined by the specific time and culture in which they lived. But the content of what they wrote is the Word of God. He is the ultimate author, who inspired all the authors of the Bible (CCCC 18).

This becomes clear when we take a closer look at the word *inspiration*. It is derived from the Latin *spiritus*, which means "spirit" or "ghost". To be inspired, therefore, means that the Holy Spirit is working in and through you: "No prophecy ever came by the impulse of man, but men moved by the Holy Spirit spoke from God" (II Pt. 1:21). This is why the Bible is also called Sacred Scripture or the Word of God.

Divine dictation?

This does not mean that God dictated the text of the Bible. The authors wrote in their own languages, used their own words, and were participants in their own cultures and circumstances. Jesus himself sometimes told parables, allegories easily understood by his

What is the Bible?

The Bible contains many texts. These originate from many different periods in history up to about A.D. 100 (SEE TWEET 1.27). The word *Bible* comes from the Greek *biblia*, which means "books". It is a collection of 73 books that were written by various authors. The books were later divided into chapters and verses for easy reference (SEE TWEET 1.10). The common theme of the Bible is God revealing himself to us and inviting us to share in his love. The Bible consists of two parts:

- The Old Testament contains 46 books about the history of the people of Israel and their relationship with God. These books were mostly written during the 1,000 years before the birth of Christ.
- The New Testament contains the 27 books about Jesus and his followers, the first Christians (SEE TWEET 1.18), written mostly between A.D. 50 and 70.

You won't find the word *Bible* in the Bible: the word used there is *Scripture* (JN. 2:22). The first texts were written on clay tablets or on papyrus scrolls. A special example of papyrus scrolls containing verses from the Scriptures are the ones that were found in clay pots in Qumran (near the Dead Sea) in the Holy Land (SEE TWEET 1.20).

listeners that illustrate a truth about God. Other stories in the Bible record historical events, for which we have some archaeological evidence (SEE TWEET 1.20). Every book in the Bible has something important to tell us about our relationship with God.

Our lives

The books of the Bible do not merely form an historical collection of texts. They contain the Word of God that he is speaking to us here and now. Through the inspired work of the authors, God reveals to us the deepest truths about himself and us. The Scriptures are "unfaltering, true and without error" (DEI VERBUM, 2). The Holy Spirit not only inspired the authors to write down the texts (SEE TWEET 1.12), but also helps us to read them in the right way (SEE TWEET 1.20), so that we can embrace our lives with God at this very moment and our future with him in heaven. The purpose of the Bible is to help us to know, to love, and to serve God, and thus to find our true happiness. In order to understand what we are reading, it is important that we pray – just as Jesus himself did (MK. 1:35; LK. 6:12).

> The Spirit of God inspired the biblical authors, from different times and places, to spread his message without error but in their own words.

Read more

Author of the Bible: CCC 105–108, 135–136; CCCC 18; YOUCAT 14.

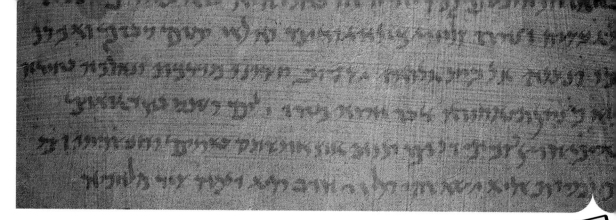

SCAN

 ## 1.13 In what language was the Bible written?

Most of the books of the Old Testament were written in Hebrew, a language of the people of Israel, between 1200 and 100 B.C. This language has an alphabet of 22 letters and, unlike our alphabet, is written from the right to the left. Have a look at Psalm 119 sometime: each paragraph refers to one of the letters of this alphabet. Only consonants were written down, which makes Hebrew tricky to translate. Abbreviations in text messages or tweets, for example, can mean different things with different vowels between the other letters. In the same way, one word in the Bible can be interpreted to mean different things about God. This can sometimes make an exact translation very difficult. At the same time, it can help us to keep thinking about God in new ways. For his being can never be fully expressed in human words (SEE TWEET 1.20).

Hebrew is the sacred language of the Jews. From the sixth century B.C. onward, however, Jews increasingly began to use a different language for daily life, Aramaic. By the time of Jesus' birth, Aramaic was the common tongue of the Jewish people. Later, some parts of the Old Testament were written in Aramaic (EZRA 4:8–6, 18; 7:12–26; DAN. 2:4–7, 28). The Aramaic script looks like Hebrew but is in fact a separate language.

An ancient world language

As the use of Hebrew as a spoken language declined, Greek became more and more important. For this reason, between 300 and 100 B.C. parts of the Old Testament were translated into Greek. The first complete translation of the Old Testament in Greek is the Septuagint (SEE TWEET 1.16). Greek slowly became a world language, like English today. As a result, the entirety of the New Testament was written in Greek (as were some Old Testament texts [SEE TWEET 1.15]).

Although Jesus' mother tongue was Aramaic and he learned Hebrew at the synagogue, he probably also spoke Greek. This is because after the Romans defeated the Greeks and

Old Testament: 46 books

Most of the Old Testament books were written in Hebrew between roughly 1200 and 100 B.C. Below is an example of Hebrew:

אֶהְיֶה אֲשֶׁר אֶהְיֶה

"I AM WHO I AM"
(Ex. 3:14; SEE TWEET 1.24)

New Testament: 27 books

The books of the New Testament were mostly written in Greek between roughly A.D. 50 and 70. Below is an example of Greek:

Ἐν ἀρχῇ ἦν ὁ λόγος

"In the beginning was the Word"
(JN. 1:1; SEE TWEET 1.29)

conquered their lands, Greek, not Latin (the language of the Romans), became the common language of the people of the Roman Empire, while Latin remained its administrative and legal language. That's probably why St. Paul wrote in Greek, even in his letters to the Christians in Rome, the capital of the Roman Empire.

But still some Aramaic

In the Greek texts of the New Testament we can still find some Aramaic expressions. For example, here are some of the words witnesses heard Jesus himself say: "Talitha cumi" ("Little girl, I say to you, arise") (MK. 5:41), "Ephatha" ("Open") (MK. 7:34), and "Eloi, Eloi, lama sabachthani?" ("My God, my God, why have you forsaken me?") (MK. 15:34). The texts also have individual Aramaic words, such as "Abba" ("Father") (GAL. 4:6) and "Maranatha" ("Come, Lord") (I COR. 16:22).

Latin for the people

By the fourth century A.D. Latin had become increasingly important as a common tongue. At the pope's request, St. Jerome (†420) translated the whole Bible into Latin. This Vulgate (related to the Latin word for "common") remains very important today. St. Jerome wrote the following about the Bible to his apprentice St. Eustochium: "Read often and learn as much as you can. Let sleep steal over you with the book still in your hands and let the sacred page catch your falling head" (LETTER 22.17).

> The Old Testament was mostly written in Hebrew, and the New Testament was mostly written in Greek.

Read more

Books of the Bible: CCC 120; CCCC 20; YOUCAT 16. *Old Testament:* CCC 121–123; CCCC 21; YOUCAT 17.
New Testament: CCC 124–127, 139; CCCC 22; YOUCAT 18.

1.14 What is the difference between the Bible and the Qur'an?

The Bible was written by people who were inspired by God (SEE TWEET 1.12). When we quote from the Bible in our prayers, we turn the words into our own prayers to speak to God from our hearts. Muslims, on the other hand, believe that the Qur'an is the literal text from God himself, which an angel dictated to Muhammad (†632) in Arabic at the beginning of the seventh century (QUR'AN 2.97). For this reason, Muslims ascribe healing and protective powers to reciting parts of the Qur'an in Arabic.

Handbook or holy book?

If nobody reads it, the Bible is of little value. Muslims, however, treat the text of the Qur'an itself with great reverence. True, during the celebration of the Eucharist, the text of the Gospel is kissed and incensed (surrounded by sweet-swelling smoke) as a sign of reverence and prayer (SEE TWEET 3.21). But especially since the invention of the printing press, the Bible has become for Christians like a handbook, something to take with you wherever you go and to read whenever you can. We do not need

to wash ourselves before reading it, but we do need to have the right frame of mind – an open mind to listen carefully and honestly in order to appreciate the Word of God (MK. 7:14). Muslims, on the other hand, treat the Qur'an itself with great reverence and ritually wash themselves before reading it (QUR'AN 56.77–79). They do not simply store it on a shelf with other books, and they never place it on the floor, which they consider impure.

Does God speak Arabic?

For Christians, Jesus is the Word of God, and the Bible tells us about him. For Muslims, the Qur'an is the spoken word of God. It is perfectly fine for Christians to read the Bible in translation. In whichever language we read the Bible, it is the living Word of God. By thinking about verses and using them in prayer, we can always find a new meaning in them that is relevant to us, through the help of the Holy Spirit. The Church helps us by providing guidance, and also by setting limits to our interpretations (SEE TWEET 1.20). Muslims, however, prefer to read the Qur'an

The Qur'an

The Arabic word *Qur'an* means "recitation". The Qur'an consists of verses, or *ayat*, that make up 114 chapters, or *suras*, of varying lengths. According to Muhammad, these were dictated to him in the Arabic language by the angel Gabriel between A.D. 610 and 632 in Mecca and Medina (QUR'AN 2.97). After the death of Muhammad, around the year 650, the texts were collected and organized on the basis of their length.

in Arabic, because they believe that God literally dictated the text in that language. This gives the Arabic text an absolute authority. Translations of the Qur'an can be informative, but the translated text is no longer holy. Not just anyone may interpret the text either. Muhammad and his followers explained the text of the Qur'an. These explanations and clarifications were written down in the *hadith*. After the Qur'an, the *hadith* is the most authoritative text in Islam (SEE TWEET 2.26).

Bible or Qur'an?

The Bible is mentioned and quoted in the Qur'an, but it is also rejected in it. According to Islam, the Bible is a counterfeit that distorts the truth; the real truth is found only in the Qur'an. The Qur'an speaks of Jesus, for example, and honors him as an important prophet, but explicitly denies that he is the Son of God (QUR'AN 5.116; 19.34–35). It also denies that Jesus rose from the dead; according to the Qur'an, somebody else died on the cross instead of him (QUR'AN 4.157). Thus, the Qur'an rejects the very core of our faith. The Bible tells us the only complete truth: that God came to live among us out of love and became a man through Jesus Christ (Jn. 3:16). In contrast to Islam, Christianity is not really a "religion of the book" (QUR'AN 49.46; SEE TWEET 2.26). Quoting St. Bernard of Clairvaux (†1153) the *Catechism* states that "Christianity is the religion of the 'Word' of God, a word which is 'not a written and mute word, but the Word which is incarnate and living'" (CCC 108; SEE TWEET 1.29). Without Jesus (God's living Word), and the help of the Holy Spirit, the Bible is just a book with a lot of dead words. They only come alive when we read them. You may take that as an urgent invitation to get the Bible from your bookshelf and to start reading it now!

The New Testament says Jesus is the Son of God, which is denied in the Qur'an. God inspired the writers of the Bible. He did not dictate the text.

Read more

The role of the Bible in the Church: CCC 103–104, 131–133, 141; CCCC 24; YOUCAT 19.

1.15 What is the structure of the Old Testament?

SCAN

The Bible: true or false?

The Old Testament consists of four parts. The first five books are the Pentateuch. This Greek word literally means "five scrolls". The Jews call them the (Five) Books of Moses or Torah, which means "teaching" or "law". The Pentateuch includes the foundational stories of the Jewish people and the laws God gave to Moses. The next part of the Old Testament consists of the Historical Books. These record the history of the people of Israel. Jews refer to them as the Early Prophets, as they are concerned with Samuel, Nathan, Elijah, and Elisha. The Prophetic Books mainly deal with the prophets who warned the people about their sins and foretold the destruction of Israel and the coming of the Messiah (Jesus [SEE TWEET 1.27]). Jews refer to them as the Late Prophets. Some of their prophecies came true when the people of Israel were conquered by the Babylonians and taken into captivity in 587 B.C. Note however that a prophet is not a kind of fortune-teller, but rather a person who speaks and acts in the name of God. Lastly, there are the Books of Wisdom, which the Jews call

The numbering of the psalms

There are 150 psalms. Their numbering differs in the Hebrew and Greek versions, as they are divided differently.

The Greek numbering merged the Hebrew Psalms 9 and 10 into one, which is why from Psalm 9 to Psalm 147 the Greek numbering is always one number lower. The Greek Psalm 138 is thus the Hebrew Psalm 139. Since the Hebrew Psalm 147 was split into two Greek parts, the numbering comes back to a total of 150 psalms.

In most modern translations of the Bible, the Hebrew numbering is followed. Some Bibles show both numbers like this: Psalm 138(139).

The 46 books of the Old Testament

Pentateuch:	*Books or Law of Moses*	Genesis, Exodus, Leviticus, Numbers, Deuteronomy	
Historical Books	*Early Prophets*	Joshua, Judges, Ruth, I and II Samuel, I and II Kings	
Prophetic Books	*Late Prophets*	Isaiah, Jeremiah, Ezekiel, and the 12 prophets (Hosea, Joel, Amos, Obadiah, Jonah, Mica, Nahum, Habakkuk, Zephaniah, Haggai, Zechariah and Malachi)	Jewish canon or Tanakh
Books of Wisdom	*Writings*	I and II Chronicles, Psalms, Job, Proverbs, Song of Solomon, Ecclesiastes, Lamentations, Esther (Hebrew parts), Daniel, Ezra, Nehemiah	
	Deuterocanonical Books:	*Judith, Tobit, I and II Maccabees, Wisdom, Sirach, Baruch, Esther (Greek parts)*	

Writings. These contain a wealth of questions, insights, poetry, and moral wisdom from people of faith. Seven of these books (and parts of others) were written in Greek by the Jewish community in Alexandria, Egypt. They are known as the Deuterocanonical Books (SEE TWEET 1.16) and belong to the Scriptures of the Catholic and Orthodox Churches (SEE TWEET 2.30). Jews and Protestants, however, consider them apocryphal, that is, of doubtful authenticity.

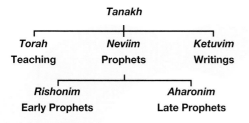

The Jewish Tanakh

The Jews call the Old Testament the Tanakh, which is an acronym of the first letters of the titles of the three most important parts: teaching or law (*Torah*), prophets (*Nevi'im*), and writings (*Ketuvim*). These texts are on scrolls that are read, or chanted, publically in the synagogue, the way Jesus did in the Gospel of Luke (4:16–21).

> The 46 books of the Old Testament are separable into 4 parts: Pentateuch, Historical Books, Prophetic Books, and Books of Wisdom.

Read more

Books of the Bible: CCC 120; CCCC 20; YOUCAT 16. *Old Testament:* CCC 121–123; CCCC 21; YOUCAT 17.

1.16 What is the difference between the Catholic Old Testament and the Jewish Tanakh?

The Jewish Tanakh comprises 39 of the 46 books of our Old Testament (SEE TWEET 1.15). The content of the Tanakh was established long after the death of Jesus. After the Romans destroyed the Temple in Jerusalem in A.D. 70, the Jews were in need of stability and a source of guidance, and so the Tanakh in its current form was put together. All of these 39 books are included in our Old Testament, which contains seven other books as well (SEE TWEET 1.15).

70 wise translators

The Tanakh has not always been limited to these 39 books. An old translation comprises all 46 books of the Catholic Old Testament. Starting in 300 B.C, the Jewish Community in Alexandria began translating the books of the Tanakh into Greek. The resulting translation is the Septuagint, or LXX, which is derived from the Latin *septuaginta*, meaning "seventy", after the 70 scholars said to have worked on it. This translation was very important, especially for the Greek-speaking Jewish communities

outside the Holy Land who no longer spoke or read Hebrew. But the Septuagint is also very important for us because it includes all 46 books of our Old Testament, exactly as they were used from 300 B.C. onward.

The translators of the Septuagint included seven books that were not in the oldest Hebrew collection of writings. This shows that, long before Jesus was born, they already considered these books to be inspired by God. These seven are the Deuterocanonical Books, which means "books of the second list (or canon)" (SEE TWEET 1.15). Later, when the New Testament was written, the authors referred to the Greek text of the Septuagint, thus including the seven Deuterocanonical Books. This shows that the first Christians fully accepted the entire Septuagint. Therefore, the Catholic Old Testament consists of 46 books.

Protestant Bible?

Given this history, it is rather surprising that in the sixteenth century Martin Luther did not consider the Deuterocanonical Books to be Holy Scripture and inserted them between the Old and New Testaments in his German translation of the Bible. Many later Protestant editions did not include them at all. The argument was that the Jews would have known best which original books made up the Old Testament. But given that these books were included in the Septuagint translation 300 years before Christ, the Church believes that these books had in fact once formed part of the Jewish Scripture, even if they were excluded later.

The Catholic Bible

Another difference between the Tanakh and the Catholic Bible is the order of the books. In the Bible the books of the Late Prophets are placed at the end, rather than the Writings (SEE TWEET 1.15). The reason is that the Late Prophets serve as a preparation for the New Testament. Because of the many references to the coming of the Messiah (Jesus our Redeemer [SEE TWEET 1.27]), it makes sense for Christians to place them right before the New Testament. All in all, the differences are rather small. The Tanakh and the Old Testament describe the same relationship between God and his people. But it's crucial to realize that the New Testament completes and helps us to understand the Old Testament. With Jesus, the Old Testament gains an added dimension because he completes the self-revelation and salvation of God that was begun with the Jews (SEE TWEET 1.26).

Synagogue

Jesus often went to the synagogue, the Jewish house of prayer (MK. 1:21). Just as a church is set apart for the liturgy, a synagogue is used only for prayer (SEE TWEET 3.20 AND 3.24). In addition to a large hall for prayer, there usually are smaller rooms used for meetings or study.

The most important place in a synagogue is the Ark, where the scrolls of the Torah are stored. This Ark points toward Jerusalem, so that when they pray toward it, Jews face the location of the original Temple. The Ark in the synagogue is a reference to the Ark of the Covenant in the Temple, where the Ten Commandments were stored (SEE TWEET 1.24 AND 1.27).

In the center of the synagogue, there is a platform with a lectern (*bema*), from where the scrolls are read.

 The Catholic Bible comprises all 46 books of Hebrew Scripture known in 300 B.C. 39 of these form the Tanakh, which was compiled in A.D. 70.

Read more

Books of the Bible: CCC 120; CCCC 20; YOUCAT 16.

1.17 How and when did the New Testament come into being?

The Bible: true or false?

The books of the Old Testament were the only Scriptures of the first Christians. In those early days of the Church, the events involving Jesus were still passed on by word of mouth. Most books of the New Testament were written between 20 and 40 years after the death and Resurrection of Christ.

Among the first of these are the Epistles of St. Paul: letters he wrote in about the year 50, during his travels to the various Christian communities he guided. By the time the first generation of Christians began to grow old, people had started to write down their experiences so as not to forget them. This is how the other books of the New Testament came into being.

Copied and handed on

These texts were copied by hand and passed on to other Christian communities, where they were read aloud at prayer meetings. Gradually, the realization grew that these texts about Jesus had a particularly holy status and authority. The

originals have not survived. But early copies of New Testament texts remain, which prove that the content has never significantly changed. Not all the texts with accounts of the life of Jesus became part of the New Testament (SEE BOX). In order to ascertain which texts were truly inspired by God, and thus ought to be included in the Scriptures, the early Church considered several things. First of all, it was important to know that the texts were written by the Apostles themselves or by their disciples. The importance of the Christian community for which they were written was also considered. Next, it was determined which texts the Christian communities used most often in the liturgy. In the process of establishing which Bible passages were inspired by the Holy Spirit, it was also very important that the content of the texts corresponded with the whole teaching of Jesus (SEE TWEET 1.12; SEE BOX).

The New Testament fulfilled

A number of early Christian writers can help us to discover when the New Testament was

Could new books be added to the Bible?

Besides the books in the New Testament, there are many texts from the first centuries after Christ that contain stories about Jesus and claim to have been written by one of the Apostles. In addition, there are texts from the Apostolic Fathers (SEE TWEET 2.24). Although these texts can be very interesting, they were not considered Scripture by the early Church. As Catholics we believe that in determining which texts were inspired by God, the early Church was led by the Holy Spirit (SEE TWEET 1.32). That is why we can be sure that there is no extra book of the Bible lying hidden somewhere. The fact that no new books have been added to the Bible in nearly two millennia is in itself proof that the Bible is complete. This is a good example of how Scripture and Tradition work together (SEE TWEET 1.11). Without the Sacred Tradition of the Church, there would never have even been a Bible! In the fourth century, the wise St. Augustine wrote: "I would not have believed the Gospels, had the authority of the Catholic Church not urged me to do so" (FUND. 5:6).

completed. St. Ignatius of Antioch (†c. 100), St. Clement of Rome (†c. 101), and St. Polycarp (†155) often cited the four Evangelists and the Epistles of St. Paul. Other important sources include the work of St. Irenaeus (†202) and a manuscript dating from the year 170 called the Muratorian fragment. The works of all these early authors tell us that from the end of the second century onward, almost all the books of the New Testament were regarded as divinely inspired Holy Scripture and were widely used by Christians.

Exactly 27 books

The oldest complete Greek manuscript of the whole Bible that still exists is the Codex Vaticanus from the fourth century. Such manuscripts show that by the time of the fourth century, exactly the same list of 27 books was used almost everywhere. Not everything is known about the compilation of this list. What we do know for certain is that these 27 books comprise the New Testament, which has played an immensely important role for almost two millennia! (SEE BOX). These books have allowed billions of people from different times and places to come into contact with Jesus and his first followers.

St. Paul wrote his Epistles in about A.D. 50. Soon thereafter, other authors wrote the rest of the 27 books of the New Testament.

Read more

Books of the Bible: CCC 120; CCCC 20; YOUCAT 16. *New Testament:* CCC 124–127, 139; CCCC 22; YOUCAT 18.
Explaining the Bible: CCC 119; CCCC 19; YOUCAT 16.

SCAN

1.18 What are the parts of the New Testament?

The Bible: true or false?

The New Testament can be divided into four parts: the Gospels; The Acts of the Apostles; the Epistles of Paul, James, Peter, John, and Jude; and The Revelation to John.

Gospels and Acts

The Gospels are four accounts of the life, death, and Resurrection of Jesus Christ. They were written by the four Evangelists (SEE BOX). The word *gospel* means "glad tidings", or "good news", which refers to the message of God's love and salvation that Jesus brought (SEE TWEET 1.27).

The Gospels of Matthew, Mark, and Luke are very similar and are known to scholars as the Synoptic Gospels. It is often argued that they had a common source, which has since been lost. The Gospel of John has a somewhat different, more theological style and content. It does not mention several of the things already mentioned in the other three Gospels.

The four Evangelists

Traditionally, the four Evangelists have been depicted symbolically as winged creatures (Ez. 1:10; Rev. 4:7):

- A man (Matthew): his Gospel begins with a long list of Jesus' forefathers.
- A lion (Mark): he begins his Gospel with John the Baptist preaching like a roaring lion.
- An ox (Luke): an ox was a sacrificial animal such as the one Zechariah offered up in the temple.
- An eagle (John): his Gospel begins with a bird's-eye view showing Jesus as the eternal Word.

You can often see these symbols in churches. For instance, many lecterns are adorned with the image of an eagle, as a sign of the Word of God (Jn. 1:1).

The 27 books of the New Testament

Gospels:	*Synoptic:*	Matthew, Mark, Luke
	Other:	John

Acts of the Apostles

Epistles:	*By St. Paul:*	Romans, I and II Corinthians, Galatians, Ephesians, Philippians, Colossians, I and II Thessalonians, I and II Timothy, Titus, Philemon
	Other authors:	Hebrews and the Catholic Epistles (those written to the whole Church) James, I and II Peter, I, II, and III John, Jude

Apocalypse The Revelation to John

The Acts of the Apostles was also written by Luke and gives the early history of the Church. Acts is about the first Christians in Jerusalem, who were under the leadership of St. Peter. Here we also read about the first missionaries, St. Paul (SEE TWEET 1.11) in particular, who were sent to spread the Word of God.

Epistles and Revelation

St. Paul travelled and preached throughout Asia Minor and the northeastern Mediterranean and visited local churches, some of which he had established himself. Afterward, he wrote letters to these young Christian communities, to guide them on their path of faith. These letters are the Epistles of St. Paul. Today it is known that St. Paul did not in fact write the Epistle to the Hebrews, though it has long been attributed to him. The other Epistles were written by various authors.

These are more general in content, and most were not addressed to a specific community.

Lastly, The Apocalypse, or The Revelation to John, is the last book of the Bible. It contains prophetic visions of the end of the world and the final battle against evil. Its language is highly symbolic, and it concerns the Last Judgment and the heavenly Jerusalem (SEE TWEET 1.44).

> The New Testament consists of 4 Gospels, The Acts of the Apostles, 21 Epistles by St. Paul and others, plus The Apocalypse.

Read more

Books of the Bible: CCC 120; CCCC 20; YOUCAT 16. *New Testament:* CCC 124–127, 139; CCCC 22; YOUCAT 18.

1.19 Should I follow all the rules in the Bible?

Jesus said: "Do not think that I have come to abolish the law and the prophets; I have come ... to fulfil them. For truly, I say to you, till heaven and earth pass away, not an iota, not a dot, will pass from the law" (Mt. 5:17–18). That seems to indicate that all the commandments of the Old Testament still apply. But Jesus also said: "The law and the prophets were until John; since then the good news of the kingdom of God is preached" (Lk. 16:16). It is clear that something fundamental changed with the coming of Jesus.

A sacrifice of love

Jesus fulfilled the law and the prophets by offering himself up for mankind out of love, in obedience to the Father. From the moment that Jesus was sacrificed on the cross, we have been reconciled with God (SEE TWEET 1.26). For that reason the Jewish laws about burnt offerings and sacrifices are no longer required of us. Under the Old Covenant (as described in the first books of the Old Testament), people gained temporary reconciliation with God through sacrificed animals. But Jesus fulfilled all of these sacrifices for all time. The same is true for a number of other laws. However, the Ten Commandments are still as valid as when God gave them to Moses (SEE TWEET 4.9).

The double commandment

The Bible should be read in its entirety. The New Testament sheds new light on the Old (SEE BOX). Jesus summed up the Ten Commandments when he answered the question: "Which commandment is the first, or greatest, of all?" Jesus answered with a double commandment: "The first is, 'Hear, O Israel: The Lord our God, the Lord is one; and you shall love the Lord your God with all your heart, and with all your soul, and with all your mind, and with all your strength.' The second is this, 'You shall love your neighbor as yourself.' There is no other commandment greater than these" (Mk. 12:29–31).

Here, Jesus did not say anything new with regard to Jewish Scripture, our Old Testament.

How do I reconcile "tooth for tooth" with "turn the other cheek"?

Why did God allow a rule such as an "eye for eye, tooth for tooth" (Deut. 19:21) to apply in the Old Testament and then have Jesus say that you should turn the other cheek to your enemy? (Mt. 5:38–41). Why did God previously urge war and destruction? (Deut. 7:1–2). We do not have a complete answer, but we can think of this in several ways. You could say that the path God takes with his people is composed of phases. In preparation for Christ's coming, God wanted the Jews to distance themselves from the Gentiles who worshipped idols and who behaved immorally. That explains the severe commands against idolatry and the wars that Israel waged against pagan peoples. The laws, practices, and customs of the Old Testament were intended to combat the worst of sinful excesses.

With the coming of Christ these harsh laws were definitively replaced by the most important law: love of God and neighbor. This command already existed in the Old Testament (Lev. 19:18; Deut. 6:5), but Jesus made it the most important law (Lk. 10:25–28). Furthermore, the harsh punishments of the Old Testament help you to realize how bad sin is. For example, the punishment for adultery was death by stoning. When an adulterous woman was brought before Jesus, he said to the crowd that he who was without sin should throw the first stone (Jn. 8:7). They all left without stoning her, and Jesus said to the woman: "Neither do I condemn you; go, and do not sin again" (Jn. 8:11). Jesus brought us something radically new: although sin is a very bad thing, Jesus can forgive us and thus reconcile us with God (see Tweet 3.38 and 4.13). Therefore we must always read the Scriptures with Jesus' teachings in mind.

But at another time, Jesus asked his listeners to surpass the Old Law: "You have heard that it was said, 'You shall love your neighbor and hate your enemy.' But I say to you, Love your enemies" (Mt. 5:43–44).

Last word to the Church

Love God and your neighbors: that is the essence of being a Christian. In doing this, we do not stand alone, but rather form a community of believers who try to love each other and everyone. This community is the Church, which is led by the Holy Spirit in his wisdom (see Tweet 1.31). For that reason we can trust the judgments of the Church (see Tweet 1.20) that teach us which commands of the Old Testament apply to us, and which do not.

The New Testament throws new light on the Old: certain rules have been abolished while others have been reaffirmed. Love is the main command.

Read more

Importance of the Bible: CCC 106–108, 115–119; CCCC 18; YOUCAT 15.
Unity between Old and New Testament: CCC 128–130, 140; CCCC 23; YOUCAT 17–18.

SCAN

1.20 How can you know what is literally true in the Bible, and what is not?

The Bible is the Word of God, but it was written down by people (SEE TWEET 1.12). How do I know when God is speaking and when the human authors are? How do I know what is history, what is narrative, what is poetry, and what is parable? How do I know the right way to interpret these?

Reading the Bible well

If you want to read the Bible well and to understand it, there are at least three important things to remember. First of all, we must give thought "to the content and unity of the whole Scripture" (CCC 112; SEE DEI VERBUM, 12). Any text that is divided up into pieces can twist the truth and transmit a false message. Through the ages people have twisted the Word of God to match their own opinions by citing passages of the Bible without taking into account the underlying message (SEE TWEET 1.11). The Bible is one coherent whole, such that all parts must be read with reference to each other and the whole.

Second, we need to read the Bible within the Tradition of the whole Church (CCC 113; SEE DEI VERBUM, 12; SEE TWEET 1.11). Scripture and Tradition are two ways in which God has revealed himself to us. Throughout the centuries saints, popes, and Church Councils have written beautiful commentaries on the Bible. Their words can help us to delve deeper into the truths about God that are found in the Scriptures.

Third, it is important to realize that the truths of the faith are parts of a larger whole, which is God's plan of salvation. We know of this plan through divine revelation (CCC 114; SEE TWEET 1.27).

The Holy Spirit and the Church

When trying to understand the Bible, we have help from our common sense and from the many wise people who throughout the centuries have correctly interpreted it. But above all we need help from the Holy Spirit, who will guide us on our way with God.

Excavations as evidence

There are many places named in the Bible that have been excavated by archaeologists. These include, for instance, the Temple Mount in Jerusalem, where remains of the palace of King Herod were found (Lk. 23:7). An inscription on a stone in Caesarea testifies that Pontius Pilate was indeed the governor of Judea in the first century (Mt. 27:11). There is also evidence for the existence of many of the kings who are named in the Old Testament. For example, seals have been found from the time of King Hezekiah of Judah (II Kgs. 18:1).

Between 1946 and 1956, the Dead Sea Scrolls were found in caves of the Holy Land, near Qumran. These papyrus scrolls contain Jewish Scriptures that were probably written in the century before Jesus lived. To date, these are the oldest known Jewish Scriptures. The texts on the scrolls correspond to our Old Testament.

This is the Helper whom Jesus promised to the Apostles, who helped them to comprehend and to proclaim the gospel (SEE TWEET 1.31). From Jesus the Church received the fundamental task (SEE TWEET 2.11) of interpreting the Scriptures without error. With the aid given by the Holy Spirit, the Church helps us to comprehend the Word of God properly, in harmony with all the faithful and in light of Sacred Tradition.

Prayer: a word with God

It is important to find out what the God-inspired authors meant when they wrote the books of the Bible. In order to do so, you can read and study about their backgrounds and the times in which they lived. But the main thing is to listen to God, the ultimate author, who is not bound by time and place. You do that not so much by studying the Bible as by reading it prayerfully, so to speak (SEE TWEET 3.8).

Scripture is meant for people of all times and all places, including you. It is not for nothing that we speak of the "Word of God". In the words of the Bible you can hear God himself speaking! For that reason, the Scriptures say: "Blessed is the man who walks not in the counsel of the wicked ... his delight is in the law of the LORD, and on his law he meditates day and night" (Ps. 1:1–2).

> The Church, aided by the Holy Spirit, helps us to read the Bible well and to comprehend it in its entirety within the Tradition.

Read more

Reading the Bible correctly: CCC 109–114, 137; CCCC 19; YOUCAT 16.

1.21 Aren't those incredible Bible stories just fairy tales?

Eve was created from Adam's rib (GEN. 2:21–22); giants lived on earth (GEN. 6:4), and Jonah was not only swallowed by a great fish, but even spit out alive after three days (JON. 2). More important than the question as to whether these incredible tales happened exactly as told is their deeper meanings. Just like Jesus, who wanted to make some of his messages clearer by expressing them in the form of parables, some Old Testament texts reveal deeper truths about God in a poetic way. They are not, therefore, just fairy tales.

Connection to the New Testament

Eve's creation from the rib of Adam does not mean that she is his inferior, but that they are equal, united: "Flesh of my flesh", said Adam (GEN 2:23; SEE TWEET 1.2 AND 3.43). Some see in the image a symbolic correspondence to Jesus, whose side was pierced with a lance until blood and water flowed from it (JN. 19:34), giving birth to the Church. The three days and three nights that Jonah spent in the stomach of the huge fish, Jesus linked to his Passion and death (MT. 12:40).

Another connection is the experience of the Israelites when they were once again complaining to God. Suddenly poisonous snakes appeared and started biting the Israelites (SEE TWEET 1.24). Answering their prayers, God helped his people by telling Moses to put a bronze serpent on a pole; anyone who looked at it would live (NUM. 21:4–9). This prefigures the cross on which Jesus was crucified: anyone who looks upon him with the eyes of faith will be granted eternal life (JN. 3:14–15).

Fact or fiction?

All of the stories and images in the Bible were inspired by God and have something important to tell us. Even if stories such as the Creation (GEN. 1:1–2:4) or the Tower of Babel (GEN. 11:1–9) do not describe exactly what happened, they are still true: the core message is true. There is always the danger of being so proud that we

Do the Gospels contradict each other?

It sometimes appears as if the Gospels contradict each other. Matthew, for example, describes Jesus sending his disciples out to preach the gospel, telling them to take neither "sandals, nor a staff" (Mt. 10:10). Mark, on the other hand, has Jesus saying that they should carry only a stick and wear sandals (Mk. 6:8–9). These texts were written on the basis of the varying memories of different eyewitnesses. That is why slight differences between the texts can sometimes be found. Still, a number of apparent or actual contradictions can easily be explained. You could imagine, for instance, that Jesus sent his Apostles out a number of times, sometimes with sandals and a stick and sometimes without.

Such differences are of secondary importance to the core message, which is always the same: Jesus came to deliver people from evil and sin; his gospel must be preached throughout the world. John wrote, for example, that "these are written that you may believe that Jesus is the Christ, the son of God, and that believing you may have life in his name" (Jn. 20:31). This central truth was documented without error or disagreement by all four Evangelists. This is due to divine inspiration: the Holy Spirit inspired the human authors to record the saving words and deeds of Jesus, and the same Holy Spirit helps us to understand them.

think we can climb up to God all by ourselves, a danger illustrated by the Tower of Babel. All the stories in the Old Testament contain lessons about our relationship with God.

Evidence

The Old Testament has many independently verified historical facts. Archaeologists have been able to find clues as to persons, places, and incidents referred to in the Bible (see Tweet 1.20). However, the path that God treads with his people is much more important than knowing what precisely happened at any given moment. The core message of the Old Testament is that God continues to love his people despite all their faults; he always gives them another chance. That is the most incredible message of the Bible – and yet, it is true!

Not everything in the Bible is to be taken literally, but there is an important message about God's love on every page.

Read more

Usefulness of the Old Testament: ccc 121–123, 128–130, 140; cccc 21, 23; youcat 17.
Gospels: ccc 124–127, 139; cccc 22; youcat 18.

SCAN

1.22 Why did the Great Flood take place in the time of Noah?

The book of Genesis tells of Noah and his family. In those times, many generations after the fall of Adam and Eve (SEE TWEET 1.4), God saw how badly the people were behaving and how wicked they had become. It made him sad, and he regretted ever having created man (GEN. 6:7).

Seeing that Noah was the only righteous person left, that is, someone whose actions were good, God decided to destroy everyone except Noah and his family. God told him: "Make yourself an ark of gopher wood.... I will bring a flood of waters upon the earth, to destroy all flesh in which is the breath of life from under heaven; everything that is on the earth shall die. But I will establish my covenant with you; and you shall come into the ark, you, your sons, your wife, and your sons' wives with you. And of every living thing of all flesh, you shall bring two of every sort into the ark, to keep them alive with you" (GEN. 6:13–19).

One long rainstorm

Noah did as God had asked, and on the seventh day (a special day in the Bible) it began to rain. The rain lasted 40 days and 40 nights. Then everything was flooded, and Noah's ark drifted on an enormous sea. After 150 days, the ark came to rest on a mountain top. These periods of time do not necessarily need to be taken as days from sunrise to sunset (SEE TWEET 1.2).

Noah sent out a dove to see if the time had come when they could return to the land. The dove came back with an olive branch in its beak. This symbol is often used today to represent peace, since God was no longer angry with his people.

The rainbow

God said: "I will never again curse the ground because of man, for the imagination of man's heart is evil from his youth" (GEN. 8:21). That day God made a covenant with Noah. God promised that he would never again send rain

Water in the Bible

Water plays an important role in the Bible. On the one hand, its lack can cause death (GEN. 6:17); on the other, it is dangerous as we can drown in it (MT. 14:28–32).

Just think back on the Exodus from Egypt that took place through the parted waters of the Red Sea: "The Lord drove the sea back.... And the sons of Israel went into the midst of the sea on dry ground, the waters being a wall to them on their right hand and on their left" (EX. 14:21–22). When the Egyptians went after them, the waters flowed back in and they were drowned.

In spite of this miraculous event, later in the desert, the Israelites complained of thirst. Once again, God helped his people. He told Moses to take his staff to "the rock at Horeb" and to "strike the rock". He said: "Water shall come out of it, that the people may drink" (EX. 17:6).

Yet, the most significant role water has in the Bible is in the deliverance that Jesus brings through Baptism, which opens the path to salvation: "Let us draw near with a true heart in full assurance of faith, with our hearts sprinkled clean from an evil conscience and our bodies washed with pure water" (HEB. 10:22).

to destroy the earth. He sent the rainbow as a sign of the new covenant he had made with his people (GEN. 9:16). God has kept this promise. Despite the fact that people have continued to sin ("their hearts remained inclined toward evil" [PS 141:4; SEE TWEET 1.4]), God has continued to show them mercy (SEE TWEET 1.27). Although little can be known of an event that happened so long ago, it is interesting to note that the broad outline of the Bible account of the Great Flood also occurs in other stories from the ancient Near East.

God's promise fulfilled

St. Peter saw the ark as an image of Baptism. Eight people were kept safe in the ark, but anyone can be saved through Baptism (I PT. 3:20–21; SEE TWEET 3.36). The Church has taken the place of the ark: we can see the Church as a ship that brings us to the right destination – our ultimate salvation in God (SEE TWEET 1.27). By instituting the Church, God has kept his promise to care always for his people.

Because of the people's sins, God destroyed them with the Flood. Noah was righteous, however, so God saved him and his family.

Read more

Noah: GEN 6–9; CCC 56–58, 71; CCCC 7; YOUCAT 8.

`SCAN`

1.23 Why is Abraham so important?

Just when Abraham thought that he had everything he could ever wish for, he heard God's voice say: "Go from your country … to the land that I will show you. And I will make of you a great nation.… [A]nd by you all the families of the earth shall bless themselves" (GEN. 12:1–3). Imagine God telling you this out of the blue!

On his way

Abraham left with his wife, Sarah, his family, and his livestock, just as God had commanded – leaving everything behind and without knowing where he was going. He first went to Canaan and then to Egypt, through the dry Negev Desert, and then back to Canaan. At every step, God showed him the way. One day, God promised Abraham that his reward was going to be great, but Abraham answered: "O Lord GOD, what wilt thou give me, for I continue childless" (GEN. 15:2). God told Abraham to trust that his descendants would be as numberless as the stars (GEN. 15:5). And so Abraham chose to trust God again. That night, God made a covenant with Abraham in order to confirm his promise (SEE BOX). God kept his promise, and even though Abraham was well on in years, he had a son, whom he named Isaac (GEN. 21:2–3).

Fighting with God

One day God ordered Abraham to go up a mountain to offer him his son Isaac as a sacrifice (SEE PICTURE). Although heartbroken, Abraham was ready to obey God's command. But then, just as he took the knife and was about to offer God the one he loved the most, God intervened and stopped him, saying: "Now I know that you fear God" (GEN. 22:12). You may ask yourself: Am I ready to give up everything for God? Isaac later married and had twins: Esau and Jacob. One night, Jacob fought with an angel. Afterward the angel told Jacob that he was henceforth to be called Israel (GEN. 32:28). Similarly, our path with God is sometimes a struggle! Jacob's 12 sons became the leaders of the 12 tribes of Israel, forerunners of the 12 Apostles. Abraham, Isaac, and Jacob are the three great patriarchs of God's people.

How did God make a covenant with Abraham?

Abraham's trust in God was confirmed by God's covenant with him. God asked Abraham to fetch a heifer, a goat, a ram, a turtle dove, and a young pigeon. He split these in two and lay the halves down in opposing rows. After sunset, Abraham saw that "a smoking fire pot and a flaming torch passed between these pieces" (GEN 15:17–18). This "passing between the pieces" was an old ritual whereby the person making the promise walked through the rows of dead animals. It represented a potential curse: "If I do not keep my promise, then may the same happen to me as with these animals." By "passing between the pieces" God made an unbreakable promise, a covenant, with Abraham.

It pays to be obedient

Because Abraham trusted God, he was given the Promised Land and made the founding father of the people of Israel. God kept his promise: Abraham has a multitude of descendants. We too are descendants of Abraham; all the faithful are. His example is very important to us. Through his obedience to God, he was given the privilege of participating in God's plan of salvation. That plan was completed in the life, death, and Resurrection of Jesus, who leads us step-by-step to heaven (SEE TWEET 1.27). If we can be as obedient to God as Abraham was, then God will also achieve great things through us.

> God called Abraham to be our "Father in Faith". He was obedient to God and was rewarded for his trust in ways he never could have imagined.

Read more

Abraham: GEN 12–36; CCC 59–61, 72; CCCC 8; YOUCAT 8. *Obedience:* CCC 145–147; CCCC 26; YOUCAT 20.

1.24 Why did the people of Israel wander in the desert for 40 years?

SCAN

Joseph, one of Jacob's sons (SEE TWEET 1.23) was living in Egypt after his brothers sold him into slavery (GEN. 37–39). Later, when a famine broke out in their homeland, Joseph's 11 brothers joined him in Egypt (GEN. 42–47).

Their descendants eventually became so numerous that Pharaoh made them slaves. God knew how much the people of Israel suffered under this oppression. When the people he loves suffer, he also suffers (SEE TWEET 1.37).

Moses

God chose Moses from his people in Egypt to lead them toward a better life. Moses, however, was afraid to undertake this task. He didn't have enough faith in God or himself. He complained: "They will not believe me or listen to my voice" (EX. 4:1). God then gave him signs by which he could prove to the people that he was acting in God's name. When Moses threw his staff on the ground, it changed into a snake (EX. 4:3). His hand became leprous after placing it in his cloak. When he again placed his hand in his cloak, the leprosy disappeared (EX. 4:6). But still Moses resisted, arguing that he wasn't a good speaker. Then God became irritated and told Moses that his brother Aaron could serve as his spokesman. In spite of his doubts and weaknesses, and with God's help, Moses eventually succeeded in fulfilling the task that was given to him.

First: through the desert

God helped the people of Israel to free themselves from their bondage in Egypt. Moses approached Pharaoh and told him to release the Israelites in the name of God. But Pharaoh refused. Then God sent 10 plagues to Egypt, and Pharaoh finally – but reluctantly – let the people go.

After they had fled Egypt, the Israelites began a journey that would last for 40 years. Every day God sent them an edible substance they called *manna*. That was a lesson in trust: they could not keep this "bread from heaven", for

What is God's name?

Moses was wandering through the desert with his sheep when he suddenly saw a burning bush. As he walked toward it, he saw that its branches were not being consumed by the flames. Then he heard the voice of God: "Do not come near; put off your shoes from your feet, for the place on which you are standing is holy ground" (Ex. 3:5).

When Moses asked God to tell him his name, God said: "I AM WHO I AM" (Ex. 3:14). God is the one who is. He is Being. And he is there for all people in all times. He is also there for you! In Hebrew, God's name is written as YHWH. These letters are unpronounceable without vowels. This indicates that we cannot completely know or understand God, that he cannot be expressed fully in human words. God is always greater than our conception of him.

it would go bad. It was exactly enough for one day (Ex. 16). On Mount Sinai, God dictated the Ten Commandments to Moses. Thus he entered into a new covenant with the people (Ex. 19–20; 24; SEE TWEET 1.27). The stone tablets with the Ten Commandments were stored in the Ark of the Covenant, which the people carried with them during their wanderings in the desert and later placed in the Temple of Jerusalem. Because the people kept breaking the Commandments and failing to trust God, they were punished by having to wander for 40 years. After that, Moses and the Israelites reached the border of the land that God had promised to Abraham, Isaac, and Jacob (DEUT. 34:4). Moses died before the people entered the Promised Land and built a new future for themselves. The other books of the Old Testament tell the rest of that story.

From the Promised Land to heaven

God promised yet another covenant to his people (JER. 31:31). Jesus came to fulfill this promise by freeing the people from the bondage of sin – just as God had freed the Israelites from bondage in Egypt. He founded his Church, the new Israel, not on 12 tribes, but on the 12 Apostles. By the covenant he made with God on our behalf on the cross, Jesus wants to take all of us to the Promised Land of heaven. Because he gave his life for us, we can trust and rely on him (SEE TWEET 1.28). Therefore, we never have to lose hope, even in the face of the greatest adversity.

> After God freed his people from bondage, as punishment for their disobedience, it took 40 years for them to reach the Promised Land.

Read more

Israel: Ex. 1–24; CCCC 8, 38–40; YOUCAT 8.

SCAN

1.25 What is the moral of the story of Job?

Job was a pious man who had trusted in God all his life. Misfortune struck him and his family, however. One messenger after another came to bring him terrible news: theft and fire had deprived him of his property; a house had collapsed and killed his children. Although shaken, Job said: "The LORD gave, and the LORD has taken away; blessed be the name of the LORD" (JOB 1:21). Then Job himself became covered in sores from head to toe, and his wife mocked him for his faith. Yet Job remained confident in God.

The origins of Job's suffering

Where did this awful suffering come from? Why did it happen to Job? Trying to find an explanation, Job's friends told him that he must be guilty of something, since God is always just. But as readers of the story, we already know that the suffering that befell Job was caused by Satan, or "the tempter", the enemy of God (JOB 1:6–12). Satan told God that Job loved him only because he had such a good, happy life. God then gave Satan power

over everything Job had, but not over his life. Satan used this power to harm and to taunt Job in the most dreadful way.

Dealing with suffering

The book of Job does not completely answer all of our questions about suffering. God allows the devil, and human beings, to do evil, but the question of why remains unanswered (SEE TWEET 1.34). The largest part of the book of Job is taken up by Job's discussion with his friends who argued that all suffering is punishment for sins. But because Job knew that he was innocent, he even dared to challenge God to prove he had done wrong (JOB 31). When one of his friends argued that God punishes sins but rewards the righteous, he unknowingly predicted Job's future: "Though your beginning was small, your latter days will be very great" (JOB 8:6–7). Job's story tells us how confusing and chaotic life can often be, but also how faith in God eventually brings a happy end. Job firmly believed that God would eventually restore him. His suffering transformed him. Before it, he asked all kinds of earthly blessings from God, while afterward he had only one desire: to see God. In the end he received both. God blessed the last part of Job's life even more than his earlier days (JOB 42:12).

The moral of the story

In Job's case, we know where his suffering came from. But what about the suffering in our own lives? When someone you love very much suddenly dies? Or when you see in the news how many people are injured and killed in wars or disasters? Where is God at such times? We don't have the full answer. But as Christians we do know that our hope points beyond our current life. When you are suffering, you can remember Job, who eventually came through it all happier than he was before. Through Jesus, suffering can acquire an additional meaning because he was willing to suffer for others (SEE TWEET 1.37). With Jesus our suffering can be redemptive like his (SEE TWEET 1.28), that is, it can help to save ourselves and others.

> Job shows that, also during times of pain or sorrow, you can put your faith in God. Trusting God is always rewarded, now and in heaven.

Read more

Job: JOB 1–42.

1.26 Why did Jesus die for us?

With the arrival of Jesus in the world, God offered his people, the Jews, and all of mankind a new and everlasting covenant (SEE TWEET 1.27). This covenant was sealed by Jesus' sacrifice on the cross and his Resurrection on the third day. Because he loves us so much, God wanted to save us for eternal life: "For God so loved the world that he gave his only-begotten Son, that whoever believes in him should not perish but have eternal life" (JN. 3:16). In Jesus, God became a man so that he could die for us and reconcile us with himself and thereby open the way to heaven (SEE TWEET 1.45).

A clean slate

St. Paul wrote that sin and death came into the world through one man, Adam (SEE TWEET 1.4), and were also taken away by one man, Jesus (ROM. 5:12–13). The first sin of Adam weighs on all his descendants as the original sin (SEE TWEET 1.4) and subjects them to death. Jesus changed that. He gave his life "as a ransom for many" (MT. 20:28), for "the forgiveness of sins" (MT. 26:28). On the cross, he took the blame for the sins of all people – present, past, and future. So that includes our sins! As a result, when we are baptized, we are cleansed from original sin and from all of the sins we have personally committed up to that point (SEE TWEET 3.36). We thereby start our relationship with God – as his children through Jesus – with a clean slate.

The ultimate sacrifice

The escape of the Jews from their oppression in Egypt served as a confirmation of their covenant with God (SEE TWEET 1.24). The people would often break this covenant, however, by sin. So, under the Old Covenant sacrifices to God for sins were repeated constantly (HEB. 10:1).

The death of Jesus on the cross brought about a new and everlasting covenant between God and man (SEE TWEET 1.27). Jesus himself was the ultimate sacrifice. But of course, he was much more than that: "Greater love has no man than this, that a man lay down his life for his friends" (JN. 15:13). The sacrifice of Jesus on the cross, out of love, is his incredible gift to us and to God. Through it, Jesus entered into the New Covenant with God on our behalf, which can never again be broken by us. Because of the sacrifice of Jesus, we can be freed from the burden of sin and become children of God through Baptism (SEE TWEET 3.36).

Lamb of God

With good reason, St. John the Baptist spoke of Jesus as "the Lamb of God, who takes away the sin of the world" (Jn. 1:29). The prophet Isaiah had said that the Lord would lay the blame for all our misconduct on his servant. Just like that servant, Jesus was "like a lamb that is led to the slaughter" (Isa. 53:7). During the celebration of the Eucharist, the sacrifice of the Mass is united with the sacrifice of Jesus on the cross. On the cross, Jesus allowed himself to be "broken" for our sake (SEE TWEET 3.45 AND 3.48), and to signify this the Host is broken by the priest during Mass. At that moment in Mass we say: "Lamb of God, you take away the sins of the world, have mercy on us." Jesus does indeed have mercy on us: with our sins forgiven, we are destined to live with him forever.

> By his death and Resurrection, Jesus restored our relationship with God. Because of his sacrifice, all who turn to God can go to heaven.

Read more

Baptism and washing away of sin: CCC 1250, 1282; CCCC 258; YOUCAT 197. *Fullness of revelation:* CCC 65–67, 73; CCCC 9–10; YOUCAT 9–10. *Jesus takes our sins upon himself:* CCC 613–617, 622–623; CCCC 122; YOUCAT 101.

1.27 What is the covenant? And what is God's plan of salvation?

God has been involved with mankind since the beginning. Loving us yet knowing that we would reject his love, and separate ourselves from him, God made a plan for our salvation, which we can find in the Bible. The Old Testament begins with the Creation and the Fall (SEE TWEET 1.1–1.4). After the Flood (SEE TWEET 1.22) it is mostly concerned with the formation of the Jewish people, the people of Israel, the Israelites (SEE TWEET 1.23–1.24). This nation was chosen by God, from all the earth's peoples, to fulfill a special purpose.

Connected to God

God sealed his selection of the Israelites through a covenant, which is not so much like a contract, but more like a spiritual marriage in which God would love and care for his people no matter what and they would love him in return. This covenant was initially made with Abraham and then renewed through the Exodus (SEE TWEET 1.23–1.24). The people, however, did not remain faithful to God. They turned away from him to worship other gods,

to do as they pleased, and brought misery and suffering upon themselves. God forgave Israel and reestablished the covenant by giving Moses the Ten Commandments, which were chiselled into two stone tablets (SEE TWEET 1.24 AND 4.9). The rest of the Old Testament tells of how God's people repeatedly sinned against him, harming themselves and each other, and how, each time, God forgave them and renewed his covenant with them.

The plan of salvation

Whenever God's people strayed away from him, God called upon prophets to speak on his behalf and to bring his people back. The prophets told the people that God had a big plan for them: he wanted to save not only them but through them all the peoples of the earth. A large part of the Old Testament is devoted to the prophets, through whom God prepared the people for the biggest part of his plan of salvation, the coming of Jesus, the Savior, who would bring redemption from sin and lasting happiness. In the fullness of time, Jesus was born into a Jewish family, and God sent

What does
Anno Domini (A.D.) mean?

A.D. is an abbreviation of the Latin *Anno Domini*, meaning, "in the Year of our Lord". Our calendar begins with Jesus' year of birth. This is not an accident; it is the way we indicate how important the birth of Jesus is to the human race. It was then that our calendar began anew, because mankind was presented with a new future. This is the reason why historical dates sometimes include A.D. or B.C., which means "before Christ".

This dating system was devised in the year 525 by the monk Dionysius Exiguus. He counted backward from his time to the time of Christ. The reason he did this was to ascertain the date of the first Easter. The outcome of his calculations was to serve as the beginning of our calendar. Note that at the time there were several calendars in use.

It is interesting to note that, due to an error in the calendar, we do not know exactly in what year Jesus was born. We know that he was born during King Herod's reign. However, King Herod died in about 4 B.C., so most scholars assume, then, that Jesus was born around the year 6 B.C. and not in what we would call the year 0.

the last of his prophets, St. John the Baptist, to prepare the people to accept Jesus as their awaited Savior. Some Jews accepted Jesus, but many did not, and yet God's plan of salvation continued to unfold. In fact, because Jesus was rejected by the leaders of his people, he was condemned to death, and his execution was the very means by which the whole world could be saved (SEE TWEET 1.26). In this way, Jesus made a covenant with God on our behalf, a covenant that no longer could be broken by human sin.

#The plan continues

After Jesus rose from the dead, he commissioned his Apostles to spread the good news of his death and Resurrection to all the peoples of the earth. Early on, this mission seemed doomed to failure as the Apostles were persecuted by their own people wherever they went, but again God used rejection to fulfill his purpose: he inspired the Apostles to spread the gospel to the Gentiles, that is, non-Jews. The missionary zeal of the Church continued through the ages, and as a result the prophecies of old have come to pass: God's offer of salvation has spread throughout the earth!

> God's covenant with Israel set them apart for the salvation of the world. Salvation history = the unfolding of God's plan to save mankind.

Read more

Covenant with Israel: CCC 62–64, 72; CCCC 8; YOUCAT 8. *Plan of Salvation:* CCC 51–55, 68–70; CCCC 6–7; YOUCAT 7–8.

1.28 Why did Jesus have to die such a horrific death?

One thing is certain: in his humanity Jesus awaited his suffering and death on the cross with pain and anxiety. He even asked God not to let it happen. While praying in the Garden of Gethsemane he said: "Father, if you are willing, remove this chalice from me" (Lk. 22:42). Did he doubt whether he was strong enough to bear this inhumane suffering? Perhaps, but because he was still prepared to suffer in obedience to the Father and out of love for us, he added: "Not my will, but yours, be done" (Lk. 22:42). And so Jesus went to his death.

Gruesome

The Bible says that in this way Jesus obtained forgiveness for our sins and thereby saved us from death (SEE TWEET 1.26). We could ask ourselves whether God, who is almighty (SEE TWEET 1.35), could have redeemed us in another way. We don't know the answer, but Jesus' prayer in Gethsemane suggests that the answer is no, not because God is limited but because a perfect offering was needed to reunite God and sinful man; thus God provided this perfect offering – himself. The Jewish religious leaders saw it as an insult to God (or blasphemy) that Jesus presumed to forgive sins and called himself the Son of God (SEE BOX), which is the reason they demanded his death. Through the Resurrection, God showed that Jesus really is his Son, who really does have the power to forgive sins and to grant eternal life. The murder of God's only Son is the greatest sin imaginable. Yet Jesus forgave those who did it (Lk. 23:24), proving that there is, then, no sin too great to be forgiven by God.

Holy Wounds

St. Peter told of how we have been healed by the wounds of Jesus (I Pt. 2:24). In this way, Jesus brought God and man together. The sacrifice on the cross could be seen as the answer Jesus gave on behalf of mankind to God. The Resurrection is God's answer to mankind. The five Holy Wounds in Jesus' hands, feet, and side are signs of our redemption. This is why, for example, a bishop

Is Jesus the Son of God?

Before the time of Jesus, the Jews had already spoken of some special persons as "sons of God". In Scripture, Israel is called God's "first-born son" (Ex. 4:22). Kings were also sometimes called God's sons (Ps. 2:7). However, when we call Jesus the Son of God, this is not just a cultural or honorary title. The relationship between Jesus and the Father is different from our bond with God, because Jesus himself is also God. Thomas, one of Jesus' Apostles, known as "Doubting Thomas", proclaimed to Jesus: "My Lord and my God!" (Jn. 20:28). God himself called Jesus his "beloved Son" (Mt. 3:17). Peter even said to Jesus: "You are the Christ, the Son of the living God" (Mt. 16:16). And Jesus confirmed that. Many who heard Jesus say that he was the Son of God did not believe him. They even wanted to stone him for blasphemy, saying: "You, being a man, make yourself God" (Jn. 10:33). They would have never wanted to stone him if the expression "Son of God" was merely an honorific title. In this way, Scripture confirms that Jesus is truly God. The belief that Jesus Christ is the Son of God is the essential criterion for being a Christian (CCC 454). In the Nicene Creed (SEE TWEET 1.31), we speak of Jesus being "true God from true God, begotten, not made, consubstantial with the Father".

anoints an altar with chrism before it is first used: he makes five crosses on the altar's surface to represent the five wounds of Christ.

Life from death

The greatest suffering of Jesus was caused not by his physical wounds but by the desolation and rejection that he experienced on the cross. Though God, Jesus in his humanity experienced abandonment by God, which is what we ourselves would suffer for our sins without the forgiveness offered through Christ. In our place Jesus said: "My God, my God, why have you forsaken me?" (Mk. 15:34). Jesus, without guilt or blame, became "sin" for us (Heb. 9:28; SEE TWEET 1.26). It is our sins, and their punishment, that he bore on the cross. He stayed to the last moment faithful to God (II Tim. 2:13), and with his last breath he said: "Father, into your hands I commit my spirit!" (Lk. 23:46). By offering his love to God in our place, he made our reconciliation with God possible (Col. 1:20). Jesus made a new covenant with his Father on our behalf that will last for all time (Heb. 9:15; SEE TWEET 1.27).

By suffering and dying in our place, Jesus has reconciled us with God. He destroyed sin so that we may live forever.

Read more

Jesus takes our sins upon himself: CCC 613–617, 622–623; CCCC 122; YOUCAT 101. *Sacrifice on the cross:* CCC 616–618, 623; CCCC 122–123; YOUCAT 101–102. *Son of God:* CCC 441–445, 454; CCCC 83; YOUCAT 74.

1.29 Wasn't Jesus really just a good person and a wise guru?

Some say that Jesus was just a man who had a calling – like the prophets – to speak about God. However, if Jesus was *really* a good person, he could not have claimed that he was God: that would have been a lie, and a liar is not a good person.

Crazy as a poached egg?

The English author C. S. Lewis warned those who were willing to accept Jesus as a great moral teacher but not as God: "A man who was merely a man and said the sort of things Jesus said would not be a great moral teacher. He would either be a lunatic – on the level with the man who says he is a poached egg – or else he would be the Devil of Hell. You must make your choice. Either this man was, and is, the Son of God: or else a madman or something worse" (MERE CHRISTIANITY).

Thus, according to Lewis, there are three possibilities: (1) Jesus was crazy, (2) Jesus was evil, or (3) Jesus was (and is) God (SEE TWEET 1.27).

A madman, evil, or God?

In the Gospels, a few people called Jesus a madman (JN. 10:20). Most people, however, recognized that he engaged in rational debate and therefore was not mad. Even his enemies could not accuse Jesus of being evil in the strict sense of the word. On the contrary, he did good things of a supernatural nature. When he was asked whether he was the Christ, or the Messiah, he referred to his miracles: "The blind receive their sight and the lame walk, lepers are cleansed and the deaf hear, and the dead are raised up, and the poor have good news preached to them" (MT. 11:4–5). For ages the prophets had predicted that God would someday send the Savior who would do those things (ISA. 29:18–19). And then it happened! Seeing this, people said: "These are not the sayings of one who has a demon. Can a demon open the eyes of the blind?" (JN. 10:21). Most extraordinary were the things Jesus said of himself (SEE TWEET 1.28), namely that he was one with God. He did great miracles and spoke about God as someone who knows him intimately. Someone who can do all that has to be more than just a wise guru: he must be God himself!

Was Jesus a person, a Word, or God himself?

Some people say the Church determined that Jesus was God only several centuries after his death. This is not true. The New Testament tells us that the first Christians already believed that Jesus was God (Rom. 9:5; Col 2:9). Jesus said: "I and the Father are one" (Jn. 10:30). John spoke of Jesus as being the "Word": "In the beginning was the Word, and the Word was with God, and the Word was God" (Jn. 1:1). Jesus is the Word that God spoke when he created the world (see Tweet 1.2). The ancient Greeks understood the term *Word* (*Logos*) to mean a bridge connecting God and the material world. Jesus is not only a bridge and mediator between God and man, he is also God. Early texts show that the first Christians believed this. St. Ignatius of Antioch, for example, wrote in around A.D. 108 that Jesus is God, and that he was born not only of a human being (Mary) but also of the Holy Spirit of God (Lk. 1:35). Another example is the early report of the Roman historical scholar Pliny, a pagan who wrote to Emperor Trajan that the Christians worshipped their leader "as a god" (Letters 10:96).

Jesus was also, however, fully human. He was born from a woman, Mary (Lk. 2:7). He grew up as normal children do (Lk. 2:40–52). He experienced hunger and thirst (Mt. 4:2; Jn. 19:28). He got tired (Jn. 4:6). He was afraid (Lk. 22:44). And, he eventually died (Lk. 23:46). Even when he rose from the dead on the third day, he had a human, albeit glorified, body (Lk. 24:39; Jn. 20:20–27). As a human being, Jesus is like us in everything but sin (Heb. 4:15). The conclusion is that Jesus is both God and man at the same time! Jesus is one person with two natures: a divine nature and a human nature. In this he is unique.

God and man

God fulfilled his promise to send the Savior when Jesus was born in Bethlehem (Lk. 2:1–7; Jn. 1:1–14). Jesus is God himself made man (see box). Not only did Jesus teach us how we should love one another, but he practiced what he preached as no other person ever has. In his humanity, he demonstrated how a perfect human being lives. We can also strive for this, and in doing so, take part in our own redemption. Precisely by becoming man, God redeemed us from the limitations of this life, which are brought about by sin and error. He opened the way to eternal life in heaven (see Tweet 1.45). A mere human being could never have done these things.

 A good and wise person cannot reconcile us with God the way Jesus did. Jesus is both man and God: he desires, and IS, our redemption.

Read more

God and mankind: CCC 464–469, 480–482; CCCC 89–91; YOUCAT 77.

 ## 1.30 Did Jesus have brothers and sisters?

People in Nazareth said about Jesus: "Is not this the carpenter's son? Is not his mother called Mary? And are not his brethren James and Joseph and Simon and Judas? And are not all his sisters with us?" (Mt. 13:55–56; see Mk. 6:3). At a certain point, Jesus was told that his mother and his brothers stood outside, asking to speak with him (Mt. 12:46). We also read about Jesus' brothers going to a feast while he himself stayed behind (Jn. 7:3–9). One could wonder, therefore, whether Mary had borne other children besides Jesus, meaning that she did not remain a virgin as we Catholics believe (see Tweet 1.40).

Brother or nephew?

In the Scriptures we come across hundreds of occasions when the word *brother* refers to a relative other than a sibling. Sometimes it refers to persons who have the same parents, such as Cain and Abel (Gen. 4:2; see Tweet 1.2), but often it does not. Tobit, for example, called the angel Raphael "my brother" (Tob. 5:11). He didn't know at that time that he was an angel,

but it was clear to him that they did not share the same parents! When the Gospels speak of the brothers and sisters of Jesus, they are not referring to children of Joseph and Mary, but rather, to other relatives: cousins, nieces and nephews, uncles and aunts. In Hebrew, the same word was usually used for all these relations. In the Septuagint (see Tweet 1.15) and in the New Testament it was translated into the Greek word for brother (*adelphos*).

The brothers of Jesus

The names of Jesus' "brothers" are used in Nazareth, where everyone knows him. Because more than one of Jesus' disciples is called James (Jacob), the modifiers "the Greater" and "the Lesser" have been added to their names (see Tweet 2.15). Matthew spoke of the "brothers" James (the Lesser), Simon, and Joseph (whom Mark calls Joses and Judas) (Mt. 13:55; Mk. 6:3). The confusing thing is that their mother is also called Mary. She is "Mary, the mother of James [the Lesser] and Joseph" (Mt. 27:56) (or Joses [Mk. 15:40]); and elsewhere

"Mary, the mother of James [the Lesser]" (Mk. 16:1; Lk. 24:10). This Mary was probably the cousin of Jesus' mother, because in the Gospel she is called "his mother's sister, Mary the wife of Clopas" (Jn. 19:25).

The mother of James (the Greater) and John was also a close follower of Jesus. She was married to Zebedee (Mt. 20:20, 27:56; Mk. 10:35). She stood at the foot of the cross, together with Jesus' mother (Jn. 19:25; Lk. 24:10). Perhaps it was because they were cousins of Jesus that James (the Greater) and John, "sons of Zebedee", dared to ask him whether they could be seated at his left and at his right in the Kingdom (Mk. 10:35–37; Mt. 20:20–21).

Who is my mother?

None of these "brothers" was a child of Joseph and Mary. Jesus was their only child. Otherwise would he not have entrusted his mother to his brother(s) while hanging on the cross, instead of to the Apostle John? (Jn. 19:27; SEE PICTURE). James, the "Lord's brother", was still alive, because Paul later came across him (Gal. 1:19). When Jesus' mother and brothers wanted to see him, he said: "Who is my mother, and who are my brethren?" He answered this question himself: "Whoever does the will of my Father in heaven is my brother, and sister, and mother" (Mt. 12:48–50).

Jesus himself calls us all "brother, and sister, and mother". In doing so, he is showing us that blood relations are not as important as

following him. This becomes concrete in the Sacrament of Baptism (SEE TWEET 3.36). Together we make up one big family of God's children, and we are thus brothers and sisters of Jesus. This is also why Jesus' mother Mary is the mother of us all.

> Mary & Joseph conceived no children together. Jesus' "brothers" and "sisters" are other relatives. You too can be brother or sister of Jesus!

Read more

Mary's Virginity: CCC 496–498; CCCC 98; YOUCAT 80. *Brothers and sisters of Jesus:* CCC 499–501, 510; CCCC 99; YOUCAT 81.

1.31 Who is the Holy Spirit?

Most people can form an idea of God the Father. We can picture what Jesus, God the Son, looks like, because he is a man. But who is the Holy Spirit? The first book of the Bible, Genesis, tells us that "in the beginning ... the Spirit of God [the Holy Spirit] was moving over the face of the waters" (GEN. 1:1–2). Just as God the Father and God the Son have always existed, God the Holy Spirit, or Holy Ghost, has also always existed. He is the third Person of the Holy Trinity (SEE TWEET 1.33).

From Father and Son

The Holy Spirit is a Person, with his own personality and gifts (SEE TWEET 1.32). St. Thomas Aquinas called the Holy Spirit the fruit of the love between the Father and the Son. The Holy Spirit comes forth from the Father and the Son, as the sun produces warm rays of light. We confirm this every Sunday when we pray the Creed (SEE BOX). Because the Holy Spirit is God himself, he understands God completely (I COR. 2:10).

Waves on the beach

To help you imagine the Holy Spirit, think of the beach. Can you see a wave, without seeing the sea? The Holy Spirit is like the wave, and the sea is like the Word of God.

Through the Holy Spirit, life came into the world. He speaks to us, but not about himself: he merely allows us to hear the Word of the Father. He is the Spirit of God who approaches us invisibly and wants to help us to understand the Word of God and to accept it in faith (CCC 687; SEE TWEET 1.20).

In the Old Testament, kings received the Holy Spirit by being anointed. This was the same Spirit who helped prophets such as Moses, Elijah, Isaiah, Ezekiel, Jeremiah, and many others. Bravely, the prophets even criticized kings. The Holy Spirit enabled them to inspire countless people.

The same is true for the Apostles, who went forth to spread the gospel with the help of the

"I believe in the Holy Spirit"

Every Sunday, the Nicene Creed is prayed in all Catholic churches, as well as in many other Christian communities. With the Creed we express our faith in God the Father, the Son, and the Holy Spirit.

"I believe in one God, the Father almighty, maker of heaven and earth, of all things visible and invisible. I believe in one Lord Jesus Christ, the Only Begotten Son of God, born of the Father before all ages. God from God, Light from Light, true God from true God, begotten, not made, consubstantial with the Father; through him all things were made. For us men and for our salvation he came down from heaven, and by the Holy Spirit was incarnate of the Virgin Mary, and became man. For our sake he was crucified under Pontius Pilate, he suffered death and was buried, and rose again on the third day in accordance with the Scriptures. He ascended into heaven and is seated at the right hand of the Father. He will come again in glory to judge the living and the dead and his kingdom will have no end. I believe in the Holy Spirit, the Lord, the giver of life, who proceeds from the Father and the Son, who with the Father and the Son is adored and glorified, who has spoken through the prophets. I believe in one, holy, catholic and apostolic Church. I confess one Baptism for the forgiveness of sins and I look forward to the resurrection of the dead and the life of the world to come. Amen."

Holy Spirit. Even today, the Holy Spirit still helps us through his gifts (SEE TWEET 1.32).

Breath of Life
The story of Creation tells us that God made man from the dust of the ground and breathed his breath (the Spirit) into him to bring him to life (GEN. 2:7). The Holy Spirit is often called "the breath of God".

Because he is known by what he does, symbols are often used to express the Holy Spirit: a breath, the air or the wind, water, fire, light, and clouds. He is also often depicted as a dove, as when he descended on Jesus when John baptized him (MT. 3:16).

With the Father and the Son, the Holy Spirit is God. He comforts us, lets us share in God's love, and helps us.

Read more
The Holy Spirit: CCC 687–688; CCCC 137; YOUCAT 116. *Names and symbols of the Holy Spirit* CCC 691–701; CCCC 138–139; YOUCAT 115.

1.32 What does the Holy Spirit do? Do I need him?

SCAN

John the Baptist spoke about Jesus: "I baptize you with water for repentance, but he who is coming after me is mightier than I, whose sandals I am not worthy to carry; he will baptize you with the Holy Spirit and with fire" (Mt. 3:11). Long before that time, the prophet Isaiah had already spoken of the expected Savior: "The Spirit of the Lord shall rest upon him, the spirit of wisdom and understanding, the spirit of counsel and might, the spirit of knowledge and the fear of the Lord" (Isa. 11:2).

Promise fulfilled

This promise became reality with Jesus, who was full of the Holy Spirit (Lk. 4:18–19). Mary became pregnant through the Holy Spirit (Lk. 1:35); she "conceived in her womb and bore a son" (Lk. 1:31). When Jesus was baptized, the Holy Spirit descended on him (Mt. 3:16). Jesus preached the Kingdom of God and performed many miracles with the help of the Holy Spirit. He cured blind people, gave cripples the use of their legs, and cast out demons. But the Holy Spirit was not only meant for Jesus. After his Resurrection, Jesus gave the gift of the Holy Spirit to all of his followers.

The workings of the Spirit

God gives us the Holy Spirit so that we can live good Christian lives. The Holy Spirit is especially given through the Sacraments of Baptism and Confirmation, which fortify us with his gifts (SEE BOX; SEE TWEET 3.36–3.37). The clearest sign of the Holy Spirit is the life of a saintly person. For example, St. Maximilian Kolbe (†1941) exhibited the greatest Christian charity, a fruit of the Spirit, when he traded

....

12 fruits of the Holy Spirit

- charity
- joy
- peace
- patience
- kindness
- goodness

- generosity
- gentleness
- faithfulness
- modesty
- self-control
- chastity

(Gal. 5:22–23; CCC 1832)

7 gifts of the Holy Spirit

1   *Wisdom*: the knowledge of God's plan and purposes.
2   *Understanding*: the grasp of revealed truths, especially those in Scripture.
3   *Counsel*: the knowledge of the best course of action as God sees it.
4   *Fortitude*: the strength in the face of difficulties to do what is right in the service of God.
5   *Knowledge*: the knowledge of created things in right relation to God.
6   *Piety*: reverence for God, as the Creator and Lord of all, and for men and women as his children who have been created in his image.
7   *Fear of the Lord*: the dread of offending God because he is all good and deserving of all our love.

(Isa. 11:2; ccc 1831)

his life for that of someone else (SEE TWEET 4.41). Nobody can have even Christian faith without the Holy Spirit (I COR. 12:3). And it's the Holy Spirit that teaches us to pray from the heart: "God has sent the Spirit of his Son into our hearts, crying, 'Abba! Father!'" (GAL. 4:6).

The Comforter and Helper

Before he died, Jesus promised that an Advocate, a Helper, would come to assist his followers (JN. 14:16–17). This is what we celebrate every year on Pentecost (SEE TWEET 3.34). Because God respects our freedom, we are free to cooperate with the Spirit or to go against him: we have the choice. Every day, in many different ways, we are faced with such choices. That is the basis of what it means to lead a Christian life. The Holy Spirit gives us gifts that help us to choose what is right (SEE BOX). The evidence of his working through us is

what St. Paul called the fruits of the Spirit (SEE BOX). The Holy Spirit helps us to pray, because we cannot do that alone. As St. Paul said: "The Spirit helps us in our weakness; for we do not know how to pray as we ought, but the Spirit himself intercedes with sighs too deep for words" (ROM. 8:26). He also helps us to explain our faith: "Do not be anxious about how or what you are to answer or what you are to say; for the Holy Spirit will teach you in that very hour what you ought to say" (LK. 12:11–12).

Every right choice we make is inspired by the Holy Spirit. You need his help to live a truly Christian life. Ask for it!

Read more

'Conceived of the Holy Spirit': CCC 484–486; CCCC 94; YOUCAT 80.
Gifts of the Holy Spirit: CCC 1830–1831, 1845; CCCC 389; YOUCAT 310. *Fruits of the Holy Spirit*: CCC 1832; CCCC 390; YOUCAT 311.
Fruits of Confirmation: CCC 1302–1305; CCCC 268–269; YOUCAT 205.

1.33 God is one, and at the same time he is three. Isn't that nonsense?

SCAN

There is only one God, but in him are three Persons: God the Father, God the Son, and God the Holy Spirit. Together, they are the Holy Trinity. But how can we imagine something that is both one and, at the same time, three? Ultimately, we cannot fully grasp this.

St. Augustine once walked along a beach, pondering the Holy Trinity. He came across a little boy walking to and fro with a tiny bucket. The boy said he wanted to put the whole sea into the hole he had dug in the sand. When Augustine said that the sea would never fit in the hole, the boy replied that, similarly, he would never be able to fit the whole mystery of the Trinity in his mind.

Images of God

Nevertheless, certain images can help us to understand something of what it means that God is both one and three. For example, the three sides of a triangle form one whole. In this sense, they are one, because if you remove one of the sides, you no longer have a triangle. Also, the space any material thing takes up is one, but has three dimensions.

In the fifth century, St. Patrick used a shamrock to explain the Trinity: it is one clover, but it consists of three leaves. In some paintings of the Trinity, God the Father is depicted as an old man with a white beard, and Jesus as a younger man. Such images might help us to think about the fatherhood of God and the manhood of the Son in Jesus, but the Persons of the Trinity have always existed, and will continue to exist for all time: they are without beginning or end.

Sharing love

The loving relationship between Father, Son, and Holy Spirit is the very essence of God, and he does not want to keep that love just for himself. He created us so that we could share in his love. By uniting ourselves with Jesus, we enter into the communion of love that is the Trinity.

The Apostles' Creed (12 articles of faith)

1. I believe in God, the Father almighty, Creator of heaven and earth,
2. and in Jesus Christ, his only Son, our Lord,
3. who was conceived by the Holy Spirit, born of the Virgin Mary,
4. suffered under Pontius Pilate, was crucified, died and was buried;
5. he descended into hell; on the third day he arose again from the dead;
6. he ascended into heaven, and is seated at the right hand of God the Father almighty;
7. from there he will come to judge the living and the dead.
8. I believe in the Holy Spirit,
9. the holy catholic Church, the communion of saints,
10. the forgiveness of sins,
11. the resurrection of the body,
12. and life everlasting. Amen.

....

A special connection

In the famous icon of the Trinity by Andrei Rublev († c. 1430), the three angels who visited Abraham and foretold the birth of Isaac (Gen. 18:1–15), symbolize the Father, the Son, and the Holy Spirit (SEE PICTURE). Their postures and looks show the connection between them, and Abraham participated in their communion when they shared a meal together. In the icon, the angels form a loving unity, but each one is also fully and entirely himself. On the left, the Father is depicted with his heavenly abode above him, where we are all welcome (Jn. 14:2–3). On the right, there's the Holy Spirit

with a mountain, which symbolizes our ascent to God through prayer (Lk. 6:12). The Son sits in the middle, with the tree of life, symbolizing the cross. He points to the chalice, which represents his sacrifice on our behalf. The open space between the Father and the Spirit forms a cup holding the Son. Just like the Persons of the Trinity, in heaven we will have a perfect connection with God and with each other (SEE TWEET 1.45), and we will be fully ourselves.

As three Persons, in himself God shares love between the Father, the Son, and the Holy Spirit. He wants to share that love with you too!

Read more

Holy Trinity: CCC 232–267; CCCC 45–49; YOUCAT 35–39.

SCAN

 ## 1.34 Did God create evil?
What does it have to do with my sins?

If God is utterly good, how could he permit evil to exist? If he can do anything, why does he allow people to do terrible things? Why doesn't God intervene? We are unable to know fully the answers to these questions. We refer to them as the "mystery of evil" (in Latin: *mysterium iniquitatis*). We do know, however, that evil is the corruption, or perversion, of good, and does not correspond with God's Will.

Origin

Before he became a Christian, St. Augustine "strove to understand where evil comes from, but found no answer" (CONFESSIONS 7,7.11). After his conversion, he saw that the best thing to do when faced with the question of evil, is to try to understand it from the perspective of God's love. Without the light of divine revelation, it's very difficult to see that the source of evil is sin (CCC 387; SEE TWEET 1.4).

God made us in order to love him and to love each other. We have the freedom to love, but we can also abuse that freedom by making bad

A very important bath

Because Jesus gave his life for our sins, both original sin (SEE TWEET 1.4) and our personal sins can be washed away through Baptism. This is the beginning of a Christian life (SEE TWEET 3.36). In this way we become children of God. Even after Baptism, our tendency toward evil remains (SEE TWEET 1.4). We are easily persuaded to do something wrong. To remove sins committed after Baptism, Jesus gave us another sacrament: Reconciliation, also known as confession (SEE TWEET 3.38-3.39). In all the sacraments of the Church, Jesus gives us grace, which is a share in his own life (SEE TWEET 4.8). Grace makes the difficulties we face, including temptations, easier to overcome. The Holy Spirit (SEE TWEET 1.32), received in Baptism, helps us to be open to receive God's grace.

choices. All of us have had the experience of doing something we knew was wrong. Deep down we knew were making a bad choice, but we went ahead and did it anyway. We allowed ourselves to go along with it, almost against our own wills. This is how we personally participate in evil.

Good and evil

The struggle between good and evil takes place in the hearts and minds of every person. While the biblical story of Adam and Eve falling into sin doesn't have to be taken literally, it does reveal important truths (SEE TWEET 1.2). It shows that even the first man and woman were tempted to choose evil rather than good; thus, nobody can avoid temptation. The story also shows *how* our first parents were tempted. First of all, Satan lied to Eve, telling her that she would not die if she disobeyed God, as God himself had said, but would instead become like God. Behind every temptation is a lie that says something bad is good. Eve was being deceived when she saw that the forbidden tree "was good for food, and that it was a delight to the eyes, and that the tree was to be desired to make one wise" (GEN. 3:6). These three desires at the root of every sin are "the lust of the flesh, the lust of the eyes, and the pride of life" (I JN. 2:16).

Because of the Fall, mankind is prone to sin (SEE TWEET 1.4). We inherited this tendency from our ancestors. As St. Paul said: "By one man's [Adam's] disobedience many were made sinners" (ROM. 5:19). And the tendency toward evil remains in us after Baptism (SEE BOX). That is why our struggle against sin is often so difficult (SEE TWEET 4.13).

Evil and Jesus

We have reached the core reason why Jesus came into our world: to save mankind from the burden of sin (SEE TWEET 1.26). What's most important is not our sins, but the forgiveness and the redemption that Jesus offers us: "Then as one man's [Adam's] trespass led to condemnation for all men, so one man's [Jesus'] act of righteousness leads to acquittal and life for all men" (ROM. 5:18).

By accepting forgiveness and redemption from Jesus, and by uniting ourselves with him, we can overcome our sinful tendencies, conquer the evil at work in the world, and become the man or the woman God intended us to be from the beginning. That's why St. Thomas Aquinas could say: "God allows evils to happen in order to bring a greater good therefrom" (SUMMA III.1.3 AD 3). And St. Paul said: "Where sin increased, grace abounded all the more" (ROM. 5:20).

> God created everything good. He gave us free will so that we can choose to do what is good. Evil results when we abuse our freedom to sin.

Read more

Abuse of our freedom: CCC 386–387; CCCC 73; YOUCAT 67. *Evil in the world:* CCC 309–314, 324; CCCC 57–58; YOUCAT 51. *Necessity of Baptism:* CCC 1257–1261, 1281, 1283; CCCC 261–262; YOUCAT 199.

1.35 If God is all-powerful, why do disasters happen? Why is there evil?

Is God omnipotent? In other words: Can God do anything? A great philosopher once asked whether God could create a stone so heavy that he couldn't lift it. If we take this tricky question seriously, we must conclude that God is not omnipotent. But can we really capture God in a trick of human words?

Many people wonder why God doesn't take away the evil in our world. When we try to figure out an answer, we have to distinguish between the evil that people do themselves (moral evil) and other things that we experience as evil, such as natural disasters (physical, or natural, evil).

Disasters as punishment?

There are people who consider natural disasters such as earthquakes, tsunamis, and hurricanes as punishments from God. That is absolutely wrong. It is true that God can influence the weather (Deut. 11:17; Jas. 5:17). And in the Old Testament, some natural disasters were punishments for the sins of people. Think of

the Great Flood, for example (SEE TWEET 1.22). But all of that was part of the history of the people of Israel, who were being prepared for the birth of Jesus (SEE TWEET 1.24). The coming of Jesus is the ultimate evidence of God's love for mankind. The suffering and sorrow that is caused by disasters do not correspond to that love. Therefore, we cannot regard such disasters as punishments from God. He suffers with the people who are struck by these disasters. And he inspires other people to help the victims. In this way, something good can come of this evil. God needs our help for that. But why does God allow such natural disasters to occur in the first place? Ultimately, we don't have the answer to that. It has to do with the origin of evil, which remains a mystery to us.

Human freedom limits God?

Why doesn't God stop people who are about to do harm? The short answer is that people are not puppets controlled by God. People have free will so that they can choose to do what is good. But this same freedom enables them to

God is almighty and merciful

It is precisely through of our weakness that God can show his omnipotence and mercy. Think of what God told Abraham, when he could not believe he would become a father at his old age: "Is anything too hard for the LORD?" (GEN. 18:14; SEE TWEET 1.23). At the Annunciation, Mary could hardly believe she would give birth to a son. The angel Gabriel said: "With God nothing will be impossible" (LK. 1:37; SEE TWEET 1.39).

Abraham and Mary had faith. That is why God could prove his omnipotence to them and through them. The secret lies in our surrender to God. If we can manage to rely on God, he can do great things! Then disasters and evil can never depress us totally and take away our hope. God is omnipotent because he can bring good out of evil. He is the one who gives people the inspiration and the strength to do good, even in the most desperate circumstances. The evil in the world remains a great mystery. But it cannot even begin to offset God's unending love for us.

choose to do what is evil. If we freely choose to go our own way, God will not intervene – because otherwise, we would not be truly free. You could say that this is an inability to act. But God isn't a dictator who violently forces us to do his Will. Our freedom to choose is the consequence of his unending love. Because he loves people so much, it hurts him to see the suffering that is caused by our evil choices.

Good or evil?

People can choose to do what is good, but often they choose to do what is evil. Murder, theft, rape, and slander – all of these are choices that people make when they want to get something for themselves at the expense of others. When we think only of our desires, with no regard for the Will of God and the harm that we do, we are full of pride, which

is what caused the downfall of Adam and Eve when they thought they could "be like God" (GEN. 3:5; SEE TWEET 1.4). There is only one way to counter evil: to be humble by choosing to love God and to do what he wants. Jesus is our example. Although he was God, equal to the Father, he humbled himself by taking on our humanity and obeying the Father, even unto death on a cross (PHIL. 2:8; SEE TWEET 1.26).

> Neither the world nor the people in it are perfect, hence bad things happen. God proves his omnipotence by bringing good out of evil.

Read more

Evil in the world: CCC 309–314, 324; CCCC 57–58; YOUCAT 51.

1.36 Is it the Will of God that people die?

God created us for life. Death came into the world with sin: "For the wages of sin is death" (ROM. 6:23; SEE TWEET 1.4). God is the source of life. If we turn against him, we also turn against life itself. But the opposite is also true!

The moment sin came into the world, death became the fate of mankind. But that was not God's intention when he created the earthly paradise, Eden. Even so, he respected man's freedom to choose something other than him (SEE TWEET 1.2 AND 1.34). In the world as it is now, with suffering and death, we cannot live forever. Every man must die eventually. But as Christians, we know that death is not the end but rather a new beginning. As Jesus said: "I came that they may have life, and have it abundantly" (JN. 10:10). Because Jesus sacrificed his life for us, and then rose from the dead, after our own death we can live forever with him in heaven. The grave could not hold Jesus, and it will not hold those in union with him. That is the reason for our hope (SEE TWEET 1.50).

Hatching

So death is part of human life as we know it. The English writer C. S. Lewis once wrote: "It may be hard for an egg to turn into a bird; it would be a jolly sight harder for it to learn to fly while remaining an egg. We are like eggs at present. And you cannot go on indefinitely being just an ordinary, decent egg. We must be hatched, or go bad" (MERE CHRISTIANITY).

Even though we understand that death is inevitable, and that eternal life awaits those who die with hope in God, we are still sad when someone dies. People often say that someone died "too young" or "too soon". Even when a very old person dies, we experience grief. That is understandable.

We might wonder if mourning the loss of someone is a criticism of God's plan for that person, but it is only natural to mourn for a loved one. Even Jesus grieved over Lazarus when he died (JN. 11:35).

Miracles in death

While the soul goes to God when someone dies, the body remains and decomposes (SEE TWEET 1.43). But sometimes a miracle happens with the body of a deceased saint. For example, after St. Teresa of Avila (†1582) died, a wonderful, sweet smell lingered around her for a long time, instead of the stench that dead bodies usually emit. The blood of St. Januarius (†305) still mysteriously turns to liquid every year on September 19, his feast day. The bodies of St. Catherine of Siena (†1380) and St. Bernadette of Lourdes (†1879) did not decompose immediately after they died. They are *incorrupt*. Although they had not been embalmed, they remained beautiful and whole.

A mystery

Why do some people die young and others when they have grown old? Why do criminals stay alive while good people die? Why do illnesses and accidents tear people away from us? Why doesn't God intervene? We do not know the answers. We experience death as evil, and this brings us back to the mystery of evil (SEE TWEET 1.34). But our perspective is limited; if we could grasp the whole picture, we would surely be comforted and awed by God's wisdom.

Perspective

In spite of everything that happens to us, we can be sure that God loves us and wants the best for us. He has destined us to live forever in heaven (SEE TWEET 1.45). That is all we really need to know. He said: "My thoughts are not your thoughts, neither are your ways my ways" (ISA. 55:8–9). The Resurrection changed the reality of death, giving whoever strives to live a saintly life the prospect of gaining heaven (SEE TWEET 1.45 AND 1.50). God doesn't want death for us, but life. That is why St. Paul said: "For to me to live is Christ, and to die is gain" (PHIL. 1:21).

> Death is not what God wants for us. It came into the world with sin. We all die, but through Jesus' Resurrection, we can live forever.

Read more
Evil in the world: CCC 309–314, 324; CCCC 57–58; YOUCAT 51. *Death:* CCC 1005–1014,1019; CCCC 206; YOUCAT 155.

 ## 1.37 Can suffering help us to come closer to God?

Evil and suffering

Everybody suffers at some point in life. But suffering is not what God intended for us. It's important to realize that suffering is not a kind of personal punishment. It came into the world when Adam and Eve fell into sin (SEE TWEET 1.27). Now that suffering is part of life, it is unavoidable. To save us from the victory of evil, Jesus chose to suffer for all people and to die on the cross. He did so out of love.

Thus, God did not remove suffering from the world but bore it himself, making it the means of our redemption. Jesus knew ahead of time that he would be rejected and killed (MT. 16:31; MK. 8:31). He accepted suffering as part of his mission on earth (SEE TWEET 1.28). Through his suffering and death, he opened for us the way to eternal life in heaven (SEE TWEET 1.26). Even during the most dreadful suffering, we can look forward to a different life: one without suffering in heaven! By uniting our suffering with that of Jesus, we can unite ourselves to his saving mission.

Understanding suffering

Jesus suffered and died on the cross out of love. By reflecting on his sacrifice, we can gain a deeper understanding of our own suffering. According to Pope Benedict XVI: "It was in this way that he gave meaning to our suffering, a meaning that many men and women of every age since have understood and made their own, experiencing profound tranquillity even in the bitterness of harsh physical and moral trials" (ANGELUS, FEB. 1, 2009). In this way, although suffering is always ultimately caused by evil, it can still be a way to grow closer to God. Thus, something good can come of something bad. We must try to avoid pain and suffering, especially for others (SEE TWEET 4.39). Even so, there will always be plenty of suffering left. We can offer up (dedicate) our suffering to God, with the words of St. Paul: "In my flesh I complete what is lacking in Christ's afflictions for the sake of his body, that is, the Church" (COL. 1:24). This way our own suffering can become meaningful along with the suffering of Jesus on the cross. Luckily, God has promised that we

Who was St Thérèse of Lisieux?

The young French nun Thérèse of Lisieux (†1897) suffered intensely during her short life. At the age of 23 she contracted tuberculosis. That illness slowly destroys the lungs, and at that time there were no medicines with which to treat it. But Thérèse looked beyond the pain and went in search of meaning for her suffering. She found this meaning in the cross of Jesus. This allowed her to suffer with him for the redemption of the world. About her suffering with Christ she wrote: "In order to suffer in peace it is enough to want all that Jesus wants." Thérèse died at the age of 24. Her feast day is October 1.

will not be tested beyond what we can handle, and that he will give us strength (I Cor. 10:13). That is why St. Paul said: "I can do all things in him who strengthens me" (Phil. 4:13).

Asking for suffering?

You can even go one step further, and ask God to send you suffering because you want to offer it up for your salvation and that of others. That is a fine prayer, because God gives us only what is good for us. The tradition of fasting, abstinence, and other forms of self-denial can also be seen in this light (see Tweet 3.19). With regards to the practice of some Christians who deliberately harm themselves physically in order to share in Jesus' suffering, we have to be much more careful. Although some saints have done this, we could argue there is enough suffering in the world already. St. Thérèse of Lisieux preferred humbling herself by doing works of charity to doing physical penance (see box). The danger of seeking physical suffering is that we might become proud of our own ability to withstand it. And that is precisely the kind of sin for which Jesus had to die on the cross!

Hope

Suffering is a trial – at times a very hard one – to which we all at one time or another are subjected (Salvifici Doloris, 23). But because Jesus rose from the dead, suffering and death do not have the last word; in the face of our suffering and death we can therefore look forward to our resurrection (see Tweet 1.50). We can do so particularly if we offer up our suffering to God. We hope for the joy of eternal life not because we deserve it, because of our own merits, but because of the merits of Jesus. St. Paul said: "I will all the more gladly boast of my weaknesses, that the power of Christ may rest upon me" (II Cor. 12:9).

 Jesus' suffering out of love for each of us saves us. Our suffering becomes meaningful if we offer it to God with Jesus.

Read more

Suffering: ccc 1500–1505; youcat 241.

1.38 Why is Mary so important?

Mary and the angels

Mary played a crucial role in our history. God chose her to cooperate in the salvation of mankind. The Bible speaks of Mary as "a virgin engaged to a man whose name was Joseph" (Lk. 1:27). According to Church tradition, Mary's parents were St. Joachim and St. Anne, the grandparents of Jesus.

Mary and Jesus

Jesus did not begin publically preaching and performing miracles until he was 30, and there is a lot about his life before that, often referred to as his "hidden life", that we do not know. We can learn the most about his childhood and his mother, Mary, from the Gospel of Luke. We first meet Mary at the Annunciation, when an angel told her she would give birth to the Savior and she answered, "Behold, I am the handmaid of the Lord; let it be to me according to your word" (Lk. 1:38). When Jesus was born in Bethlehem, shepherds adored the holy infant and said angels had told them that the baby was the Savior. Mary "kept all these things, pondering them in her heart" (Lk. 2:19). Forty days after Jesus was born, Joseph and Mary dedicated him to God in the Temple, according to Jewish custom. At that moment, the prophet Simeon spoke these words to Mary: "This child [will be] ... a sign that is spoken against (and a sword will pierce through your own soul also)" (Lk. 2:34–35). This foretold how Mary would suffer with her son (SEE BOX).

Mary's suffering

Mary's suffering had already started when the Holy Family fled to Egypt in order to avoid the soldiers sent to kill her newborn son (Mt. 2:13–15). On another occasion, when Jesus was 12 years old, his parents lost him during a visit to Jerusalem. After three days of desperate searching, Joseph and Mary found him in the Temple, where he was busy listening and talking to Jewish teachers. In this too, Mary "kept all these things in her heart" (Lk. 2:51). She always kept faith in God. When her son was executed, Mary stood beneath his cross. Joseph had already died; otherwise he would have certainly been there with her.

What are the Seven Sorrows of Mary?

On September 14, the Church celebrates the Feast of the Exaltation of the Holy Cross. The next day, we remember the suffering of Mary by reflecting on her Seven Sorrows:

- The prophecy of Simeon (Lk. 2:22–35).

- The flight into Egypt (Mt. 2:13–15).

- The loss of Jesus in the Temple (Lk. 2:41–51; SEE PICTURE).

- Mary meeting Jesus on the way to the cross (Jn. 19:25).

- The crucifixion and death of Jesus (Mk. 15:24–37).

- Mary receiving the dead body of her son (Mk. 15:46).

- The burial of Jesus in the tomb (Jn. 19:38).

Jesus told the Apostle John: "Behold, your mother" (Jn. 19:27; SEE TWEET 1.30). His purpose was not merely to ensure that his mother would be provided for after his death, but also to make Mary John's mother and the mother of all of us, who are brothers and sisters in Christ (SEE TWEET 1.30). *Compassion* literally means "to suffer with". Pope John Paul II said that the suffering of Mary with her son, her compassion, especially as she stood below the cross, "reached an intensity which can hardly be imagined from a human point of view but which was mysterious and supernaturally fruitful for the redemption of the world" (SALVIFICI DOLORIS, 25).

Mary's prayer

Through her faith and closeness to Jesus, Mary can intercede for us in a special way. For example, at Mary's request Jesus performed his first miracle by changing water into wine at the wedding in Cana (Jn. 2:1–12). Because Mary is with Jesus in heaven, we can ask her to pray for us "now and at the hour of our death" (SEE TWEET 1.39). Of course, we can pray to Jesus directly, but God also listens to people who pray for others (SEE TWEET 3.9). Moses prayed regularly for the people of Israel (Ex. 32:11–14; NUM. 14:13–20). Jesus himself told us to pray for others (Mt. 5:44), and St. Stephen prayed for the people who were stoning him (ACTS 7:60). Asking Mary to pray for us is a very good habit.

> Mary is unique and important for us. She is "full of grace" (Lk. 1:28), "blessed among women" and "the mother of the Lord" (Lk. 1:42–43).

Read more
Role of Mary: CCC 972, 974–975; CCCC 199; YOUCAT 147.

1.39 Mary is not God — so, why all this devotion to her?

Mary and the angels

Mary is called Mother of God. She is not a goddess, but a human being. Only God may be worshipped (Rev. 19:10). Therefore we do not worship Mary, but venerate her. We are devoted to her, because God chose her for an absolutely unique role. She is the Mother of the Son of God (SEE TWEET 1.38). When she was pregnant with Jesus, Mary said: "Henceforth all generations will call me blessed" (Lk. 1:48).

Hail Mary!

Devotion to Mary is based on Scripture. The prayer to Mary that is most commonly used is based on biblical verses (SEE BOX). The archangel Gabriel told Mary: "Hail, full of grace, the Lord is with you!" (Lk. 1:28). And Mary's cousin Elizabeth said: "Blessed are you among women, and blessed is the fruit of your womb!" (Lk. 1:42). Elizabeth also called Mary the "mother of my Lord" (Lk. 1:43). The term *Lord* (*Kyrios*, in Greek) was also used for God. Jesus is God (SEE TWEET 1.29), so Mary is the Mother of God (*Theotokos*, in Greek). This does not make Mary a goddess: she has always been completely human. Because Mary is the Mother of God, we can honor her, just as Elizabeth did.

Old habits

From the very beginning, the Church has been devoted to Mary and has asked for her

Hail Mary

(ENGLISH) Hail Mary, full of grace, the Lord is with thee. Blessed art thou among women, and blessed is the fruit of thy womb, Jesus. Holy Mary, Mother of God, pray for us sinners, now and at the hour of our death. Amen.

(LATIN) Ave Maria, gratia plena, Dominus tecum. Benedicta tu in mulieribus, et benedictus fructus ventris tui, Iesus. Sancta Maria, mater Dei, ora pro nobis peccatoribus, nunc et in hora mortis nostræ. Amen.

What are we to think of Marian apparitions?

When someone claims that Jesus, Mary, or one of the saints has appeared to him, the Church sometimes conducts an inquiry to determine whether this was truly a supernatural occurrence sent by God. If this is so, the apparition is approved as worthy of belief. This means that everybody is permitted to visit that special place to pray. The most famous apparitions are of Mary. For example, she appeared to the 14-year-old Bernadette Soubirous in 1858 in the French town of Lourdes. The Church recognized this apparition, and Bernadette was eventually declared a saint. Miracles continue to happen in Lourdes, which became a prominent place of Marian pilgrimage. Other approved apparitions of Mary have occurred in Fatima, Guadalupe, Paris, La Salette, and in Champion, Wisconsin. When the last Apostle died, public revelation was completed (SEE TWEET 1.11). Therefore, an apparition can never add anything new to the deposit of faith. Everybody is free to believe in the apparition of Mary, or not. Apparitions are private revelations, as opposed to the public revelation in the Bible. But there are many people who grow in their faith by going on a pilgrimage to such places. Just give it a try!

....

prayers. In the second century, St. Irenaeus called her "our advocate". He also called her the "second Eve", because Jesus came as a second Adam (I COR. 15:45) to liberate mankind from the consequences of the Fall (SEE TWEET 1.4). A Marian prayer from the third century shows us that Christians then were already passionately praying to Mary: "Beneath your compassion, we take refuge, O Mother of God: do not despise our petitions in time of trouble: but rescue us from dangers, only pure, only blessed one" (SUB TUUM PRAESIDIUM).

Feast!

Many feast days are devoted to Mary. Let's look at some of them to understand her better. *Immaculate Conception* (SOLEMNITY, DEC. 8): this celebrates when, in anticipation of the Redemption, Mary was conceived without original sin (SEE TWEET 1.38). *Annunciation* (SOLEMNITY, MAR. 25): nine months before Christmas, the Church celebrates when an angel announced to Mary that she would give birth to the Savior. *Mary, Mother of God* (SOLEMNITY, JAN. 1): we honor Mary by this title on the eighth day of Christmas, when the baby Jesus was circumcised according to the Law of Moses (SEE TWEET 1.38). *Assumption* (SOLEMNITY, AUG. 15): this celebrates when Mary, having never sinned, "was assumed body and soul into heavenly glory" after completing her earthly life (MUNIFICENTISSIMUS DEUS, 44; SEE TWEET 1.40).

> Jesus gave us Mary as our mother. Therefore we can pray to her and ask her to put in a good word for us with her son, Jesus.

Read more
On the Hail Mary: CCC 2676–2679, 2682; CCCC 563; YOUCAT 480. *The Rosary:* CCC 2678; CCCC 563; YOUCAT 481. *Devotion to Mary:* CCC 971; CCCC 198; YOUCAT 149.

1.40 Did Mary always remain a virgin and never sin?

Some people find it hard to believe that Mary was a virgin when she gave birth to Jesus. They also find it hard to accept that she remained a virgin afterward. They have difficulty with these Catholic dogmas because they seem so unnatural. But for those who believe that God himself was born as a man, it is no problem to believe in Mary's virginity.

Always a virgin?

On behalf of God, the angel Gabriel told the Virgin Mary that she would bear his Son. She said to the angel: "How can this be, since I have no husband?" (Lk 1:34). The angel answered: "The Holy Spirit will come upon you" (Lk. 1: 35). God himself, not a human being, would be the Father. Through Mary's collaboration with God, Jesus would receive his human nature. Although Mary had many questions at the time and could have objected, she was sure that "with God nothing [is] impossible" (Lk. 1:37). Thus, the Church believes that the Virgin Mary conceived Jesus "by the Holy Spirit without human seed" (SEE Lk. 1:34; CCC 496; COUNCIL OF THE LATERAN). The Church's Tradition teaches that Mary also remained a virgin after the birth of Jesus. The Bible speaks of Jesus' brothers and sisters. These are, however, not Mary's children but other relatives (SEE TWEET 1.30). Hundreds of years before the birth of Jesus, the prophet Isaiah had already foretold the virgin birth: "Behold, a virgin shall conceive and bear a son, and shall call his name Immanuel [God with us]" (ISA. 7:14; Mt. 1:23). That is one of the names given to Jesus in the Bible. Following the command of the angel of the Lord, Joseph gave him the name Jesus, which means "God saves" (Mt. 1:21).

Immaculately conceived

God and sin, perfection and imperfection, repel each other like the two poles of a magnet. Yet God needed a human mother in order to become a man. Given these two truths, the Church believes in Mary's Immaculate Conception, that unlike every other human being since the Fall, Mary was conceived without original sin (SEE TWEET 1.4

Did Mary actually die?

Mary completely dedicated herself, body and soul, to God alone until the time of her Assumption into heaven. With the Fall, death came into the world, so death is therefore the direct consequence of original sin (Rom. 5:12; see Tweet 1.4).

Mary did not have to die, because she was without sin: at the end of her earthly life she was taken up (assumed) into heaven, body and soul.

The Eastern Churches have a slightly different approach that was also liked by St. John Paul II: although Mary did not have to die, as do the rest of us, it is assumed that she freely chose to share in the suffering and death of her son. The Eastern Churches therefore speak of the "falling asleep" (*dormitio*) of Mary. At that moment her soul went to heaven. After God raised her on the third day, her body was also taken up into heaven.

In his great vision of heaven, John saw that Mary was there (Rev. 12:1). Jesus wanted to encourage mankind in this way, because at the end of time he wants to take all of us, body and soul, into heaven (see Tweet 1.49). He has prepared a place for each of us (Jn. 14:3).

and 1.38): the grace won by Christ's death and Resurrection was applied to her in advance. For how could God spend nine months in a sinful human being? The Church further believes that Mary remained free from personal sin throughout her whole life, also thanks to God's grace (see Tweet 4.12).

Holy, without sin?

It is sometimes asked: "Did Mary ever have a chance to sin?" That is a very good question, and the answer is very important. Let's first recall that Eve also came into the world without original sin, but she chose to disobey God (see Tweet 1.4). Mary, on the other hand, chose to obey God, particularly when at the Annunciation she said: "Let it be to me according to your word" (Lk. 1:38). With those words she freely chose to follow God's plan. She therefore also chose not to sin. Just as Mary said yes to God, thereby making our redemption possible, we too should answer the same. Just as she said to the bridegroom's servants at the wedding in Cana, she also says to each of us: "Do whatever he tells you" (Jn. 2:5). She could not give us better advice!

> Mary remained a virgin and never sinned. She was dedicated to God in everything. This is why she went to heaven, body and soul.

Read more

Immaculate Conception: ccc 487–493, 508; cccc 96; youcat 83. *The Virgin Mary:* ccc 499–501, 510; cccc 99; youcat 81. *Virgin and mother:* ccc 501–507, 511, 963–966, 973; cccc 100, 196; youcat 85.

 ## 1.41 Are there really angels in heaven?

Mary and the angels

Like us, angels are persons: they have intelligence and free will. But unlike us, angels do not have bodies. They are in heaven with God. Angels have made a definite choice to stay with God and to serve him (SEE TWEET 1.42). The Greek word for angel (*ángelos*) means "messenger": in the Bible, angels often bring God's messages to people.

Angels everywhere

We find angels everywhere in the Bible. At the gates of paradise there is an angel (GEN. 3:24). Angels surround the throne of God in heaven (ISA. 6:2). Angels also play a part in the life of Jesus. The angel Gabriel announced his birth (LK. 1:26), and angels sang on the night he was born: "Glory to God in the highest heaven, and on earth peace among men with whom he is pleased!" (LK. 2:14). An angel comforted Jesus when he spent the night in mortal fear, praying in the Garden of Gethsemane (LK. 22:43). Angels also announced his Resurrection when a group of women wanted to pray by his grave (MT. 28:2–6). At the

Second Coming, an angel will announce the return of Jesus (I THES. 4:16; SEE TWEET 1.49).

Known angels

The names of three archangels are mentioned in the Bible: Michael, Gabriel, and Rafael. St. Michael is the commander of the heavenly forces against the devil (REV. 12:7). His name means "Who is like God?" You can often find the Latin version in paintings or inscribed on statues: "Quis ut Deus?" You may pray to St. Michael and ask him for help in the struggle against evil; doing so is a good idea (SEE TWEET 3.18). He is venerated all over the world in shrines and sanctuaries, such as Mont St. Michel in France or Sacra di San Michele in Italy. Pope Benedict XVI reminded us that St. Michael is also the defender of the people of God (DAN. 10:21; SEPT. 29, 2007).

The archangel Gabriel announced the birth of Jesus (LK. 1:26). His name means "God is my strength." St. Raphael cured a man's blindness (TOB. 3:17). His name means: "God heals." The archangels are part of "the seven holy angels who present the prayers of the saints and enter into the presence of the glory of the Lord" (Tob. 12:15). In the Eastern Churches, four other archangels are venerated because of this passage. But their names are known only from nonbiblical books. Catholics stick to the three mentioned above. The feast day of the archangels is September 29.

Your own guardian angel

God entrusts the angels with very important tasks, though "surely it is not with angels that he is concerned but with the descendants of Abraham" (Heb. 2:16). From the very beginning of our lives, we have been protected by angels. Everybody has an angel watching over him: his own guardian angel (Mt. 18:10; Acts 12:15). These guardian angels are ordered by God to look after people: "He will give his angels charge of you to guard you in all your ways" (Ps 91(90):11). Their feast day is October 2. Because they surround the throne of God, we can always ask them to pray for us. It is a very good idea to pray for the guidance of angels, especially of our guardian angels. There is a well-known prayer for this: "Angel of God, my guardian dear, to whom God's love commits me here, ever this day (or night) be at my side, to light and guard, to rule and guide."

Angels are everywhere in the Bible, worshipping God in heaven and bringing us messages. They watch over us. You, too, have a guardian angel!

Read more

Angels: CCC 328–336, 350–325; cccc 60–61; youcat 54–55.

1.42 What's this business about fallen angels?

Mary and the angels

According to the Bible and Church Tradition an angel rebelled against God and became known as Satan, or the devil. People have always had the experience of a tempting voice opposed to God (GEN. 3:1–5). That voice has been attributed to Satan, the fallen angel who became the tempter of mankind. Satan had originally been created by God as a good angel. But he chose to reject God and his love in a radical way. The consequence of that choice was that "he was thrown down to the earth, and his angels were thrown down with him" (REV. 12:9). With these "fallen angels" an evil force came into the world. Their leader, Satan, is given many names in the Bible: Beelzebub, the devil, the tempter, the father of lies, and the lord of darkness.

Definitively against God

The choice that these angels made against God and his merciful love is final. That is why their sin cannot be forgiven. St. John of Damascene wrote: "After the fall [of the angels] into sin, repentance is no longer possible, as is the case for people after they died" (DE FIDE ORTHODOXA 2,4). And the Scriptures tell us: "The angels that did not keep their own position but left their proper dwelling have been kept by him in eternal chains in the deepest darkness until the judgment of the great day" (JUDE 1:6).

A demonic angel

St. John said that the devil "has sinned from the beginning" (I JN. 3:8), and Jesus himself said that the devil is a "liar and the father of lies" (JN. 8:44). Adam and Eve were seduced by the devil (the serpent), with the lie: "You will be like God" (GEN. 3:5). Wanting to become like God means wanting to reject his authority. This is the same pride that caused the devil's downfall. That is why the sin of Adam and Eve was so serious (SEE TWEET 1.4).

The power of Satan is not infinite. He is still a creature and is ultimately powerless to oppose the coming of the Kingdom of God. Jesus came to the world to "destroy the works of the devil" (I JN. 3:8). At the end of time, at the

The devil in the Bible

The devil assumed the form of a snake to tempt Eve (SEE TWEET 1.4). He caused the evil that afflicted Job to (SEE TWEET 1.25). A verse from the book of the prophet Isaiah is sometimes understood to apply to the fall of the devil, also called Lucifer, which means "morning star": "How you are fallen from heaven, O Day Star, son of Dawn!... You said in your heart, 'I will ascend to heaven; above the stars of God I will set my throne on high....' But you are brought down to Sheol [the realm of the dead], to the depths of the Pit" (ISA. 14:12–15).

According to the New Testament, the devil tempted Jesus (MT. 4:1–11). On many occasions, Jesus cast out the demons of possessed people with commands such as this: "Come out of the man, you unclean spirit!" (MK. 5:8). It was the devil who urged Judas to betray Jesus (LK. 22:3). Nevertheless, we do not have to be afraid. Jesus is stronger than the devil because he is God, who *is* love! (I JN. 4:8). He became man "that through death he might destroy him who has the power of death, that is, the devil" (HEB. 2:14).

Last Judgment, God will destroy the forces of evil. But until that happens, we have to take the presence of evil in the world into account. Why God allows the devil to operate in the world remains a great mystery. But "we know that in everything God works for good with those who love him, who are called according to his purpose" (ROM. 8:28).

Be realistic and watchful

We have to take the presence of evil in the world seriously (SEE TWEET 1.34). Just as he tempted Adam and Eve, the devil tempts us to reject God. Of course, he doesn't tempt us as a silly little critter with horns on his head, brandishing a pitch fork and urging us to sin. The influence of evil is real, and we experience it both in and around ourselves. Sometimes we feel an urge to do what we know is wrong and will harm ourselves and others. And in spite of all that, we are inclined toward these sins! As St. Peter said: "Be sober, be watchful. Your adversary the devil prowls around like a roaring lion, seeking some one to devour. Resist him, firm in the faith" (I PT. 5:8–9).

> Angels were created good, but some abused their freedom and chose against God. These fell from heaven, and they tempt us to share their fate.

Read more
Fallen angels: CCC 391–395, 414; CCCC 74.

1.43 What happens when we die?

Many of us find it difficult to believe that death is really the end, especially when someone we love dies. How could that love really be over? At such a moment, people feel deep inside themselves that there must be something more. Jesus confirmed there is more and promised all believers that death is certainly not the end: after death, their life continues with God in heaven. Jesus said "I am the resurrection and the life; he who believes in me, though he die, yet shall he live, and whoever lives and believes in me shall never die" (Jn. 11:25–26).

Fear of death

Most people are at least a little afraid of death, even if they believe in the Resurrection (see Tweet 1.50). Death is so definitive, so mysterious. It means separating from everything that we know and crossing into an unknown state. You die alone, taking neither your loved ones nor your possessions with you. Even Jesus was afraid when he approached his own suffering and death (Mk 14:33–36). Yet this angst that most

of us feel, while understandable and very human, is not necessary. While life changes at the moment of death, it still continues!

For this reason, at the Mass for the dead, the priest prays: "Indeed for your faithful, Lord, life is changed not ended, and, when this earthly dwelling turns to dust, an eternal dwelling is made ready for them in heaven" (Preface I for the dead).

Four last things

The Sacred Tradition of the Church speaks of the "four last things": death, judgment, hell, and heaven (CCCC appendix b). Some skeptical people say that there are only two certain things in life: death and taxes. Death is a reality for everyone. Death is also definitive: after death you cannot change anything about your former earthly life (CCC 1021). During that life, you were free to respond positively or negatively to the love of God, but after death comes judgment (Heb. 9:27).

Can I prepare myself for death?

Because we will all have to face God after we die, the Church urges us to prepare for the moment of our death (CCC 1014). Thus, when we pray the Hail Mary, we ask Mary to pray for us "at the hour of our death" (SEE TWEET 1.39). We can also pray to St. Joseph, the patron saint of a good death.

Thomas à Kempis (†1471) wrote that being aware of the reality of death can help us to be good Christians: "In every deed and every thought, act as though you were to die this very day. If you had a good conscience you would not fear death very much. It is better to avoid sin than to fear death. If you are not prepared today, how will you be prepared tomorrow? Tomorrow is an uncertain day; how do you know you will have a tomorrow?" (THE IMITATION OF CHRIST). St. Francis of Assisi mentioned death in his praises to God: "Praised be you, my Lord, through our sister Bodily Death, from whom no mortal can escape: woe to those who die in mortal sin; blessed are they she finds doing your will, no second death can do them harm" (CANTICO DELLE CREATURE; SEE TWEET 1.44).

Death as something good

At death the soul departs from the body and goes to its final destination, heaven or hell. If a person who accepted the mercy of God still needs to be purified before entering his presence, he will go to heaven by way of purgatory (CCC 1010; SEE TWEET 1.44). In heaven our salvation in Christ is complete, and we remain with God forever (SEE TWEET 1.45). Looking forward to heaven, some Christians long for death, just as St. Paul did: "My desire is to depart and be with Christ, for that is far better" (PHIL. 1:23). In another place he said: "If we have died with him, we shall also live with him" (II TIM. 2:11). By this he meant that through our Baptism we have "died with Christ" in order that we may begin a new life in him that will continue after death (SEE TWEET 3.36). In spite of his longing to be with the Lord, St. Paul persevered in his calling, trusting that God knew best how long he should live on earth (PHIL. 1:24).

When you die, you leave everything and everyone behind: your soul is separated from your body and appears before God.

Read more

Preparing for death: CCC 1014; CCCC 206; YOUCAT 155. *Death and resurrection:* CCC 992–1004, 1016–1018; CCCC 205; YOUCAT 154. *Christian death:* CCC 1010; CCCC 206; YOUCAT 155.

1.44 Will we be judged immediately after we die?

SCAN

In the end, the most important question we can ask of ourselves is this: Do we choose for or against the love of God? As St. John of the Cross (†1591) wrote: "In the evening of our lives, we shall be judged on our love" (DICHOS, 64).

Particular judgment

God is good, and this means that he is also just. Immediately after we die, we face God's particular judgment, when we are confronted with the consequences of the choices we made during our lives (MT. 12:36). It is "particular", because it refers to everything about our individual lives: the words we have spoken (MT. 12:36), our thoughts (I COR. 4:5), our actions (MT. 16:27; ROM. 2:6; II COR. 5:10), and also what we failed to do (MT. 25:35–47).

Does this scare you? The good news is, you can still turn toward God! The best moment to ask for God's forgiveness is now, and you can do this through the Sacrament of Reconciliation (SEE TWEET 3.39). Based on our

particular judgment, our soul will either enter "into the blessedness of heaven" – immediately or after our purification in purgatory – or be condemned to "immediate and everlasting damnation" (CCC 1022; SEE TWEET 1.45–1.47). Our judgment will be completed at the Last Judgment after the resurrection of our body, when soul and body are joined once more (SEE TWEET 1.50).

Redemption for all

If you honestly try to have faith and to live a good Christian life, you do not need to fear God's judgment. It is very reassuring to read in the Bible: "The Lord ... is forbearing toward you, not wishing that any should perish, but that all should reach repentance" (II PT. 3:9). God wants all of us to live forever (JN. 3:16). Through his death, Jesus overcame sin, death, and the devil, "who has the power of death" (HEB. 2:14). Thereby, Jesus opened up the way to heaven for all who believe in him and show it through their actions (SEE TWEET 1.45 AND 4.8).

Are we predestined for heaven or hell?

Anyone may choose God, but each of us can also persist in mortal sin, which is the rejection of God. In either case, the individual bears the responsibility of the choice he makes. Knowing how many temptations there are in this life, Jesus urged his followers to "enter by the narrow gate" that "leads to life". He warned that "the gate is wide and the way is easy, that leads to destruction, and those who enter by it are many" (Mt. 7:13–14).

Those and other Bible verses led the Frenchman John Calvin (†1564) to believe that God predestines everyone for either heaven or hell (double predestination [SEE TWEET 2.36]). According to him, God has determined in advance the few people who are going to heaven and the many (the damned masses) who are going to hell. The Catholic Church explicitly rejects this.

Calvin's idea directly contradicts God's desire that everyone be saved (I Tim. 2:3–4). "God predestines no one to go to hell; for this, a willful turning away from God (a mortal sin) is necessary, and persistence in it until the end" (ccc 1037; SEE TWEET 4.13). Instead, for every human being Jesus has prepared a place in heaven (Jn. 14:2–3).

Last Judgment

So what then is the Last Judgment? At the end of time, when Jesus returns to us in glory (SEE TWEET 1.49), there will be a new heaven and a new earth, and evil will be no more. Then our bodies and souls will be reunited, and "the truth of each man's relationship to God will be laid bare" (ccc 1039). The Last Judgment is not another judgment: we will only be judged once. But at the Last Judgment, as Jesus said: "Nothing is covered up that will not be revealed, or hidden that will not be known" (Lk. 12:2). Thus all the good you have done or have neglected to do during your life on earth will become public, so to speak, as the Kingdom of God and your place in it comes into its fullness. The future Kingdom in heaven that God first promised to the Jews and then to the whole world though the words and actions of Jesus is a mystery, but it will be very good. Until Jesus returns, we are "awaiting our blessed hope, the appearing of the glory of our great God and Savior" (Ti. 2:13).

After we die, God confronts us with our choices. Those who refuse God's love & mercy go to hell. Those who accept God go to heaven.

Read more

Particular judgment: ccc 1021–1022, 1051–1052; cccc 208; youcat 157. *No predestination:* ccc 1037; cccc 213; youcat 161.
Last Judgment: ccc 1038–1041, 1058–1059; cccc 214–215; youcat 163.

1.45 Heavens! What on earth would eternal life be like?

SCAN

To have life abundantly, forever (Jn. 10:10) – that is the vision of heaven that the Bible offers us. Eternal life begins on earth, when you decide to believe in Jesus and are baptized. Jesus spoke to God about us: "This is eternal life, that they may know you" (Jn. 17:3). Only in heaven can we fully know God and know ourselves and become all that God intended us to be. When we go to heaven, we literally return home to the "Father's house", where Jesus has prepared a place for us (Jn. 14:2–3).

Angels on fluffy clouds?

It's very hard to imagine what heaven looks like. You have probably seen pictures of cute little angels frolicking on fluffy clouds, and other such images. But nowhere in the Bible is there such a scene. The prophets of the Old Testament used colorful images when they spoke of heaven, such as life, light, peace, a wedding feast, the house of the Father, the heavenly Jerusalem, and paradise. But still, we don't know what heaven actually looks like: "No eye has seen, nor ear heard, nor the heart of man conceived, what God has prepared for those who love him" (I Cor. 2:9).

Staring at God

In heaven we will be with God forever, and we will be like him, "for we shall see him as he is" (I Jn. 3:2) and come "face to face" with him (I Cor. 13:12). This is what we call the "beatific vision". Don't worry: it is something that will never bore you! It therefore makes a lot of sense to search for God during your life on earth, a search that will be completed in heaven (ccc 1024). Heaven is communion with God, Mary (the Queen of Heaven), the angels, and everyone else who is there. We will not be alone; we can expect a joyful reunion with those who have died in the embrace of God's love and mercy. Jesus spoke of some who will be called "least" and others who will be called "great" in heaven (Mt. 5:19). For some, a special place has been reserved (Mk. 10:40). Still, we will all be equally happy there.

What is limbo?

Limbo is a theoretical answer to the question of what happens to people who die without having been baptized, through no fault of their own. On the one hand, there is the underworld, where Jesus "descended into hell" (APOSTLES' CREED; I PT. 3:18–19). That is the place where the souls of the people who died before his Resurrection remained until he came to open up the way to heaven for them (*limbus patrorum*). After he died on the cross, Jesus remained in the underworld until the third day. And when he rose again, he took those who had been righteous with him to heaven.

There is also the question of what happens to infants who die before being baptized. Jesus said that Baptism is necessary for salvation (JN. 3:5). This led some theologians to speculate that these children would go to a special, separate place (*limbo puerorum*). There they would be happy forever, but not be able to see God face to face. However, this theory is not present in the *Catechism*, which teaches that infants who die without Baptism are entrusted by the Church to the mercy of God (CCC 1261). It is unthinkable that his desire for all people to be saved would exclude infants who die without Baptism. At the same time this underlines the importance of Baptism!

A ticket to heaven?

People often say that by living a good life, you can earn your way to heaven. But that is not quite true. We can never "earn" entrance to heaven. Heaven can only be given to us as a gift. We will be "justified by his grace as a gift, through the redemption that is in Christ Jesus" (ROM. 3:24). When someone asked the Apostles what he must to do to be saved, he was told: "Believe in the Lord Jesus, and you will be saved" (ACTS 16:31). The only thing that God asks of us is to have faith in Jesus and to follow him. Jesus said: "No one comes to the Father, but by me" (JN. 14:6). When people choose to follow Jesus, they are baptized. The Sacrament of Baptism is not an automatic "ticket to heaven", however, our choice for Jesus must be expressed in what we do (SEE TWEET 4.8). Baptism is a very important start, which is intended for everybody (SEE TWEET 3.36). Nevertheless, we do not have to despair for people who, through no fault of their own, die without having been baptized (SEE TWEET 2.14). God's compassion is so great that these people may still go to heaven. How this may happen is known only to God.

> Eternal life means to live forever with God in joy, peace, and happiness, together with the saints and the angels.

Read more

Heaven: CCC 325–327, 1023–1026, 1053; CCCC 59, 209; YOUCAT 52, 158.

SCAN

 ## 1.46 What is hell like?

Hell is for people who consciously and definitively decide not to love God. We don't know what hell looks like. We do know that it is separation from God's love forever. That must be horrible, because only in God can we find the life, love, and happiness that we were created for (ccc 1057). In the Bible, hell is mentioned as a state of being excluded from the heavenly Jerusalem. "The door was shut" (Mt. 25:10) for the foolish bridesmaids in the parable, who were not prepared for God's arrival. And of the servant who wasted his talents it was said: "Cast the worthless servant into the outer darkness" (Mt. 25:30). On Judgment Day, the Lord will divide mankind into the righteous and the unrighteous. To the latter the Lord will say: "Depart from me you cursed, into the eternal fire prepared for the devil and his angels" (Mt. 25:41).

Painful fire

Jesus spoke of hell as "the unquenchable fire" (Mt. 5:22, 29; Mt. 13:42, 50; Mk. 9:43–48). But this fire is not necessarily like the fire we know. After

Who's in hell?

The Church has never said which individuals are in hell, only those who are in heaven (see Tweet 4.15). We do not know who is in hell, but we know it exists. The Bible is clear about the existence of hell and warns that people can end up there. The Bible also speaks of demons (fallen angels) that have been condemned forever and must therefore be in hell (Mt. 25:41). Furthermore, holy people, such as St. Faustina (†1938), have had visions of hell.

the Last Judgment, all souls will be given their physical bodies (see Tweet 50). Therefore, in hell one could suffer physical pain, but the worst pain of hell is the realization that contact with God is no longer possible. Because everybody

106

in hell is concerned only with himself, it is a dreadfully lonely place. A greater contrast with heaven is impossible! That is why Jesus warned against the temptations of the devil, "who can destroy both soul and body in hell" (Mt. 10:28).

Casually?

The existence of hell should instruct us not to be too casual about our lives: "God is not mocked, for whatever a man sows, that he will also reap" (Gal. 6:7). Jesus keeps urging us to turn to God: "Repent, and believe in the gospel!" (Mk. 1:15). Conversion must be renewed constantly, because we keep sinning. If you do not repent of your sins, and you refuse to ask for forgiveness for them, you turn away from God. If we persist in that attitude, God will respect our decision: in his infinite justice, God respects our freedom. The result is that eventually we will be separated from God's love forever in hell. But at the same time, we should remind ourselves that God is infinitely good. Everywhere in the Bible he tells us not to be afraid (Gen. 15:1; Mt. 10:28). God loves us immensely, so much that he even became human and died for us (Jn. 3:16). He passionately wants everybody to be saved (I Tim. 2:4). But it is up to us to accept his offer!

In a state of grace?

Thankfully, nobody knows exactly what happens during the final moments of life. Until our very last breath – even if nobody can see it – we have the chance to repent from our sins and to allow God's love to flood into us. Then you die "in a state of grace", in friendship with God (see Tweet 4.12). To the good thief who defended Jesus on the cross, Jesus said: "Truly, I say to you, today you will be with me in Paradise" (Lk. 23:43). But if someone persists in denying God, until the very end, he will die in a "state of mortal sin" (ccc 1033). That means that one deliberately chose to go against God's commandments, fully knowing what he was doing, and refused to ask for forgiveness. He has made a definite choice to be excluded from communion with God. That is a choice against life itself. Therefore, mortal sin eventually leads to eternal death in hell.

> Hell is permanent separation from God's love, where one is stuck in the pain and unhappiness of pride and selfishness.

Read more

Mortal sin: ccc 1033, 1854–1861, 1874; cccc 212, 394–395; youcat 161, 316–317.

Existence of hell: ccc 1036–1037; cccc 213; youcat 162. *Hell:* ccc 1033–1035, 1056–1057; cccc 212; youcat 161.

 ## 1.47 Should I be afraid of purgatory?

Purgatory exists because of God's infinite compassion and mercy: he wants everyone to be saved (I Tim. 2:4). But God is also infinitely just. Whoever is completely free from the effects of sin can go straight to heaven when he dies. But almost no one is.

Swept away!

Purgatory is the solution. If when you die you are still burdened with the consequences of your sins, which if you are on your way to heaven have already been forgiven, you go to purgatory for purification. This purification is necessary because God and imperfection are opposed to each other, like the two poles of a magnet. They cannot remain in each other's presence. Therefore, you have to be cleansed of the effects of your sins before you can be in God's presence: they have to be swept away. The purpose of our Christian life on earth is to grow toward perfect love – through, with, and in Jesus. That takes some time, and sometimes we die before the process is completed, but what is a little more time spent in purgatory

compared to the eternity of heaven? (See Tweet 1.45.)

Place and time

Purgatory is best imagined as a preparatory phase, as the antechamber of heaven. Purgatory is like a mirror where you have to face yourself and the way you have lived your life: you are being prepared and purified before crossing the threshold of the house of God. A priest once said purgatory is for everyone who is too good for hell, but not good enough for heaven.

Time in purgatory cannot be compared to our own time, because purgatory participates in eternity in some way, where there are no hours and years like those in our world. But "time" in purgatory can be shortened in different ways. Christians have always prayed for the souls of the deceased, that they may speedily be made ready for heaven. We can do this by having Holy Mass offered for them (ccc 1032). We can also help them through works of penance (see Tweet 1.37), by fasting (see Tweet 3.19), through

Is purgatory described in the Bible?

The word *purgatory* does not appear in the Bible, but we can deduce its existence from a number of verses. For example, Sacred Scripture speaks of atonement for the dead, "that they might be delivered from their sin" (II Mc. 12:45). If these people had been in hell, prayers would not have been able to help them, and if they had been in heaven, prayers would not have been necessary. Therefore, there must be a purgatory! This is confirmed in the New Testament. St. Paul spoke of the salvation of souls "as through fire" (I Cor. 3:15), and St. Peter of a "testing fire" (I Pt. 1:7).

Jesus said that, if repented, "every sin and blasphemy will be forgiven men." Then he added: "Whoever speaks against the Holy Spirit will not be forgiven, either in this age or in the age to come" (Mt. 12:31–32; CCC 1864). From Jesus' words we may take it that certain sins are forgiven after death (in the time to come), in the state we call purgatory.

indulgences (SEE TWEET 2.35), or by giving alms to the poor (SEE TWEET 3.50).

Hell on earth

Some people experience terrible suffering in their lives. But instead of calling this "hell on earth", we should call this "purgatory on earth". Your sufferings in this life can serve to purify you for the afterlife and to prepare you for heaven. Jesus said: "Blessed are the poor in spirit"; "those who mourn"; "those who hunger and thirst for righteousness"; and "those who are persecuted for righteousness' sake, for theirs is the kingdom of heaven" (Mt. 5:4–10; SEE TWEET 1.37). Purgatory is a cleansing fire. But it cannot be compared to actual fire. It is like the compassionate fire of Jesus' love (Lk. 12:49). After Peter denied knowing Jesus three times, Jesus looked at him, and Peter "went out and wept bitterly" (Lk. 22:62). The experience of purgatory is something like that: burning shame and painful remorse about your failure to love (YOUCAT 159). Only after experiencing this cleansing pain will we be able to respond to Jesus' loving gaze without fear, without having to hide anything. Then we can be happy forever in heaven.

Don't be afraid, God wants you in heaven. In purgatory, your remaining imperfections are removed to prepare you for eternal life with God.

Read more

On purgatory: CCC 1030–1032, 1054; CCCC 210; YOUCAT 159.

Helping those in purgatory: CCC 1032, 1055, 1414; CCCC 211, 281; YOUCAT 159–160.

 ## 1.48 Will I meet my pet in heaven?

God appointed man to be the steward of animals (Gen. 2:19–20). The Church teaches that we must take care of animals, as St. Francis did. But there are limits: "One can love animals; one should not direct to them the affection due only to persons" (ccc 2418).

Humans and animals

There is a fundamental difference between human beings and animals (see Tweet 1.3). Think about it: although some animals show signs of advanced intelligence, they cannot reason or argue rationally as people can. They don't have free will and cannot be held responsible for their actions. Animals follow their instincts; people follow their reason (well, at least they should).

Immortality as the difference

Animals are clearly quite different from people. Whereas the Bible mentions animals only by the names of their species, it tells us that God knows every unique human being by his individual name and calls him into a personal relationship with him: "I have called you by name, you are mine" (Isa. 43:1; see Tweet 1.2). God directly created our immortal souls at the moment of our conception (see Tweet 1.3 and 4.26). Because God gave us minds and wills, we can know him and love him. The animals give glory to God by their very existence. They serve him by acting completely unthinkingly in accordance with their nature. In giving us minds and wills like his own, God asks more of us than to exist on the level of an animal. He even asks more than that we serve him: he asks that we be his friends (see Jn. 15:14 –15). Our

....

Is it permissible to kill animals?

God has forbidden murder, which is the unjustified killing of human beings, whom he created in his own image (Gen. 9:5; Ex. 20:13; see Tweet 3.43). Though, like all creation, animals carry some traces of their Creator, God said that animals may be killed for food (Gen. 9:3; Acts 11:7) or for an offering to God (Lev. 1:2). We must care properly for animals, however, and we may not make them suffer needlessly (see Tweet 4.48).

What about reincarnation?

Reincarnation is the idea that the soul can live on after death in a different body. This could be the body of another human being or of an animal. Usually, to be reincarnated as a human being is seen as the highest possibility, and a further distinction is often made between "higher" and "lower" humans. The Church does not teach this, however. This doctrine of reincarnation goes against the Catholic conviction that a person has one soul and one body, which together form one unified whole (CCC 365; SEE TWEET 1.3). Body and soul belong together and make up one unique person. We die only once, according to Scripture (HEB. 9:27). When we die, our body and soul are temporarily separated from each other. After all, the soul cannot die. The body is buried, and the soul will (hopefully) go to heaven. There, the soul remains without the body until the resurrection at the end of time (SEE TWEET 1.49–1.50).

greatest task on earth is to learn how to know and to love God so that we can be with him in heaven forever (SEE TWEET 1.46).

The purpose of life

Unlike human beings, animals have no purpose beyond their earthly lives. They did not receive an immortal soul from God. But we won't miss them in heaven, where we will, together with the angels and the saints, be completely happy in the presence of God. It may be difficult to imagine, but we won't need anything other than God, who will fulfill our every desire. So, we will not be longing to see our pet dog or cat again. If you don't know what to say to someone who is inconsolable because his pet died, think of the following story. Once, a churchgoer, in tears, complained to her parish priest that the assistant priest had just said that her dear deceased cat would not go to heaven. The old priest answered that God, out of love, had made heaven as a place of perfect happiness. "So *if* you need your cat to be perfectly happy," he said, "you will find it there!"

Unlike people, animals do not have immortal souls. Death is final for them.

Read more
The place of animals in creation: CCC 2416–2418, 2456–2457; CCCC 506; YOUCAT 437.
The soul: CCC 362–368, 382; CCCC 69–70; YOUCAT 62–63. *Reincarnation:* CCC 1013.

SCAN

 # 1.49 When will the end of time come about?

When Jesus ascended to heaven, a new age began: our age. Now is the time for the Church to spread and to proclaim the message of Jesus throughout the world (SEE TWEET 2.11). "When we eat this Bread and drink this Cup, we proclaim your Death, O Lord, until you come again." We say these words of St. Paul when we celebrate the Eucharist (SEE I COR. 11:26).

Jesus promised that he would return to earth. Thus we await in hope his Second Coming (*parousia* in Greek). When he returns, the bodies of the dead shall rise again (SEE TWEET 1.50) and the Kingdom of God will be complete. Every year we celebrate Advent: four weeks of looking forward to the coming of Jesus (SEE TWEET 3.28). During this season, we not only anticipate the celebration of his birth on Christmas, we also look forward to his return in glory at the end of time.

When, O Lord?

Nobody knows when the Second Coming will be. Jesus said: "It is not for you to know times or seasons which the Father has fixed by his own authority" (ACTS 1:7). It could be today or tomorrow or in a thousand years. From the beginning, Christians have been taught to live daily with the real possibility of Jesus' Second Coming. Whether he comes today or tomorrow, this should not make any difference to our way of living. At the same time, we should not be impatient, since God's time is not like our time. After all, Jesus said: "Heaven and earth will pass away.... But of that day or that hour no one knows, neither the angels in heaven, nor the Son, but only the Father" (MK. 13:31–32). In spite of that clear statement, new sects continue to claim that they can predict when the end of time will occur. In every case, the facts prove them wrong. The return of our Lord is not something we can bring about, after all. Only God knows the day and the hour when the world, which he himself created, will end.

Prophesying the end

When the end of time will occur is a question that has troubled people for centuries. The biblical verses that speak of the end of time are meant to be understood symbolically, although they give a general idea of what to expect. For instance, Jesus said: "Nation will rise against nation, and kingdom against kingdom; there will be great earthquakes, and in various places famines and plagues; and there will be terrors and great signs from heaven" (Lk 21:10–11). And St. Paul spoke of moral decay: "For men will be lovers of self, lovers of money, proud, arrogant … haters of good, treacherous, reckless, swollen with conceit, lovers of pleasure rather than lovers of God, holding the form of religion but denying the power of it" (II Tim. 3:2–5).

Keep alert!

If you ponder these texts, it sounds like we're already living during the end times! But disasters, wars, and loss of faith have always been present! It is important that we do not try to interpret these texts literally, as specific, cryptic indications about when the time has arrived. Their purpose is to urge us to be prepared: you have to try to be ready to meet Jesus at all times!

As Christians, we look forward to the coming of Jesus and the fulfillment of creation. One thing we can never pray too often is "Come, Lord Jesus!" (Rev. 22:20). After all, he himself said: "Surely I am coming soon" (Rev. 22:20). He also urged us to keep alert for we "do not know when the time will come" (Mk. 13:33).

Why is Jesus taking so long to return?

The longer Jesus waits, the more opportunities sinners have to repent and to receive the mercy of God. That may be the reason why Jesus has not returned to us yet. We don't know. We do know that he will come; we don't know when. St. Peter wrote: "With the Lord one day is as a thousand years, and a thousand years as one day. The Lord is not slow about his promise as some count slowness, but is forbearing toward you, not wishing that any should perish, but that all should reach repentance" (II Pt. 3:8–9). And St. Paul said: "May the Lord make you increase and abound in love for one another and for all, just as we abound in love for you. And may he so strengthen your hearts in holiness that you may be blameless before our God and Father at the coming of our Lord Jesus with all his saints" (I Thes. 3:12–13).

At the end of time, the dead will rise and Jesus will return. Nobody knows when this will happen: so be prepared and choose to follow God!

Read more

Resurrection of Christ: CCC 651–655, 658; CCCC 131; YOUCAT 108.

 SCAN

1.50 How important is the Resurrection?

Jesus rose from the dead and in doing so conquered the power death has over us (SEE TWEET 1.36). Because of the Resurrection, if we accept the gift of God's mercy we will live forever with him in heaven. The opposite is also true: if there had been no Resurrection, we would be unable to enter heaven. St. Paul explained: "If Christ has not been raised, then our preaching is in vain and your faith is in vain" (I COR. 15:14). The Resurrection of Jesus is the very core and foundation of our faith.

Sin and death

In God's original plan, there was no death. Death came into the world as a consequence of the Fall (SEE TWEET 1.4). That is why St. Paul called death "the wages of sin" (ROM. 6:23). Before Christ, the souls of the dead went to the underworld (SEE TWEET 1.45), where they remained far removed from God and heaven. Jesus changed this, however: "As in Adam all die, so also in Christ shall all be made alive" (I COR. 15:22). When Jesus died,

he descended into the underworld to free the souls of the people who had lived righteous lives and to take them with him to heaven (SEE TWEET 1.45).

The promise of our resurrection

The promise of the resurrection of the dead had already been made in the Old Testament. Isaiah wrote: "Your dead shall live, their bodies shall rise. O dwellers in the dust, awake and sing for joy!" (ISA. 26:19). And Ezekiel said: "Thus says the Lord GOD to these bones: Behold, I will cause breath to enter you, and you shall live" (EZ. 37:5).

The Resurrection of Jesus forms the basis for the promise of our own resurrection, which fulfills the promises of both the Old and the New Testaments (I COR. 15:4). Jesus said he is "the resurrection and the life" (JN. 11:25). From the earliest days of the Church, she has preached "that what God promised to the fathers, this he has fulfilled to us their children by raising Jesus" (ACTS 13:32–33).

The communion of saints

The communion of saints comprises all the faithful, both living and dead. The one Church of Jesus consists of three states:

- The visible Church, the Church on earth, comprises all the faithful, who form the Church Militant (SEE TWEET 2.11).

- The Church in purgatory comprises the souls who are being prepared for heaven. They form the Church Suffering (SEE TWEET 1.47).

- The Church in heaven consists of the angels and saints who are already gathered around the throne of God. They form the Church Triumphant. On earth we honor the saints in heaven and ask them to pray for us (SEE TWEET 1.45).

When we celebrate the Eucharist, the souls in heaven, in purgatory, and on earth are connected in a very special way through the single sacrifice of Jesus. Thus it becomes clear that the Church is the single Body of Christ (EPH. 1:22–23; SEE TWEET 2.1 AND 4.15).

Incomplete until Jesus comes

Upon death the soul is separated from the body. The body decomposes, while the immortal soul goes to God (CCC 997). Because body and soul are one, until the moment of our resurrection we are still in a state of incompleteness. Only after the Second Coming of Jesus at the end of time will our bodies rise. But then they will be glorified bodies: "The dead will be raised imperishable, and we shall be changed. For this perishable nature must put on the imperishable, and this mortal nature must put on immortality" (I COR. 15:52–53).

This new, glorified body will be reunited with our soul. It will be freed from all limitations and imperfections. Everyone will rise again, "both the just and the unjust" (ACTS 24:15). "All who are in the tombs will hear his voice and come forth, those who have done good, to the resurrection of life, and those who have done evil, to the resurrection of judgment" (JN. 5:28–29). With the exception of those who have deliberately and persistently chosen against God (SEE TWEET 1.46), after being resurrected, we will be happy with God forever in heaven.

> Jesus' Resurrection is the foundation of our faith. Because Jesus rose from the dead, we too can rise again to live with God forever.

Read more

Resurrection of Christ: CCC 651–655, 658; CCCC 131; YOUCAT 108. *Resurrection of the dead:* CCC 997–1001, 1017; CCCC 205; YOUCAT 153–154. *Communion of saints:* CCC 946–959; CCCC 194; YOUCAT 146.

Part 2

Tweets about the Church: Origin & Future

Introduction

The Church exists to evangelize. This is the truth that we learn when we study the Church's origins and mission. The Church's mission of evangelization is ever ancient and ever new. Evangelization is the mission that Jesus entrusted to his first disciples in the last words he spoke on earth, on the mountain near Jerusalem 2,000 years ago: "Go therefore and make disciples of all nations, baptizing them in the name of the Father and of the Son and of the Holy Spirit, teaching them to observe all that I have commanded you; and behold, I am with you always, to the close of the age" (Mt. 28:19–20).

Jesus gave his Church a structure, building on the foundation of his twelve Apostles and the "rock" of the Apostle St. Peter. He gave St. Peter the keys to the Kingdom and gave his Church the power to forgive sins and to open the gates of heaven. He established his priesthood, a chain of apostolic succession, and the sacraments, especially the Eucharist, to sanctify men and women and to draw all peoples into communion with him. He filled his Church with his Holy Spirit to guide her so that she always teaches his truth. Throughout history, the Church has continued to walk with Jesus, guided by his Spirit, serving his mission and carrying his gospel to the ends of the earth. As Jesus did, we walk with the people we are called to serve. As Jesus did, we share in their hopes and joys, their worries and sufferings.

Through the Church's mission, the men and women of every time and place still know the joy of the encounter with Jesus, the Son of the living God. Through the Church's witness, people still hear the good news of God's mercy, his forgiveness and love. In everything the Church serves God's plan of salvation – helping him to create, from out of the world's many peoples, a single family of God.

The mission of the Church is *our mission*. Every one of us has a duty to evangelize. This has been an important theme in the teaching of our Holy Father Pope Francis. By our Baptism, the pope tells us, we are made "missionary disciples" – called to be *missionaries of the everyday*, missionaries in all the ordinary circumstances in our daily lives.

We have to go out and meet people wherever they are at. In our homes. At school. In the places where we work. In the shadows and margins of our society. We are called to tell others about Jesus Christ and the love he shows us. We are called to spread the blessings of God's love and mercy to the whole world.

May Our Lady of Guadalupe, the Mother of the Americas and the Mother of the New Evangelization, help all of us in the Church as we carry out our mission to evangelize the world.

✠ José H. Gomez
Archbishop of Los Angeles

SCAN

2.1 What is the Church? Who is in the Church?

The Church is the community of the baptized, who believe in Jesus and want to follow him in their lives. But the Church is not just a human institution: she is a supernatural society, through which God wants to bring all believers into communion with himself and with each other as brothers and sisters in Christ. Jesus himself established the Church in order to bring all people to the Father through him (SEE TWEET 1.45). That makes the Church essential for everyone (SEE TWEET 2.14 AND 4.12).

Body of Christ

The Apostle Paul often spoke of the Church as the Body of Christ: Jesus is the head and we are the members of his body (I COR. 12:12–13; SEE TWEET 2.12). We need all the members of the Church, whether they are strong or weak. The Bible says that whichever members seem to be weaker are actually indispensable (I COR 12:22). Every believer has equal worth, and each has his own task (I COR. 12:29).

All should become holy

The Bible speaks of the most important task of every believer. It says that "this is the will of God, your sanctification" (I THES. 4:3). All believers have the responsibility to do their

....

What are lay movements?

The term has been applied to groups within the Church that have been established and grown rapidly in recent decades. The members often agree to pray and to receive sacraments regularly and to meet or even to live together. Usually there are some priests connected to these groups, which otherwise consist mainly of lay people, both singles and families. Examples of lay movements are the Chemin Neuf Community and the Emmanuel Community in France, Focolare and Communione e Liberazione in Italy, the Neo-catechumenate in Spain, and the Shalom Community in Brazil. Many of these movements have spread beyond the countries in which they began and are committed to a global New Evangelization (SEE TWEET 2.49 AND 4.49).

The Faithful, "the people of God" (100%)
All persons who have received the Sacrament of Baptism are called to follow Jesus as members of the Church. Everyone is of equal worth. Yet there are different vocations and forms of service (SEE TWEET 4.4).

Lay people (99.89%)	Religious persons (±0.08%)		Deacons, priests, and bishops (±0.03%)		
married or unmarried	Sister Brother Friar	Father	Deacon	Priest	Bishop
acolyte or lector catechist or pastoral worker missionary youth group leader member of a new movement sacristan — accountant, mechanic, homemaker, etc.	Dominicans Franciscans Benedictines etc. — prior, teacher, missionary, etc.	Dominicans Franciscans Jesuits etc. — abbot, teacher, pastor, missionary, etc.	parish deacon — possibly a husband and father, baker, engineer, etc.	pastor diocesan bishop cardinal chaplain rector prefect vicar	
NUMBER IN 2012: 1,213,591,000 catechists: 3,125,235 lay missionaries: 381,722 movements: 25,297	sisters: 713,206 brothers: 55,085	fathers: 135,072	deacons: 40,914	priests: 278,346	bishops: 5,132
Vocation: to live as Christians in the community, to proclaim the gospel while working and caring for a family.	**Vocation:** to dedicate themselves in a particular way to God, sharing in the poverty, chastity, and obedience of Jesus.		**Vocation:** to bring people to God through the sacraments, to lead the Church by proclaiming and teaching the gospel.		

best to live as Christians, to become more like Jesus by being sanctified (being made holy), and to treat other people with love (LUMEN GENTIUM, 40). There are currently more than one billion Catholics in the world, which is around one-sixth of the world's population. If we all really tried to live as Christians, then the world would certainly be a bit better!

> Jesus established the Church as a community of people who believe in him and follow him. We come to God through the Church.

Read more
The Church of Jesus: CCC 763–766, 778; CCCC 149; YOUCAT 123.

SCAN

2.2 How is the Church governed?

The Church is governed by the pope, who is the successor of St. Peter, to whom Jesus entrusted the leadership of the Church (SEE TWEET 2.17). Just as Peter worked together with the other Apostles, so the pope continually works with their successors, the bishops. The most important decisions regarding the faith and governance of the Church are made by the pope and the bishops together during a Council, a worldwide gathering (SEE TWEET 2.22).

Because Councils are rare, the pope has some small permanent councils of cardinals from around the world to advise him, and from time to time he convenes all the cardinals in an official meeting (consistory). Every five years the bishops of each Church province visit the pope to tell him how things are going in their country (an *ad limina* visit).

Diocesan bishop
The world is divided into dioceses, and each is led by a bishop appointed by the pope. Large and important dioceses are archdioceses,

led by an archbishop. Some dioceses are so large that one or more auxiliary bishops are appointed to assist the bishop. The bishop is assisted in the administration of his diocese by the vicar general and sometimes also by episcopal vicars, who along with other ecclesiastical officials, form the diocesan curia, or chancery, the governing body of the diocese. Several dioceses together form a Church province, headed by a metropolitan (SEE TWEET 2.21). The bishops in a Church province gather together from time to time for consultation in a Bishops Conference. Worldwide, there are more than 3,000 dioceses and over 5,000 bishops.

Sitting on the chair
The main church of the diocese is the cathedral, where the seat (Latin: *cathedra*) of the bishop is located. The bishop appoints a number of priests (or canons) in the cathedral chapter (SEE TWEET 2.8). Each diocese is divided into parishes. The bishop appoints a parish priest (sometimes called a pastor) as the head

of the parish. The other priests in a parish are assistant priests (sometimes called assistant pastors). If a diocese is large, the bishop may decide to divide it into deaneries, clusters of parishes led by deans.

Priests and deacons

There are over 400,000 priests in the world and more than a billion Catholics, each of whom belongs to a diocese (SEE TWEET 2.1). A delegation of the priests of the diocese, gathered as a council of priests, regularly gives the bishop advice on the management of the diocese. Permanent deacons are male ministers with special concern for the poor or other people with particular pastoral needs, such as the sick or couples preparing for the Baptism of their child. They also play a role in the Mass. Any Catholic who has the appropriate gifts and training could work as a parish catechist, pastoral worker, clerk, and so on. Many people play their parts as volunteers in the community of the Church.

....

Continental bishops' meetings

Bishops from the same province gather together, for example, in meetings of the United States Conference of Catholic Bishops (USCCB), and so do bishops from the same continent. There is the CELAM in Latin America, the FABC in Asia, and the CCEE in Europe, all of which bring together bishops from neighboring countries to exchange knowledge and experience relevant to leading the Church.

Functions in a diocese

Bishops
- Diocesan bishop
- Vicar general
- Episcopal vicar
- Auxiliary bishop

Priests
- Vicar general
- Canon, or dean
- Parish priest, or pastor
- Assistant priest, or assistant pastor

Deacons
- Parish administrator
- Catechist

Lay men and women
- Acolyte
- Lector
- Extraordinary minister of the Eucharist
- Catechist
- Other kinds of volunteers

The Church is governed by the pope and the bishops, each with his own diocese, which is divided into parishes led by parish priests.

Read more

Church hierarchy: CCC 874–879, 935; CCCC 179–181; YOUCAT 140.
Tasks of the bishops: CCC 883–896, 938–939; CCCC 183–187; YOUCAT 142, 144.

2.3 Who "sits" on the Chair of St. Peter, the Holy See?

The Holy See is the chair of the bishop of Rome, the pope. Since he is the successor of the Apostle Peter, it is also spoken of as the Apostolic See. It is a bit like a throne from which a king rules, assists, and judges his people.

Driver's seat

Usually when we speak of the Holy See, we do not primarily mean a chair. The Holy See is the center of administration for our Church. If the pope dies (or resigns, as did Pope Benedict XVI), the seat becomes vacant (*sede vacante*). Then the Holy See as an institution, with all the cardinals collectively, continues to govern the Church until a new pope is chosen. At that time only urgent matters are dealt with: the rest must wait until there is a new pope (SEE TWEET 2.4). The insignia of the Holy See is formed by two crossed keys. The keys are a reminder of those that Jesus gave to Peter (SEE TWEET 2.17). Above the keys is the three-tiered crown (tiara) or the special mitre of the pope.

Vatican or Holy See?

According to international treaties, the Holy See is a legal entity that can enter into diplomatic relations with other countries. But the Holy See itself is not a state, which makes its position unique. Vatican City, however, is a state, which is represented by the Holy See (SEE TWEET 2.6). So, when you hear it said that the Vatican has decided something or does not want something, the speaker almost always means that the Holy See has decided for or against something.

That the Holy See, rather than Vatican City, is the entity involved in the international diplomatic relations of the pope, has to do with history. Between 1870 and 1929, the Papal States were occupied, and the pope officially had no country. Yet, the Holy See continued to maintain diplomatic relations with many countries (SEE TWEET 2.44–2.45). In 1929, the Lateran Treaties stipulated that the Holy See would have an independent state, Vatican City (SEE TWEET 2.6).

Why papal diplomacy?

You may wonder why the Church puts so much energy into maintaining a diplomatic network in many countries that often do not agree with the Church. It is precisely through this network that the Church lets a clear voice be heard in a society that often otherwise has little regard for the weak and needy. Topics such as freedom of religion, disarmament, the right to life, food and shelter for all, must always be given renewed attention.

A good example is the papal encyclical (papal letter) *Caritas in Veritate* (*Charity in Truth*) of Pope Benedict xvi. In it he spoke about contemporary issues such as globalization, the market economy, and alternative energy sources. The pope called on people to be less greedy, to share more, and to be guided by their consciences in decisions about the economy and the environment. He also discussed disarmament, peace, and securing food sources for all. *Caritas in Veritate* aroused widespread interest, partly because the pope called for a reform of the United Nations. The pope had not written anything new; he based this document on Catholic social teaching, which is a practical application of the gospel (SEE TWEET 4.45).

The Pope as a negotiator

Why would a country like to have diplomatic relations with the Church? Sometimes you hear ambassadors say that the Holy See is better informed than any secret service agency, because so much information is brought together through local churches and missionaries throughout the world.

Also, the position of the Holy See on human rights, for example, is appreciated by many countries. Its neutral position with respect to governments or political parties can be of great help in crisis situations or in negotiating peace between countries at war. The Church can fulfill this Christian task, because in these situations she can stand above the political factions.

> The Holy See is the central administration of the Church. Through it the pope makes contact with bishops and heads of state.

Read more

The pope as successor of Peter: CCC 880–882, 936–937; CCCC 182; YOUCAT 141.

 ## 2.4 How does someone get to be pope?

When the pope dies, there is suddenly much to do. His body is vested as usual for Holy Mass, and he is laid out before St. Peter's altar. After the death of Pope John Paul II, many millions of people stood in line day and night, waiting hours on end, to say good-bye and to pray for him (SEE TWEET 2.50). Popes are usually buried in the crypt under St. Peter's Basilica.

An empty chair!

Naturally, the pope must be buried properly, but the necessary preparations for his succession must also be taken care of. The seat of the pope is then, after all, empty (*sede vacante*). Cardinals from around the world come to Rome (SEE TWEET 2.2). For nine days (the *novemdiales*), a daily Holy Mass is said for the deceased pope. Then the conclave begins. This is the meeting of all cardinals younger than 80, who will together elect a new pope. In theory, every Catholic man is eligible to become pope – at his election, he would be ordained a bishop if necessary!

In practice, however, one of the cardinals is elected.

Offline

During the conclave, the cardinals live in a hotel within the walls of the Vatican and officially meet in the morning and the afternoon in the Sistine Chapel. For as long as the conclave lasts, they may not come into contact with anyone on the outside. Newspapers, Internet, TVS and mobile phones

....

What's the hammer for?

Once the pope is deceased, it is the task of the chamberlain (*camerlengo*) to destroy the signet ring of the pope with a silver hammer. This prevents false documents from being fraudulently authenticated with the "ring of the fisherman". Formerly, the hammer was also used to determine whether the pope was dead. Three gentle taps were made on the head of the pope as he was called by his Christian name. If he had not yet responded after the third tap, the pope was declared dead.

are out of the question during a conclave. The word *conclave* comes from the Latin words *cum clave* ("with a key"), because the cardinals are locked in until they have chosen a new pope. Meanwhile, the outside world waits for and speculates about the outcome. Of course there are favored candidates for the papacy (*papabili*). But an ancient Roman proverb says that whoever enters the conclave as pope comes out merely as a cardinal. The reverse also happens: in 2013 almost everyone thought that Jose Cardinal Bergoglio, a favorite at the preceding conclave in 2005, was too old to be pope. But he became Pope Francis!

Voting

Before each round of voting, cardinals get a piece of paper that says: "Eligo in ultimate pontificem …" ("I choose as pope …"). One by one they come forward to place their folded ballots on a paten, a small plate made from precious metal. After this, each ballot is deposited in a golden chalice. The rounds of voting continue until a candidate is elected by a two-thirds majority. If a candidate is elected, he is first asked whether he will accept the papacy (he can say no). If he says yes, then he is asked for his new chosen name. After he puts on a white cassock, each cardinal presents himself to honor the new pope. The doors on the balcony of St. Peter's are then opened to the world, and the traditional words are proclaimed: "Habemus papam" ("We have a pope!").

Where does the white smoke come from?

For the conclave, a large stove with a chimney that reaches through the roof is placed in the Sistine Chapel. Over the years, tourists in St. Peter's Square have, alas, searched in vain for that famous chimney. Every morning and afternoon of the conclave the ballots from the two rounds of voting are burned. If no pope is chosen, the smoke is dark in color, so that the people in St. Peter's Square know that they should continue to ask the Holy Spirit to guide the conclave. White smoke indicates that the pope has been chosen. But producing white or black smoke is not always as easy as you might think. During the conclave of 2005, something went wrong with the stove, causing the whole Sistine Chapel to fill with smoke, while outside nothing was seen. It was not a surprise that something went wrong: it had been 27 years since the previous election!

 The pope is elected by the cardinals at a conclave in the Sistine Chapel. He is presented to everyone with the words Habemus papam!

Read more

Hierarchical structure of the Church: CCC 874–879, 935; CCCC 179–181; YOUCAT 140.

2.5 What is the Roman Curia?

Formally, the pope is the absolute monarch of the Church. But, of course, he does not govern the Church alone. He has a collection of ministries (dicasteries) in Rome, which help him with the government of the Church. These departments together form the Roman Curia.

Secretariat of State

The Roman Curia is headed by the secretary of state. His function resembles that of a modern prime minister, but he is not a kind of "shadow pope". There is only one pope! The Secretariat of State oversees simultaneously domestic and foreign affairs. This ministry is located in the building where the pope has his official apartment. The First Section, for General Affairs, maintains contact with the Church throughout the world. The Second Section, for Relations with States, focuses on international diplomatic relations of the Holy See. Both sections are in continuous contact with the worldwide network of nunciatures (SEE TWEET 2.8).

Congregations and councils

Within the Curia, there are several congregations and pontifical councils. Each of these takes responsibility for a different part of the life of the Church. Thus, the Congregation for the Doctrine of the Faith helps to answer contemporary questions relating to the faith. The congregations for bishops, clergy (priests and deacons), and religious (brothers and sisters) follow issues pertaining to these specific vocations within the Church. The same applies for the dicasteries responsible for laity, youth and family, migrants, and Christian unity, for example. The Congregation for the Evangelization of Peoples maintains contact with all Catholic missions and missionaries worldwide. Each of these dicasteries focuses on a particular administrative or policy area. For example, one of them is – among others – responsible for the organization of World Youth Day (WYD) on behalf of the pope. Part of the organization of each WYD is in the hands of the host country, but oversight of the WYD is in the hands of the Roman Curia. The dicastery

Some ministries of the pope

Secretariat of State

Secretariat for the Economy

Themes dealt with by congregations and pontifical councils:

- Doctrine of the Faith
- Eastern Churches
- Divine Worship and the Sacraments
- Causes of Saints
- Bishops
- Evangelization of Peoples
- Clergy
- Religious Brothers and Sisters
- Catholic Education
- Laity, Youth and Family
- Culture
- Promotion of Christian Unity
- Justice and Peace
- Migrants and Itinerant People
- Health Care Workers
- Legislative Texts
- Interreligious Dialogue
- Social Communications
- Promotion of the New Evangelization
- Papal Charity

Tribunals:

- Apostolic Penitentiary
- Apostolic Signatura
- Roman Rota

responsible for social communications helps the pope to use all the available media for proclaiming the gospel in our time, for example through the Twitter channel of the pope (SEE TWEET 4.49).

Tribunals

Although dioceses have their own ecclesiastical courts, some cases are presented to the Roman Rota, the central or supreme court. But the highest court where an appeal against a decision of the Rota may be made is the Apostolic Signatura. On behalf of the pope, the Apostolic Penitentiary forgives, in the name of God, certain very grave sins and grants indulgences for special occasions (SEE TWEET 2.35). In addition there are a number of other organizations in the Curia that have a lot of influence, such as the Secretariat for the Economy, which is responsible for all economic and administrative affairs of the Holy See and the Vatican state. The objective of all these organizations is to help the Church to focus on its key task of proclaiming the gospel and assisting the faithful on their path to God.

The Roman Curia is the system of ministries (congregations and councils) that helps the pope to lead the Church.

Read more

Organization of the Church: CCC 874–879, 935; CCCC 179–181; YOUCAT 140.

 ## 2.6 Is the Vatican a real state?

With little more than 100 acres, Vatican City, although the smallest state in the world, is nevertheless a real state! At about the size of 20 football fields it has nearly 1,000 inhabitants, the greater part being priests or bishops. Some people, such as certain cardinals and diplomats of the Holy See, have a Vatican passport. You cannot just walk into Vatican City as a tourist. So, you probably won't ever get to see most of what follows.

Gardens and politics

More than half of Vatican City is occupied by the Vatican Gardens, which date back to the Middle Ages and were replanted in the Renaissance and Baroque eras. Another large part is occupied by St. Peter's Basilica and St. Peter's Square. Then there is the official apartment of the pope, the Secretariat of State, the Secret Archives, and the Vatican Library, as well as the Vatican Museums and many offices. The political organization of Vatican City is unique in the world. The pope is the head of state as an absolute monarch. He is represented by the Governorate, which is led by a cardinal. The Secretariat of State is responsible for the external relations of Vatican City, which coincide with those of the Holy See (SEE TWEET 2.3). The postal code of Vatican City is SCV-00120, which stands for Stato della Città del Vaticano. The official license plates of the cars of the Holy See also begin with SCV, other licence plates begin with CV.

Self-sufficient

Vatican City has its own "bank", IOR (Istituto per le Opere di Religione). It isn't a bank in the normal sense: it enables financial transactions between parts of the Church. The ATM asks

INSERITO
SCIDULAM
QUAESO UT
FACIUNDAM
COGNOSCAS
RATIONEM

you in Latin to insert your bank card: "Inserito scidulam quaeso" (SEE PICTURE). Although Latin is the official language of Vatican City, most personnel come from Italy. So, you get much further with a smattering of Italian. The Vatican has its own euros with a picture of the pope on the coins. One rarely encounters such a coin in Europe. Because only small numbers of coins are minted, they are very popular among collectors. The post office sells the most beautiful stamps. Through a partnership with the Swiss Post, the Vatican mail service ensures that the letters posted from the Vatican arrive on time and in good order.

The *gendarmeria* are the Vatican City police, who are responsible for protecting public order, regulating traffic, and investigating crimes committed within the territory of the Vatican. There even is a jail, but because of an agreement with Italy, you will visit an Italian prison if you have to serve a longer term! Meanwhile, the fire brigade stands ready to extinguish fires, and there is an ambulance service for people who faint (or worse) within the walls of the Vatican. Finally, there is a grocery store, a department store, and a pharmacy, along with a large garage, a helicopter landing pad, and a train station.

Pontifical media

The Italian inventor of radio, Guglielmo Marconi, built one for Pope Pius XI. Currently, Radio Vaticana is available in almost all countries of the world. There is also a

television station (CTV) and a newspaper (*L'Osservatore Romano*). Long lines of Internet servers ensure that www.vatican.va and other official sites can remain in operation. These media are not actually part of Vatican City, but are part of the Holy See (SEE TWEET 2.3).

The Swiss Guard

The Swiss Guard is the army that protects the pope, and it has done so since 1506. New Guards swear that they will protect the pope, with their lives if necessary. The recruits must be Swiss Catholic men between the ages of 19 and 30. If you were not born in Switzerland, you don't have much of a chance to get in! Besides the famous dress uniform with blue and yellow stripes, is the much simpler daily uniform in dark blue with a white collar. The men in neat dark suits who walk next to the pope are usually also Swiss Guards. In total there are about 100 guardsmen and five officers.

 Vatican City is a real state with about 1,000 inhabitants, radio & TV stations, an army & a police force, a helicopter pad, a bank, etc.

Read more

Social doctrine of the Church: CCC 2419–2423; CCCC 509; YOUCAT 438.

2.7 Isn't it unchristian for the Church to be so rich?

Some people say that the Church should sell her possessions and give the money to the poor. That is in itself a beautiful thought. But can you express the wealth of the Church in terms of money? The greatest treasure that the Church has is the faith. The desire of Jesus is that everyone should believe in him (SEE TWEET 1.44). The Church does what she can to make this a reality and, in the process, uses all the means available.

Unmarketable wealth

In Vatican City you can find some of the most famous art in the world. St. Peter's, the Sistine Chapel, and the *Pieta* of Michelangelo, as well as the frescoes of Raphael and the other pieces in the Vatican Museums – there is just too much to mention! The Vatican Library preserves rare, ancient manuscripts, which contain much valuable historical information. These are some of the most important collections of Western cultural heritage. As with the Louvre in Paris or the National Museum in London, it is the task of the Vatican to preserve this heritage for posterity and to make it accessible now.

All of these treasures are invaluable in the sense that their value could never be adequately measured in terms of money; it is therefore unthinkable to sell them for money.

It is inconceivable that the pope would sell St. Peter's or the Vatican Museums, which by the way appear on the Vatican balance sheet as being worth one cent. The pope is the steward of this treasury for us and for the future. The same applies to the bishops who oversee Church property around the world, most of which is currently in use as churches, schools, hospitals, and so on. In most cases Church facilities are badly needed for these institutions. And they are not money-making assets for the Church, in fact, the maintenance of these properties costs a lot of money annually.

Two budgets

It is sometimes said that the Vatican is overly rich, but the Vatican City's annual budget of 300 million euro paints a very different picture. In comparison, the yearly budget of Harvard University, for example, is around 10 times as high. Some 2,000 employees are paid from the Vatican City budget, which is also used to maintain and to restore the beautiful buildings and other art treasures.

The revenue generated by the Vatican comes in part from the sale of Vatican City stamps and coins and the entry fees paid at the Vatican Museums. There is also a certain annual return on investments and real estate. The Holy See has its own budget. While it has a lot of expenses due to employees and the diplomatic network, it has few income streams. So, the modest profit of the Vatican City is partly used to supplement the annual loss in the budget of the Holy See.

Revenues of the pope

Dioceses and individual faithful support the pope financially with the St. Peter's Pence. This is based on the custom of the first Christians. Pope Benedict XVI wrote: " 'Peter's Pence' is the most typical expression of the participation of all the faithful in the bishop of Rome's projects of good for the universal Church. The collection is a gesture that not only has practical value but is also highly symbolic as a sign of communion with the pope and attention to the needs of the brethren" (FEB. 25, 2006).

Does the pope do development work?

The pope has his own office for charity to the poor, the Elemosineria Apostolica. Furthermore, the sisters of Blessed Mother Teresa (†1997), the Missonaries of Charity, daily open a door in the wall of Vatican City. There they give out food to hungry homeless and other people in need.

The pope also provides disaster relief. Thanks to donations from the faithful, the pope is able to help those who are suffering in the midst of great difficulties. Papal charity encourages people to reflect on the need for Christian charity.

It is not only the pope who contributes such relief: a large number of the charitable organizations of the world are Catholic. This is no coincidence, because Jesus calls us to commit ourselves to the good of our neighbors (LK. 10:29–37).

> The budget of the Holy See and the Vatican is smaller than that of many other states. Worldwide the Church gives a lot of money to charity.

Read more

Social doctrine of the Church: CCC 2419–2423; CCCC 509; YOUCAT 438.

2.8 What is a nuncio?

The highest representative of the pope in any given country is the nuncio. Actually, he is the representative of the central administration of the Church, the Holy See (SEE TWEET 2.3). *Nuncio* literally means "messenger". Because he represents the pope, who is a successor of the Apostles, he is an apostolic nuncio. Usually, the nuncio is an archbishop. His house, where he does his work, is a nunciature.

The Church

The nuncio's first responsibility is to maintain contacts between the local church and the ministries of the pope in Rome (the congregations and councils [SEE TWEET 2.5]). He informs Rome about what is happening in the local church and relays messages from Rome to the local bishops. A very important task of the nuncio is to advise the pope on the appointment of new bishops in his assigned country (SEE BOX). The nuncio knows the local situation well because he himself lives there and is in contact with many people both inside and outside the Church.

The world

Secondly, the nuncio is the ambassador of the Holy See to the country in which he has been appointed. He takes care of the relations between the pope and the country's head of state and/or government. Currently, the Holy See has official diplomatic relations with some 180 countries.

Sometimes a nuncio is invited by the local government to give an explanation or commentary on certain pronouncements or decisions made by the Church. From time to time the Church asks the same of a foreign ambassador to the Holy See, who usually lives in Rome.

Although they are not nuncios, diplomats of the Holy See represent the pope to important international organizations, such as the United Nations, the World Health Organization, and the Arab League.

How does someone become a bishop?

An important task of the nuncio is to advise the pope on the appointment of new bishops in the country where he is assigned. He must make sure he is well informed about all possible candidates. If a new bishop needs to be named, the pope asks the nuncio to draw up a list of three candidates, which is called the *terna*. The main criteria here are the personal faith and holiness of the candidate, but his human qualities are also important. The nuncio first asks the bishops of the country to make a *terna* with three candidates. In some countries, the cathedral chapter (SEE TWEET 2.2) has the right to send in such a list. Based on these submissions, the nuncio then makes his *terna*. This he sends to the Congregation of Bishops (SEE TWEET 2.5), which gives the pope advice on the best candidate. The pope is always free to deviate if he himself knows a better candidate.

The difference between secular and religious priests

The priests of a particular diocese are secular, or diocesan, priests, because they live in the world. Their boss is the bishop. On the day of their ordination, diocesan priests promise to remain unmarried and to be obedient to their bishops. Most secular priests belong to the diocese in which they were ordained for the rest of their lives. They live alone or with other priests and usually work in a parish.

Priests who belong to an order or a congregation are religious, or regular, priests because they follow the rule of their order. They promise to remain unmarried and to be obedient to their superior. They also take the vow of poverty: they promise not to own property and to share everything they have with the other members of their order. They usually live in a community with other priests and brothers. After their name is the abbreviation of their order, such as O.S.B., O.F.M., S.J., or S.D.B. (SEE TWEET 2.9).

How do you become a nuncio?
The Academia Pontificia Ecclesiastica in Rome is the place where ecclesiastical diplomats are trained. They are almost always secular priests (SEE BOX) who are sent to Rome by their bishops to study canon law and international diplomacy. After several years of study, such a priest is appointed to a nunciature somewhere in the world. After working in various countries as the second in command, he is himself appointed nuncio.

A nuncio is the contact person between the pope and the Church in a given country. He is also an ambassador of the Holy See to that country.

Read more
Ordained bishops, priests and deacons: CCC 1554–1580, 1593–1600; CCCC 325–334; YOUCAT 251–256, 258.

 ## 2.9 What kinds of monks, nuns, and friars are there?

 SCAN

Religious have chosen to live completely for God. They have no spouse or children to take care of: they consecrate, or dedicate, themselves to God alone. Therefore, we speak of the "consecrated life".

Most religious make three vows, the three evangelical counsels of poverty, chastity, and obedience. With the vow of poverty they promise not to own any property and to share everything they have. With the vow of chastity they promise to remain unmarried and to live in purity. And with the vow of obedience they promise to follow the rule of life of their community and to do what their superior asks of them.

Order or congregation

Those who have taken the same vows form an order or a congregation (these are not the same as the congregations of the Roman Curia [SEE TWEET 2.5]). The character of each order or congregation depends on the type of vows, their way of prayer, and the specific work they do. Daily life is governed by an order, or rule of life. This rule tells the members how they are supposed to follow Jesus together. For example, there are many hospitals in America that were founded by orders with a rule that asks them to care for the sick. Other orders run schools or take care of elderly people. In many developed countries, the government takes care of education and healthcare; thus, there are new movements in the Church that focus on what is most needed in our time, especially the spreading of the gospel (SEE TWEET 2.49 AND 4.49).

Passive?

Nuns are women who live in a convent or cloister and do not regularly go out into the world. Monks are male religious who also live in this way. Monks can be either fathers or brothers: the fathers are ordained priests, the brothers are not. The life of nuns and monks is primarily contemplative, that is, devoted to prayer. They come together in their chapel up to seven times a day for communal prayer, and

Some large orders and congregations

- **Benedictines (O.S.B.)** These are monks and nuns who, like their twin founders, St. Benedict (†547) and St. Scholastica, live in a monastery governed by the Rule of St. Benedict. Their motto is *Ora et labora* (Latin for "Pray and work"). They sometimes have been called "intellectuals with dirt under their fingernails" (SEE TWEET 2.25) because of the works of scholarship they copied or produced.

- **Franciscans (O.F.M.)** Their order was founded by St. Francis of Assisi (†1226), who wanted to follow Jesus by being poor, preaching the gospel, and serving the needy (SEE TWEET 2.29). St. Clare founded a branch for women who want to live in the spirit of St. Francis.

- **Jesuits (S.J.)** Founded by St. Ignatius of Loyola (†1556) as the Society of Jesus, the Jesuits are scholars, educators, and missionaries. St. Ignatius' *Spiritual Exercises* are famous for helping people to find God's Will for them. Probably they can also help you! (SEE TWEET 2.40 AND 3.8)

- **Salesians (S.D.B.)** These are followers of St. John Bosco (†1888), who worked primarily with young people and children. His greatest desire was that all of them would get to know Jesus. He urged them to go often to Holy Mass and the Sacrament of Reconciliation (SEE TWEET 2.43).

....

they also pray privately. In between prayer they work: in the garden, in the library, in a sewing workshop, or in various other places. Such a lifestyle can hardly be called passive! For example, Benedictine brothers and sisters in Europe and North America farm or raise livestock. The Trappists in Belgium and the Netherlands are famous for their beer (SEE BOX).

Action

Consecrated women who, like the Apostles, serve God in the world outside their convents are apostolic sisters. Besides participating in daily communal prayer, they work in schools, hospitals, hospices, and chanceries. A good example of a recently founded order of apostolic sisters is the Missionaries of

Charity, which was begun by Blessed Mother Teresa to serve the "poorest of the poor" in India. These sisters have spread throughout the world and can be found in the most neglected places tending the sick, the dying, and the destitute, in whom they see the "suffering Jesus in disguise".

> There are many kinds of religious who give all to God and live by a rule. They pray, live, and work together to proclaim the gospel.

Read more

The consecrated life: CCC 873, 914–933, 934, 944–945; CCCC 178, 192–193; YOUCAT 138, 145.

SCAN

 ## 2.10 What do all the colors mean? Who's who?

Red sashes, black cassocks, purple skullcaps, white robes: there is a lot to see when the ministers of the Church dress up in their Sunday best.

The Church is a hierarchical organization, and the division into various clerical ranks includes distinctive and often colorful clothes. And we have not even mentioned the colors used in the liturgy (SEE TWEET 3.25). But who are all these people? And how do you address them properly? (SEE APPENDIX 2).

The pope is always dressed in a white cassock, or long robe. Earlier popes kept their red cardinal's clothing once they were elected. That was the tradition until in 1566, when Pope Pius v (†1572) decided to keep his white Dominican habit. From that moment on the pope dressed in white. Yet, if you look closely, you may see that the pope's mantle is still red. You address the pope as "Holy Father".

Cardinals

Cardinals are the closest collaborators of the pope. In a sense, you could say that they are his ministers. From time to time the pope calls the cardinals for a meeting (consistory) to ask for advice. Only the pope can appoint, or create, a cardinal. Usually the pope chooses cardinals from among the bishops, although someone does not necessarily have to be a bishop to be chosen. Cardinals wear a red, or scarlet, cassock as a sign of their devotion to the Church, since they are in principle willing to give their blood and even their lives for her. A cardinal is addressed as "Your Eminence".

Bishops and monsignors

The ordinary cassock of a bishop is black with purple piping, and he wears a purple sash (SEE PICTURE). On his chest he wears a cross. During the liturgy the cassock of the bishop is purple. His purple skull cap, a zucchetto, is sometimes called a solideo (from two Latin words meaning "for God alone"), which he removes only for God. A bishop is addressed

How do you recognize religious?

Almost every religious community has its own distinctive clothing. By its habit (religious garb), you can recognize an order or a congregation. The Benedictines wear black, Franciscans brown, the Dominicans white. The Missionaries of Charity wear a white sari (a traditional dress in India) with blue stripes along the edges. The Holy Spirit Adoration Sisters, or "pink sisters", of Steyl, Netherlands, are so called because of their pink habits.

as "Your Excellency". Sometimes the pope names an ordinary priest a monsignor because of his service to the Church. Depending on his role in the Church, such a priest may have red or purple elements in his clothing. He is not a bishop and therefore wears no pectoral cross or solideo. You may have guessed he is addressed as "Monsignor".

Priests and deacons

Ordinary priests and deacons dress soberly: they have a black cassock with a black sash. Incidentally, in daily life cardinals, bishops, priests, and deacons usually wear a priestly collar with a cassock or dark suit. The religious orders and congregations, for men and women, also bring lots of color into the Church, but there are so many of these that it is impossible to describe them all here!

Clerical dress and religious habits have to do with the external: they make visible each person's task and vocation in the Church. But they also show devotion to Jesus, the desire to serve him and his people in many different ways.

> The pope wears white, cardinals red, bishops purple, priests and deacons black. Religious often wear habits of distinctive colors.

Read more

Bishops, priests and deacons: CCC 1554, 1593; CCCC 325; YOUCAT 251.

2.11 What are the origins of the Church? How did it all start?

SCAN

When you hear the word *church*, you may think first of a big building with a steeple, a bell, and a cross. We have a lot of these in the Western world. However, there is only one Church (with a capital *C*). The Church is the community of all who believe in Jesus and want to follow him in everything they do (SEE BOX; SEE TWEET 2.1).

Origin

God's great desire is that one day all people will live in heaven with him (SEE TWEET 1.45). In preparation for this, he wants everyone to be gathered together in the Church. The first Christians believed that the world was created with an eye toward the Church (CCC 760). Jesus himself established the Church. He called the first Apostles, teaching them how to proclaim his message to everyone, and thereby beginning an ever-growing community of people who belong to him (the Church). Jesus still teaches all his disciples how to live and to pray by means of the Church (MT. 6:5–6).

Church or church (building)

Our English word *church* comes from the Greek *kyriakon*, which literally means "of the Lord". The Church is the community of the Lord, and the church building is the house of the Lord (SEE TWEET 3.20). In the New Testament, the community of Jesus is usually called *ecclesia*. The Greek word literally means "gathering", and is still recognizable, for example, in the French word *église*. In the Church God calls together his people from all the corners of the earth (CCC 751).

When we talk about the church building, then, *church* begins with a lowercase letter. And when we talk about the community of believers and the Church as a whole, we use a capital letter.

138

God	Creation	Formation	Incarnation (Annunciation)	Redemption (Easter)	Consummation
↓	↓	↓	↓	↓	↓

A	**B**	**C**	**D**	**E**	**F**
God in secrecy	Beginning of revelation	God forms his people	Revelation by Jesus	The Church as instrument of salvation	Jesus comes again: God's Kingdom is complete

Church

In the beginning, the one Church was led by the Apostles and later by their successors, the popes and the bishops who came after them. At various times in history, certain Christian communities broke away from the Catholic Church to govern themselves or to form new churches (SEE TWEET 2.12). Almost no organization has continuously existed as long as the Church has. That the Church still exists after 2,000 years, in spite of many internal divisions and outside attacks, can be seen as a kind of proof that she is not merely a human organization, but established and protected by God.

Salvation history

God's interaction with mankind over time is called salvation history (SEE TWEET 1.27). This is the history of God's plan for us (SEE BOX). God has always existed (A). At Creation (B) he started to reveal himself to man as he sought a relationship with him. God then formed his chosen people (C) through a covenant with Abraham and his descendants, who were often unfaithful to him (SEE TWEET 1.23–1.24). Over the centuries God sent prophets to lead his people back to him and to proclaim the coming of the Savior. Eventually, God entered the world as Jesus in order to save mankind. This historical event is the Incarnation (D) and marks the beginning of a new era. Through the sacrifice of his life (SEE TWEET 1.26), Jesus brought about the Redemption (E), sealing a new and eternal covenant between God and man. Jesus established the Church so that everyone can come to the Father through him. The Consummation (F) of God's union with mankind will take place at the end of time, when Jesus will come again (SEE TWEET 1.49–4.50) and the Kingdom of God will be completed.

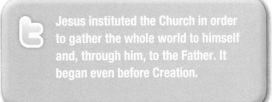

Jesus instituted the Church in order to gather the whole world to himself and, through him, to the Father. It began even before Creation.

Read more

Meaning of Church: CCC 751–752; CCCC 147; YOUCAT 121. *God wants the Church*: CCC 760; CCCC 149; YOUCAT 122.

2.12 One Church – then why all the division among Christians?

The main cause of division among Christians is the stubbornness and sinfulness of men. Often a lack of charity, rather than a disagreement on the substance of the gospel, caused Christians to be divided. The division of Christians shows that the Kingdom of God is far from complete!

Not in the plans

Jesus and the Church cannot be separated from each other: together they form an inseparable unit. Just as God in the Trinity is one (SEE TWEET 1.33), the Church is also one in Jesus (GAL. 3:28). The members of the Church together form the Body of Christ, of which Jesus is the head (COL. 1:18; SEE TWEET 2.1). Thus we are all united in "one Lord, one faith, one baptism, one God and Father of us all, who is above all and through all and in all" (EPH. 4:4–6). Jesus prayed that all Christians would be one in God (JN. 17:20–23).

Discord

It is therefore very painful to see that Christians are so divided. The whole Church is harmed by quarrels. There are now many churches and communities that gather, separately, in the name of Jesus. This is not as God intended it. And it is even worse when such division is used as an excuse to wage war. Precisely because of the love of Jesus and the unity he wanted, the Church must always continue to work for unity among Christians, by seeking reconciliation by asking for forgiveness.

In this context, Pope Francis called us to be "all united in our differences, but united, always: this is the way of Jesus. Unity is superior to conflict. Unity is a grace for which we must ask the Lord that he may liberate us from the temptation of division, of conflict between us, of selfishness, of gossip.... Never gossip about others, never! So much damage to the Church comes from division among Christians, from biases, from narrow interests.... [W]e have to pray together as Catholics and also with other Christians, pray that the Lord gives us the gift of unity, unity among us" (AUDIENCE, JUNE 19, 2013).

According to the Creed, the Church is one, holy, catholic, and apostolic

One, because Jesus has established the Church. The many different talents and ways of life that Christians practice enrich the Church. Yet the unity of the Church remains the starting point. That is why St. Paul said: "As in one body we have many members, and all the members do not have the same function, so we, though many, are one body in Christ" (ROM. 12:4–5; SEE TWEET 2.1).

Holy, because God himself is holy. Fortunately, the sanctity of the Church is not dependent on the holiness of the faithful, who are sinners. The Church is more than the sum of all believers, because Jesus is the founder and the head of the Church. It is not through man's efforts that the Church is holy, but through the merits of Christ, which he shares with us through his grace (SEE TWEET 2.14 AND 4.12).

Catholic, or universal, because the Catholic Church is complete in herself. Since Jesus established her, the Church has been made for all people in all lands at all times. Jesus established the Church to bring all people to God. Without her, this would not be possible (SEE TWEET 2.14).

Apostolic, because the Church is built upon the Apostles. Jesus called each of them personally to be his witnesses throughout the world (LK. 6:13–16; MK. 3:16–19). Before their deaths, the Apostles gave this task to other men, who received the title of bishop (SEE TWEET 2.15). The office of the pope also comes from a long line of successors who have carried on the work of the Apostle Peter, who had received a special responsibility for the Church from Jesus (SEE TWEET 2.15) (SEE APPENDIX 3).

....

Ecumenism

When seeking Christian unity (ecumenism) we depend on the help of the Holy Spirit. The goal of ecumenism is not to mix opposing doctrines for the sake of a false unity.

Although the separation of Christians is sometimes the result of human error, it also is sometimes the result of misunderstanding. It takes effort to overcome both; we ourselves cannot force unity to happen.

Nevertheless, the desire for unity is a good one (JN. 17:21). The one Church of Christ remains, and Jesus will gather his whole flock together one day. Until then, as long as we are not yet fully one Church, we cannot, for instance, share in all the sacraments (SEE TWEET 3.49). However, we must ceaselessly continue to work prayerfully for the one Church of Christ.

> Jesus wants one Church, but our sinfulness causes divisions. We must pray and work for unity, but only God can give it.

Read more

Separation and unity of Christians: CCC 817–822; CCCC 163–164; YOUCAT 130–131. *The Church is one:* CCC 811–822, 866, 870; CCCC 161–164; YOUCAT 129–131. *The Church is holy:* CCC 823–829, 867; CCCC 165; YOUCAT 132. *The Church is catholic:* CCC 830–838, 868; CCCC 166–168; YOUCAT 133–134. *The Church is apostolic:* CCC 857–865, 869; CCCC 174–176; YOUCAT 137.

2.13 How can I be sure that the Church is telling the truth?

You probably know from experience how difficult it can be to discover or to know for sure what is true. Sometimes opposing views may all sound very logical.

St. Paul warned Christians to avoid "insubordinate men, idle talkers and deceivers" and not to pay attention to the "commands of men who reject the truth" about Christ (Tɪ. 1:10, 14). In our own time there is also a danger of losing sight of the truth, especially when many people say contradictory things. So many people, so many opinions! But isn't there only one truth? (Sᴇᴇ Tᴡᴇᴇᴛ 1.8.)

Bulwark of truth

Jesus established the Church so that we could know him and be in relationship with him. Jesus placed great emphasis on the Church, which Scripture calls "the Church of the living God, the pillar and bulwark of the truth" (I Tɪᴍ. 3:15). He entrusted her leadership to Peter (Mᴛ. 16:18–19), the other Apostles, and their successors (sᴇᴇ Aᴘᴘᴇɴᴅɪx 3). They have the

responsibility to guard everything Jesus said and did and to pass it on. So that the Church could do this without error, Jesus promised his Holy Spirit, the "Spirit of truth" (Jɴ. 14:17), to the Church (sᴇᴇ Tᴡᴇᴇᴛ 1.31). Anyone who stands against the Church stands against Jesus, who is one with the Church (Eᴘʜ. 5.23). Pope Paul ᴠɪ said that only by presenting the truth about Jesus that he has given to his Church will we truly respect everyone's religious freedom, by proposing it to them (Eᴠᴀɴɢᴇʟɪɪ Nᴜɴᴛɪᴀɴᴅɪ, 80).

Tried and tested

From the moment that the Church was instituted by Jesus, she has continued to expand. Just as a firm oak tree grows from a little acorn, likewise over the centuries the Church gradually became the Catholic Church that we see today.

Holy Spirit

Contrary to what is sometimes claimed, the Church has never changed the core of her official doctrine. As time has passed the

How can I still believe the Church with all those evil priests?

The media is full of indignation when a priest or a bishop has committed or covered up a crime – and rightly so! We should expect priests and bishops to lead holy lives and to tell the truth. But despite the great gift of the priesthood (SEE TWEET 3.41), priests and bishops are weak men who can commit grievous sins like anybody else. Although man is created good, he is inclined to evil (SEE TWEET 1.4). The history of the Church shows that in every age there have been rotten apples among Christ's followers, and even among the clergy. It started with the terrible betrayal of Judas (MT. 26:14–16). But Peter also made mistakes; he even denied Christ! The same applies to his successors: no man is without sin (I JN. 1:8–10). It is clear that crimes must be punished, both by man and by God (SEE TWEET 4.42). St. Augustine said: "God will call the bad shepherds to account for his sheep and for their deaths" (SERM. 46:20). You may wonder why Jesus allows bad apples in the Church. He wants as many people as possible to turn away from sin and to accept his love. Bad apples are tolerated because they need saving too. St. Paul exhorted the leaders of the Church: "Take heed to yourselves and to all the flock, in which the Holy Spirit has made you guardians, to feed the Church of the Lord" (ACTS 20:28).

Although individuals in the Church may sin, the Church itself is without sin. This is because Jesus is without sin, and the Church is his Body (COL. 1:18; SEE TWEET 2.1). So, you can believe the Church, even if priests or other Catholics sometimes sin grievously. The Church proclaims the words of Jesus without error; the Holy Spirit is the guarantee of this (SEE TWEET 1.32). Therefore, we can take to heart the words of St. Augustine about bad priests: "Do whatever they say, but do not do what they do" (SERM. 46.21; MT. 23:3). Jesus makes sure that, however bad a priest may be, he still gives us access to fully valid sacraments (SEE TWEET 3.35). Jesus chose Peter to lead the Church, despite his human weakness, and said: "I have prayed for you that your faith may not fail; and when you have turned again, strengthen your brethren" (LK. 22:32). You are also asked to pray that the pope, bishops, and priests can continue to fulfill their great duty with honesty, faith, love, and fortitude.

Church has certainly understood the various elements of the faith better. This is due to the constant help of the Holy Spirit, who guides the Church into all truth (JN. 16:13). Through the Holy Spirit, Jesus continues to lead the Church. Because of this the Church is indestructible (CCC 869).

The Holy Spirit ensures that the Church teaches the truth about the faith, even when priests or bishops are sinful.

Read more
Christ governs the Church today: CCC 869; CCCC 173; YOUCAT 137. *Holiness of the Church:* CCC 829; CCCC 165; YOUCAT 132.

2.14 Can I be a good Christian without the Church?

SCAN

We cannot do it all alone; we need God's help to live well. And he gives this help through the Church. You could say that the Catholic Church is a kind of highway to heaven. Through the sacraments and the instructions she gives, believers can more easily find their way through life to their proper end in God.

However, this does not happen automatically: we ourselves must continue to be careful to live in the right way. Remember that sometimes serious accidents can happen on the motorway! But the alternative to membership in the Church in this analogy is even riskier: the non-Catholic depends on winding country roads, where he can easily get lost.

Not without the Church

Jesus and the Church cannot be separated from each other. Jesus established the Church so that through her "the manifold wisdom of God might now be made known" (EPH. 3:10). Because the Church represents Jesus, whoever persecutes her also persecutes him (ACTS 9:4–5; 26:14–15). Jesus told his disciples that those who reject him will reject them as well (JN. 15:18–21). In the third century, St. Cyprian said that God cannot be your father if the Church is not your mother (DE CAT. ECCL. UNITATE, 6). He even said that no one can be saved without some connection to the Church! And St. Paul said that without Jesus, no one can be saved (ACTS 4:12). Whoever rejects the Church, also rejects Jesus, and thus cannot be saved (LK. 10:16).

That does not mean that people who through no fault of their own are not Catholic are automatically lost and have no future with God (SEE BOX). But it shows how important the Church is! It is in fact very logical, when you realize that Jesus set up the Church to bring all people to him (SEE TWEET 2.1).

A close relationship

The relationship between Jesus and the Church is so powerful that St. Paul compared it to the love between husband and wife (EPH. 5:25).

Can non-Catholics go to heaven?

Jesus instituted the Church so that we can live good lives and go to heaven. Through the Church, we receive his strength in the sacraments (SEE TWEET 3.35), the correct interpretation of his Word (SEE TWEET 1.20), and help with difficult choices (SEE TWEET 4.6). Also the Church community supports us when life is difficult. Jesus wishes to give everyone this indispensable help of the Church. It is therefore our duty to share with everyone the importance of being or becoming Catholic (SEE TWEET 3.50).

God "desires all men to be saved and to come to the knowledge of the truth" (I TIM 2:4). While we do our part to achieve that goal we do not judge people who do not (yet) know Jesus or the Church. Everyone deserves our respect, as he is created in the image of God (GEN. 1:26). We trust that the future of those who do not know Jesus and of those who do not know him in the same way we do, lies in the hands of God, who loves them.

If we want to be in a close relationship with Jesus, then we must also be in one with the Church. Indeed, we are asked to love the Church as Jesus loves her! Jesus wants us to be connected to him and each other, fastened together like the branches of a vine, without which the branches could not live (JN. 15:5). Pope Benedict XVI said that the Church is "communion of life with Jesus Christ and for one another" (SEPT. 22, 2011).

Follow the Church

If you really love someone, you are willing to give up a lot for that person. You stop living only for yourself and start living for that other person too. It is the same if we truly love Jesus. Being a Christian is a paradox: in losing ourselves we find ourselves. If we follow Jesus by living according to what the Church teaches – even though it is sometimes very difficult – we discover our best selves. Jesus invites us to take up our cross, to die to our sinfulness, in order to receive eternal life. He also promises that anyone who gives up for his sake even good things, such as family and possessions, will "receive a hundredfold" (MT. 19:29). As St. Paul said: "I rejoice in my sufferings for your sake ... for the sake of his body, that is, the Church" (COL. 1:24).

> Jesus founded the Church as a reliable way to God, with everything we need to reach our final destination in heaven.

Read more

Holiness of the Church: CCC 829; CCCC 165; YOUCAT 132. Church as sacrament of salvation: CCC 774–776, 780; CCCC 152, YOUCAT 123. "Outside the Church there is no salvation": CCC 846–848; CCCC 171; YOUCAT 136. The Church and other religions: CCC 836–845; CCCC 168–170; YOUCAT 134–136.

2.15 Who are the Apostles? Who are their successors?

SCAN

The word *Apostle* means "one who is sent". At the beginning of his public ministry Jesus chose 12 men to follow him closely (Mk. 1:16–19; SEE TWEET 2.11). After teaching them, he sent them out to heal, to drive out demons, and to proclaim the gospel in places where he himself could not be (Mt. 10:5–7). These men lived with Jesus for three years and were witnesses of what he said and did. After the Resurrection, Jesus told them to teach and to administer the sacraments, and he appointed Peter to be their leader (Mt. 16:18; SEE TWEET 2.17).

The Twelve

Just as God began his people in the Old Testament with the 12 tribes of Israel (SEE TWEET 1.23), he began his Church with 12 Apostles (CCC 765; SEE BOX). Simon Peter and his brother Andrew were fishermen, and so were the two brothers John and James (Mt. 4:18–21). To distinguish the latter from the other Apostle James, "the Greater" is added to his name (SEE TWEET 1.30). Matthew was a tax collector before becoming an Apostle (Mt. 10:3). Doubting

Thomas would not believe that Jesus had risen until he could place his finger in the Lord's wounds (Jn. 20:24–25). The other Apostles were Philip, Bartholomew, Simon the Zealot, James (the Lesser), and his brother Judas Thaddaeus (Jude) (Lk 6:14–16). Judas Iscariot, the traitor, was replaced by Matthias after Jesus ascended into heaven (Acts 1:26). Paul never met Jesus during his earthly life, but through a mysterious encounter with the Risen Christ he was made an Apostle (Acts 9:1–22).

Successors

The Apostles passed on the office that they had received from Jesus to their successors, the

....

Apostle, apostle, and disciple

Only the Twelve, Matthias, and Paul (Gal. 1:1) were Apostles with a capital A. Other followers of Jesus, disciples or apostles, are also mentioned in the New Testament. In one of his letters St. Paul named Andronicus and Junias as "noteworthy men among the apostles" (Rom. 16:7).

Recognizing the Apostles

St. Philip	sword and lance	May 3
St. James (the Lesser)	knots and fuller rod (or a bat)	May 3
St. Matthias	axe	May 14
St. Peter	keys (Mt. 16:18–19) or rooster (Mk. 14:30)	June 29
St. Paul	sword (Eph. 6:17)	June 29
St. Thomas	sword and square	July 3
St. James (the Greater)	great scallop shell	July 25
St. Bartholomew	knife	August 24
St. Matthew	moneybag (Mt. 9:9)	September 21
St. Simon	saw	October 28
St. Jude	knots	October 28
St. Andrew	Andrew's cross and sword	November 30
St. John	chalice	December 27

bishops, who did the same in their turn. This apostolic succession has continued through the ages down to our own day (cccc 176). Pope Francis said that "it is through an unbroken chain of witnesses that we come to see the face of Jesus" (Lumen Fidei, 38). Because the Christian world was (and is) growing, an increasing number of bishops were needed to continue the work of the Apostles.

successors, the bishops are connected with Jesus and his Church in a special way. To express this mystery, around the year 107 St. Ignatius of Antioch wrote: "Let the community come together where the bishop is, for where Jesus is, there is the Catholic Church" (The Church of Smyrna, 8).

Tasks

The tasks of the bishops are still the same as those of the Apostles: leading the Church (governing), making Jesus present in the sacraments (sanctifying), and preaching the Word of God (teaching). As the Apostles'

> Jesus chose 12 Apostles to lead the Church, to administer sacraments, and to preach the Gospel; their successors are the bishops.

Read more

Choice of the Twelve: ccc 551–553, 567, 765, 858–860; cccc 109, 175; youcat 92, 137.

Apostolic succession: ccc 861–862, 1087; cccc 176, 222; youcat 137.

SCAN

2.16 Was Jesus against women?

Looking at the list of Apostles (SEE TWEET 2.15), some say Jesus valued women less than men. Looking more closely at the Gospels, however, we see that Jesus highly valued and respected women and that women played an important role in his life and mission. First of all, Jesus, like any human being, was born of a woman. Because his mother, Mary, played such a critical role in his mission, the Church believes she occupies the highest place among the saints in heaven (SEE TWEET 1.38).

In addition to his mother, other women were disciples of Jesus. A well-known example is St. Mary Magdalene, who along with several other women travelled with Jesus and financially supported his ministry (LK. 8:1–3). She was one of the few disciples to remain with Jesus as he died on the cross.

Martha and Mary

Among the close friends of Jesus were the sisters Martha and Mary (LK. 10:38–42). When Jesus visited their home, Mary attentively listened to him, while Martha occupied herself with preparing dinner. When Martha complained that Mary wasn't helping her, Jesus said that spending time with him is more important than doing even necessary tasks. Martha and Mary have long been reverenced by the Church. A medieval fresco by Fra Angelico (SEE PICTURE) contrasts the praying sisters with the sleeping Apostles during the agony of Jesus in the Garden of Gethsemane (LK. 22:43).

Equally valued

Neither Jesus nor his Church is against women. On the contrary, Jesus reached out to women, even sinful women, with openness, respect, acceptance, and tenderness. For her part, the Church has improved the treatment of women in many places of the world. Christianity is the reason women have more civil rights in Western societies than they do in parts of Asia, Africa, and the Middle East. Women have always played an important role in the transmission of the faith. St. Timothy, for example, received the faith from his mother and grandmother (II Tim. 1:5). Thus the Church honors countless female saints; some she even names in the Mass. First, the Virgin Mary is mentioned (see Tweet 1.38), then Felicity, Perpetua, Agatha, and Lucy, who all gave up their lives for their faith in the first centuries of the Church (Eucharistic prayer I). In later centuries untold numbers of Catholic women committed themselves to the care of their neighbors, in hospitals and schools, for instance. Others were great scholars, such as Maria Agnesi (†1799), the first woman to be a professor of mathematics at any university. And then there are the many religious sisters who have given their lives to Jesus through prayer and service on behalf of the Church (see Tweet 2.9).

But not the same

But why then did Jesus choose only men as his Apostles? Some say that Jesus limited the priesthood to men out of respect for the customs of his time, but many of his actions defied prevailing customs. After the Resurrection, Jesus first appeared to Mary Magdalene, instructing her to tell the Apostles that he had risen from the dead (Mk. 16:7; Mt. 28:7; Jn 20:11–18). He thus made Mary Magdalene an "apostle to the Apostles" (see Tweet 2.15) in a society that gave the testimony of a woman less value than that of a man. Because Jesus chose only men to be Apostles, their successors – the bishops along with their priests and deacons – are only men (see Tweet 3.41). From the Creation and the Redemption

we can see that men and women are of equal worth in the eyes of God. At the same time, it is clear that men and women are not exactly the same (see Tweet 3.41). Men are made for fatherhood, women for motherhood, and Jesus calls both to follow him in accordance with these complementary vocations.

Jesus highly valued women. Women and men are of equal worth in the eyes of God, who gives them different but complementary vocations.

Read more

Equal worth of man and woman: CCC 2334–2335, 2393; CCCC 487; YOUCAT 401.

2.17 Is the pope a successor of St. Peter?

There was one among the 12 Apostles whom Jesus gave a special task. The fisherman Simon Peter was married and lived in the home of his in-laws (Mt. 8:14), where Jesus was a regular guest. Jesus called him and his brother Andrew to follow him (Mt. 4:19). It is striking that the Gospels give more detail about Peter, and especially about his journey of faith with Jesus, than about the other Apostles. He is mentioned more than all the others put together. And, he is always mentioned first (Mt. 10:2; Lk. 6:14). Apparently the Evangelists, who wrote the Gospels, saw Peter as the chief among the Apostles (Mk. 16:7).

Rock

Simon was renamed Peter by Jesus. The Greek word *petra* means "rock". In Aramaic the word is *cephas*. Peter was appointed by Jesus to be the rock-solid foundation of the Church. Jesus said to him: "You are Peter, and on this rock I will build my Church, and the gates of Hades shall not prevail against it. I will give you the keys of the kingdom of heaven, and whatever you bind on earth shall be bound in heaven, and whatever you loose on earth shall be loosed in heaven" (Mt. 16:18–19).

Peter and the Christians

In the early Church the Apostles were often spoken of as "Peter and his companions" (SEE Lk. 9:32). Despite their occasional disagreements, Paul always talked about Peter as the rock of the Church (Gal. 1:18; 2:7–8, I Cor. 1:12). Whenever ther e was a problem, Peter was there looking for a solution. And so here it is shown how, despite his human weaknesses, Peter provided leadership to the early Church. He was appointed the leader by Jesus, and other Christians accepted and obeyed him in this role.

Rome

After the Resurrection, Jesus said to Peter: "Feed my lambs", "Tend my sheep", and "Feed my sheep" (Jn. 21:15–17). Three times he expressed very clearly that Peter should lead the Church the way a shepherd cares for his sheep. Before each of these three commands, Jesus asked Peter whether he loved him. Peter answered that he did, and his love for the Lord's sheep would follow from this and would be the true basis of his leadership. As a shepherd, Peter would keep the Lord's flock, the Church, together. To do this, he had received from Jesus the Lord's own authority as represented by the "keys to the kingdom of heaven".

Peter was leader of the church in Rome, where he died a martyr's death around the year 64. The special role of the bishop of Rome, the pope, is due to the special role of Peter among the Apostles. Already in A.D. 107, St. Ignatius of Antioch said that the bishop of Rome took precedence over the bishops in the other cities where the Church was established. The name *Roman Catholic* signifies the relationship between Rome and the universal Church: all the Catholic bishops throughout the world are bound to the pope, the successor of the Apostle Peter and the bishop of Rome.

Successors

Early Christian writings list the successors of Peter, those who took his place as the bishop of Rome (SEE APPENDIX 3). Around A.D. 180, St. Irenaeus wrote that, since its foundation,

the church in Rome had had a continuous line of successors from Peter (ADV. HAER. III.3). He underlined the importance of each local church remaining connected to the church of Rome. He also said that the church of Rome was to be the measure of the correct interpretation of the faith. The fact that the late first-century Pope Clement I intervened with authority in the problems in the Corinthian church, is seen as an expression of the special task of the bishop of Rome in relation to other churches. Both the pope and the Corinthian Christians were apparently aware of the special position of the successor of Peter. When Jesus personally installed Peter as head of the Church, he promised that the Church would last until the end of time (SEE TWEET 2.11). Peter's singular role did not disappear when Peter himself died. Rather it has continued through the office of the pope down to our own day. The title *pope* is of later date, but the office goes back to the selection of Peter by Jesus himself.

> Jesus appointed Peter as leader of the Apostles and of the Church as a whole. Peter's role was passed on to his successors, the popes.

Read more

Organization of the Church: CCC 874–879, 935; CCCC 179–181; YOUCAT 140.

Pope as successor of Peter: CCC 880–882, 936–937; CCCC 182; YOUCAT 141.

 2.18 How did things proceed after Pentecost?

SCAN

Just before his ascension, Jesus commanded the Apostles to wait for the promise of the Father, about which he had told them (Acts 1:4). That promise was the Holy Spirit – the Helper, or Comforter, of the Church, who 10 days after Jesus' ascension was poured out on the Apostles. On this day, Pentecost, the Church definitively began its work on earth.

Christian or Jew?

With the help of the Holy Spirit, the Apostles preached the message of Jesus wherever they could. They established local churches in cities throughout the Roman Empire and beyond. John went to Ephesus. Peter and Paul arrived after some time at Rome, where Peter became the leader of the local church as well as of the universal Church. From the beginning, the church of Rome had a special place among the local churches (SEE TWEET 2.17). The first Christians were Jews who believed Jesus is the Savior (the Messiah) whom God had promised to the people of Israel through the prophets (SEE TWEET 1.27). They continued to gather in

synagogues, as well as in private houses (SEE TWEET 3.20), and to observe many Jewish customs. Naturally, the Apostles at first shared the gospel only with their fellow Jews. But then Peter had a vision from God that he came to understand when he visited the Roman centurion Cornelius, who was not a Jew. Cornelius recognized the importance of faith in Jesus and was baptized. This event showed Peter, and eventually the other Apostles, that Jesus is the Savior of everyone and that the gospel should be preached to the entire world (ACTS 10 AND 11).

Meetings and prayer

Around the year 50, the Apostles held several large meetings (ACTS 15:6). At the first of these, sometimes called the Council of Jerusalem, St. Peter had a significant role (SEE TWEET 2.22). Some believers at the meeting insisted that Gentiles (non-Jews) could not be saved unless they were first circumcised according to the Law of Moses, as was obligatory for Jews. Peter disagreed and said that grace through

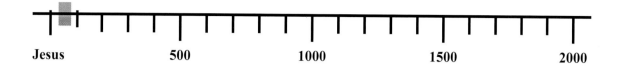
The deaths of Peter and Paul

The Apostles Peter and Paul were killed in Rome around the year 64 during Emperor Nero's persecution of Christians (SEE TWEET 2.19).

Because Paul was a Roman citizen, he had the right to a trial and to a humane execution, a swift beheading rather than a long and tortuous crucifixion. Legend has it that his head bounced three times, and that springs arose in those three places. The site of Paul's martyrdom is marked by the Church of St. Paul at the Three Fountains in Rome. Paul was buried in the place where later the Basilica of St. Paul outside the Walls was built. Originally, this church was outside the city.

Peter was not a Roman citizen and was crucified. According to legend, Peter requested to be crucified upside down, because he did not believe himself worthy to die the same death as Jesus. St. Peter's Basilica was later built at the site believed to be his tomb, with the altar just above his grave. Archaeological excavations between 1940 and 1950 have shown that it is very likely that St. Peter is indeed buried in that place.

Jesus, not the Law, saved everyone, whether Jew or Gentile (ACTS 15:7–12). In the end the Apostles followed Peter's lead and decided that the Gentiles did not need to be circumcised before entering the Church. They needed only to follow the moral laws of God and to avoid any behavior involved in the worship of idols. As more non-Jews became Christians, the Church began to lose some of its Jewish character and increasingly developed its own identity and forms of prayer.

Preaching

The Roman Empire's good roads made travelling relatively easy, so the message of the gospel quickly spread. Added to that, the *Pax Romana* ("Roman Peace") of the first two centuries of the Christian era ensured a certain tranquillity throughout the Roman Empire. What also helped was that Greek (and later Latin) was spoken almost everywhere. The message of Christ appealed to the poor, slaves, and day-laborers, but also spread among the upper classes. In the first centuries most Christians lived in the cities, where local churches were formed.

> After Pentecost, the Apostles began proclaiming the gospel to everyone everywhere. Churches arose, especially in urban areas.

2.19 Why were Christians persecuted by the Romans?

Despite the relative calm of the *Pax Romana* (Roman Peace), the life of Christians in the first century was not always easy. According to the Roman historian Tacitus, in A.D. 64 Emperor Nero accused the Christians of starting the fire that destroyed much of Rome. He did this in order to combat rumors that he had started the fire himself. Many Christians, including Peter and Paul, died as martyrs during the persecution that followed (SEE TWEET 2.18).

End of the peace

Around 180 the stable period of the Roman Empire came to an end. One bad and weak emperor followed another, and for Christians life could be very hard at times. Christians were persecuted because they refused to worship the emperor as a god, along with the other Roman gods, which was considered a civic duty. Thus until about 250, Christians were prosecuted as criminals mainly by local administrators and tribunals, but sometimes by special order of the emperor.

Modern martyrs

Even in our time Christians are persecuted for their faith. In 2011 the Afghan Said Musa was held for six months in Kabul, suspected of having converted from Islam to Christianity, a crime punishable by death according to Islamic law (SEE TWEET 2.26). Musa was released after an appeal from the international community led by the media.

In 2014 the Dutch Jesuit Fr. Frans van de Lugt was brutally murdered in Syria, where he had served people with disabilities regardless of their religious background. As Pope Francis remarked, he "always did good to everyone generously and with love" (AUDIENCE, APRIL 9, 2014).

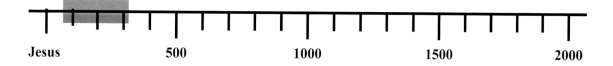
Martyrs and heroes

In the first centuries of the Church, it took a lot of courage and persistence to be a Christian. Christians often had to practice in secret to avoid arrest and execution. The martyrs who died because they would not negate their faith became the heroes, or saints, of the Church (SEE TWEET 4.15–4.17). The Greek word *martyr* means "witness". Martyrs witnessed that eternal life with God is more important than earthly life. Remarkably, their perseverance and example kept encouraging people to become Christians. Therefore, the Christian writer Tertullian (†225) said: "We multiply whenever we are mown down by you. The blood of Christians is seed" (APOLEGETICUM 50.13). A martyr follows the path of Jesus, who was willing to sacrifice his own life for others. In the first centuries, martyrdom was an important element in the spiritual life of Christians.

Imperial persecution

During the reign of Emperor Decius (249–251), the persecution of Christians increased. After years of weak governance, Decius wanted to magnify the power of the emperor. Tens of thousands of Christians died because they refused to obey his command to worship him and the Roman gods. An imperial command of Decius' successor, Valerianus (253–260), stated that it was a crime to be a Christian and ordered Church leaders to be executed.

After a quieter period, Emperor Diocletian (284–305) wanted to destroy the Church. Around 303, he issued several edicts against the Christians. The persecutions that followed were the most violent so far. Churches were closed, books confiscated, bishops prosecuted, and gatherings banned. Diocletian divided the Roman Empire into two parts (East and West), controlled by two equal leaders, both named Augustus. They were each assisted by two junior emperors, named Caesar. The rivalries between these four leaders, the Tetrarchy, would soon cause division and war in the empire.

Change

Diocletian's successor, Emperor Galerius, was first a staunch opponent of the Christians, but just before his death, after he had seen that his persecutions had had little effect, he chose a different strategy. On April 30, 311, he issued an edict of toleration. He even asked the Christians to pray for him and the empire.

In spite of persecutions, the Church continued to expand. She could not be destroyed because God guides her and protects her through the assistance of the Holy Spirit (SEE TWEET 2.13).

> Initially the Roman emperors saw the increase of Christians as a threat and persecuted them because they refused to worship them as gods.

155

SCAN

2.20 What changed with Emperor Constantine?

On October 28, 312, Constantine defeated his rival for power over the Western Roman Empire. Before the decisive battle, Constantine had dreamed of a cross bearing an inscription: "With this sign you shall conquer" ("In hoc signo vinces"). Believing that he owed his victory to Christ, Constantine became sympathetic to Christianity, although he refused to be baptized until the end of his life.

End of the persecutions

In January 313, Emperor Constantine called off the persecution of Christians with the Edict of Milan. Christians were no longer to be treated as criminals, and their seized property was to be returned. Constantine's rule brought not only legitimacy to Christianity but stability and peace throughout the empire (SEE TWEET 2.19).

At last Christians could openly live their faith and be involved in the government of the empire. The number of Christians grew rapidly, as did the need for large, well-lit buildings for the liturgy. Major basilicas, such as St. John Lateran in Rome and the Holy Sepulchre in Jerusalem, were built during this time (SEE BOX).

Constantinople

After Constantine took control of the Eastern Roman Empire, he moved the capital to the city of Byzantium, renaming it Constantinople after himself. We know it today as Istanbul, Turkey. Most successors of Constantine were Christians. Only the emperor Julian the Apostate (†363) tried unsuccessfully to reinstate paganism.

In 380 Emperor Theodosius (379–395) confirmed by edict the truth of the Creed of the Council of Nicaea, a large Church meeting that took place in 325 (SEE TWEET 2.23). With the declarations of Emperor Theodosius, the Catholic faith became the state religion. St. Ambrose (†397), bishop of Milan, had a significant influence on the emperor.

St. Helena and the true cross

St. Helena was the mother of Constantine. She was appointed empress by her son, and she gained unlimited access to the treasury to fund her quest for Christian relics. Around 326 she went to the Holy Land, where according to the historian Eusebius, she had the Church of the Nativity and a church on the Mount of Olives built.

Legend has it that she found three crosses buried in the place where Jesus had been crucified. A woman near death was placed on each of the three crosses in turn and was healed when she touched the third one. By this miracle, St. Helena identified the true cross of Christ. Her son Constantine ordered that the Holy Sepulchre be built in that place in Jerusalem. Helena brought part of the cross and other relics of Jesus' Passion to Rome.

East and West

Invasions and internal conflicts prevented the empire from remaining united, and it split again into East and West. Over time the differences between the eastern and western parts of the empire increased and weakened the unity of the Church.

The eastern part of the Roman Empire consisted of several important ecclesiastical territories, called patriarchates: Alexandria, Antioch, and Jerusalem. Later Constantinople became a patriarchate (SEE TWEET 2.21).

The pope, the bishop of Rome, was the patriarch of the West. Even as the Western Roman Empire began to collapse, and the city of Rome itself was invaded multiple times, he led the Church and protected civilization. Pope Leo the Great, for example, convinced Attila the Hun not to sack Rome in 452.

In 313 Constantine gave Christians legal recognition and protection. The Church grew rapidly and became influential.

 ## 2.21 How was the early Church organized?

SCAN

In the first century, there was a lot of contact between the Christian communities that the Apostles had founded in various cities. These churches had been organized hierarchically, and each was under the leadership of an Apostle. The Apostles were succeeded by the local bishops, from the Greek word *episkopoi* (PHIL. 1:1; ACTS 1:20; I TIM. 3:1–2). Helping the bishops were *presbyteroi*, which is where our word *priest* comes from (I PT. 5:1–2; ACTS 15:2). There were also deacons, the *diakonoi*, whose main task was to provide for the poor (PHIL. 1:1; I TIM. 3:1–2). St. Ignatius of Antioch wrote of the trio of bishop, priest, and deacon in about the year 107 (SEE TWEET 3.41).

Division of labor

The original division of labor between bishop, priest, and deacon is not entirely clear, but it is clear that the essence of the structure of the Church today was present from the very beginning. From the outset, the bishops passed their duties on to their successors through prayer and the laying on of hands (SEE TWEET 2.13

AND 3.41). Gradually the organization of the Church as we know it today came to be.

There were many other roles within the early Church community besides the three already mentioned: "God has appointed in the Church first apostles, second prophets, third teachers, then workers of miracles, then healers, helpers, administrators, speakers in various kinds of tongues" (I COR. 12:28). Also today, everyone has a special role in the Church (SEE TWEET 3.42). All these tasks are performed in accordance and in consultation with the leaders of the community: the bishops and their priests.

Synod

As the Church became more organized, the synod – a meeting of Church leaders – came to be a new form of regional discussion. In this way, the churches in a given region (or province) could be called together by the bishop to discuss current problems and to deal with questions that had arisen. The first synod was held around 170. Here, the starting

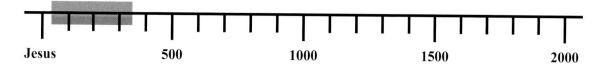

point was what Jesus himself said: he would be present where two or three gathered in his name (Mт. 18:20).

Church province

An ever-increasing experience that the Church is one came through the regional synods. Just as the Roman Empire was organized into provinces, the Church was organized into ecclesiastical territories. A Church province usually consisted of several dioceses, each with their own bishops (see Tweet 2.2).

By the end of the third century, the leadership of a Church province was entrusted to the bishop of a large city (or metropolis, hence the title *metropolitan*). The various ecclesiastical provinces were grouped together under the guidance of a patriarch (see Tweet 2.20). The five patriarchates were Rome, Alexandria, Antioch, Jerusalem, and Constantinople. These last four, and especially Constantinople, tried to increase their own influence and power at the expense of Rome.

> From the beginning, the Church consisted of the faithful, led by Apostles and later bishops. Everyone had a role in the community.

159

 ## 2.22 What is a Church Council?

A Council is a meeting or series of meetings of bishops and the pope (or his representative), often assisted by experts and theologians. The Apostles held a first series of meetings in Jerusalem (Acts 15:6; see Tweet 2.18). There they had to provide answers to questions related to faith that could not be readily found in the Scriptures. The responses the Councils gave are part of the Tradition of the Church (see Tweet 1.11). Councils were often convened in response to a heresy, that is, to a denial or a distortion of the truth about God. Heresy is the result of an erroneous understanding of faith, and it is a very serious matter because it leads believers astray. Therefore it is also referred to as a false doctrine.

Gnosticism

Gnosticism is an example of an early Christian heresy. Gnostics claimed that they were saved by knowledge and that they possessed a higher form of wisdom, which was accessible only to a limited group of initiates. This stands in complete contrast to Jesus' intention that the gospel be preached to everyone. Gnostics denied the teaching authority of the Apostles and adopted only those Christian beliefs that suited their own understanding. Many Christian writers of the first centuries, such as St. Paul (I Tim. 6:20–21) and Justin Martyr (†c. 165), reacted very strongly against this heresy.

Arianism

In the fourth century Arius, a priest from Alexandria, Egypt, claimed that Jesus and the Holy Spirit were created by God and therefore were not the same as, or equal to, God himself. This heresy, known as Arianism, has important implications. For example, if Jesus is not also God, then there has been no Incarnation or Redemption: in other words, Jesus could not have saved us! Because Arianism was closely related to Platonism, the branch of Greek philosophy begun by Plato, it spread particularly rapidly among educated men, including priests and bishops of the Church. The issue sowed

Western heresy

The first Councils were held in the East. Nicaea is in present day Turkey. Other places of the early Councils are Constantinople, Ephesus, and Chalcedon (SEE TWEET 2.23). There were mainly Eastern bishops present. By ratification of the pope, the outcome of such Councils applied to the whole Church.

A more Western theological question concerned the teachings of Pelagius. This monk put much emphasis on the ability (or efficacy) of man to get to heaven merely through his own efforts, without needing God's grace. According to him, the grace of God was not as necessary as many had thought. St. Augustine fought fervently against this doctrine.

The (Western) Council of Orange in 529 stated that a man cannot go to heaven merely by his own efforts. At the same time, the Council rejected the idea that only a few people are destined for heaven (predestination). The idea of predestination to hell was also condemned. In the sixteenth century, these heresies would resurface in Calvinist teachings about double predestination (SEE TWEET 1.44).

such discord within the whole Church, that a Council was convened to settle the matter.

Ecumenical Councils

As a regional synod (SEE TWEET 2.21) could not speak for the whole Church, the emperor convened an Ecumenical Council at Nicaea in 325. It was called "ecumenical" (as opposed to "regional") because it gathered representatives of the whole Church.

Representatives of the pope, more than 300 bishops, and the emperor came together to discuss the claims of the Arians. The conclusion of the pope and the bishops together was that Jesus himself was God. Jesus had not been created but has always existed as the second Person of the Trinity. At the Incarnation, the Son of God took flesh and became man; thus Jesus was also fully man. Jesus, clarified the Council of Nicaea, was both God and man at the same time (SEE TWEET 1.29). The Council Fathers wrote most of our Creed, which was completed during the following Council, that of Constantinople in 381 (SEE TWEET 2.23).

A Church Council is a meeting of the pope and the bishops to answer definitively questions about faith and morals for the whole Church.

2.23 What were the main Church Councils?

SCAN

When there were important matters of faith that needed to be discussed, the emperor or the pope called a worldwide Church meeting, an Ecumenical Council.

During the Councils, no new doctrines were invented by the pope and the bishops present. After all, the faith does not change! Instead, they clarified what had already been believed from the very beginning of Christianity. Up to that point no one had yet seen fit − or had a reason − to declare it officially and write it down. St. Vincent of Lerins (†c. 445) said that such developments in teaching "must truly be development of the faith, not alteration of the faith: development means that each thing expands to be itself, while alteration means that a thing is changed from one thing into another" (Commonitorio I,23).

The first Councils

Reasons for convening a Council were questions regarding certain matters of faith, or controversies that arose. Together the assembled bishops and theologians intended to answer the questions before them within the boundaries of the entirety of the faith. In order to do so, what exactly we believe as Christians had to be clearly defined. What does it actually mean for God to be both three and one, for instance? (See Tweet 1.33.) Are Father, Son, and Spirit equal?

And so, step-by-step, the knowledge of God grew and the correct interpretation of his revelation expanded. That revelation comes to us through both Scripture and Tradition (see Tweet 1.11). Many truths about faith were settled during the first Ecumenical Councils. For example, the first two Councils resulted in the Creed, the great confession of faith that we still pray today (see Tweet 1.31).

Subsequent Councils

The Council of Trent was very important, because it gave answers to the questions that were raised by the Reformation (see Tweet 2.41). The most recent Ecumenical Council, the

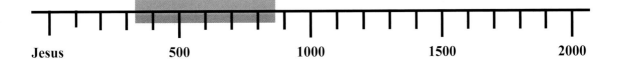

Jesus   500   1000   1500   2000

The first eight Ecumenical Councils

	Year	Council	Important decisions	Reaction against
1	325	Nicaea I	Christ is fully God and "one in essence with the Father" (consubstantial).	Arianism, which denied the divinity of Christ
2	381	Constantinople I	The Holy Spirit is fully God; Jesus is fully human (and fully God).	Apollinaris, who said Jesus was not fully human, and the Pneumatomachi, who said the Holy Spirit is not God
3	431	Ephesus	Jesus is both man and God, therefore Mary is the Mother of God (*Theotokos*).	Nestorius, who said there were two different persons in Christ, human and divine, and Mary was the mother of only the human one
4	451	Chalcedon	Christ is God, but also man. He is one person with two natures (divine and human).	Eutyches, who said Christ was only a divine person
5	553	Constantinople II	Christ is truly only one person.	Followers of Nestorius (see above)
6	680–681	Constantinople III	Christ is fully God and fully man and therefore has both a divine and a human will.	Monothelitism, which said Jesus had only a divine will, and thus was not fully human
7	787	Nicaea II	Because Jesus is human, he can also be depicted in pictures. Images may be venerated (but not worshipped) (SEE TWEET 3.9 AND 3.22).	Iconoclasm, a movement against religious images
8	869–870	Constantinople IV	Each human being has one body and one soul. Constantinople was recognized as a patriarchate, which solved the schism (split) caused by Photius.	Photius who rejected the special authority of the pope (see Tweet 2.30)

Second Vatican Council, was held between 1962 and 1965 (SEE TWEET 2.48). The decisions of Vatican II still have great influence on the daily life and the liturgy of the Church. The Council renewed interest in the role of the laity in the Church, in dialogue with society and other religions, and in the preaching of the gospel.

> The first 8 Councils laid out the core Christian beliefs in response to attacks. When more questions arose, Councils followed with answers.

SCAN

2.24 What are Church Fathers?

The Fathers of the Church are great teachers of the faith who lived in the first few centuries of Christianity. They were men of great sanctity and wisdom. Their work has helped Christians in every age to understand better the message that Jesus gave to the Apostles, and their writings are still invaluable to us.

To illustrate the Church's debt to these great teachers, Bernini's *Chair of St. Peter*, a sculpture in St. Peter's Basilica in Rome, is carried by statues of four Fathers of the Church: Sts. Athanasius and John Chrysostom from the East, and Sts. Ambrose and Augustine from the West (SEE PICTURE).

Apostolic Fathers

The first great Christian teachers after the Apostles are the Apostolic Fathers. These men were taught by one or more of the Apostles or at least lived in the same period. Among them was Pope Clement I, who was ordained by St. Peter. Around the year 96 he wrote to

the Christians of Corinth, exhorting them to be obedient to their leaders. Around the year 100, St. Ignatius of Antioch wrote a series of letters, which demonstrate that from the beginning the Church has always taught the same things about herself, the sacraments, and the role of the bishops. A third Apostolic Father was St. Polycarp, a bishop who had been a disciple of the Apostle John. After the Apostolic Fathers

Greek Church Fathers

St. Athanasius (295–373)
Bishop of Alexandria

- opposed the Arian heresy (SEE TWEET 2.22)
- played a key role in the first Council of Nicaea

St. Gregory of Nazianzus (329–389)
Patriarch of Constantinople

- one of the three Cappadocian Fathers (from Cappadocia, Turkey)
- studied the essence of the Trinity

St. Basil the Great (330–379)
Bishop of Caesarea

- brother of St. Gregory of Nyssa and one of the Cappadocian Fathers
- studied the Trinity and wrote an influential monastic rule (SEE TWEET 2.25)

St. John Chrysostom (345–407)
Patriarch of Constantinople

- complained of abuses in the Church and stood up for the poor
- was nicknamed Chrysostom (meaning, "golden mouth") because of his gift for preaching

Latin Church Fathers

St. Ambrose (339–397)
Bishop of Milan

- stood up against Emperor Theodosius on matters of the faith
- said to have written the Te Deum (song of praise to God) when he baptized St. Augustine

St. Jerome (347–420)
Priest

- translated the Bible into Latin (the Vulgate), which is still used in modified form

St. Augustine of Hippo (354–430)
Bishop of Hippo

- preached much about theology, ethics, and the daily life of the Christian
- described the story of his conversion and vocation in the *Confessions*, in which his mother, St. Monica, played an important role

St. Gregory the Great (540–604)
Pope

- sent the first missionaries to England
- Gregorian chant is named after him

there were the Greek Fathers in the East and the Latin Fathers in the West. One of the first was St. Irenaeus, who was bishop of Lyon in the second century and wrote a strong work against the distortions of the faith, *Against Heresies* (c. 180).

> In the first centuries, the Church Fathers were holy men who thought and wrote deeply about Christ and the faith of his Church.

 ## 2.25 How did monastic life begin?

From the beginning of the Church there were men and women who wanted to follow Jesus as closely as possible. Instead of marrying, or remarrying if they had been widowed, they devoted themselves completely to God by praying, living simply, and giving generously to the support of the Church and to the poor. Their unsought martyrdoms made their total dedication to Jesus complete (SEE TWEET 2.19).

Only with the Lord

With the end of the persecutions of the first centuries, Christians wondered how to follow Jesus perfectly without physically dying for him as martyrs. And so other ways of giving oneself entirely to God came about.

In the third century there were men and women who retreated into the solitude of the desert in order to focus on God alone. A famous early hermit was St. Anthony the Abbot (†356). He heard the words of Jesus to the rich young man: "If you would be perfect, go, sell what you possess and give to the poor, and you will have treasure in heaven; and come, follow me" (MT. 19:21). In response, St. Anthony went to live in the Egyptian desert to be alone with Jesus.

Community

In 325 the Egyptian St. Pachomius began to live in community with other hermits. They promised obedience to a prior and dedication to the gospel. Other communities were soon founded, including those by St. Basil the Great (†379), the father of Eastern monasticism. In the fourth century St. Augustine, bishop of Hippo, together with the priests of his diocese, led a communal life. His starting point was the description of the early Christians, who were "of one heart and soul, and no one said that any of the things which he possessed was his own, but they had everything in common" (ACTS 4:32).

Care for the poor

Although non-Christians would care for their own families, and the rich were sometimes very generous, in much of the ancient world,

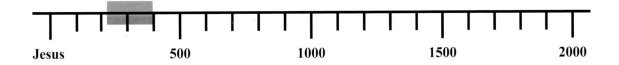

Jesus 500 1000 1500 2000

Living according to a rule

A monastic rule is the set of instructions and agreements that help monks to live together as a community of fellow religious. Inspired by the rules of St. Pachomius, St. Basil, and St. Augustine, in the sixth century the monk St. Benedict wrote a rule for his community. Obedience, poverty, and chastity have important places in this rule. Together these are the three evangelical counsels, which form the core of religious vows. Through his rule and the monasteries he founded, St. Benedict became the father of Western monasticism.

The Rule of St. Benedict has been a major influence on the Order of St. Benedict (o.s.b. for short) and other monastic orders. His Rule helps monks and nuns to grow closer to God. The followers of St. Benedict, called Benedictines, vow to live together in the same place (*stabilitas loci*) and not to run away because of difficulties in community life.

there was no organized charity. This changed with the rise of Christianity, following the words of Scripture: "If any one has the world's goods and sees his brother in need, yet closes his heart against him, how does God's love abide in him?" (I Jn. 3:17).

The early Church chose some men to be deacons, who concentrated on caring for the poor (Acts 6:2–3). St. Basil the Great, a monk, founded the first hospital in the fourth century.

In Western Europe, monasteries became centers of not only charity but also culture. There monks became skilled in medicine, engineering, architecture, art, agriculture, and animal husbandry. At the same time they fostered intellectual culture with their libraries and *scriptoria*, where books were written by hand and studied. This is the origin of the first Christian schools, and later universities in the cities grew up around monasteries.

> Monastic life began when men and women set themselves apart from the world in order to dedicate themselves completely to God.

 ## 2.26 What are the origins of Islam?

SCAN

The word *Islam* means "submission"; a Muslim is literally one who submits to *Allah* (Arabic for "God"). In the seventh century Muhammad, an Arab from Mecca, claimed that revelations from God were dictated to him by the angel Gabriel (*Jibreel*) (Qur'an 53.4,10,11). After the death of Muhammad, these were collected in the Qur'an (SEE TWEET 1.14). For Muslims, Muhammad is the greatest prophet. Other prophets include Abraham, Moses, and Jesus (*Isa*). There are recognizable influences in the Qur'an of Jewish, Christian, and pagan texts. Besides the Qur'an, there are the *hadith*, the explanations of the Qur'an by Muhammad and his followers. The *sharia*, or Islamic law, is composed of the Qur'an and hadith together.

Militant faith

Some Arabs were impressed by Muhammad and willingly followed him, but hostility from others caused Muhammad to flee to Medina in 622. While there, Muhammad called for *jihad* ("struggle") against those who refused to accept his religion, or infidels (Qur'an 61.10–12). Using violence, he and his followers overcame pagan, Jewish, and Christian communities and in 630 entered victoriously into Mecca. Before he died in 632 Muhammad had conquered all of Arabia.

There are crucial differences between Jesus and Muhammad. Jesus claimed to be the Son of God (SEE TWEET 1.28), spread his message without war, allowed himself to be killed in order to redeem mankind, and even prayed for his enemies (LK. 23:34; SEE TWEET 4.43). Muhammad claimed to be a prophet with orders from God to spread his message with violence (Qur'an 8.60) and to kill his enemies (Qur'an 8.12,15,17). He denied that Jesus is God, that he died on the cross, and that he rose again (SEE TWEET 1.26).

Growth of Islam

After the death of Muhammad, campaigns of Muslim warlords overwhelmed much of the Christian East. They also invaded the West, first Spain and then France. In 732 Charles Martel pushed them back in a great battle at

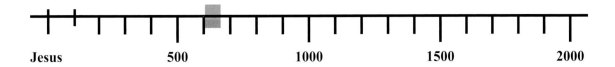

Poitiers. By the tenth century, Islam had spread across Western Asia, North Africa, most of Spain, and Sicily. Islamic law applied in those places. Muslim Turks captured Constantinople in 1453, renaming the city Istanbul and making it the capital of their Ottoman Empire. At their peak, the Ottomans controlled most of southeastern Europe. Only in 1653 were they finally defeated at the gates of Vienna. The Ottoman Empire was dissolved after World War I. Although most Muslim areas of Europe returned to Christian rule, in the East, Christianity is almost completely gone.

Holy war

Jihad against the infidels, or holy war, is a duty for Muslims. According to the Qur'an, violence may be used against non-Muslims in order to make them submit to Allah (Qur'an 8.59; 66.9). Muslims consider Christians "people of the book", that is, the Bible. Since Muslims respect certain Bible passages and consider Jesus a prophet, they do not always force Christians to convert; however, Christians are second-class citizens under Islamic law. They must pay extra taxes and endure restrictions on the practice of their faith (Qur'an 9.29). In our time there are Muslims who advocate holy war and Muslims who want to live in peace with those who do not practice their religion. As Christians, we must do everything possible to live peacefully with everyone regardless of faith. Every recent pope has called upon political leaders everywhere to assure religious freedom for all. At the same time, they have stressed the

Virgins and pillars

According to Islam, everyone will be judged by Allah at the end of time. Those who lived justly will go to paradise, a place of physical and spiritual pleasure where they will lie on couches, eat sumptuous food, and be served by young and beautiful attendants, or virgins. The wicked will go to hell. Islam has five main practices or "pillars". These are professing the faith (*shahadah*), praying five times a day (*salat*), giving alms (*zakat*), fasting during Ramadan (*sawm*), and making a pilgrimage to Mecca (*hajj*). Friday prayer in the mosque is obligatory. This is accompanied by an extensive sermon by an imam, whose words are considered very important.

importance of spreading the Christian faith through peaceful evangelization, as Jesus has commanded the Church (Mk. 16:15; see Tweet 4.50).

 In the seventh century Muhammad spread a religion confessing one God, but without Jesus as our Lord and Savior.

2.27 How did Northern Europe become Catholic?

As the Western Roman Empire collapsed, Christianity spread to lands and tribes never conquered by Rome. Early in the fifth century, St. Patrick (SEE TWEET 1.33) brought the gospel from England to Ireland, where he had been a slave, and the faith took root, thrived, and produced many monasteries.

In turn, Irish monks headed out to preach the faith in Scotland and mainland Europe. They put much emphasis on the personal experience of one's relationship with God and the forgiveness that he gives in the Sacrament of Reconciliation (SEE TWEET 3.38).

Franks and Frisians

Late in the sixth century, the holy Pope Gregory the Great carried out a drastic reform of ecclesiastical structures. The Church began again to focus more on the mission to proclaim the gospel to the world. In 596 the pope gave Augustine of Canterbury the mission to preach among the Anglo-Saxon tribes in England. The pope also sent other missionaries to northern Europe. Around 635, Amandus (†675) was sent from Maastricht to proclaim the gospel to the Franks in the south and the Frisians in the north of the Low Countries. However, it is mainly through the work of Irish and English missionaries that northern Europe became Catholic.

St. Willibrord

In 690 the missionary Willibrord landed on the coast of West Friesland in the Low Countries. He had come from Ireland with 12 companions. On his evangelistic journey he worked closely with the king of the Franks.

Five years after his arrival in Friesland, Willibrord was ordained a bishop by Pope Sergius I in Rome and his seat (*cathedra* [SEE TWEET 2.2]) was in Utrecht. His main residence was in Echternach, Luxembourg, where he had a monastery built. Here he could rest between his various missionary journeys. These brought him also to Denmark, from where the faith was further passed

on to Norway. Willibrord died in 739 in Echternach, where his relics are honored with an annual procession. He is the patron saint of the Dutch church, celebrated on November 7.

St. Boniface

In 716, when he was 36 years old, the English Benedictine monk Boniface crossed the North Sea to preach the gospel to the Germanic peoples. In 732 he was appointed archbishop of Mainz, Germany, and from there he travelled to preach and to support other missionaries. Thus he also went to preach the gospel to the Frisians in the north.

In 754 he was killed by pagans in Dokkum, along with 52 other Christians. According to tradition, he held a heavy Bible above his head to ward off the first sword. There is still a large Bible in Dokkum, Netherlands, with a giant gash in it. The feast day of this patron of the Church in Germany is June 5.

> In the eighth century, missionaries from England and Ireland, such as Willibrord and Boniface, proclaimed the faith in Northern Europe.

SCAN

2.28 What was the relationship between king and pope during the Middle Ages?

Christianity spread gradually throughout Europe. Often the conversion of the chief or king played an important role. When Clovis, king of the Franks, was baptized around 500, both the Western and Eastern Roman Empires had Catholic emperors. The conversion of the Magyars (Hungarians) began with the Baptism of their king, St. Stephen (†1038). And Christians flourished in Bohemia thanks to holy King Wenceslaus (†935).

Frankish kings

In the early Middle Ages, the role of the Franks became increasingly important. In 754 Pope Stephen II anointed Pepin the Short as king of the Franks. When, two years later, Rome was besieged by the Lombards, Pepin came to the rescue of the pope and gave him control over Rome and much of northern Italy. This was the beginning of the Papal States, which existed until 1870 (SEE TWEET 2.44–2.45). At Christmas in the year 800, Pepin's son Charlemagne was crowned emperor of the Holy Roman Empire by Pope Leo III in

St. Peter's Basilica (SEE PICTURE). That empire included a large part of Western Europe. So the West now had a leader on par with that in the East, in Constantinople (SEE TWEET 2.20). Charlemagne was a fervent Christian. He helped with the implementation of many reforms in the Church and in society, including the introduction of Christian marriage in the Germanic tribes.

Nobles and vassals

After the death of Charlemagne, his great empire soon fell apart. A social structure came about in which the nobility had all the power. There were small kingdoms in which lords protected their subjects (vassals) in return for their services and loyalty.

These noblemen also wanted ecclesiastical control in their fiefdoms, for instance, by having the right to appoint the priests in their churches. The pope, who no longer had a strong patron, was dominated by powerful families. This was reinforced by the fact that

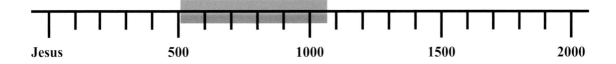

Gregorian reforms

Pope Gregory VII (†1085) called to order clerics that did not keep their promise of celibacy (SEE TWEET 2.25). He also strongly opposed the sale of religious offices and other sacred things (the sin of simony). Thirdly, he wanted to stop the appointment of clergy by secular rulers. Gradually the emperor and the lower nobles had increased their say in the appointments of bishops and priests. Pope Gregory wanted to restore the correct order of appointments to sacred offices.

Pope Gregory VII reformed the Church and restored the independence of the pope, even in the naming of bishops. The latter led to a fight with Emperor Henry IV (†1106), because bishops often had control over a given territory. Gregory then announced officially that the pope had both spiritual and secular power over Christians (DICTATUS PAPAE).

German kings

In 962 the pope crowned German King Otto I as emperor, and the leadership of the Holy Roman Empire came into German hands. When bishops were then given noble titles and territory to control, some of the clergy became still more worldly. At the time, the pope crowned the emperor, and the emperor made sure that the papal elections were fair. However, this cooperation led to tensions, because both claimed to have the final say. There were also all kinds of abuses in the Church. It was high time for a great reform, which was initiated by the election of Pope Gregory VII in 1073 (SEE BOX).

Some early Christian kings were saints. In the Middle Ages kings and popes often contended with each other.

the popes themselves were not very decisive then. It was a time of moral decline among believers, clergy, and monastics. So this was truly a "dark age".

2.29 What was the spiritual rebirth that happened in the Middle Ages?

SCAN

In the Middle Ages the Catholic faith experienced low points and high points. One of the high points was a renewed interest in the life of Christ. People wanted to learn more about Jesus and to imitate him more closely. Many new religious communities were founded during this time, but also lay faithful went in search of the meaning of Jesus in their lives and of the right way to follow him.

Monasteries and religious

In the tenth century, the Benedictine Abbey of Cluny was founded. This abbey, which would become a center of a renewal of faith, culture, and art, was under the direction of the pope. Many monasteries joined the Order of Cluny. At its peak, more than 1,200 monasteries were attached to this order.

In the twelfth century many new religious orders were founded, which would have a big impact on Christendom. The Cistercians wanted to go back to the original simplicity of the Benedictine life. They reacted against the grandeur and splendor of the Order of Cluny. Under the influence of leaders such as St. Bernard of Clairvaux (†1153), the Cistercians devoted much time to prayer and worked hard on the land. Their approach reflected the original Benedictine motto: *Ora et labora* ("Pray and work").

The thirteenth century brought the mendicants (beggars): the followers of St. Francis of Assisi (Franciscans) and St. Dominic (Dominicans) went around preaching to anyone who wanted to hear the gospel (SEE TWEET 2.9). They lived on whatever people gave them. They had no monasteries at first, and they called themselves friars (related to the Latin word for brother).

Faith seeking understanding

In the thirteenth century there was a revival of the study of the faith. The Dominicans and Franciscans played a large role in this. Theology was supposed to deepen the knowledge of the faith with reasoned debate consisting of theses on a given topic, reasoned defenses, and opposing arguments. This method of searching for the truth, which was developed in the Middle Ages, is called Scholasticism. Great thinkers such as St. Thomas Aquinas (†1274) studied the writings of the Church Fathers (SEE TWEET 2.24) and those of ancient Greek philosophers, particularly Aristotle. Even today, the works of St. Thomas are studied by all Catholic seminarians and theologians. In this intellectual environment, the first universities were founded. In 1215 Pope Innocent III recognized the University of Paris as the first ecclesiastical university. Not long after came the universities of Oxford, Bologna, and Salamanca. By 1450 there were over 50 universities in Europe.

Modern Devotion

The spiritual movement Modern Devotion (*Devotio moderna*) originated in the Low Countries in the fourteenth century. Geert Grote (†1384) of Deventer founded the community of Brothers and Sisters of the Common Life. The members were laymen who had taken no religious vows. They did not withdraw from the world, but rather led Christian lives of prayer and simplicity in the midst of ordinary tasks. There were also convents that joined the movement. The ideas of the Modern Devotion spread mainly in Northern Europe and influenced the Dutch philosopher Erasmus (†1536) and the painter Hieronymus Bosch (†1516), among others. The book *The Imitation of Christ* (*De Imitatione Christi*) by Thomas à Kempis comes from this tradition and is still read all over the world.

Medieval art

Almost all the art in the Middle Ages was religious in nature. Huge cathedrals and churches were erected in cities.
The round Romanesque arches were replaced by the pointed Gothic ones, while architects tried to let more and more light into the building.

Stained glass windows, sculptures, and paintings illustrated the mysteries of the faith. Their beauty reflects the supernatural.

New orders were founded to follow Christ. Catholic universities were founded to promote the exchange of knowledge and understanding.

2.30 How did the Orthodox Churches come into being?

Muslims, barbarians, and the Orthodox

As the Western Roman Empire began to collapse, the differences between it and the Eastern Empire grew. It all started with language: in the East, Greek was predominantly spoken and in the West, Latin. Mutual understanding was not as easy as it had been.

Constantinople versus Rome

After Constantine made Constantinople his capital, the city of Rome began to decline in importance. When the empire broke again into two parts, the West and Rome itself were invaded by various tribes. During all this upheaval, however, Rome remained the "eternal city" and the spiritual center of the Church. By 451, the patriarch of Constantinople was claiming that he, not the patriarch of Rome, should have primacy in the Church. During the centuries that followed, the tensions between East and West, which were mostly political, continued to grow. Then in the ninth century, Photios, patriarch of Constantinople, chose to join the party against the pope in a dispute over whether the Holy Spirit proceeds from the Father alone or from the Father and the Son together (SEE TWEET 1.31).

Orthodox Churches

In 1054 there was a definite schism (split) between the Eastern and Western halves of the Church. Emotions ran high in a conflict between the patriarch of Constantinople, Cerularius, and the envoy of the pope, Cardinal Humbert, and each excommunicated the other. It is not clear to what extent the envoy, an ambassador, could speak on behalf of the pope, but the harm was done. Christianity was from then on divided into the Western Latin Church (Roman Catholics) and the Eastern Greek Church (Orthodox Christians).

The Orthodox Churches still do not accept the supreme authority of the pope, but recently Catholics and Orthodox have come closer together through various efforts at

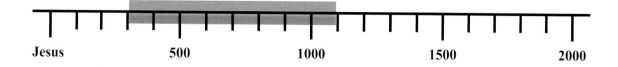

Orthodox or Catholic?

Broadly speaking, Catholics and Orthodox are in agreement about the faith. They both believe in the triune God, salvation through Jesus (SEE TWEET 1.27 AND 1.33), and the presence of Christ in the sacraments (SEE TWEET 3.35). Orthodox (and Eastern Catholic) liturgies differ from Catholic ones, as do the shape and design of their church buildings. At their Baptism, Orthodox babies immediately receive Confirmation and Communion (SEE TWEET 3.49). However, the Orthodox, in contrast to the Protestants, have the same seven sacraments as we Catholics, and they are all valid from the Catholic point of view. Jesus is truly present with his Body and Blood in the Eucharist in the Orthodox Churches (SEE TWEET 3.48). If you cannot find a Catholic priest, you can go to an Orthodox one and ask to receive the sacraments (SEE TWEET 3.49).

The Orthodox Churches are organized differently from the Catholic Church. Just as with us, their bishops and priests are ordained into the ministry dating back to the Apostles, which has been passed down through successive generations (SEE TWEET 2.15). Patriarchs and bishops lead geographical, or even national, churches, but there is no central leader, although occasionally a patriarch tries to take up this role. After the Catholic Church, which has more than a billion faithful (SEE TWEET 2.1), the Orthodox Churches are the largest group of Christians in the world, with about 300 million believers.

dialogue and reconciliation (SEE TWEET 2.12). Praying for a future reconciliation between the Eastern and Western Churches remains very important.

Eastern Catholics

Since the Council of Brest in 1596, some Orthodox Churches have come back into communion with the Catholic Church. These are Eastern Catholics who recognize the pope, while they continue to celebrate their Eastern liturgies and have their own Code of Canon Law approved by the pope (SEE TWEET 4.11). Thus Roman Catholics and Eastern Catholics form one Church.

In 1054 a schism between the Catholic Church and the Eastern Orthodox Churches arose. We do not differ in faith, but in form of government.

 ## 2.31 Why were there violent Crusades?

From the third century on, pilgrimages to the Holy Land (Palestine) were becoming increasingly popular among Christians. It is a unique experience to walk in the footsteps of Jesus in the holy places spoken of in the Bible. In the seventh century Islam came into existence (SEE TWEET 2.26) and rose to power in the Middle East. It made these trips more difficult, but the tradition continued.

Jihad

By the tenth century more and more people were going on pilgrimage to the Holy Land. Under the Arab Fatimid Dynasty, Christians were welcomed, partly because of the valuable trade that could be conducted with them. However, this period of relative peace came to an end in the eleventh century with the rise of the Turks (SEE TWEET 2.26). These Muslims preached a *jihad* (holy war) and wanted to spread the teachings of Islam with the sword to the "infidel" Christians. The goal of these Muslims was to convert the entire world to Islam. The Turks oppressed Christians in the Holy Land, and pilgrimages became very dangerous. Christians were cruelly tortured and slain if they refused conversion.

Crusades

News of the atrocities by Muslims led to the belief in Europe that something must be done to defend Christians in the Holy Land and to make pilgrimages there possible. Thousands of Christians volunteered to fight the Muslims for control of the Holy Land. Especially in the beginning, this initiative was a matter of faith, an act of mercy done for God and neighbor. In 1095 Pope Urban II gave his blessing to the First Crusade in response to a call for help from the Byzantine emperor. It was partly a pilgrimage, which helped people on their personal path to God, and partly a military draft. Three years later the Muslims were defeated and Jerusalem was conquered by the crusaders. More Crusades occurred in the two centuries that followed.

Violence

But how could Christians take up arms against their fellow men? Well, it was all started as a Christian ideal, namely, the protection of Christians and the reclamation of the sacred ground where Jesus had walked from the anti-Christian invaders. However, this ideal sometimes degenerated into cruel massacres and raids. Some crusaders wore the cross unworthily, which cannot be justified. Concerning the evil deeds that were sometimes committed in the name of God by both Muslims and Christians, during a visit to a mosque Pope John Paul II said: "For all the times that Muslims and Christians have offended one another, we need to seek forgiveness from the Almighty and to offer each other forgiveness" (MAY 6, 2001). It's good to note that the end of the armed Crusades coincided with the beginning of the peaceful preaching of the gospel in Muslim regions, especially by the new mendicant orders (SEE TWEET 2.9), including the Franciscans.

Knights Templar

After the First Crusade (1095–1101) the Order of the Templars was founded by nine French nobles. They wanted to serve the Church by liberating the Holy Land. Because of the well-trained knights, who courageously leaped into battle, the Templars were very successful. Many believers wanted to support the knights wearing the white uniform with the red cross, so the order soon amassed great wealth. They answered directly to the pope. King Philip IV, "the Fair", (†1314) borrowed money from the Templars. That, together with the power and independence of the order, might have been the reason that King Philip falsely accused the Templars of heresy and ecclesiastical disobedience. His troops arrested and tortured knights all over France on Friday, October, 13, 1307 (since then Friday the thirteenth is associated with bad luck). In 1312 the pope formally disbanded the order.

> The Crusades were intended to protect Christians in the Holy Land against oppression by Muslims, but crusaders often used the wrong means.

2.32 What was the Spanish Inquisition?

SCAN

After the heresies of the first centuries died down, the Middle Ages saw new forms of false teaching. The southern French Cathars preached a form of Gnosticism (SEE TWEET 2.22) and essentially rejected the Old Testament. The English scholar John Wycliff (†1384) and a priest from Prague named Jan Hus (†1415), spread a message that was a sort of precursor of Protestantism (SEE TWEET 2.36).

In the twelfth century kings increasingly took action against heresy and errors in belief. Local governments established courts and prosecuted heretics. In the thirteenth century Pope Gregory IX (†1241) gave orders to the Dominicans to defend the faith as inquisitors (judges of belief) and to combat heresy.

Roman Inquisition

Early in the sixteenth century Pope Paul III established a commission of six cardinals whose job was to watch over matters of faith. This committee became known as the Roman Inquisition. In the twentieth century

it was succeeded by the Congregation for the Doctrine of the Faith, which is responsible for safeguarding the truths of the faith and taking disciplinary measures against serious violations of it within the Church (SEE TWEET 2.5).

Spanish Inquisition

The Spanish Inquisition was a wholly different organization. It was founded by the Spanish king in 1480 to ensure the purity of the Catholic faith in his realm. The aim was to expose false Christian converts, who secretly practiced Judaism or Islam. It also restored the good names of those who had been falsely accused of heresy.

Though originally the king had obtained the support of Pope Sixtus IV, this same pope protested two years later: "The Inquisition has for some time been moved not by zeal for the faith and the salvation of souls but by lust for wealth" (APR. 18, 1482). However, the king refused to listen to the pope's request for justice, and the Spanish Inquisition continued.

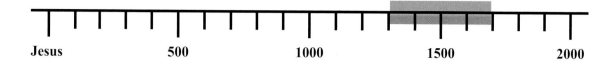

No good words

The errors of the Inquisition can never be condoned. However, it is good to know the facts. It is often said that the Inquisition killed millions of people, but modern researchers speak of hundreds or thousands of deaths as a more realistic count.

The courts of the Inquisition were known as cruel and unjust, but secular courts were reportedly even worse. So, people often preferred to be tried by an ecclesiastical court. Protestants also had inquisitions, in which "heretical Catholics" were tortured and killed. A lot of terrible things were done in the name of Christ during that time.

During the reign of Philip II, the Inquisition extended into the north of Europe. People who were accused of heresy, superstition, bigamy, witchcraft, sodomy, or blasphemy appeared before its courts. Between 1560 and 1700 these courts saw nearly 50,000 cases. In too many cases those who worked for the Inquisition committed terrible crimes against their fellow man in the name of the Church. Anti-Semitism (hatred of Jews), the burning of people presumed to be witches, and the use of torture make the Inquisition a black chapter in Church history.

Perpetrators may perhaps have been misled by the false idea of some theologians that their actions were justified based on passages in the Old Testament. But Christians are primarily called to love, and many of the acts of the Inquisition had nothing in common with love.

An unholy Church?

The Inquisition is often the first thing mentioned when people criticize the Church. There should, however, be a distinction made between the Church that Jesus established and the people who work in and for the Church (SEE TWEET 2.13). The Church is made up of sinners, some of whom have committed terrible acts. During the Jubilee Year of 2000, Pope John Paul II expressly asked for forgiveness for all these sins (MAR. 13, 2000).

> The Spanish king established the Inquisition to keep the faith pure. It became corrupt and committed terrible acts in the name of the Church.

2.33 What happened at the beginning of the Renaissance?

Toward the Reformation

Many medieval popes were not exactly saints. For instance, Pope Boniface VIII (†1303) was more of a legal scholar than a shepherd of the faithful flock. He got into a conflict with King Philip IV of France about the power of the pope and was taken prisoner in 1303 by a representative of the king (after being slapped in the face).

Bottoming out in Avignon

In 1309 Pope Boniface's French successor, Clement V, moved the papal seat to Avignon in southern France. His six successors (SEE APPENDIX 3), all French, lived in Avignon and came under the influence of the French king. In 1377, through the intervention of the Italian St. Catherine of Siena, Pope Gregory XI returned to Rome. But that was not the end of the difficulties within the Church. A few months after the selection of Pope Urban VI as the successor of Gregory XI, the French cardinals elected their own pope, an "antipope", who again took up residence in Avignon. This was the beginning of the Great Schism (split) in the Roman Catholic Church, in which rivals claimed that they were the legitimate pope and excommunicated each other. This led to great confusion among Christians, for who was the real pope? At one point there were even three men claiming to be the pope! This situation was only resolved in 1417 with the Council of Constance, when all parties acknowledged Pope Martin V as the only true pope.

Still no renewal

After these events, the Church was in need of some real renewal, and attention needed to be given to following Jesus Christ. Such reform, however, would still be years in coming. In the fifteenth century the popes were patrons of the arts and the intellectual life in Europe, but they were getting richer and becoming worldly. It was a period when securing jobs for relatives (nepotism) and selling sacred objects (simony) often occurred. The march to the Renaissance was begun, though this did not mean a revival for the Church.

Adrian VI seeks reform

In 1522, Adrian Floriszoon of Utrecht, Netherlands, was elected pope (Adrian VI) by the cardinals (SEE PICTURE). Many of them would soon regret the choice, because he lived a very sober life in contrast to many members of the Roman Curia (SEE TWEET 2.5) at that time. That quickly led to great tensions, mainly because the pope was earnest about curbing the abuses among the clergy.

Tensions also arose with King Francis I of France; there was the threat of another schism (split) in the Church. The antipopes of Avignon were still fresh in the collective memory, and Adrian VI wanted to avoid at all costs great disagreements that could lead to divisions. The biggest threat to the Church during the pontificate of Adrian VI was the Reformation. In just a few years' time, the teachings of Luther had gained a large following, especially among the German princes (SEE TWEET 2.36). In 1523, merely a year and two weeks after his election, Pope Adrian died. He is buried in the church of Santa Maria dell'Anima in Rome. It would take until 1978, with the election of John Paul II, for a non-Italian again to sit on the Chair of Peter (SEE TWEET 2.50).

Renaissance

The Renaissance saw a revived interest in the wisdom of the ancient Greeks and Romans. Together with the discovery of new continents, this developed into a new approach to science, art, and Church life. There were many paintings, sculptures, and buildings created during this time, which even today are considered masterpieces. There was one big problem: with the renewed interest in the art of antiquity, earthly things began to take on more importance. Not God, but man took center stage.

> The Renaissance was man-centered (forgetful of God?). As in the Middle Ages, Church leaders were sometimes weak or even bad.

2.34 Why was the Church so cruel to the Native Americans?

Once explorers such as Columbus had discovered new continents, Europeans realized that the world was bigger than they had imagined. In the late fifteenth and early sixteenth centuries there were many missionaries heading out to preach the faith in North and South America, Asia, Africa, and Oceania.

The ideal was that the finest treasure that the Europeans possessed – faith in Jesus Christ – should be proclaimed to all people, especially those who had not heard about him. This was also the command that Jesus gave to his Apostles (Mt. 28:19–20; SEE TWEET 2.18). Unfortunately, political and economic factors also often played a role, and in many places the natives were mistreated and exploited.

A real world deal

After Columbus' discovery of America in 1492, the pope divided most of the colonial rights to the New World between Spain and Portugal. The conquistadors were commissioned to preach the faith in the newly discovered regions. Most of them, however, were more interested in looting villages, looking for gold, silver, and other riches. The kings of Spain and Portugal seized large areas of North and South America. The local population was often suppressed with violence and forced into slavery. The Native Americans were so brutalized that in 1537 Pope Paul III had to explain that the indigenous people are human persons and as such had dignity.

Royal interference

The kings of Spain and Portugal had great influence on the Church in the new mission territories. The king decided which missionaries were sent, founded dioceses, and suggested bishops. In this way, the interests of the Church were subordinated to those of the king. This is how the Church was misused in the conquest and oppression of the indigenous people. Unknowingly, Europeans also brought another evil to the Americas. The natives had no resistance to certain European diseases and many of them died from them. The tomb

Toward the Reformation

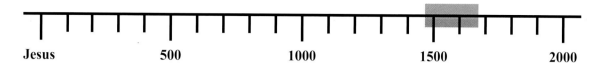

of Pope Gregory XIII (†1585) in St. Peter's in the Vatican depicts a discussion about the discovery of the New World (SEE PICTURE).

Missionaries

Only at a later stage did the Church herself send missionaries to preach the gospel. In the early sixteenth century Franciscans, Jesuits, Dominicans, and other orders set themselves up for the proclamation of faith in overseas territories, as well as for the establishment of schools, hospitals, and the like. For example, in Paraguay the Jesuits built Christian communities for the Native Americans, but they were brutally attacked by slave traders. Many natives voluntarily embraced the faith, and some of them were later recognized as saints, such as St. Kateri Tekakwitha (†1680) in North America. In 1568, with

the establishment of what later became the Congregation for the Evangelization of Peoples (SEE TWEET 2.5), the pope was then in more direct control over the missionary activities. Preaching Christian faith and teaching that the natives had human dignity were important tasks of the congregation. Spain and Portugal were not well pleased by the papal interference with "their" overseas mission territories. This often led to conflicts.

> Spain and Portugal often sought wealth before converts, without caring for people. The pope condemned the mistreatment of the natives.

2.35 What was the business with the Church selling indulgences as tickets to heaven?

Toward the Reformation

In the context of the Renaissance, an incorrect use of indulgences arose. Jesus himself had given the command to the Apostles to forgive sins in his name (Jn. 20:22–23). But although the sins are forgiven, the consequences of the sins still exist. Take for example your aunt's beautiful vase that you broke when you threw it in anger: it remains broken, even if she forgives you! And you still have a bad temper! (See Tweet 4.13.)

To undo the damage done by your sin, the priest gives you something to do for penance or atonement in the Sacrament of Reconciliation (see Tweet 3.38). In this sacrament, the priest freely forgives you in God's name when he gives you absolution. The penance, which may consist of prayers or good works, is meant to help you to overcome your faults. Any imperfection still left in you at the time of your death can be purified in purgatory (see Tweet 1.47). There is hope for everyone: only one who persists in mortal sin cannot be saved (see Tweet 1.46).

Earn indulgence!

The remission of all or part of the purification you need in purgatory can happen with an indulgence. Normally, such indulgences can only be obtained from the pope. For instance, to gain an indulgence you may be expected to say certain prayers, do an act of charity, or go on pilgrimage. The principle of the indulgence is the mercy of God, who desires all men to be in heaven as soon they are able. Clearly this is a very good starting point.

Abuse

In the late Middle Ages, however, abuses were made of this mercy of God. Indulgences were promised for improper reasons, for example, to those who gave money to the Church. Pope Leo x (†1521) promised indulgences to those who gave financial contributions to the construction of St. Peter's in Rome. These were sold for big money as tickets to heaven by, for example, the Dominican Johann Tetzel in Germany. The purchaser was promised: "In the authority of all the saints, and in compassion toward you, I absolve you from all sins and misdeeds, and remit

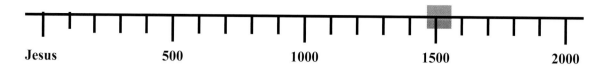

all punishment for ten days" (SEE PICTURE). The sale of sacred things (simony) is strictly forbidden by the Church and a great sin. Indulgences themselves were not the problem, but the poor way in which Church leaders greedy for money dealt with the task that they had received from Jesus. It is understandable that protests were lodged.

Erasmus

Erasmus of Rotterdam (†1536) (SEE PICTURE), was one of the most important Renaissance thinkers. He criticized the sale of indulgences and other ecclesiastical abuses in his book *In Praise of Folly* (1509). He is often regarded as a precursor of the Reformation. Erasmus was a humanist, someone who highly valued the human ability to reason and to create beauty. According to him, man himself could

contribute to the meaning of his life. He was particularly interested in the ancient Greeks and Romans. He travelled a lot and carried on extensive correspondence with other humanists. Martin Luther initially wanted to rely on humanistic principles in his criticism of the way indulgences and other abuses were handled (SEE TWEET 2.36). But he soon complained that Erasmus was a skeptical theologian who was not firm in his faith. Erasmus always remained a Catholic, although sometimes he was at odds with the ecclesiastical authorities. Yet, he was more scholar than reformer. Despite his sometimes sharp criticism of the sale of indulgences and other abuses in the Church, he also criticized certain ideas of Luther, such as the restriction of human freedom and thought.

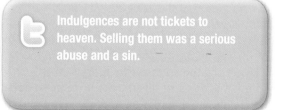

Indulgences are not tickets to heaven. Selling them was a serious abuse and a sin.

2.36 What are the ideas that set off the Reformation?

Toward the Reformation

In 1517, the German monk, priest, and scholar Martin Luther detailed and denounced many abuses in the Church in his "Ninety-Five Theses". The direct cause of his writing was the sale of indulgences (SEE TWEET 2.35) and religious offices (simony), and the corruption of the clergy that he had seen in Rome. So far the indignation of Luther was well founded and good.

Deception and superstition?

The problem is that Luther not only objected to real abuses but also dismissed true parts of our faith as delusions and superstitions. He rejected most sacraments, the special role of Mary, the communion of saints, the authority of the pope, and the priesthood. Luther also rejected apostolic succession (SEE TWEET 2.15) and the interpretation of the faith by the Church (SEE TWEET 2.13). He placed his trust only in the Bible (*sola scriptura*). Because of the bad behavior of some of the clergy, he distanced himself from the Church and the sacraments. Luther, however, forgot that a priest, despite his sinfulness, passes on the good grace of God in the sacraments (SEE TWEET 3.35). The sacraments should not be abolished, but the priests who abuse them should be corrected.

Sola gratia et fide

According to Luther, we can be saved only by God's grace (*sola gratia*) and faith (*sola fide*). However, the Catholic Church has always taught that our faith must necessarily lead to good deeds. St. James said: "You see that a man is justified by works and not by faith alone" (JAS. 2:24; SEE TWEET 4.8). In the years following the publication of his theses, Luther moved further away from the Catholic faith and became more radical in his mockery of the pope and the Church. Due to his extreme views, Luther placed himself outside the communion of the Church, which was confirmed by his official excommunication in 1521.

Politics and reformation

Political tensions between pope and emperor and local rulers were an important reason

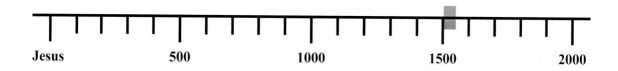
John Calvin

The Frenchman John Calvin (†1564) had ideas similar to Martin Luther, but he went one step further. He said that God in his omnipotence decided in advance who would go to heaven and who to hell. The future of any person would thus be predetermined (predestined). Calvin based his doctrine of double predestination on his own interpretation of certain passages from the Bible and from the writings of St. Augustine (SEE TWEET 2.22). The great sinfulness of man meant, according to Calvin, that he had to lead a strict and austere life of hard work.

This doctrine of predestination is in complete contrast with the goodness and mercy of God, "who desires all men to be saved" (I TIM. 2:4). The Church has always taught that God has given us a free will in the hope that we will choose to receive his love. We must say yes to God's grace and thus cooperate in our own salvation (SEE TWEET 1.38).

authority. Unfortunately, when they threw out the secular authority of the pope, they also discarded his spiritual role. Sometimes without being aware of it, they placed themselves outside the Church. Moral reasons also played a role: many priests and religious were losing the original fire of their vocation. Jesus Christ, to whom they had dedicated their lives, was often placed on the back burner. For many in these circumstances, it was liberating to hear that Luther had abolished celibacy (SEE TWEET 2.25) and the monastic life. However, it is questionable whether they really found peace by abandoning their original vows to the Lord in this way.

Luther was right to denounce certain abuses in the Church, but in his search for reform he also denied important truths and caused a schism.

for the rapid spread of Luther's ideas, and through the recent invention of the printing press, his writings could be easily distributed. The Reformation gave secular leaders the opportunity to loose themselves from papal

2.37 What is the difference between Protestants and Catholics?

The Reformation was a protest movement (SEE TWEET 2.36), but the protesters were not always in agreement with each other. While there is one Catholic Church, there are many different Protestant Christian communities. Luther and Calvin, for instance, each had their own group of followers, who themselves in later years often further divided when no agreement could be reached about issues of faith. The unifying role of the pope is missing in these communities.

Lutheranism and Calvinism

Lutheranism spread mainly in Germany and Scandinavia. Later, immigrants from these countries took their faith to America. In 1999, a joint declaration was signed between the Lutheran World Federation and the Catholic Church. Here, particular attention was given to what unites us, although it became clear once again that we have major differences. There is not a Calvinist Church. The followers of Calvin are spread primarily across Europe and North America in many different Christian communities, in Reformed, Presbyterian, and certain Baptist churches.

Protestant or Catholic?

Like practicing Catholics, devoted Protestants want to have Jesus Christ at the center of their lives. This is something of great importance that we share. However, there are some essential differences between Protestants and Catholics that should be clearly understood (SEE BOX).

Unity

It's good to know these differences, but it is also good to know that we can still pray together. We all believe that Jesus was born to save mankind, and many Protestant communities pray the same Creed we do (SEE TWEET 1.31 AND 1.33). Precisely because Jesus longed for one Church, we have the task to work toward unity (ecumenism) (SEE TWEET 2.12). Prayer is the most important part: the separation caused by people can only be resolved with the help of the Holy Spirit.

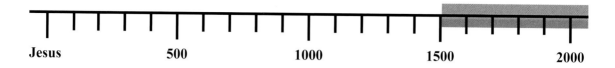

Jesus   500   1000   1500   2000

Most Protestants believe ...

- God's revelation, after the Incarnation, comes only through the Bible.

- Man is saved by Jesus (through grace and faith). Good deeds have no influence here.

- Individual churches govern themselves (sometimes in consultation with other churches).

- A minister (or pastor) is accountable chiefly to the local community (his employer).

- There are two sacraments: baptism and communion (sometimes called the Lord's Supper). Their communion is not truly the Eucharist (thus we cannot receive communion together with Protestants [SEE TWEET 3.48]).

- Depictions of Jesus on the cross are not permitted for certain Protestants, because Jesus accomplished his sacrifice once and for all. The cross is then empty.

- They do not, broadly speaking, accept the special place of Mary in Christian devotion, the intercession of the saints, statues, purgatory, certain sacraments, and the unique authority of the pope.

Catholics believe ...

- Revelation comes through the Bible *and* Tradition (SEE TWEET 1.11).

- Man is saved by Jesus, and he cooperates in his salvation through performing good deeds with the help of grace (SEE TWEET 4.8).

- Parishes are fully part of the Catholic Church and fall under the authority of a bishop and the pope (SEE TWEET 2.2).

- A priest is accountable to the bishop (his "employer") (SEE TWEET 2.2).

- There are seven sacraments (SEE TWEET 3.35). In the Eucharist, bread and wine are changed (SEE TWEET 3.48) into the actual Body and Blood of Christ. (Most Protestants do not believe this.)

- Crucifixes, depictions of the body of Jesus on the cross, are widely used: Jesus' sacrifice (once and for all) is still operative, and we participate in it in the Eucharist.

- The Catholic Church proclaims the fullness of the truth of Christian faith (SEE TWEET 2.13–14).

> **Protestants reject some aspects of Catholic faith, especially the pope as a sign of unity & the sacraments as a source of grace.**

2.38 What were the consequences of the Reformation?

German rulers and local leaders saw in Luther's ideas a good opportunity to rebel against the pope and his influence, for instance, by limiting the appointment of bishops. In other places, too, the Reformation had political overtones (SEE TWEET 2.36).

The Low Countries

That was the case in the Low Countries. The national government was in the hands of Philip II, the king of Spain who persecuted those who supported the Reformation. This increasingly brought the relationship between Catholics and Calvinists to a head. Soon, a legitimate struggle against Philip's law and taxes morphed into an unjust rejection of the Church. In 1566, furious crowds stormed churches to destroy statues and paintings. King Philip II sent the Duke of Alva to restore order. Alva mercilessly cracked down on the "heretical Calvinists". In 1568 William of Orange led a revolt against his brutal policies and additional taxes. Thus began the Eighty Years War. Soon came a split between the North and South Netherlands. In the northern Republic of the Seven United Netherlands, Calvinism prevailed (SEE BOX). The Southern Netherlands remained Catholic and under the rule of Philip and his successors.

The Nordic countries

In Scandinavia, too, the events surrounding the Reformation had a political and economic background. In the course of the sixteenth century, the monarchs of the northern countries embraced Lutheranism and made a state church out of it. Bishops were deposed, priests pursued, and monasteries closed. Remarkably, in later years, oppressed Catholics found refuge in what was then a somewhat milder Netherlands. For centuries the law in much of Scandinavia allowed no other religion than Lutheranism. Only in 1956 were Jesuits again allowed to settle in Norway.

Mission Area

Since normal ecclesiastical governance by local bishops was not possible, the pope

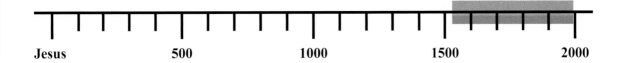
Martyrs and hidden churches in the Low Countries

Some Catholics categorically refused to accept the Reformation. As in England (SEE TWEET 2.39), the situation in the Low Countries was particularly grim. Calvinists conquered many Dutch cities from King Philip II of Spain, and then often cruelly tortured and put to death Catholics, especially the clergy. In 1572, Gorcum was occupied by Calvinists who arrested Catholic clergy. The priests refused to renounce the pope and to mock the Eucharist and were therefore tortured by the Protestants and hung in a barn. Their dead bodies were defiled and maimed. Later they were buried in the same barn. The 19 martyrs of Gorcum were canonized by the pope in 1867 (SEE TWEET 4.17).

In the Republic of the United Netherlands, all Catholic churches were confiscated by the Calvinists. Catholic worship was officially banned in 1581 and Catholics were expected to accept Calvinism. Yet many Catholics continued to stand up for their beliefs and thus created clandestine churches, where they could celebrate the Holy Mass in secret and could receive other sacraments. In the beginning, the government inveighed against

these hidden churches. In later centuries, they were unofficially allowed and tolerated, often after paying a fine. In any case they were not recognizable from the outside as churches. In order not to disturb the Protestants, singing and organ music were not allowed to be heard on the streets. Catholics first gathered in large houses, and later in hidden, but beautifully decorated, churches that stood behind nondescript façades, of which there are still some standing today.

Church and state were formally separated in 1796, but it would be years before Catholics actually experienced the freedom to practice their faith. Processions and other public expressions of Catholic beliefs were strictly prohibited in the Republic. The societal consequences of this were long-lasting. Only in 1983, for example, was the ban on Catholic processions removed from the Constitution. Even when the worst persecutions were over, Catholics were still subordinated and discriminated against in public. For a long time they were not eligible for certain public positions.

....

declared different countries to be mission areas. The result was that certain areas fell directly under the papal Congregation for the Propagation of the Faith (SEE TWEET 2.34), which appointed an apostolic vicar, as for example in the Netherlands (1581) and Sweden (1783). This situation lasted until well into the nineteenth century (SEE TWEET 2.44).

> Politics and the struggle over faith went hand in hand with the spread of Protestantism, resulting in martyred and oppressed Catholics.

SCAN

2.39 What is the Anglican Church?

At the beginning of the sixteenth century King Henry VIII of England (†1547) (SEE PICTURE) no longer wanted to accept the authority of the pope, and so he proclaimed himself head of the Church in England. Thus began the Anglican Church, or Church of England, of which the Queen is still the head.

Initially, Henry VIII was an ardent defender of the Catholic Church against the ideas of Luther (SEE TWEET 2.36). Pope Leo X gave him the title "Defender of the Faith" (*defensor fidei*). But he later changed his attitude toward the Church.

A bond for life

Henry VIII was given papal permission (a dispensation) to marry Catherine of Aragon, the widow of his older brother, Arthur. By her marriage to Arthur, Catherine was regarded as a relative of Henry. And without a dispensation, marriage between close relatives is not possible according to canon law (SEE TWEET 4.11). Henry wanted a male heir to succeed him, but Catherine and Henry had no surviving sons. Therefore, he asked Pope Clement VII to declare his marriage to his sister-in-law invalid so that he could marry again. According to Jesus marriage is a lifelong bond, so only with an annulment would the king have been able to marry again in the Church (SEE TWEET 3.43). Because Henry and Catherine had already been married through a papal dispensation, the pope could do nothing but reject the request of the English king.

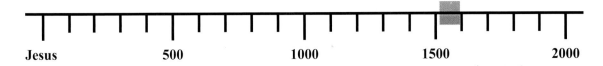
His own judge

Henry VIII seized the pope's refusal as a reason to reject papal authority. In 1534, with the Act of Supremacy, he proclaimed himself the supreme leader of the Church in England. Now he could give himself permission to marry again. Desperately seeking a male heir, Henry married six times. Catholics in England that remained faithful to the pope were treated harshly. This included the chancellor St. Thomas More (SEE PICTURE), who quietly opposed Henry's break with the pope. Because More would not publically acknowledge the king as head of the Church, he was executed for treason. Bishop John Fisher and others who remained faithful to the pope suffered the same fate.

Bloody Mary and Elizabeth I

In the years that followed, the Anglican Church became more Protestant. Only during the short reign of Henry's daughter Queen Mary I (1553–1558) was England again Catholic, returning to communion with the pope. She had always disagreed with her father's break with Rome and with the Protestant institutions that were established under the leadership of his successor, her brother, Edward VI (†1553). Queen Mary later became known as "Bloody Mary", because of her severe persecution of people who did not want to swear allegiance to Rome. Her successor and half-sister, Queen Elizabeth I, reaffirmed the Act of Supremacy and thus broke again with Rome. The Anglican Church was now definitively Protestant. Elizabeth was strongly opposed to the Catholics, who were considered traitors and who were cruelly persecuted and killed during her reign. This is why English seminaries were founded in Rome, France, and Spain. After their formation abroad, the young Englishmen returned to their homeland to be priests with the prospect that they would die as martyrs for their fidelity to Christ and the Church. Some of them were later canonized (SEE TWEET 4.17).

> In 1534, English King Henry VIII rejected the pope and named himself head of the Church of England. Faithful Catholics opposed this.

 ## 2.40 What was the Counter-Reformation?

SCAN

Luther had one thing absolutely right: some of the clergy behaved disgracefully (SEE TWEET 2.36). The Church certainly needed to be reformed. That happened in the Catholic Reformation, or Counter-Reformation. During this period conscious attention was again given to the essence of the faith, in part as a response to the teachings of the Protestants.

Royal resistance

From the beginning, Luther and other reformers found a great opponent in Emperor Charles v (†1558). Wherever he could, the emperor stood against Lutheranism and Calvinism. The Spanish monarchs Ferdinand and Isabella, however, were committed to the reform of the Church. And changes got underway also because bishops were no longer appointed simply because of their noble families but, rather, because of their holiness and knowledge. Intellectual life and the study of theology were stimulated. As a response to the Reformation, old religious orders were reformed and new ones were established. The

reform of the ecclesiastical structures by the Council of Trent (SEE TWEET 2.41) paid attention to the formation of believers, especially of priests, and to one's personal relationship with Jesus. There was also a revival of devotion to the Virgin Mary.

Ignatius of Loyola

The Spanish soldier Ignatius of Loyola (†1556) was wounded in battle and experienced a profound conversion. He began the Society of Jesus, the Jesuits, an order of men willing to take the gospel into the toughest places. Their focus on prayer, discipline, and education is the reason the order quickly grew into an influential organization. Jesuits such as St. Francis Xavier (†1551) worked as missionaries in the distant lands of Asia and America. Other Jesuits went to the Protestant areas of Europe to bring Catholics back into the fold. Many of them were martyred because of their fidelity to Jesus and the Church. Often Jesuits were appointed as confessors and advisers to kings. They were assigned teaching

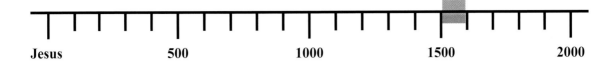
positions in colleges and universities. In our time, the Society of Jesus is the largest single religious order of men within the Church.

Even more saints

Other saints made important contributions to reforming the Church. St. Teresa of Avila and St. John of the Cross reformed the Carmelites in Spain. Their goal was to bring Carmelite monks and nuns back into line with their order's original rule of life. In many communities the observance of the rule had weakened to the detriment of their faith. As bishop of Geneva, St. Francis de Sales (†1622) tried to convince Calvinists of the truth of the Catholic Church. In Rome St. Philip Neri (†1595) founded the Congregation of the Oratory, groups of diocesan priests who pray together. He was known as a holy priest who helped the poor, the sick, and children. His cheerful character and sense of humor made a big impression on many. The fundamental understanding of the

Baroque

Whereas the Renaissance often reverted to pagan antiquity, Baroque architecture was very Catholic (SEE PICTURE). Churches from the time of the Counter- Reformation are large and wide, so that everyone has a good view of the mystery that takes place in the liturgy. Through images, God's greatness was to be celebrated, hence the grandiose style of Baroque art and architecture. It may also have been a reaction against Protestant iconoclasm (SEE TWEET 2.33). Many Jesuit churches were constructed in this style. In these churches, attention was also given to the acoustics, so that all could clearly follow the sermon in which the priest explains the truths of the faith.

Counter-Reformation saints was that Christ needed to be in the center of people's lives.

> In the Counter-Reformation the Church was reformed from within, with great attention to the faith and a personal relationship with Jesus.

Canon Missae.

...rdos extendens, elevans et ...s manus, elevans ad cœlum ...et statim demittens, profunde ...us ante Altare, manibus su- ...ositis, dicit :

re dignéris toto orbe terrá una cum fámulo tuo P...stro N. et Antístite n... et ómnibus orthodóx... cathólicæ et Apostó... cultóribus.

E ígitur, clemen- tíssime

COMMEMOR...

SCAN

2.41 What was the Council of Trent?

The Council of Trent played an important role in the Counter-Reformation (SEE TWEET 2.40). This Council was the meeting of bishops called by Pope Paul III in 1545 at the insistence of Emperor Charles V. As with previous Councils, the relations between the pope and the emperor were again the reason for the political and diplomatic tensions that the Council was meant to alleviate (SEE BOX).

Rules and visitations

During the Council of Trent certain abuses in the Church were dealt with, as were questions that were put forward by the Reformation (SEE TWEET 2.36). Bishops and priests were called to order: they had to live in their own diocese or parish in order to exercise more care over the people who were entrusted to them. Their possibilities for financial gain were limited by the Council, which penalized the sale of indulgences (SEE TWEET 2.35). Controls and visitations were added to strengthen these rules. Training for the priesthood had to take place in a seminary, where young men

could receive good spiritual and intellectual formation. Even the laity, adults and children, were to receive religious instruction from their priests. A good example of a bishop who faithfully put these reforms into practice is St. Charles Borromeo (†1584). As archbishop of Milan he devoted himself to his role as shepherd of his diocese. He attended to the formation of priests and, to that end, founded new seminaries. He also drew up very influential guidelines for building churches.

Sacraments and preaching

Trent put renewed emphasis on the essentials of the faith, the sacraments, and the structure of the Church. The Council taught that God reveals himself both in Scripture and through the Tradition of the Apostles (SEE TWEET 1.11). In response to the Reformers (Protestants), Trent confirmed that people can and should cooperate with the divine grace of Jesus, who wants to redeem them (SEE TWEET 4.8). Also, the Council clearly identified and described the seven sacraments of the Church (SEE TWEET 3.35).

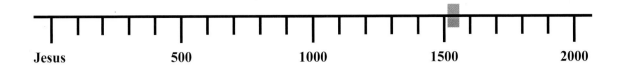

A long breath

Participants in the Council of Trent had a lot of patience, since it would eventually take 18 years before the Council ended. It was originally convened by Pope Paul III in the Italian city of Trento on December 13, 1545. In 1547 the tensions between the pope and the emperor grew, and a very contagious disease broke out. It was therefore decided to continue the Council in Bologna. Because of the difficult relationship with the emperor, the pope suspended the Council at the end of that year.

In 1551 Pope Julius III called the Council together in Trento to continue discussions. But a year later Emperor Charles V was defeated and the Council was again suspended. In 1562, under Pius IV, the last sessions of the Council were held, and it was officially closed on December 4, 1663. Despite the difficult course, the decisions of the Council led to many good changes and adjustments in the Church.

The real presence of Jesus in the Eucharist – Body, Blood, Soul, and Divinity – was reaffirmed (SEE TWEET 3.48). The main message of the Council was that the Church must proclaim the gospel of Jesus to all peoples (MK. 13:10) and make Christ present among the faithful. All in all, the Council of Trent had a very positive and significant impact on the Church.

The Catechism and other books

After the Council of Trent, a book explaining the faith – the *Roman Catechism* – was issued by Pope Pius V. The invention of the printing press, which had played such a large role in the Reformation, meant that this information could be spread rapidly through Christendom and beyond. Pius V also approved liturgical books for use in the whole Church. These included the *Roman Missal*, with the texts for the Holy Mass, and the *Roman Breviary*, containing daily prayers for priests. With some minor changes these books would be used throughout the Church until 1969 (SEE TWEET 3.13).

> Trent wanted to give an answer to the Reformation; it deepened the understanding of faith and reformed Church practices.

2.42 What role did the Church play in the Enlightenment?

Through scientific developments in the seventeenth century, the world came to be seen as less mysterious, and man himself was thought to be not merely a creature but also a creator. This raised new questions. Not only were certain elements of Catholic doctrine being questioned, as the Protestants had done (SEE TWEET 2.36), but faith in God itself came under fire. It was the time of the Enlightenment, which elevated the ability of man to think for himself above everything else. The Enlightenment was critical of faith in anything that could not be proved scientifically or considered rational. The result was hostility to the Church in general and the pope in particular.

Rationalism

Rationalism, which was promoted by René Descartes (†1650) and other thinkers, placed human reason on a divine level. As Descartes said: "Cogito ergo sum" ("I think, therefore I am"). In other words, reality is made certain by man's thinking not the other way around.

Rationalism rejected anything that could not be scientifically, or mathematically, demonstrated. Thus the revelation of God, and therefore Christianity, had to be rejected as a source of truth. In addition, ideas like those of the Dutch philosopher Baruch Spinoza (†1677) led to deism, which sees God as unknowable and unreachable. Because divine intervention in this life seems doubtful, God appears to be far away, if he exists at all. The naturalistic rationalism of Jean-Jacques Rousseau (†1778) led to revolutionary ideas about social organization. Church leaders were not the only authority figures brought into question, but kings as well. Voltaire (†1778) attacked the Church, made fun of her, and wanted to destroy her. And the French Revolution tried to do exactly that when it brought down the French monarchy, sacked monasteries, and killed religious and clergy.

Politics

Along with the relativistic ideas of the Enlightenment was a growing focus on the

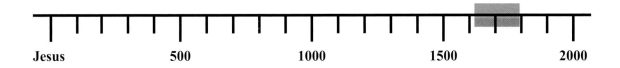

Jesus   500   1000   1500   2000

Gallicanism and Jansenism

Gallicanism, named after the French Gauls, was a seventeenth-century movement that sought to give national civil authorities the same power over the Catholic Church in their respective countries as that exercised by the pope. When French seminaries were obliged by their government to teach these nationalist ideas, Gallicanism spread widely among the French clergy and would have long-lasting consequences for the whole Church.

Jansenism was a kind of Calvinist Catholicism based on the ideas of the Dutchman Cornelius Jansen (†1638). Jansen's belief in the predestination of man by God minimizes or even denies the role of man's free will in his salvation (SEE TWEET 2.36) and was rejected by the Church as a heresy.

individual and his rights. Political leaders affirmed their independence from religion, especially from the pope and the bishops of the Catholic Church, and set up secular governments. The Jesuits, who fiercely defended the pope, were expelled from various European countries. They were abolished by Pope Clement XIV in 1773. Forty-one years later the order would be reestablished by Pope Pius VII. Despite everything, the Enlightenment failed to destroy the Church.

Toward tolerance?

By the time of the Enlightenment, most religious wars that followed on the heels of the Protestant Reformation had come to an end, although other wars followed. Certain governments in Europe were allowing for various degrees of religious toleration, for example in the Netherlands and Germany. In other places, persecution of Catholics by Protestants or Enlightened leaders and vice versa continued, while Protestants also persecuted each other. In this environment a number of Protestants and Catholics fled to North America, where they hoped to find a more tolerant society. As a result, the founding of the United States was, in part, a result of the Enlightenment.

The Enlightenment put faith and reason into conflict. Worldly leaders opposed the pope and wanted to limit his influence.

2.43 What were the consequences of the French Revolution?

The response of the Church

The French revolution of 1789 was violently anticlerical. The ideas of Enlightenment thinkers such as Rousseau and Voltaire contributed to extreme attacks on the Church (SEE TWEET 2.42). Church possessions were confiscated, religious life was banned, monasteries and convents were destroyed, and priests and religious were banished or murdered. They were forced to swear an oath of allegiance to a new religious organization that excluded the pope.

When many priests then remained loyal to the pope, this led to a new wave of persecutions. Many thousands of Catholics were executed. The revolutionaries wanted France to be a state without hierarchical authority, including that of God and the Church, and therefore tried to eradicate every trace of Christianity. They even initiated a new calendar that no longer started with the birth of Christ, but with the birth of the new French Republic in 1792. Notre Dame, the cathedral in Paris, was renamed as the Temple of Reason.

Napoleon and the Papal States

Napoleon Bonaparte took over France in the wake of the French Revolution. He went to war with his European neighbors, conquering Rome and the Papal States. The old and sickly Pius VI was taken as a prisoner to France in 1799, where he died soon after. His energetic successor Pius VII subsequently made a treaty with Napoleon in 1801, which heralded the beginning of a resurgence of the Church in France. New bishops were appointed, but many rules remained in place to prevent the Church from reestablishing herself, especially with regards to monasteries. When Pope Pius VII refused to support Napoleon in his war against England, he too was imprisoned in France. It took six years before the pope was freed by allied soldiers. Shortly after he returned to Rome, Napoleon was defeated at Waterloo in 1815. The Congress of Vienna, held that same year, wanted to restore the map of Europe to what it was before Napoleon's time. Thus, almost all the territory of the Papal States again came under the control of the Holy See (SEE TWEET 2.3).

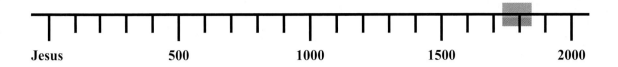

Jesus   500   1000   1500   2000

Liberalism and positivism

The political attacks on the Church were followed by a different ideological threat. As a result of the Enlightenment of the eighteenth century (SEE TWEET 2.42), liberalism became increasingly important in Europe. Focusing on the freedom of the individual and seeing religion as a purely private matter, liberalism seeks the separation of Church and state. Faith was no longer the organizing principle of society, and the sciences came to be seen as the only reliable source of knowledge. The philosophy of positivism completely rejected the supernatural, assuming that everything is material and measurable. In this way, the Christian faith took a backseat to the natural and social sciences.

A thriving Church

Given this context, it is truly remarkable that Christianity actually blossomed again during the nineteenth century. In 1833, the French priest Prosper Guéranger restored the Benedictine monastic tradition in the Abbey of Solesmes. To this day the abbey is renowned for its rediscovery of Gregorian chant and its study of the liturgy.

Around the same time the Italian priest John Bosco was evangelizing and educating poor and sometimes delinquent boys. Like his order, the Salesians, many other missionary orders were founded at this time. These spread throughout the world, sharing the gospel, educating the poor, and nursing the sick.

Liberalism and the Church

Around 1830, the philosopher and priest Felicité Robert de Lamennais tried to reconcile liberalism and the Church. However, Pope Gregory XVI disapproved of his approach and spoke out against the total separation of Church and state. He also rejected the notion that all religions would lead to eternal salvation; he warned that this would lead to religious indifference.

This was also the time of the Risorgimento in Italy, the political unification movement that threatened the Papal States and lead to the founding of the Italian state in 1870. This certainly influenced the stern response of the pope.

Neither the ideas of the French revolutionaries nor liberalism could wipe out Christianity.

 The French Revolution led to the oppression of the Church. Popes and bishops took defensive stances. Religious life soon bloomed again.

 ## 2.44 What was the First Vatican Council?

Between 1869 and 1870, the pope and the bishops gathered for the First Vatican Council. At that moment, there were still vivid memories of the oppression of the Church during the French Revolution and its aftermath (SEE TWEET 2.43). In addition, anti-Church policies were still in place in Italy and other countries (SEE BOX).

Since liberalism and rational philosophies denying the revelation of God led to persecutions of the faithful, these ideologies called for a clear and explicit response. The Council focused on the dangers of these developments and not on the possibilities for dialogue with society. That would have to wait until the Second Vatican Council (SEE TWEET 2.48).

Faith and reason

Because science was seen as a rival to faith, the First Vatican Council tried to formulate the proper relationship between faith and reason. Scientists often blindly discarded faith, because not everything that Christians believe can be measured; this position is called positivism (SEE TWEET 2.43). On the other hand, there were also Christians who claimed reason was completely irrelevant to faith; this position is called fideism. Both positions are in error. In the document *Dei Filius*, the Council explained that both faith and reason are necessary to understand Jesus' message properly (SEE TWEET 1.5).

Infallibility

Because the teaching authority of the Church was questioned, the Council confirmed her authority. Jesus had ordained that St. Peter would have the final word, should conflicts arise between Christians about the faith (SEE TWEET 2.17).

That authority extends to the successors of St. Peter, the popes. The Council confirmed this by clarifying the doctrine of papal infallibility, the belief that certain formal papal teaching is free from error because the Holy Spirit guides the Church (SEE TWEET 2.13). Not everything the pope says is infallible, however. Only when he makes a specific statement on faith or morals

The Papal Zouaves

The Papal Zouaves were a regiment of soldiers that defended the Papal States during the second half of the nineteenth century. They were unmarried Catholic volunteers. About a third of the soldiers were Dutch; others were French, Belgian, or Italian, and there were usually some Americans as well.

Their primary task was to defend the Papal States against the attacks of an Italian king, Vittorio Emmanuele II (†1878), and Giuseppe Garibaldi (†1882). In this, they were often supported by the French Army. The Papal Zouaves were inspired by the Zouave regiment in the French Army, which was originally composed of Algerian Berbers. When France needed its soldiers in its war with Prussia, the Italians seized their chance and defeated the Papal Zouaves. Rome was occupied on September 20, 1870. The next day, the Zouave regiment was disbanded.

as the shepherd and teacher of all Christians, speaking from the Chair of St. Peter (*ex cathedra*), does he teach infallibly. This happens very rarely. As Pope Benedict XVI said: "The pope is not an oracle" (JUL. 29, 2005). In fact, since 1870 it has happened only once, when in 1950 Pope Pius XII officially declared the dogma of Mary's bodily Assumption into heaven (SEE TWEET 1.40), which theologians and faithful had already believed for centuries.

Appointing bishops

There is another way in which the pope grew more powerful in the nineteenth century. He could directly appoint bishops, increasingly without kings having a say in the matter. This was particularly important after the reestablishment of the Catholic hierarchy in countries such as England (1850), the Netherlands (1853), and Bosnia (1881). Ties with the pope were further strengthened because more and more new bishops had studied in Rome. After the Belgian College in Rome was established in 1844, many other countries also opened their own seminaries there.

> Vatican I responded to ideological changes by formulating the proper relationship between faith and reason and the authority of the pope.

2.45 How did the Church respond to the developments of the nineteenth century?

The response of the Church

In 1870, Rome was incorporated into the Kingdom of Italy. That meant the end of the Papal States and therefore of the temporal power of the pope. The pope retreated to the Vatican, like a prisoner. It is curious that as the worldly power of the pope diminished, his moral influence actually grew. The First Vatican Council was interrupted and some business was unfinished. It was never reconvened, though, and only formally closed in 1960 prior to the Second Vatican Council.

Theology and science

The years after the First Vatican Council (SEE TWEET 2.44) saw a wave of new ideologies that criticized faith. Despite these attacks, the Church blossomed in those years. New orders arose. Thinkers such as Blessed John Henry Cardinal Newman (†1890) defended the truths of faith against its critics (SEE PICTURE).

It became necessary to find new ways and arguments to explain the faith, to show that it is not irrational as many made it out to be.

Special attention was again paid to the intellectual formation of priests. The encyclical *Aeterni Patris* (1879) of Pope Leo XIII made it obligatory for all seminarians to study the works of St. Thomas Aquinas (SEE TWEET 2.29). The pope also encouraged scientific research.

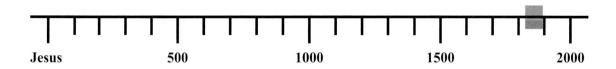
Socialism and communism

The Industrial Revolution of the nineteenth century led to new social problems and tensions, particularly because factory workers frequently had to work and to live in miserable conditions. Karl Marx responded by urging the workers to overthrow the capitalist owners of the factories. He also urged them to rebel against religion, which he called the "opium of the people" because it made them passive. Marxism laid the foundations for socialism and communism, which led to new kinds of oppressive regimes, such as those in the Soviet Union, China, Cuba, North Korea, and Vietnam.

The answer of the Church

The Church had a different answer to the problems caused by the Industrial Revolution. The Society of St. Vincent de Paul had been working since 1833 to provide both aid and spiritual guidance to the poor.

In 1891, Pope Leo XIII wrote the first social encyclical, *Rerum Novarum*, which urged factory workers and owners to work together to improve society. Instead of remaining on the sidelines, as liberalism taught, the state also had an important role to play, according to the pope. Workers were urged to start Catholic labor unions. This encyclical was the beginning of Catholic social teaching (SEE TWEET 4.45), which was further developed during the twentieth century. Thus, the moral authority of the pope grew.

Emancipation and architecture

The reestablishment of the Catholic hierarchy in England in 1850 and in the Netherlands in 1853 (SEE TWEET 2.44) was followed by movements of Catholic emancipation. Although inequality between Protestants and Catholics would long remain in place, the Church became increasingly visible in society, as Catholics built new churches and organizations.

Most of these new churches were built in the neo-Gothic style, which was inspired by the glorious architecture of the Middle Ages. The French architect Eugène Viollet-le-Duc (†1879) worked out a new way to combine Gothic principles with modern materials. He is often described as the first theoretician of modern architecture. In England, Augustus Pugin (†1852) played an important role in developing a Gothic-revival style.

In the 19th century the pope had less worldly power but greater moral influence. He defended the faith and workers' rights.

 ## 2.46 How did the Church enter the twentieth century?

 SCAN

At the dawn of the twentieth century, the scientific study of the faith, the Bible, and the liturgy had risen to great heights. There were excesses, however, and Pope Pius x (†1914) had to condemn the modernism that sought to make science the ultimate measure of faith. Meanwhile, the number of religious vocations grew enormously, as did the number of missionaries spreading the faith all over the world. Hundreds of priests, sisters, and brothers left Europe to spread the gospel in Africa, Asia, and the Americas.

Popes with prestige

Pope Pius x (SEE PICTURE), who was declared a saint in 1954, sought to promote the holiness of priests. He also lowered the age at which children could receive their First Holy Communion. He urged the faithful to receive Communion more often (SEE TWEET 3.49) and to be active as Catholics in their societies. Pope Benedict xv (†1922) tried to reconcile the belligerents of the First World War and organized aid for the victims. Pope

Americans in Rome

During the 1950s, the Pontifical North American College (PNAC) was built in Rome. The college houses about 250 seminarians and priests, who receive part of their formation there while they study at one of the papal universities in Rome.

Could it be because of their excellent sports facilities that the PNAC is always such a feared contestant in the soccer competitions that take place between the different national colleges in Rome? (SEE TWEET 2.44.)

Pius XI (†1939) promoted social justice and evangelization. Working on political and diplomatic levels, he tried to prevent the rise of totalitarian regimes and another world war.

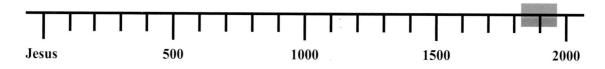

S.S. PIUS X — PONT. MAX.

Who were the popes of the twentieth and twenty-first centuries?

1878–1903:	Leo XIII	(Gioacchino Pecci)
1903–1914:	St. Pius X	(Giuseppe Sarto)
1914–1922:	Benedict XV	(Giacomo della Chiesa)
1922–1939:	Pius XI	(Achille Ratti)
1939–1958:	Pius XII	(Eugenio Pacelli)
1958–1963:	St. John XXIII	(Angelo Roncalli)
1963–1978:	Paul VI	(Giovanni Montini)
1978–1978:	John Paul I	(Albino Luciani)
1978–2005:	St. John Paul II	(Karol Wojtyła)
2005–2013:	Benedict XVI	(Joseph Ratzinger)
2013– :	Francis	(Jorge Mario Bergoglio)

Catholic Action

In the nineteenth century, lay Catholics founded Catholic Action in several countries. Their goal was to exert a Catholic influence on society, based on the social teaching of the Church (SEE TWEET 4.45). This brought into being a wide range of Catholic organizations, such as unions, political parties, newspapers, radio stations, schools, etc.

Persecutions

In France (in 1905) and Portugal (in 1910), the government confiscated Church property as it secularized society. Catholics were even persecuted. After the 1917 Russian Revolution, Communists imposed atheism on the Soviet Union and murdered many Orthodox and Catholic Christians. In the 1920s and '30s, Catholics were killed in Spain and Mexico during Communist attempts to take over those countries. The Church was restricted by the Fascist government in Italy despite the Lateran Pacts of 1929, in which the pope recognized Rome as the Italian capital and settled for Vatican City as Church territory. In Germany, after years of state opposition to the Catholic Church, an agreement was made in 1933 to protect her rights, but the rise of the National Socialists (the Nazis) soon put an end to those.

> Holiness, sacraments, and active Christians were the focus of the 20th-century Church. Catholics were persecuted in many countries.

SCAN

2.47 Why didn't the Church oppose the Nazis?

Pope Pius XI had condemned Italian Fascism in 1931 in his encyclical *Non Abbiamo Bisogno*. In 1937, he spoke out against German National Socialism and its racist ideology in the encyclical *Mit Brennender Sorge*. That was the first official statement strongly opposing Nazism; at that point, no government had denounced Nazism so clearly. In the same year, the pope condemned Marxism and communism in his encyclical *Divini Redemptoris*.

War and invasion

In 1939, Pius XII was elected pope. A week before the Second World War began, he made a last desperate call for peace: "It is by the power of sound reason, not by force of arms, that justice makes its way" (AUG. 24, 1939). His first encyclical, *Summi Pontificatus*, condemned the invasion of Poland by the Nazis in 1939. The pope pointed to the dangers of racism, anti-Semitism (Jew-hatred), and totalitarianism; described the horrors of armed conflict; and urged all Christians to come to the aid of victims of the war. The Holy See (SEE TWEET 2.3) remained neutral in the war. Nevertheless, in his Christmas speech of 1942 the pope spoke of his grave concern for "the many people who are innocently put to death or exploited, sometimes merely on account of their nationality or background" (DEC. 24, 1942). Later he also condemned the many other horrors of the war.

Diplomacy

Behind the scenes, the diplomatic network of the Holy See was working together with the Allies. Archives show that many people who were persecuted by the Nazis, including many Jews, were assisted by the Church. With good reason, the Nazis considered the pope to be their enemy. The Vatican Information Office for prisoners and refugees provided information about the fate of millions of missing persons. Thousands of Jews and other victims of Nazi or Fascist persecution found refuge in religious institutions in Rome and elsewhere (SEE BOX). Concern for their safety is one of the reasons that the pope chose to protest the Nazis through diplomatic channels instead of direct confrontation.

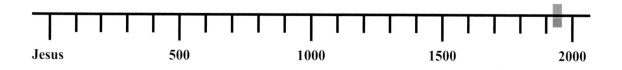

Jesus   500   1000   1500   2000

Jesus **500** **1000** **1500** **2000**

Should the Church have acted differently?

It is very hard to know in retrospect whether a different policy would have been better. In the Netherlands, bishops (directed by the pope) openly called for resistance against the Nazis, which led to severe German countermeasures and the death of many people, including Bl. Titus Brandsma (see Tweet 3.50) and Jewish converts to Catholicism such as Edith Stein (St. Teresa Benedicta of the Cross). If the pope had spoken out more, that would certainly have led to harsh reprisals and raids of religious buildings throughout Europe, with disastrous consequences for the people hidden there. The United States and England pressured the pope not to condemn Nazism. Robert Kempner, a German-Jewish lawyer and public official at the Nuremberg Tribunal, wrote in 1964: "Any propagandistic position that the Church might have taken against Hitler's government would not only have been a suicidal move, but would have hastened the execution of an even greater number of Jews and priests."

Criticism and compliments

After the war, Pius XII was praised for his actions. The state of Israel gave him its highest honor. It is remarkable that the harsh criticism of the Church arose only during the 1960s. Pius XII was accused of being insensitive about the suffering of the Jews, and even of being an accomplice in the Holocaust through his alleged silence about the matter. These allegations were also distributed and publicized through the Soviet propaganda office both during and after the war.
But the many gestures of intense gratitude to the Church during and after the war tell a very different story. For instance, in 1940 Albert Einstein, born of Jewish parents, told *Time* magazine: "Only the Church stood squarely across the path of Hitler's campaign for suppressing truth" (Dec. 23, p. 38). Many other prominent Jews also praised the pope after the war. The Jewish World Congress presented the pope with "warmest thanks for the efforts of the Catholic Church on behalf of Jews throughout Europe during the War" (L'Osservatore Romano, Sept. 23, 1945, p. 1).

> Pope Pius XII did much more to help the Jews than is commonly thought. In the first years after the war he was much praised for his efforts.

 ## 2.48 What was the Second Vatican Council?

SCAN

Shortly after his papal election in 1958, the then 77-year-old Pope John XXIII announced the Second Vatican Council. In his opening speech in 1962 the pope called for *aggiornamento*, Italian for "bringing up to date".

The pope wanted to update the ways in which the Church preached the gospel in the modern age. Representatives of other churches and ecclesial communities were invited to attend the Council as observers.

2,500 bishops

The Council was held in four sessions between 1962 and 1965. This happened in St. Peter's Basilica, where more than 2,500 bishops discussed the Church in their time. They used Latin for this conversation. Between the general sessions there were committees working on proposals that could be discussed during the next session. Among others, the future popes John Paul II and Benedict XVI participated in the Council's discussions.

Preparation and outcome

The way to the Council was prepared by new ecclesiastical developments in the twentieth century, which were at first encouraged by the Church. The mainly French *nouvelle théologie* ("new theology") was based on what the Church Fathers had taught during the first centuries of Christianity. The liturgical movement was made up of scholars who wanted to reform aspects of the liturgy and in particular the Eucharist, which the Council declared the "source and summit" of Christian life.

The main purpose of the Council was to proclaim the unchanging message of Jesus to the modern world. Its four main documents (constitutions) were on liturgy (*Sacrosanctum Concilium*), the Church (*Lumen Gentium*), divine revelation (*Dei Verbum*), and the Church in the modern world (*Gaudium et Spes*). The Council also prepared a *Decree on Ecumenism*, which promoted dialogue between Catholics and other Christians.

Aftermath of the Council

Worldwide, the Council's reforms had major consequences for the Church. In some places the renovation was carried so far that it became innovation, and the good news of salvation in Christ was pushed into the background (SEE TWEET 2.49). An example is the liberation theology that became popular in Latin America as a response to poverty and extreme social inequality. It is good to fight injustice, but some liberation theology became a form of Marxism that promised salvation through violent revolution. The Congregation for the Doctrine of Faith condemned this interpretation of the gospel.

Another version of worldly salvation is the "culture of consumption", in which man bases his happiness only on material things. This has led to extreme individualism, in which faith in God, the family, and the weakest members of society have less or no value. Such a culture leads to increasing callousness toward human life and violence. In response, the Church continues to preach the dignity of the human person as made in the image of God (SEE TWEET 4.26) and called to eternal friendship with him through Christ and his Church.

Another Mass?

After the Council, in 1969, Pope Paul VI approved the new *Roman Missal*. This replaced the missal that was approved after the Council of Trent (SEE TWEET 2.41) in 1570 and last revised in 1962. In search of a "noble simplicity", the liturgy was greatly streamlined. Where formerly the language at Mass was always Latin, local languages could now be used and the priest could celebrate Mass facing the people (SEE TWEET 3.23). In 2007, Pope Benedict XVI issued a letter stating that both the previous missal and the new one may be used. What has never changed is the essence of the Mass, the presence of Jesus in the Holy Eucharist (SEE TWEET 3.48).

Vatican II wanted to enter into dialogue with society and draw attention to the core belief in Jesus that our world so badly needs.

2.49 What happened after the Second Vatican Council?

Generally, the changes made at the Second Vatican Council (SEE TWEET 2.48) were well received, and people enthusiastically looked for the best ways to put them into practice. But in some cases, they went too far. There were many experiments with the liturgy and the design of churches, especially in Western societies. In certain places a new iconoclasm took hold, in which people whitewashed the walls of their churches, destroyed high altars, and removed paintings, statues, and stained glass windows. This was the wrong way to implement "noble simplicity" (SEE TWEET 2.48).

It is interesting that by the end of the twentieth century, a new movement sought to undo the effects of this iconoclasm, and to restore the original, beautiful interiors of church buildings as a sign of the glory the faithful wish to give to God.

Leaving the Church

During these changes many priests left the priesthood, and many religious men and women their communities. Was the fire of their dedication to Jesus – in heart, body, and soul – extinguished? Was it an act of protest against the Church? Had ecclesiastical life been too focused on worldly things and not enough on its spiritual life with the Lord? Had religious communities that were forced to update themselves lost their founding vision and zeal? There are more questions than answers, but it is clear that the large number of people leaving their vocations coincided with the declining role and status of the Church in society.

A new spirit

Meanwhile, new movements, associations, and communities were born among Catholics wanting to dedicate their lives to God (SEE TWEET 2.1). New religious orders also arose in order to renew the Church. Some groups were made up of both priests and lay people.

An interesting example is the French Chemin Neuf community, because it combines elements from several other movements.

Catholics in Eastern Europe

While the Second Vatican Council led to outward renewal in many parts of the Church, the movement of the Holy Spirit was less visible in Eastern Europe. The countries under Communist rule were separated from the rest of Europe by the Iron Curtain. Though there were differences in severity, the Communist rulers tried to diminish the influence of the Church and of faith in general. The most important task of Catholics in these countries was to fight communism to regain their freedom. The number of the faithful fell drastically, while the remaining believers were strengthened in their faith. The situation may remind us of the different persecutions Christians have had to endure over the centuries (SEE TWEET 2.19, 2.38, AND 2.43).

In Hungary, József Cardinal Mindszenty (†1975) suffered many years of imprisonment after he spoke out openly against the Communist regime and its suppression of religious freedom. Poland's Stefan Cardinal Wyszyński (†1981) played a similar role. The diplomatic activities of Pope John Paul II were very important for the eventual demise of communism in his homeland, Poland, which triggered its fall throughout Eastern Europe.

It was founded in 1973 in Lyon, France, by the Jesuit Laurent Fabre. An important characteristic of Chemin Neuf is that families and dedicated single adults live together in one community. Priests are closely tied to the group. A second characteristic is their focus on the spirituality of St. Ignatius, the founder of the Jesuit Order, and on a personal relationship with Jesus (SEE TWEET 3.8). Third, they focus on communal work and prayer for the unity of the Church: they are ecumenical. Finally, Chemin Neuf is inspired by the Charismatic Renewal, a movement that seeks the gifts of the Holy Spirit as described in the New Testament.

Jesus as a friend

Enthusiastic new Catholic movements have spread throughout the world. Although they have various charisms, they have at least one important thing in common: they place a personal relationship with Jesus at the center of their spirituality. This should be the goal of everyone, as it is the core of the Christian life and also of the New Evangelization (SEE TWEET 4.50), of which these new movements are a part.

> After Vatican II the Church sought a new balance between society and faith, focusing on the eternal core of the faith: friendship with Jesus.

215

2.50 What is so important about Pope John Paul II?

 SCAN

In 1978, a Pole, Karol Wojtyła, became the first non-Italian to become the pope since Adrian VI (†1523). In his first official sermon, Pope John Paul II urged everyone to allow Jesus into his life: "Do not be afraid. Open wide the doors for Christ!" (Oct. 22, 1978). At the core of his teaching was the dignity of man as created in the image of God, which is damaged by sin and restored by Christ.

Communism

Through his great dedication to truth and freedom for all, Pope John Paul II was able to accomplish many things. His travels to Poland and the diplomatic efforts of the Church under his leadership strongly contributed to the fall of communism in Eastern Europe, which finally happened in 1989. Communist regimes had been in power there since the end of the Second World War, when the Soviets drew the Iron Curtain across the continent. That was the time of the Cold War between the democratic West and the Communist East (see Tweet 2.48). His peaceful struggle against communism

did not make the pope popular everywhere: on May 13, 1981, he barely survived an assassination attempt.

The New Evangelization

While John Paul II was pope, the moral influence of the Church grew. He travelled extensively throughout the world, calling upon Catholics everywhere to provide answers to modern challenges. He started the worldwide New Evangelization, using modern means of communication to spread the gospel (see Tweet 4.49).

Forgiveness

The Jubilee Year 2000 brought a record number of pilgrims to Rome, 25 million in fact. This was a year of purification, as the pope asked for forgiveness for the many errors committed by members of the Church down through history, such as during the Crusades and the Spanish Inquisition (see Tweet 2.31–2.32). This same year, it also became obvious that the pope had grown old. Because of Parkinson's

Jesus   500   1000   1500   2000

WYD

At the invitation of the pope, young Catholics from the whole world gathered in Rome in April 1984 for a great festival of faith, with meetings, activities, and prayer. After a second youth meeting on Palm Sunday 1985, the pope declared a new annual event: World Youth Day (WYD, Dec. 20, 1985). Every few years, a WYD with the pope is organized.

No other pope has been able to mobilize so many people as John Paul II. At the WYD in Manila in 1995, he celebrated Mass in the presence of more than five million people. From the beginning, he told young people: "You are the future of the world and the hope of the Church! You are my hope!" (Oct. 22, 1978).

disease he walked and spoke with difficulty. Nevertheless, he continued his work and showed that human dignity is not diminished by age or illness. Even then, he continued to rely on Mary in everything. Pope John Paul II died on April, 2, 2005, with thousands of people gathered beneath his window overlooking St. Peter's Square. A total of four million pilgrims came to Rome to show their affection, to say good-bye, and to pray for him. In 2011, in the presence of millions, Pope Benedict XVI beatified him. An even larger crowd gathered for the canonization by Pope Francis on April 27, 2014.

JP2 dedicated himself to the truth of the gospel and freedom for all. He particularly called for the young to follow Jesus.

Part 3

Tweets about You & God: Prayer & Sacraments

Introduction

The Church is a supernatural institution—the Mystical Body of Christ—borne in the Incarnation, the Resurrection, and at Pentecost, in which the Holy Spirit became manifestly present among the community of Christian believers. The Church stretches beyond time and space, uniting the saints in heaven; the holy souls in purgatory; and the baptized men and women zealously pursuing holiness in life on earth. The Church is the communion of all those reborn into Jesus Christ—the adopted sons and daughters of God the Father, redeemed in the mercy of Jesus Christ.

The Church is a communion of faith, of sacraments, and of governance. As a practical matter, she is established by Christ, organized, equipped, and inspired in the fire of the Holy Spirit, and shaped by the circumstances of her history, in order to proclaim and to safeguard the saving message of Jesus Christ's birth, life, death, and Resurrection.

The Church herself is, in Christ, a kind of sacrament—a sign and instrument that unites us to God and with one another. In the seven sacraments, Christ—fully human and fully divine—is made present in our world and lives. All of the sacraments have been instituted by Christ to give us a share of his own life, which we call grace. Through the sacraments we are united with Christ and receive from him the strength we need to do the will of the Father.

The Eucharist, said the Second Vatican Council, is the source and the summit of the Christian life. In the Eucharist we receive the Lord himself, who comes to us under the appearances of bread and wine. When we receive the Body and Blood of Christ we are united with God in the most intimate way possible on this earth.

In order to prepare for this union and to benefit from it, we need to seek the Lord in daily prayer, making him a part of everything that we do. In this way, we bring Christ fully into our lives and through us into the world.

I pray that this chapter of *Tweeting with GOD* will inspire you to study and to practice your faith more deeply. And I pray that, through the intercession of the Blessed Virgin Mary, it will lead you to a deeper communion with Jesus Christ through prayer and sacraments.

✠ James Conley, S.T.L.
Bishop of Lincoln

 ## 3.1 Why should I pray and how can I do it?

Given that God knows the present and the future (SEE TWEET 1.1 AND 2.11), why should I pray? After all, God already knows what I need. Why should I have to tell him anything? Well, for one thing, because talking to God can help you a lot.

God wants to be your best friend (JN. 15:15). You can discuss anything and everything with him. Even though you may not always realize it, he is always with you, day and night! To become more aware of this, it is a good idea to pray every morning and evening. That way you can share each day with him. By praying regularly, you learn to listen to God, and you come to realize that you are not alone. By praying, you receive the strength you need to do what you must do.

In short, prayer is very good for you! Jesus often asked his disciples to pray (LK. 22:46), and he encourages us to do so, too. When the Apostles asked him how to pray, he taught them the Our Father (MT. 6:9–13; SEE TWEET 3.11). He

himself gave them an example by frequently going to a quiet place in order to be with God in prayer (MK. 1:35). The first Christians prayed constantly, both privately and together (ACTS 1:14). Prayer is a way to be with God and to serve him (LK. 2:36-37).

Understanding God's gift

One day, tired and thirsty Jesus sat near a well and asked a woman to give him a drink. When the woman protested, Jesus said: "If you knew the gift of God, and who it is that is saying to you, 'Give me a drink,' you would have asked him and he would have given you living water" (JN. 4:10). God asks us to pray so that he can give us a share in his life, which is grace (SEE TWEET 4.12). If we really understood what God wants to give us, we would pray constantly.

The special thing about prayer is that it works both ways: if we dedicate time to go toward God, he comes toward us. If we offer ourselves to him, he offers himself to us! We see this in

How do I look up a Bible reference?

The Bible is comprised of three components:

- books
- chapters
- verses

If we want to refer to the first three verses of the New Testament, for example, we list the book first (Matthew), then the chapter (1), and then the verses (1 to 3), as in the following: Matthew 1:1–3. To save space, the names of the books are often abbreviated (Mt. 1:1–3). See Appendix 1 for a full list of abbreviations.

the sacraments, where God comes close to us in a very concrete way (SEE TWEET 3.35).

You can pray too!

With a little time and effort, you too can learn to pray (SEE TWEET 3.3). When you pray, you invest in your relationship with God. By praying, you are accepting and returning the love that God has for you. God wants to help you to pray. That is why Jesus said to the woman at the well: "Whoever drinks of the water that I shall give him will never thirst; the water that I shall give him will become in him a spring of water welling up to eternal life" (JN. 4:14). The Holy Spirit will help you to let your prayers well up spontaneously from your heart. Someone in love can talk to his beloved from his heart, with or without words. This is how God wants you to speak to him. This is prayer.

Quality time with God

Making time for God is much more important than the way in which you pray. Your prayer can be very simple. As long as your prayer is honest and sincere, you are working on a relationship with God. Talking to God is perhaps the easy part, but how can you listen to him? (SEE TWEET 3.2.) How can you prevent being distracted all the time? (SEE TWEET 3.5.) Do you pray alone or with others? (SEE TWEET 3.3.) All these matters will be addressed. For the moment, it is important only to take a first step. So decide now to spend some time with God in prayer each day. He is waiting for you!

> God asks you to pray. He waits for you! Your relationship with God will bring you true & lasting joy. You can ask & tell him anything.

Read more

About prayer: CCC 2558–2565; CCCC 534; YOUCAT 469.

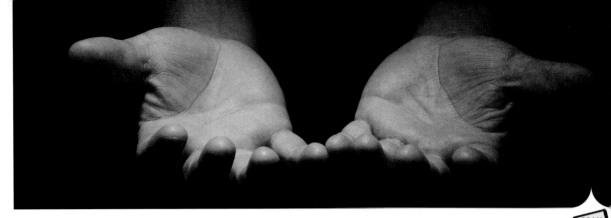

 ## 3.2 Is praying the same as talking to God?

Personal prayer

Praying is not only talking *to* God: it is speaking *with* God, which involves listening to him. It is being with him and spending time with him. You need a lot of things in your life: food, clothes, shelter, etc. God, however, doesn't need anything. He is complete in himself. Nevertheless, because he loves you, and knows that you cannot live without him, he desires that you love him too.

Being with God

If you love someone, you want to be with him as much as possible. It is the same with God. Because he loves you, he wants to be with you. And if you love God, even a little bit, you want to be with him, although you may not exactly know how to do that.

Prayer starts with a longing to be with God and to know him. That longing to be with him is something that God has placed in you, because he longs for you too.

Asking is free

We can ask God anything, as St. Paul said: "Have no anxiety about anything, but in everything by prayer and supplication with thanksgiving let your requests be made known to God" (Phil. 4:6). Jesus even said that we should be persistent in our prayers (Lk. 18:1–8). Prayer is very important.

The Bible is full of examples of people praying. If a blind man hadn't called to Jesus at the gates of Jericho, he would not have received his sight (Lk. 18:35–43). And if a mother hadn't begged Jesus for help, her daughter would not have been cured (Mk. 7:25–30). Jesus says to each one of us: "Ask, and it will be

St. Thérèse of Lisieux on prayer

For me, prayer is a surge of the heart; it is a simple look turned toward heaven, it is a cry of recognition and of love, embracing both trial and joy.

(Story of a Soul)

given you; seek, and you will find; knock, and it will be opened to you" (Mt. 7:7). But there is more. When we love someone, we do not simply ask him for what we need or want. Otherwise, a few sticky notes with scribbled requests on the fridge would be all it takes to make a marriage last. There is also need for personal contact, real communication, and most of all, love. Therefore, prayer is more than asking for what you want; it is also responding to what God wants. Love is a two-way street, and so is prayer.

Listening in silence

Prayer is more than asking God for things; it is also listening to what he asks of us. When we pray, we should not be the only ones doing the talking. Sometimes it is difficult to hear God because he speaks to us in such a subtle way, but you can be sure that he is speaking! He is discreet and wants to leave you free in everything. You can choose to live a careless life, without paying attention to God, or you can choose to become silent from time to time in order to hear him. When the prophet Elijah was asked to wait for God, he spent the night in a cave. First, he heard a heavy storm pass by, then an earthquake, and then fire and lightning. But in all that noise, God was not present. Then, he heard "a still small voice" (I Kgs. 19:12). The sign of God's presence was no more than a little breeze.

In the silence, in the stillness, is where you can hear God. The choice is yours: if you don't want to listen to God, you can ignore his voice and pretend it is not there; if you do want to listen to him, you can make some quiet time, amid the hustle and bustle of each day (SEE TWEET 3.7), and do your best to listen to what he is trying to tell you.

> Prayer is not only talking but also listening. It is working on your relationship with God, who loves you and desires your love.

Read more

Asking God questions: CCC 2629–2633, 2648; CCCC 553; YOUCAT 486.

3.3 What is the best way to pray?

Everyone can pray. You can pray either alone or with others. All of us, in fact, need to do both, just as Jesus did. Every week Jesus went faithfully to the Jewish synagogue, to pray together with other Jews and to read from the Scriptures (LK. 4:16). Also, he often withdrew to quiet places by himself for personal prayer (LK. 5:16). There are a number of ways to pray (SEE BOX). You can pray with the Bible (SEE TWEET 3.8), with the Our Father (SEE TWEET 3.11), with a rosary (SEE TWEET 3.12), and in many other ways. You can also just use your own words, simply saying what comes to mind. Don't worry about what to say: God is not easily offended by the way you say things. He is far too happy that you are there with him. The main thing is that you go to God with the simple confidence of a child, trusting that he hears you and loves you (MT. 6:5–8; 7:11).

Different kinds of prayer

Adoration: acknowledging God's greatness and praising him: he deserves it!

Supplication: asking God for a favor, for ourselves or for others: we need God!

Asking forgiveness: asking God to forgive what we have done wrong: we really need to be forgiven!

Thanksgiving: thanking God for all he gives us: there is so much to be grateful for!

How often and when?

It is a very good idea to take some time every day for personal prayer. That way, you can build a personal relationship with God and share each day with him, even though you aren't always conscious of his presence. By praying, you give God the chance to point you in the right direction (SEE TWEET 3.4). You can pray at any time, night or day. Still, many people plan their prayer in the early morning. That is smart, because then you don't risk forgetting to pray after all the stress of a busy day. It also helps to connect the whole day with your morning prayer. Appendix 4 gives some advice on how to pray.

It is a good habit to take another moment at the end of the day to pray and to reflect on all the good things that God has given you. Often, that is more than you may initially realize! If you notice something you have done wrong, you can ask forgiveness for it. And you can pray for the people you met during the day and for your plans for the following day. How to look back on your day in prayer is explained in Appendix 5.

Where?

You can pray anywhere: during a walk, on the train, on your lunch break, etc. Still, it is good to choose a quiet place for your daily personal time with God. Jesus said: "When you pray, go into your room and shut the door and pray to your Father who is in secret; and your Father who sees in secret will reward you" (MT. 6:6). You can pray in your own room, where you can prepare a corner specifically for prayer by decorating it with a crucifix, your Bible, an icon, or a candle. You can also pray in a different location. Perhaps you know of a chapel that stays open. Any place will work, so long as it is somewhere you feel comfortable and are not easily disturbed.

For how long?

Prayer can be very brief, such as when you quickly ask God: "Lord, please help me with this difficult task." But to work on your relationship with God, you need to do a bit more than that. Try to give God 5, 10, or even 30 minutes a day. It's important to determine how long you will pray at the outset, and then to stick to that plan (SEE TWEET 3.8). Taking the time for prayer is the most important part of praying. Time is precious, in the sense that you can only spend it once. Offering time for prayer to God is therefore a real gift to him and an investment in your relationship.

> There are many ways to pray. Most important is to make time for it. How you pray is less important than spending quality time with God.

Read more

Ways to pray: CCC 2626–2649; CCCC 550–556; YOUCAT 483–489. *Forms of praying:* CCC 2699, 2721; CCCC 568; YOUCAT 500.
You can pray everywhere: CCC 2691, 2696; CCCC 566; YOUCAT 498.

3.4 Can prayer help me to make the right decisions?

SCAN

Jesus prayed before he made an important decision. Before he chose the twelve Apostles, for instance, he spent a whole night in prayer (Lk. 6:12–13). Here, as in all things, Jesus is an example to us. To discover what God wants from us, we need to learn to recognize how he speaks to us. Although it may not seem like it, God really does speak to us in prayer. But he does so in a very deep and profound way. He speaks in the depth of our hearts. That way, he helps us make the right decisions.

Learning to listen

Learning to listen to God requires that we learn to listen to our deepest desires. What God asks of you can often be found in your most profound longing. The difficulty is that we often have so many different desires. But not everything we want is equally important to us. On a warm day, you may really want an ice cream. Yet you can decide not to have one because your desire to lose weight is more important to you. Everything in life is

like that. Every choice requires you to give up something else (SEE TWEET 4.3). For example, you may want to have children, but still discover that your deepest longing is not to marry, but to dedicate yourself completely to God as a priest or a nun (SEE TWEET 4.21).

Discernment

It is all too easy to fool ourselves. We often choose a superficial desire instead of that which can give us the greatest fulfillment. Still, the latter is where God's Will can be found. That is why it is crucial to learn to distinguish between the different desires you have.

For this we need discernment, that is, the ability to tell which desires come from the Holy Spirit, and which ones do not. What suits me best? How can I truly be myself? Only by listening and responding to the Will of God, can we be truly happy (SEE TWEET 4.6). Something that may help you to hear the voice of God and not to be focused only on your own thoughts,

I keep getting distracted!

Everyone who has tried to pray knows it can be difficult to focus completely on God. All sorts of thoughts keep popping up, and you keep getting distracted. You started out really wanting to give the time you reserved for prayer to God, but still your thoughts wander all over the place.

That isn't something to worry about. Quite the contrary: if you start worrying, you will be even less focused on God! If during prayer you notice that you are distracted, simply focus on God again. He alone is important: all your thoughts and desires are completely irrelevant at this moment.

During your prayer, you are with God: there is no better place to be! If, for example, you suddenly remember you have to do something, trust that God knows too and be at peace. If it is important enough, you will remember it after you finish praying. So when this happens, focus your thoughts back on God and continue to pray.

Help with discernment

You cannot discern your vocation, your specific calling from God, alone. To distinguish between your superficial desires and your deepest desires, you need God's help. This is why it is so important to build a relationship with him, by learning how to pray well (SEE TWEET 3.3 AND 3.8). It is also wise to share your thoughts with a priest or another discerning person you trust. A spiritual director can offer guidance and help you to keep track of the bigger picture (SEE TWEET 4.6). It's very easy to get carried away by all the hustle and bustle of daily life or the enthusiasm of the moment!

When you have found out what you are called to do, you will experience a real sense of contentment. Even if some things remain unclear, or if your choice means some things will be risky and difficult, deep inside you will feel you are doing the right thing. That feeling of inner peace is what God wants for each one of us. Jesus says to us what he told his terrified disciples after his Resurrection: "Peace be with you" (JN. 20:19).

> Your deepest desires are from God, who wants to help you to make decisions. When you ask him for guidance, he is sure to give it.

is to pray with a verse from the Bible (SEE TWEET 3.8 AND APPENDIX 4).

Read more

Jesus' prayer: CCC 2600–2605, 2620; CCCC 542; YOUCAT 475.

Personal prayer

3.5 Why can prayer be so difficult or boring?

SCAN

Learning any new thing is a challenge at first. But as you get the hang of something, it becomes easier. Prayer is no different. If you persevere, you will find yourself praying daily with enthusiasm and conviction. You will experience that God loves you, and that with his help, you can confidently go out into the world! You will note the immense power of prayer, the power that comes from God alone.

After becoming practiced in prayer, you might experience times when praying becomes difficult again. Praying can become stale or dry and boring (SEE BOX). At such moments, you can feel very lonely. This is normal. Every believer experiences this at one time or another.

One thing is clear: you will need perseverance (SEE TWEET 3.6). The enemy of God will try to stop you from praying (SEE TWEET 3.11). But even when you do not feel the presence of God, you may be certain that God is always there. So be persistent in dedicating time to God in prayer, even when you don't seem to experience much. You cannot determine the yield of your prayers, but you can determine the time you spend with God.

Learning to ride a bike

People often find that it becomes more difficult to pray just when things seem to be going their way. That is not something to worry about. God is with you on your journey through life. He wants to teach you how to keep going no matter what. That is why we do not always have a beautiful and inspiring experience in prayer. Think of a father teaching his child how to ride a bike. At first, he holds the shoulder of the child as he pedals. After a while, he lets go, but continues to run along the bike to catch the child when he threatens to fall over. Finally, he stops running, and the child pedals on happily – until he notices that dad is no longer running beside him. At this point he panics and falls over. Something like that often happens in our prayer life: once we no longer feel that God is there and helping us, we are tempted to lose faith.

God helps us in his own way

Do not be afraid: God is always helping you. It's just that he often helps us in a manner we don't expect. When Jesus sent Peter and a few others onto the lake on a boat, they were afraid of perishing in the waves. They became even more scared when they thought they saw a ghost approaching them from the middle of the lake. But it soon turned out to be Jesus, who said: "Take heart, it is I; have no fear" (MT. 14:27). That is exactly what he tells you when you are struggling with your prayers: "Do not be afraid; keep at it! You are not alone; trust in God." From the water, Jesus beckoned Peter to step out of the boat and to walk toward him (MT. 14:28). At first Peter was able to do this: with God's help, we can achieve the impossible – as long as it is what he asks of us. But when Peter looked around, saw the wind and the waves, he got scared and began to sink. At the moment he called for help, Jesus held out his hand and grabbed hold of him (MT. 14:31). You may be sure that God will also help you when you are in trouble and ask for his help in prayer.

Recognizing God's help

Sometimes we do not recognize how God helps us. Sometimes, we realize that he was present in a difficult time only in hindsight. Looking back after your prayer you may recognize that something good happened. You may experience this through a feeling of contentment (SEE TWEET 3.4). That also happened to two disciples who could not believe that Jesus had risen from the dead. Without knowing that it was the Lord, they ran into him on the road. Only afterward did they realize it was Jesus (LK. 24:32). The meeting had left them with peace. That deep-felt sense of inner calm is often a confirmation that you are on the right path (SEE TWEET 3.4).

> You must work at everything you do, including prayer. If you ask and do your best, God will help you. You may not notice, but he is there!

Read more

Prayer can be a struggle: CCC 2725–2733, 2753–2756; CCCC 572–574; YOUCAT 505, 508.

 ## 3.6 Why is there no answer when I pray?

Personal prayer

Sometimes it seems that God is silent. Praying can then seem as if you're talking to a brick wall. This can cause all sorts of doubts: "What if God can't hear me?" "What if there is no God?" It is normal to ask such questions. You can talk to your spiritual director about them (SEE TWEET 3.4 AND 4.6), and you can also ask God those questions in your prayer. It is important to know that God has his own way of communicating. It is he who decides when he says something and how he says it, not you – no matter how much you want to be the one in charge.

Persistence and faith

Even when it seems as if nothing much happens in prayer, it is important to persevere and to keep faith. Even the greatest saints had periods when it seemed as if God were absent. They described their prayer at such times as dry or stale. God seemed to be very far away. Their thoughts wandered all over the place. But still they persisted in their love of God and continued to pray. They knew that God

was there and that they would experience him again when they really needed him (SEE BOX). God is always there, even when you don't feel his presence. Having faith is not always easy. Even if you are very disciplined and pray every day, it can be difficult to keep going when you are having a dry phase in your prayer life. But we should not be like spoiled children. These periods can tell us that we cannot always get what we want. What matters is not feeling good when we pray, but being loyal and faithful to God. He is always loyal to us.

That is not what I asked for!

It may sometimes seem as if God is not answering your prayer. You can probably imagine why God didn't grant your request that your neighbor drop dead for refusing to turn his music down. But why didn't God listen when you asked for your aunt to recover from her illness? That is a good question, but the answer is not simple. God is capable of performing miracles (SEE TWEET 4.18), that is, of surpassing the normal workings of nature (therefore we call them *super*natural). And God wants us to have such faith in him that we would dare to ask him for miracles. Pope Francis has reminded us that Jesus himself told us to "ask" and to "knock at the door" and even to "disturb" God, trusting in his love for us. Our prayers, said the pope, need to be both "needy and confident" (HOMILY, DEC. 6, 2013). If God wants us to pray and hears all our prayers why then does he not give us all that we ask of him? St. James wrote: "You ask and do not receive, because you ask wrongly, to spend it on your passions" (JAS. 4:2–3). In other words, sometimes God does not give us what we ask because we pray in the wrong way or for the wrong things. We cannot conscript God to our own causes. Even when our intentions are good, we do not know what God knows about what is best.

The right attitude

Praying starts with total trust in God. Like Jesus we need to pray: "Not my will, but yours, be done" (LK. 22:42). Praying is not only asking for something you want for yourself or for others; above all, it is building your relationship with God, seeking his Will and trusting that he knows what is best. If we love God, how can we ask for something that goes against his Will? St. John said: "This is the confidence which we have in him, that if we ask anything according to his will he hears us" (I JN. 5:14).

The dark night of the soul

St. John of the Cross (†1591) wrote a book about his experiences in prayer. He did not seek to be happy on earth but only to be with God. That is why he wrote of the journey that his soul had to make to become one with God. That was not an easy road to travel. He encountered many difficulties before actually meeting God. John therefore spoke of the "dark night of the soul".

Only by persevering and continuing to trust in God did he finally reach his goal. Blessed Mother Teresa and other saints also experienced something similar (SEE TWEET 4.12). Still, they remained faithful to God, knowing deep inside themselves that in their lives God's love was most important to them.

Sometimes God seems silent or distant. If you persevere in prayer and trust in God, he will not disappoint you.

Read more

No answer: CCC 2735–2737; CCCC 575; YOUCAT 507.

3.7 How can I make time for prayer? Where is God in daily life?

You have a lot going on in your life. You have all sorts of important things keeping you busy. With all that happening, it can be hard to find a moment to sit down and say: "All right God, the next 10 minutes are entirely for you." The most important thing about praying is to take the time for God. That can be a sacrifice, because the time you spend praying cannot be spent doing something else.

No time?

But if you look at it in a different way, it is actually quite strange that it should be so hard to take some time for prayer. If you pray 10 minutes a day, that is a mere fraction of the 1,440 minutes you have every 24 hours (less than 1 percent!). Consider how easily you spend half an hour a day on the Internet, for example.

That is why you have to determine what is truly important in life. Is it your peace and quiet, your friends, your exams, your career?

What place do you want God to have in your life? It is important to think about priorities. No matter how important your daily affairs may be, the short time you dedicate entirely to God is the time best spent. You may believe that God can do anything.

If you take time for God in your prayer, and work hard, you can be sure that God will make certain that you can finish what you must finish. Considered thus, praying is even good for your career! That's why Blessed Mother Teresa told her sisters that they ought to pray for longer than usual on the days they have more work. If you have a lot of work to do, you also need extra help and grace from God (SEE TWEET 4.12).

Meditation and contemplation

The purpose of Christian prayer is to be with God. That is very different from the various goals of Buddhist meditation or Hindu yoga, which can be practiced with or without faith in God. As Christians, we turn toward

How can I know that my experience comes from God?

Maybe you think you are fooling yourself when you pray. Am I just talking to myself? Are the answers that seem to come really from God? What if I just made it up myself? Or maybe they come from an evil spirit? Those are important questions. But always remember Jesus' words: "Do not be afraid" (Jn. 6:20).

Everything that comes from God will give you a feeling of deep peace (SEE TWEET 3.4). In addition, there are a number of things that can help you to determine whether your experience comes from God:

- Anything God tells you will always be in line with what Jesus has said. God cannot contradict himself.
- The Holy Spirit helps the Church to tell the truth about God (SEE TWEET 2.13). Therefore, what God tells you will also be in line with the teachings of the Church.
- If you have something bothering you while you pray, speak about it to your spiritual director. He can help you to discern what is good and true and what isn't.
- Use common sense; by honestly listening to your conscience, you can find the right balance (SEE TWEET 4.6).

God in prayer in order to have a personal relationship with him. To help us to do this, we can meditate on a Bible verse, an icon, or a text from the Church Fathers or other saints (SEE TWEET 2.24). Meditation can lead to contemplation (SEE TWEET 3.3), when we focus entirely on the love God has for us and the love we have for him.

Understanding

By praying, you are developing a personal relationship with Jesus. Prayer improves your understanding of what he did to reconcile you with God and what he is doing in your life right now (SEE TWEET 1.27).

Understanding both God and yourself better begins with making time available for prayer. God will do the rest. He even helps you to pray: "The Holy Spirit helps us in our weakness; for we do not know how to pray as we ought, but the Spirit himself intercedes for us with sighs too deep for words" (ROM. 8:26).

Prioritize! What's more important: your busy life or God? Put God first and everything else will fall into place.

Read more

Daily prayer: CCC 2659–2660; YOUCAT 494. *Meditation*: CCC 2705–2708, 2723; CCCC 570; YOUCAT 502, 504.

3.8 How can I pray with a text from the Bible?

God wants to speak to you through the Bible. The Bible is not merely a collection of old stories about what God said or did in the past, it is the Word of God that he is speaking now (SEE TWEET 1.10). Every verse from the Bible has something to say to you. That is why it is so important to read the Bible regularly and to use it in your prayer. This kind of reading is not the same as scholarly study. It involves pondering a small amount of text quietly. God will help you to understand what you need at that moment. This way of praying is called *lectio divina*, which is Latin for "divine reading", or "reading with God".

Choosing a Bible text

You might be wondering about how to choose a Bible text for your prayer. A good place to start is the daily readings that have been selected by the Church for Mass. These verses are in tune with what the Church is celebrating each day (SEE TWEET 3.47). They can be found in Catholic missals, parish bulletins, and websites. You can also choose to read an

A saint prays with the Bible

St. Ignatius of Loyola (SEE TWEET 4.5) had his own way of praying with the Bible (SEE APPENDIX 4). His advice: choose a text first and decide beforehand how long you are going to pray.

The best place to start is with the Gospels. Read an episode and then imagine the scene, listening to what Jesus is saying, and observing what he is doing. Let his actions and words move you deeply, and then talk to him, telling him everything that comes to you in the moment.

St. Ignatius recommended writing down what you experienced during prayer, so that you can have a record of how God is accompanying you on your journey to him.

entire book of the Bible, a few lines every day. At any rate, it is good not to choose only texts that you like, but also to explore the richness of other texts. Any Bible text, however difficult at first sight, has something important to say. You might choose one of the four Gospels: Matthew, Mark, Luke, or John (SEE TWEET 1.17 AND 1.18). Read a few lines, think about them, and then pray. In this way you will get to know Jesus more and more each day.

Visualizing

To get to know Jesus better, it can help to visualize a situation that is described in the Gospels. If the verses say that Jesus stood on a little boat to preach while his disciples listened on the shore (LK. 5:3), try to imagine it. Close your eyes and see the boat with Jesus standing there; see the people on the shore; see yourself as one of them, feeling the wind, smelling the sea, etc. You might even crawl into the boat so that you can be very close to Jesus. Then you can listen to the words of Jesus as if he were speaking directly to you.

A chat with Jesus

If you read the text slowly, there will probably be a word or a sentence that strikes you. Maybe it brings up all sorts of questions, maybe it makes you angry, or maybe it simply feels right and you say: "Exactly, that's it!" If you are struck by a verse, stop. Maybe you can repeat the words slowly, pondering them carefully. You can ask yourself: What does God want to tell me through these words today? Why did my eyes fall on this sentence? Why does this touch me? How does this challenge me? Let it come to you. Then you can tell Jesus anything on your mind, as if you were having a chat with him.

Appendix 4 explains how you can pray with a Bible verse (SEE BOX). You do not have to finish a text, rather it is more important to fill the time you reserved for God. If you said you were going to pray for 10 minutes, then pray for 10 minutes. Otherwise, you may leave before God had the chance to speak with you! Even if you feel uninspired, if your prayer is dry and stale, simply remain attentive to God until the time is up (SEE TWEET 3.3).

When you finish praying, it is good to take a moment and look back on your prayer. What part of the Bible text was important to me? When did I feel something? In short, how did God touch me? This helps you to recognize how much God gives you in prayer.

> Take the time, read a Bible verse, and let the text speak to you. Then tell Jesus anything that comes to mind.

Read more

Praying with the Bible: CCC 1177, 2652–2653; CCCC 558; YOUCAT 491.

SCAN

3.9 Do we pray to the Father, the Son, or the Holy Spirit? To Mary and the saints?

Jesus invited us to ask God for anything we really need (SEE TWEET 3.2) – not only for ourselves, but also for others. If we pray for someone, we act as an intercessor with God, hence the term *intercessory prayer*. It is important to pray for the sick, for victims of all kinds, and for others who need or ask for our prayers. Specifically, we pray for the deceased, that they may go swiftly to heaven (SEE TWEET 1.45).

It might seem unfair that some people are prayed for much more often than others. But thankfully, there are people, both in heaven and on earth, who pray for everybody. That way, even people who don't have loved ones praying for them have intercessors. You may take this as an invitation to pray for all of those who need prayer.

Which one of the three?

We can pray to any of the three Persons in the Trinity: the Father, the Son, and the Holy Spirit (SEE TWEET 1.33). Because they form a unity, we can be sure that a prayer to any of them is a prayer to the one God. At the same time, they have distinct personalities, full of love for each other and for us, as described in the Bible. Jesus is God the Son, who leads us to God the Father. When his disciples asked Jesus how to pray, he taught them the Our Father (SEE TWEET 3.11), revealing that God deserves our reverence and obedience as he provides for our needs and forgives our sins. We can also pray directly to Jesus, as when the blind and the sick asked him for healing (SEE TWEET 3.2). For wisdom, strength, and other gifts, Jesus said that we could rely on the Holy Spirit, who

....

Glory Be

(ENGLISH) Glory be to the Father, and to the Son, and to the Holy Spirit. As it was in the beginning, is now, and ever shall be, world without end. Amen.

(LATIN) Gloria Patri, et Filio, et Spiritui Sancto. Sicut erat in principio et nunc et semper et in sæcula sæculorum. Amen.

proceeds from the Father and the Son, guiding and protecting the Church (SEE TWEET 1.32; SEE BOX).

Through Christ, our Lord

In the liturgy, we address our prayers to God the Father in the name of Jesus. In doing so, we join Jesus, the Son of God, in his constant prayer to the Father. Jesus said that God will give us all that we ask for in his name (JN. 15:16). Through Jesus, we have access to the Father (EPH. 2:18). That's why our prayers are often concluded with the words: "Through Christ, our Lord." Because the Holy Spirit is the love between the Father and the Son, we sometimes conclude with: "Through our Lord Jesus Christ, your Son, who lives and reigns with you in the unity of the Holy Spirit, one God, for ever and ever."

Mary and the saints

Prayers are continuously being said by Mary, the other saints, and the angels in heaven. That's why we can ask them to pray for us (SEE TWEET 4.15). If you don't know where to start, you might ask your patron saint to pray for you (SEE TWEET 4.16). In the Bible, we often see people going to Jesus to ask something for someone else (SEE TWEET 3.2). And Jesus listened to these intercessors. Similarly, he will listen to our prayers and those of the saints. We do not worship the saints, but we can venerate them, that is, show them our love and admiration. We worship only God, who alone has the power to answer our prayers. Thus, we pray not so much to the saints as together with the saints to God. Of course, you can always pray directly to God. But God asks the members of the Church, those in heaven and those on earth, to care for one another, and one way we do that is to pray for each other.

> You can pray to Father, Son, or Spirit, as they are one God. You can also ask Mary, the saints, and the angels to pray for and with you.

Read more

Prayer to the Father, the Son and the Holy Spirit: CCC 2664–2672, 2680–2681; CCCC 560–561; YOUCAT 495–496.
The Our Father: CCC 2759–2865; CCCC 578–598; YOUCAT 511–527. *The Hail Mary*: CCC 971; CCCC 198; YOUCAT 149.

3.10 Why do we keep repeating the same prayers?

Often, our prayer is personal, that is, in our own words (SEE TWEET 3.8). Another way of praying is through an existing prayer such as the Sign of the Cross (SEE TWEET 3.15), the Hail Mary (SEE TWEET 1.39), and the Glory Be (SEE TWEET 3.9). These formulaic prayers are sometimes called vocal prayers. The Our Father is a vocal prayer that Jesus taught his disciples (SEE TWEET 3.11).

Such prayers can be said either together with others or alone. They cannot replace personal prayer: you also should speak to God in your own words, from your heart. But you can certainly start or end your personal prayer with a vocal prayer.

Boring?

Maybe the repetition of vocal prayers sounds like a boring way to pray. It is boring indeed if all you do is mindlessly say the words. But praying is not merely intoning words! Praying needs to be done with your mind and heart. Sometimes it's hard to put into words what you want to tell God from the depths of your soul.

You can't always find the words for it. At such times, the words of a vocal prayer may help you. The repetition gives strength to your prayer. Because we can know these prayers by heart, our souls can be at rest with Jesus while we pray them. St. Josemaría Escrivá (†1975) called vocal prayers "precious gems that have a place in the routine of a life illuminated by faith" (FRIENDS OF GOD, 248).

The Angelus

The angel of the Lord declared unto Mary.
And she conceived by the Holy Spirit.

Hail Mary... (SEE TWEET 1.39).

Behold the handmaid of the Lord.
Be it done unto me according to thy Word.

Hail Mary...

And the Word was made flesh.
And dwelt among us.

Hail Mary...

Pray for us, O Holy Mother of God.
That we may be made worthy of the promises of Christ.

Let us pray:
Pour forth, we beseech thee, O Lord, thy grace into our hearts; that we to whom the Incarnation of Christ, thy Son, was made known by the message of an angel, may by his Passion and Cross be brought to the glory of his Resurrection; through the same Christ, our Lord.

Amen.

Angelus

It is a good Catholic habit to pray the Angelus regularly (SEE BOX). Maybe there is a nearby church whose bells ring three times per day at 6:00 A.M., 12:00 P.M., and 6:00 P.M. This is a call to pray the Angelus. With this prayer, we remember that God's Son, Jesus, became man in order to save us (SEE TWEET 1.26). This prayer is named after the first words in Latin, *Angelus Domini*, which mean "The Angel of the Lord".

Jesus Prayer

The Jesus Prayer is a traditional form of prayer from the Eastern Churches (SEE TWEET 2.30). Quietly praying, you continuously repeat the name of Jesus. You can do that silently, out loud, or even by singing. Its purpose is to help you to spend time with Jesus.

The complete text of this prayer of the heart is as follows: "Lord Jesus Christ, Son of God, have mercy on me, a sinner" (CCC 435). The prayer is based on the pleas of sinners and beggars in the Gospels (LK. 18:13, 38). In our prayers to Jesus, we are like beggars: we offer little, but ask much.

> Vocal prayers help you to pray with all your heart, give you words when you don't know what to say, and give strength through repetition.

Read more
Vocal prayer: CCC 2700–2704, 2722; CCCC 569; YOUCAT 501.

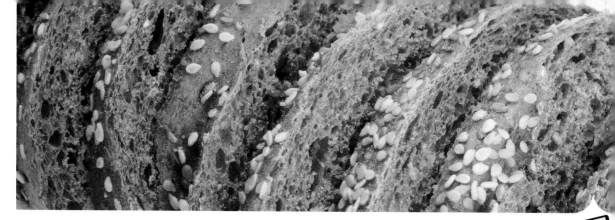

 ## 3.11 What kind of prayer is the Our Father?

 SCAN

When the disciples saw Jesus pray, they said: "Lord, teach us to pray" (Lk. 11:1). Jesus responded by giving them the Lord's Prayer, the Our Father. We can use the words of this prayer over and over again. What better way to pray, than with Jesus' own words?

Father, your kingdom

By addressing God as "Our Father" we express that God has made us and we are his children (see Tweet 1.2). When we say "hallowed be thy name" we acknowledge the holiness of God. "Thy kingdom come" means we long for the reign of God on earth, which we can already observe and experience to some degree.

Given human freedom, God's reign comes into the world only through people who try to do what is right and good. We pray for the return of Jesus at the end of time (see Tweet 1.49), because we know that not until then will the Kingdom of God be complete.

Will, bread, and forgiveness

When we say "thy Will be done" we ask God to make our will coincide with his. That is what truly matters in our life. In fact, doing God's Will is the only way we can really be happy (see Tweet 4.1). Mary gave us a great example when she said yes to God's Will without knowing entirely what that would mean for her (see Tweet 1.38). When we pray for our "daily bread" we ask for the food we need to live. That also

....

The Our Father

Our Father who art in heaven,
Hallowed be thy name.
Thy kingdom come.
Thy will be done
    On earth as it is in heaven.
Give us this day our daily bread;
And forgive us our trespasses
    As we forgive those who trespass against us;
And lead us not into temptation,
But deliver us from evil (Mt. 6:9–13).

240

includes the Word of God (the Bible) and the Eucharist (SEE BOX), which are sometimes referred to as spiritual bread.

Jesus beautifully puts us in our place when he tells us to ask for forgiveness for our sins "as we forgive those who trespass [or sin] against us". Our receiving forgiveness depends on our forgiving others. The need to forgive others is constant: forgiveness is the only way to break free from cycles of guilt and retribution (SEE TWEET 4.14). We are generous with our forgiveness because we ourselves constantly need God's forgiveness. We ask for it very concretely through the Sacrament of Reconciliation (SEE TWEET 3.38).

Temptation and evil

It is easy to fall into doubt when things are not going well. We find ourselves asking questions:

Does God really love me? Is he even there? What is the meaning of all this? The enemy of God, the devil, stirs up doubt, because that gives him a chance to tempt us (SEE TWEET 1.4). When we say "lead us not into temptation" we ask God to help us to do the right thing. To be strong, we have to stay close to Jesus, to ask ourselves what he would do (SEE TWEET 4.8). Even when Jesus was tempted, he remained loyal to the Father. We can be sure that we will never be tested beyond what we can handle, that God is near us in our difficulties (I COR. 10:13).

Evil is everywhere in the world (SEE TWEET 1.35). Every day we hear of natural disasters, terrible accidents, and horrible crimes and wars. When we pray "deliver us from evil" we put all this before God. Jesus is more powerful than evil, which he conquered by his death and Resurrection (SEE TWEET 1.26). If you follow Jesus you need not fear evil but may have confidence in God, who can bring good out of any situation. And you can look forward to the day when Jesus will return (SEE TWEET 1.35) and his triumph over evil will be complete.

Jesus gave us the Our Father, which honors God, asks for what we need, requests and promises forgiveness, and begs for protection.

Read more

The Our Father: CCC 2759–2865; CCCC 578–598; YOUCAT 511–527.

3.12 How do I pray the Rosary?

Every day, millions of people all over the world pray the Rosary. The power of this prayer lies in its simplicity. You can take your rosary everywhere; in fact, all you need are your ten fingers. Because Mary knows Jesus so well, and is so close to him in heaven, we ask her to pray for us (SEE TWEET 1.39).

What is a rosary?

A standard rosary consists of five series of ten beads. You say a prayer on every bead of the rosary. It is not about mindlessly intoning the words (SEE TWEET 3.10). When you repeat the Hail Mary (SEE TWEET 1.39) you reflect on a number of events in the lives of Jesus and Mary. We call these events "mysteries", because even as we learn more and more about the way Jesus saves us, much remains a mystery to us (SEE TWEET 1.26). We understand his great gift of salvation better by reflecting in prayer on what he does for us.

How to pray?

You start by holding the crucifix: you make the Sign of the Cross (SEE TWEET 3.15) and recite the Apostles' Creed (SEE TWEET 1.31). On the first bead, you recite the Our Father (SEE TWEET 3.11). On the next three beads, you pray the Hail Mary. Then say the Glory Be (SEE TWEET 3.9).

After this introduction, you start the first decade, or set of ten beads, which consists of an Our Father and ten Hail Marys. You start by stating which of the mysteries from the life of Jesus you will meditate upon during the decade (SEE BOX). On the single bead, you pray an Our Father, and a Hail Mary for each of the next ten beads. Then, you end with a Glory Be. You have now reached another single bead; here you start the next decade, where you say the mystery you wish to contemplate, the Our Father, ten Hail Marys, and a Glory Be.

After five decades, you will have finished one set of mysteries. After the last Glory Be, you say a Hail, Holy Queen (SEE THE APP) and the following: "Pray for us, Holy Mother of God, that we may be made worthy of the promises of Christ." When prayed together,

The Mysteries of the Rosary

The Joyful Mysteries (*Mondays and Saturdays*)

1. The Annunciation of the Lord to Mary (Lk. 1:30–33)
2. The Visitation of Mary to Elizabeth (Lk. 1:40–43)
3. The Nativity of our Lord Jesus Christ (Lk. 2:4–7)
4. The Presentation of our Lord in the Temple (Lk. 2:22–24)
5. The Finding of the Child Jesus in the Temple (Lk. 2:48–51)

The Luminous Mysteries (*Thursdays*)

1. The Baptism of Jesus in the Jordan (Mk. 1:9–11)
2. The Wedding at Cana (Jn. 2:1–11)
3. The Proclamation of the Kingdom (Mk. 1:14–15)
4. The Transfiguration of the Lord (Mk. 9:2–9)
5. The Institution of the Eucharist (Lk. 22:14–20)

The Sorrowful Mysteries (*Tuesdays and Fridays*)

1. The Agony of Jesus in the Garden (Mt. 26:38–39)
2. The Scourging at the Pillar (Mt. 27:26)
3. The Crowning with Thorns (Mt. 27:29)
4. The Carrying of the Cross (Jn. 19:17)
5. The Crucifixion of Our Lord (Jn. 19:28–30)

The Glorious Mysteries (*Wednesdays and Sundays*)

1. The Resurrection of Jesus Christ (Mk. 16:6–8)
2. The Ascension of Jesus to Heaven (Acts 1:10–11)
3. The Descent of the Holy Spirit (Acts 2:1–4)
4. The Assumption of Mary into Heaven (I Cor. 15:54–55)
5. The Crowning of Mary as Queen of Heaven and Earth (see Lk. 1:51–54)

....

the concluding prayer is usually this: "O God, by the life, death, and Resurrection of your only begotten Son, you purchased for us the rewards of eternal life; grant, we beseech you, that while meditating on these mysteries of the holy Rosary, we may imitate what they contain and obtain what they promise. Through the same Christ our Lord. Amen."

Flowers for Mary

The rose is a symbol for Mary, and the Rosary is a circle of prayers (like the petals in a flower) we can offer her while asking for her prayers. Because you can pray the Rosary every day, people sometimes compare it with the Liturgy of the Hours (see Tweet 3.13). It's

an old tradition to recite all three original mysteries of the Rosary (Joyful, Sorrowful, and Glorious), which equals 150 Hail Mary's (in place of the 150 psalms that are prayed in the Liturgy of the Hours). It is more common to pray only one set of mysteries daily.

> In the Rosary you pray an Our Father or Hail Mary on each bead while contemplating the lives of Jesus & Mary and spending time with them.

Read more

The rosary: CCC 2678; CCCC 563; YOUCAT 481.

3.13 What is the Liturgy of the Hours?

Forms of prayer

The Liturgy of the Hours, or Divine Office, is a series of prayers for specific, fixed hours of the day. That way you can dedicate the whole day to God. Hence the name: the Liturgy of the Hours. This form of prayer is primarily made up of psalms.

The 150 psalms in the Bible are prayers and songs that thank, invoke, question, beg, praise, and honor God. These texts tell us a lot about the history of the people of Israel (SEE TWEET 1.24). But they also tell us a lot about ourselves today. With poetic language, the psalms describe common feelings and experiences. They can give us words to address God if we cannot find the right words ourselves.

Origins

The Jews have long had the habit of praying and singing the psalms at sunrise and sunset, to thank God and to ask for his protection. Christians have adopted this tradition, adding a number of prayers and songs from the New

---

Magnificat

My soul proclaims the greatness of the Lord,
my spirit rejoices in God my Savior
for he has looked with favor on his lowly
    servant.
From this day all generations will call me
    blessed:
the Almighty has done great things for me,
and holy is his Name.
He has mercy on those who fear him
in every generation.
He has shown the strength of his arm,
he has scattered the proud in their conceit.
He has cast the mighty from their thrones,
and has lifted up the lowly.
He has filled the hungry with good things,
and the rich he has sent away empty.
He has come to the help of his servant Israel
for he has remembered his promise of mercy,
the promise he made to our fathers,
to Abraham and his children for ever.

Testament. The Liturgy of the Hours forms an important aspect of monastic life (SEE TWEET 2.25). In addition to Morning Prayer (or Lauds) and Evening Prayer (or Vespers), monks have other prayers for different times of the day. The Benedictines, for example, have followed the same schedule of singing psalms for centuries (SEE BELOW). Priests and deacons use a slightly shorter version of the Liturgy of the Hours (they only say the prayers between parentheses).

	Matins	(Office of Readings)
Dawn	Lauds	(Morning Prayer)
6:00	Prime	
9:00	Terce	
12:00	Sext	(Daytime Prayer which can be Terce, Sext, or None)
3:00	None	
6:00	Vespers	(Evening Prayer)
9:00	Compline	(Night Prayer)

Structure

Each of these "hours" has a fixed structure: an opening, a number of psalms, a reading from the Bible, and a number of prayers. During Lauds we say or sing the prayer of gratitude that Zechariah directed to God after the birth of his son, John the Baptist (the *Benedictus*, or Canticle of Zechariah [Lk. 1:67–79]). Vespers includes the praises Mary gave to God after being greeted by her cousin Elizabeth (the *Magnificat*, or Canticle of Mary [SEE BOX]). Compline includes the words Simeon spoke when he saw the infant Jesus in the Temple in Jerusalem (the *Nunc Dimittis*, or Canticle of Simeon [SEE BOX]).

For everybody

The Liturgy of the Hours is a good way to dedicate the day to God. Priests, deacons, and religious pray the Liturgy of the Hours every day, and many lay people do too. Although the Liturgy of the Hours is well suited to communal prayer, it can also be prayed alone, especially by priests and deacons. The texts for the Divine Office are published in a hand-held breviary. Tablets and smartphones make it even easier for anyone to pray the Liturgy of the Hours and, thereby, to consecrate the day to God.

Nunc Dimittis

Lord, now let your servant go in peace;
your word has been fulfilled:
my own eyes have seen the salvation
which you have prepared in the sight of every people:
a light to reveal you to the nations
and the glory of your people Israel. (Lk. 2:29–32)

The Liturgy of the Hours brings God into the day with psalms said at fixed times. It is prayed by priests, religious, and maybe also you?

Read more

Liturgy of the Hours: CCC 1174–1178, 1196; CCCC 243; YOUCAT 188. *Regular prayer*: CCC 2697–2698, 2720; CCCC 567; YOUCAT 499.

SCAN

 ## 3.14 How do I pass the time during adoration?

In the Eucharist, Jesus is truly present in his own Body and Blood in the form of bread (the Host) (SEE BOX). At certain times, the Host is placed in a beautifully decorated receptacle, the monstrance. This is exposition of the Blessed Sacrament. In the monstrance, Jesus is clearly visible to all, so that he can be worshipped. Apart from receiving Communion, there is no better way to get close to God on earth.

Adoration

When we kneel, sit, or are otherwise present before the Body of Christ exposed in a monstrance, we can adore him. In this way of praying, the Lord is very near to us. He is physically present with us. You can look at Jesus and tell him anything. You may put all your worries and troubles in his hands. All you have to do is quietly be near Jesus. Nothing else is important. That is silent adoration. St. John Vianney (†1859), a parish priest of Ars, France, told the story of a farmer who spent hours in the church just looking at the tabernacle (SEE BOX; SEE TWEET 3.21). When Fr.

Vianney asked him what he was doing, the farmer said: "I am here with Jesus. He looks at me, and I look at him." That farmer shows us the essence of adoration. We can show our love for Jesus simply by looking at him and being with him. This is a very personal and intimate form of meeting him. For an encounter with Jesus, you do not need words.

Boring?

It may seem boring just to kneel or to sit there in the church, doing nothing. But the point of adoration is exactly that: not doing anything, but just being there. By being with Jesus in this way we acknowledge our complete dependence on him. All of our activity is fruitless unless its source is God. By dedicating time to him in quiet adoration, we give God the chance to speak to us. You are in his presence here! This is a great moment for your personal prayer (SEE TWEET 3.8). You can silently pray the Rosary or the Liturgy of the Hours (SEE TWEET 3.12 AND 3.13). You can read from a prayer book or the Bible. But you can

What is the Blessed Sacrament?

Of the seven sacraments (SEE TWEET 3.35) only one is called the Blessed Sacrament. In all of the sacraments, God gives us grace, that is, his own life (SEE TWEET 4.12). But in the Sacrament of the Eucharist, God actually *is* the sacrament.

We see bread (the Host), but it is the Body of Christ (SEE TWEET 3.48). Therefore we give the Eucharist the same honor we would if God himself were in front of us.

After celebrating the Eucharist, the Body of Christ is preserved in the tabernacle (SEE TWEET 3.21). As a sign of the continuous and living presence of Jesus, a candle or lamp burns there, day and night. This is called the sanctuary lamp. Every time we pass, we genuflect toward the tabernacle to honor Jesus present there.

also do absolutely nothing and simply be with Jesus. This is what adoration is truly about.

Eucharistic adoration

Sometimes the Blessed Sacrament is solemnly exposed. The time of exposition of the Blessed Sacrament begins and ends with incense, singing, and public prayers led by a priest or deacon. In this way a community of believers can adore together the physical presence of Jesus in the Eucharist. On special days, such as Holy Thursday (SEE TWEET 3.30) and Corpus Christi (SEE TWEET 3.27), there may also be a procession with the Blessed Sacrament. A priest, or also a bishop, carries the Blessed Sacrament through church grounds or the streets of a city, followed by the faithful. All are literally travelling with Jesus (SEE TWEET 3.17). Pope John Paul II said: "The Church and the world have a great need of eucharistic worship. Jesus waits for us in this sacrament of love. Let us be generous with our time in going to meet him in adoration and in contemplation that is full of faith and ready to make reparation for the great faults and crimes of the world by our adoration" (DOMINICAE CENAE, 3).

> We adore Jesus in the Eucharist by quietly being with him: he looks at you and you look at him. You can tell him everything.

Read more

Worship: CCC 1378–1381, 1418; CCCC 286; YOUCAT 218.

SCAN

3.15 How is holy water made? What does a blessing do?

Jesus himself instituted the seven sacraments to give us his grace (SEE TWEET 3.35 AND 4.12). In addition, the Church has instituted sacramentals, which consist of prayers combined with certain actions or signs.

The Sign of the Cross

A good example of a sacramental is the Sign of the Cross: we trace a cross across ourselves while saying: "In the name of the Father, and of the Son, and of the Holy Spirit."

The cross of ashes traced on our foreheads on Ash Wednesday is also a sacramental, as are the blessed palm branches we receive on Palm Sunday (SEE TWEET 3.29). In our homes, we often have a crucifix, a depiction of Jesus on the cross (SEE TWEET 2.37). Every time we see it, we recall the great sacrifice that Jesus made for us (SEE TWEET 1.26). Behind the crucifix we often place a blessed palm branch we received on Palm Sunday, to remind us of Jesus' suffering, which started with his entry into Jerusalem (SEE TWEET 3.30). Just like the inhabitants of Jerusalem, at one moment we praise Jesus, and at another moment we reject him.

Holy water

Holy water is also a sacramental. The water has been blessed by a bishop, priest, or deacon. Baptismal water is holy water used to baptize people. When we enter a church, we can make

Blessing

If you receive a blessing from a bishop, a priest, or a deacon, he first says: "The Lord be with you." You answer: "And with your spirit." Now you trace the sign of the cross on yourself as he says: "May almighty God bless you, the Father, and the Son, and the Holy Spirit." Complete the blessing by saying: "Amen."

a cross with holy water, which is a reminder of our Baptism. At the entrance of every church you find holy water fonts, which are precisely intended for that purpose. You can also hang a font of holy water inside your bedroom and make the Sign of the Cross with it every day. If you take a bottle of water to a priest, he can bless it for you. The Easter Vigil is particularly suited for the blessing of water (SEE TWEET 3.32). We are sprinkled with holy water on Easter and sometimes on Sundays to remind us of our Baptism. Holy water is often used to bless people or objects.

Blessings

Blessings are sacramentals too. A blessing is not some kind of magic: it is a prayer asking for God's blessing (SEE BOX).

- *People* can be blessed in many different situations: during pregnancy, before an operation, or for an engagement, for example. Maybe you have received the blessing of St. Blaise on his feast day, February 3. For this prayer, the priest uses two candles that were blessed on the previous day, the Feast of the Presentation. He holds them near your throat, saying: "Through the intercession of St. Blaise, bishop and martyr, may God deliver you from every disease of the throat and from every other illness in the name of the Father, and of the Son, and of the Holy Spirit. Amen."
- *Devotional objects* are things such as your rosary or patron saint medal. When such objects are blessed, they are dedicated to God, that is, they are set aside to give honor and glory to him. Thus you should not use blessed objects for any other purpose. And that is why you should not sell blessed objects, although you can give them away to someone who will use them in the right way.
- Even *animals, houses, and cars* can be blessed. But be careful: you can still have an accident in a car that has been blessed. If you are driving fast on the motorway and let go of the steering wheel, assuming that God will continue to steer for you, this is not a sign of great faith, but an act of presumption. You have to cooperate with God by fulfilling your responsibilities (SEE TWEET 4.8).

You often go to a priest to obtain a blessing. But did you know that parents can also bless their children? It is a good custom for parents to bless their children before they go to bed, to school, or on a trip, by tracing a cross on their foreheads.

> A priest's blessing makes water or other objects holy. These are sacramentals (not sacraments).

Read more

Sacramentals: CCC 1667–1672, 1677–1678; CCCC 351; YOUCAT 272. Blessing: CCC 2626–2627; CCCC 551; YOUCAT 484.

3.16 What are relics?

A relic is a tangible reminder of a saint (SEE TWEET 4.15). Most relics are pieces of a saint's body or clothes (SEE BOX). That is not as strange as it may seem: think of people who keep a piece of jewelry, a lock of hair, or even the ashes of a loved one who passed away. Being close to the relic of a saint can help us in our faith: just like the saint, we try to live as the friends of God.

An old habit

The first Christians were already using relics. God performed great miracles through items touched by St. Paul: "Handkerchiefs or aprons were carried away from his body to the sick, and diseases left them and the evil spirits came out of them" (ACTS 19:11–12). The bodies of the first people who died because of their faith in Christ, the martyrs, were treated with great reverence. Just like Jesus, the martyrs were ready to give up their lives in this world for their love of God. To be near the remains of someone who shared so completely in the suffering of Christ and was therefore a powerful intercessor, the early Christians often gathered around the grave of a martyr to celebrate the Eucharist there. Jesus had been willing to sacrifice his own life for our good, showing the way to eternal life (SEE TWEET 1.26), and the martyrs joined him in this sacrifice, with which we are especially united during the celebration of the Eucharist (SEE TWEET 3.48). Thus it became a tradition to store a relic of a martyr in each altar used for Mass. Even today it is a moving experience to celebrate Mass near the grave of a martyr, for example, in the catacombs outside Rome.

Are relics real?

Because of their importance for the faith, relics require a certificate that proves they are real. The truth must be researched as much as possible. But many relics are so old that scientists cannot always prove their authenticity. That does not make them worthless. Even when the origin is uncertain, if faithful Christians have prayed near a relic for centuries, it is at least a focal point of

Kinds of relics

There are different kinds or degrees of relics:

- First-class relics are remains or objects directly associated with the life of Jesus (the cross, the manger, etc.) or parts of the body of a saint (bones, hairs, etc.).
- Second-class relics are pieces of clothing or objects that belonged to the saint.
- Third-class relics are objects that touched a first- or second-class relic.

The objects associated with Jesus' suffering and death are good examples of first-class relics: the cross, the crown of thorns, the nails that were hammered through his hands and feet, the burial cloths (e.g., the Shroud of Turin), etc. Then there are the relics of a great many saints. Underneath St. Peter's Basilica in Rome lie the bones of St. Peter, for instance. And in the French town of Nevers, the body of St. Bernadette Soubirous, to whom Mary appeared in Lourdes, has not decomposed: she is still just as beautiful as when she died (SEE TWEET 1.36). Canon law forbids the sale of relics (CIC 1190).

....

prayer and as such can bring us in touch with Jesus or a saint.

The power of touch

Only God may be worshipped and adored (SEE TWEET 4.15). In the fourth century, St. Jerome wrote: "We venerate the relics of the martyrs in order the better to adore God, whose martyrs they are" (AD RIPARIUM, I). Venerating a relic by touching or kissing it, gives you a kind of physical connection to the saint. If someone touches the photo of a loved one who passed away, he is not thinking of the photo, but of the person he loves. The same applies to venerating relics. We think of the saints and ask them to pray for us (SEE TWEET 3.9). After all, they are with God in heaven! We can also, for example, carry the relics in a procession (SEE TWEET 3.17). Relics of saints can help to draw closer to Jesus, but grace always comes from Jesus himself.
Before the relic of the Holy Cross we kneel.

We do not kneel for the piece of wood, but for Jesus, who saved us through the cross. This is to render Jesus the honor that he deserves. In the Bible we see all the human senses being employed to bring people closer to Jesus, including the sense of touch. A woman who had been sick for 12 years silently touched Jesus' garment, thinking that would make her well, and it worked! (MK. 5:28). She was cured not by the piece of cloth, but by her faith in Jesus, which allowed his power to work a miracle in her.

> Relics are tangible reminders of the saints that help us to think of them & to ask for their prayers.

Read more
Relics: CCC 1674; CCCC 353; YOUCAT 275.

SCAN

3.17 Why pilgrimages and processions? What is a retreat?

Jesus invites us to follow him and to accompany him, just like his first disciples (Mk. 1:17). A pilgrim, someone who is making a pilgrimage, is on two journeys. On the one hand, he is on his way to a sacred place. Hopefully, while on the road he will grow in his relationship with God and get to know himself better. On the other hand, he, like all the faithful, is making his way on the road to heaven, which is the final goal of our pilgrimage on earth.

Destinations

- One very special pilgrim's destination is the Holy Land (SEE TWEET 2.31). There, you can pray in the very places where Jesus lived, taught, prayed, and suffered, as well as where he died and rose from the dead. At these sites the Gospels come to life!
- You can also go on a pilgrimage to a place associated with the Virgin Mary: Lourdes in France, Walsingham in England, and Częstochowa in Poland (SEE BOX). In the Americas are the Basilica of Our Lady of

Guadalupe in Mexico City, the National Shrine of the Immaculate Conception in Washington, D.C., and the site of the first officially recognized Marian apparition in the United States, Our Lady of Good Help in New Franken, WI. At these places you may especially pray for Mary's intercession (SEE TWEET 3.9).

- Shrines connected to well-known saints also attract pilgrims. Santiago de Compostela in Spain, where the remains of St. James the Apostle are believed to be buried, has been a popular destination for pilgrims since the Middle Ages. Every year thousands of people from all over the world walk for days, weeks, or even months to get there.

Processions

A procession is a mini-pilgrimage, in which one walks solemnly with prayer and singing, inside or outside a church building. There are different occasions for processions, which often take place through the streets of a city or village. When we join clergy and other believers on such a procedure, we are reminded of the fact that we are pilgrims: we are all God's people travelling toward heaven together.

- On Corpus Christi, the pope carries the Blessed Sacrament in a procession through the city of Rome, in the presence of bishops, priests, and thousands of other faithful. The same happens in many parishes all over the world (SEE TWEET 3.27).
- On Palm Sunday, the celebration of Mass does not start at the altar, but at a different place that is often outside the church building. Singing and praying, with blessed palm branches in hand, we celebrate Jesus' triumphal entry into Jerusalem (SEE TWEET 3.29).
- Many places also have processions to honor Mary or other saints. A statue of the saint is carried on a decorated litter, accompanied by people dressed in costumes and singing. Often, special organizations take charge of planning the procession.

Places of prayer

It is a good idea to withdraw from daily life from time to time by going on a retreat. You literally retreat from the world for a couple of days in order to reflect on what is truly important in life. Monasteries and religious communities are ideal places for retreats because you can join the prayers of the people who live there. These places of prayer and silence can help you to focus on God again. And what can be more important than that?

An empty frame

A famous image of Mary is the Black Madonna of Częstochowa in Poland. In 1966, Poland celebrated the one thousandth birthday of the nation, and the faithful wanted to carry a copy of this icon in a procession through the entire country. But at that time, Poland was under Communist rule. The Communists didn't want the Poles to celebrate this event and confiscated the image to prevent the procession.

Nevertheless, the procession started exactly as planned – only with an empty frame! Still, people flocked toward this empty frame everywhere it went to honor Mary and to worship God. This goes to show that the image or the icon or the place in itself is not the most important thing, but rather what it represents: God and the many ways he reveals himself to us through his saints.

Pilgrimages & processions remind us that life is a journey with God & others toward heaven. We retreat from daily life in order to pray.

Read more

Processions: CCC 1674–1676; CCCC 353; YOUCAT 276.

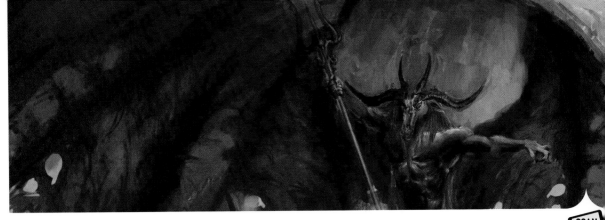

 ## 3.18 Are exorcisms to drive out devils real?

You sometimes hear scary stories of people possessed by demons or evil spirits. Filmmakers seem particularly interested in the topic. In their films you see lots of special effects as priests drive out devils and possessed persons make strange, dramatic gestures. As is often the case with films, real life is very different. Demons are angels who have rebelled against God (SEE TWEET 1.42). Their leader is the devil. In the Bible, Jesus drives out evil spirits, or demons, on a number of occasions (LK. 4:33–35). He gave his disciples authority to do the same (MK. 6:7). On one occasion, his disciples were unable to drive out an evil spirit, and Jesus had to do it himself. He said: "This kind cannot be driven out by anything but prayer and fasting" (MK. 9:29).

Being a sinner or being possessed

Everyone knows the experience of sin (SEE TWEET 1.4 AND 4.13). Being possessed by demons is something very different. The devil tempts us to sin by making something bad look good, but that does not mean he takes possession of us. When tempted, you can freely choose to sin, or with some strength of will, decide not to sin. Even if you sin, you can freely turn toward God again. Someone who is possessed by demons, on the other hand, has lost his will and can no longer control himself.

The exorcist

Real possessions are rare. Often there are medical or psychological explanations for the symptoms associated with demonic possession. Only when there is no such explanation does a parish priest refer someone to an exorcist.

An exorcist is a priest who has been appointed by his bishop to cast out demons. He has received special training to perform an exorcism in the tradition of the Apostles, who were authorized by Jesus to do this (Mt. 10:1). An exorcism is a particular prayer meant to cast out devils and to free people from demonic possession, restoring to them their freedom.

Before an exorcist begins this prayer, he performs an extensive investigation, together with doctors and psychiatrists, to determine whether the person is really possessed. An exorcism is a sacramental (SEE TWEET 3.15). In a simple form, an exorcism is performed at every Baptism: on behalf of the Church, the priest or the deacon prays that the person being baptized "be protected against the power of the evil one and withdrawn from his dominion" (CCC 1673).

But that is very different from the kind of exorcism where a demon has to be cast out. Signs that the devil is controlling a person's behavior include the ability of the person to speak in strange languages or unnatural voices, the inexplicable movement of material objects, and the presence of disgusting smells.

Defense against evil

The best defenses against evil powers are obedience to God and prayer. God is much more powerful than evil. Therefore, there is no reason to be scared of the devil. Whenever you experience temptation or fear of any kind, the best thing to do is to pray, invoking the name of Jesus. A sacramental such as a rosary, a crucifix, or holy water can help you to pray with confidence: these are all ways in which you give God the opportunity to be with you and to defend you. You can also pray to the archangel Michael, who defeated the devil and cast him out of heaven along with the other demons that had revolted against God (SEE BOX; TWEET 1.42). The most important thing is to stay close to God and to trust him completely!

> Demonic possession is rare but real. If there are no medical or psychological explanations, an exorcist can cast out demons through prayer.

Read more

Exorcisms: CCC 1673; CCCC 352; YOUCAT 273.

3.19 Muslims and Jews do not eat pork. What about Catholics?

The Old Testament says that pigs are unclean and may therefore not be eaten (Lev. 11:7). Jesus himself obeyed this Jewish law, which was later adopted by Islamic law (SEE TWEET 2.26). However, unlike Muslims and Jews, Catholics may eat pork. This is because Jesus declared all foods to be pure when he said: "Do you not see that whatever goes into a man from outside cannot defile him, since it enters, not his heart but his stomach, and so passes on?" (Mk. 7:18–19). In principle, as Catholics we are therefore free to eat anything, within reason, but we should be careful not to cause offense (Rom. 14:15).

Fish on Fridays

There are certain days, however, when Catholics make sacrifices in the food department in order to honor Jesus and to do penance for their sins. Because Jesus died on the cross on a Friday, we traditionally abstain from meat on every Friday of the year. This is a good practice even in places where it is not required by the local Bishops Conference (SEE TWEET 2.2). In the US, Catholics over the age of 14 are required to abstain at least on Ash Wednesday, the Fridays of Lent, and Good Friday. Even if you adore fish, choosing not to eat meat on Fridays because of Jesus, helps you to live more consciously with him. Two days of the year, all Catholics between the ages of majority and 60 are required to abstain as well as to fast, that is, to eat less food: Ash Wednesday and Good Friday (SEE TWEET 3.29).

More than food

After Jesus had fasted for 40 days in the desert and was tempted by the devil to turn stone into bread, he said: "Man shall not live by bread alone, but by every word that proceeds from the mouth of God" (Mt. 4:4). Thus Jesus shows us that there are more important things than food and drink, even though they can seem like the most essential things of all. To live consciously with and for God, it is good to have times when you fast, that is, eat and drink less. For this reason, the Church gives us Lent (SEE TWEET 3.29), the 40 days before Easter, as a season for fasting in imitation of Jesus.

In what other ways can I fast?

In addition to fasting from food and drink, there are many other ways of practicing self-denial. For example, you can take extra time for prayer or pay special attention to someone who needs it. Instead of watching TV or surfing the Internet, you can spend more time reading the Bible or some other book that leads you closer to God (SEE TWEET 1.10). You can decide to make more conscious choices. For example, before putting on some music, you can consider your options more carefully by asking: What is being said? Does this bring me closer to God or cause me to lose sight of him? You can also abstain from certain luxuries while praying for and giving alms to those who lack basic necessities.

Fasting constantly?

The purpose of fasting is not to lose weight or to improve your health (although that can be a pleasant side effect). The primary purpose of fasting is to grow closer to God. Hence Jesus said to fast without other people noticing (MT. 6:16–18). The money we save while fasting we can use to help those in need. Thus fasting and almsgiving, another Lenten practice, can go together. In addition to fasting from food and drink, we can also go without other things (SEE BOX). For example, we can live sustainably, by trying not to be wasteful. That way, we don't unduly burden our environment and leave more resources for others elsewhere in the world (SEE TWEET 4.48). Fasting therefore is not merely for Lent. We can make small sacrifices during the whole year – to keep God as our focus, to grow in freedom, and to care for others besides ourselves (SEE TWEET 1.37). The point is not to harm ourselves, but to live more conscious and self-disciplined lives. We do not so much impose limitations on ourselves as free ourselves from a lifestyle that is too limited. So many people appear to think that having a career, driving the latest car, wearing the best clothes, or eating the choicest food is what's most important. But as Christians, knowing that all those things are transitory, we see our lives from a different perspective: that of eternity. When we ask ourselves what lasts forever, our priorities fall into place. Our love for God and others, which begins here and now, lasts forever in heaven; and that is a joyful prospect. With that in mind, we Catholics do in fact celebrate with food and drink and merriment. In fact, we of all people have the greatest cause for celebration: God's tremendous love for us!

> By abstaining from meat on Fridays and by fasting we unite ourselves to Jesus' sacrifice and make room in our lives for God.

Read more

Days of fasting and abstinence: CCC 2043; CCCC 432; YOUCAT 345.

3.20 Why is a church the house of God?

SCAN

Jesus often went to the Temple in Jerusalem. As a twelve-year-old, he already considered it to be the house of God his Father (Lk. 2:49). Years later, when he saw that people were trading inside the Temple, he became furious and drove away the merchants. He said the house of God must be a "house of prayer", not a "den of robbers" (Mk. 11:17) nor a place for worldly affairs.

No need for a church?

As Christians we do not need the Temple of Jerusalem (SEE TWEET 1.16). With Jesus, there no longer is just one place on earth (the Temple) where we can meet God. Jesus himself is everywhere our Temple (Jn. 2:21), and we ourselves are temples of the Holy Spirit (I Cor. 6:19). All those who want to follow Jesus and are baptized form the Church (SEE TWEET 2.1). That is why St. Peter said: "Like living stones be yourselves built into a spiritual house" (I Pt. 2:5). Wherever you are – at home, in a car, on a mountain – there God is present (Ps. 139:8–10). You do not need a church to pray; but because

of the prayer of the community and especially Jesus' presence in the Eucharist, every church is the house of God and thus a unique place for prayer: here God is waiting for you. Similarly, the Mass can be celebrated in any place where you have bread, wine, and a priest. However, a church has been set apart specifically for the public gatherings and prayer of the community. For these reasons, the church building is important in your relationship with God.

Setting aside

The first Christians often came together to pray. If an Apostle visited them, they could also celebrate the Eucharist. That happened in a room at people's homes, because there weren't any churches yet (Acts 2:46). Soon the custom arose to reserve such a room for prayer and to stop using it for other purposes. What was celebrated there was so sacred that it made the room itself sacred. Thus the first churches were rooms and parts of houses that were set aside for praying to God and receiving the sacraments.

The best and most beautiful

The church is the house of God, where you can meet him. Therefore it is not surprising that a lot of attention has been paid throughout the centuries to the design of church buildings. Functionally, there are not many things required of a church: it must be large enough to house an entire community at prayer. Thus, a great deal of attention can be paid to the beauty of the building. If you build a hospital, on the other hand, there are many more practical demands to be met, making beauty a lesser concern. Function and form then are related. Since the function of a church is to worship God, it makes sense to make the building as beautiful as possible. The design and decor of churches have changed with the times (SEE TWEET 3.23). Different ages had different architectural and artistic styles. But, in every age, people strove to make the church the best, most beautiful example of the style of their day. Only the best and most beautiful building is worthy to be set aside as the house of God.

In daily life, we often reserve things for special uses: our nicest clothes for formal occasions, the best cutlery for dinner parties. Similarly we reserve things for religious uses. A rosary is blessed so it is no longer just a string of beads, but something sacred, that is, something dedicated to the worship of God (SEE TWEET 3.12 AND 3.15). Likewise, a church is consecrated before being used. A building made from stone, steel, and glass like other buildings is thereby set apart to become a meeting place between God and his people.

Coffee?

Down through the ages people have honored God by making their churches the best and most beautiful buildings of all (SEE BOX). Thus it makes sense to treat such places with respect. When we enter a Catholic church, we genuflect toward the tabernacle, where Jesus is physically present. If the tabernacle is not centrally placed and not visible when we enter the church we bow toward the altar instead (SEE TWEET 3.21). If we must speak inside a church, we whisper in order to preserve the silence needed for prayer (SEE TWEET 3.44). We organize social activities such as coffee hours, soup kitchens, or parish festivals outside the consecrated space. Catholics living within a certain geographical area, a parish, worship together as a community in a nearby church (SEE TWEET 2.2). The church building therefore brings us closer not only to God but also to each other.

> We can pray to God anywhere, but he is especially present in the places set apart by the community for prayer: churches & chapels.

Read more

House of God: CCC 1179–1181, 1186, 1197–1199; CCCC 244–245; YOUCAT 190.

SCAN

3.21 What are the most important places in a church?

When you walk into a dark Catholic church, your attention is immediately drawn to the flame of the (usually) red sanctuary lamp that burns day and night. This is in honor of Jesus, who is physically present in the Blessed Sacrament (SEE TWEET 3.14 AND 3.48). After the Eucharist is celebrated, the remaining Hosts are preserved in a beautiful box, the tabernacle. In an empty church this is the most important place. Not for nothing is it customary to genuflect as you pass before the tabernacle. During the celebration of the Eucharist three places play such an important role that they have assigned locations in the church.

Altar

A priest celebrates the Eucharist inside the sanctuary, where the altar is centrally placed. An altar is not just a table: it is the place where we are concretely connected with Jesus' sacrifice of his life, which he offered on the cross on Good Friday (SEE TWEET 1.28 AND 3.31). The altar is usually anchored to the ground and

symbolizes Jesus, who is the living stone on which our Church is built (I PT. 2:4). Therefore, we always bow before the altar as we pass (unless the tabernacle is behind it, in which

Pulpit

In older churches you often see a pulpit, that is, a raised platform or box in the church. When there were no microphones, the priest had to speak loudly. To ensure that everyone could hear him, he climbed into the pulpit. The roof above the pulpit helped the sound of his voice to bounce down to the congregation. Often it features an image of the Holy Spirit, by whom the priest is (hopefully!) inspired as he proclaims the Word of God.

case we genuflect [SEE TWEET 2.20]). To allow all the glory to go to Jesus, the altar is as empty as possible, even during the Mass. Flowers and other decorations should not be placed on the altar. Thus, the altar remains reserved for one purpose: the Holy Eucharist (SEE TWEET 3.44). In some older churches you will see several altars along the sides of the building. These date to a time when many priests were celebrating daily Masses separately. When priests celebrate Mass together around the same altar we speak of concelebration. Out of respect for Jesus' sacrifice, the priest kisses the altar at both the beginning and the end of Mass. He also incenses it several times in order to honor Jesus.

Lectern

During Mass, the Bible, the Word of God, is read from a lectern (or ambo). In some older churches it is read from a pulpit (SEE BOX). During the liturgy, the book with the Bible readings (the lectionary) rests on the lectern. Sometimes a separate book contains the readings from the Gospels. It is often beautifully decorated in honor of Jesus, the Word (SEE TWEET 1.29). There is a very special relation between Jesus' presence in the Word of God and his presence on the altar. As the altar is set apart for him, so is the lectern, from where we hear the readings, the homily, and the prayers of the faithful. For this reason, the lectern is sometimes called the table of the Word. Similar to the altar, the lectern is often flanked by candles and incense during the reading of the Gospel.

Chair

During Mass, a bishop or a priest is the celebrant. He directs prayers to God with us and for us, and he acts in the name and the person of Jesus. Because of this task, a special place has been reserved for him: during certain parts of the liturgy he sits in the celebrant's chair. If no tabernacle is in the center of the sanctuary behind the altar, then that is a proper place for the celebrant's chair. Otherwise, the chair stands usually to the right of the altar (when viewed from the congregation).

The place of the faithful is also important, so that they can participate actively in the liturgy. They are the people of God, along with the priest and the other ministers (LUMEN GENTIUM, 13). This is symbolically expressed when both the celebrant and the faithful are incensed.

Christ is present both in the priest and in every believer (I COR. 6:19). He is present in various ways during the liturgy: in the Word that is proclaimed from the lectern, in his Body and Blood on the altar, and within ourselves after we have received Communion.

> In the tabernacle Jesus is physically present. The altar, the lectern, and the chair of the bishop or priest are signs of Christ's presence.

Read more

Liturgical places: CCC 1182–1186; CCCC 246; YOUCAT 191.

3.22 What is the baptismal font?
Why are there statues in the church?

Inside the church building

In a church you can learn a lot about your faith just by looking around you. Every object tells you something about your relationship with God. If you walk into the church during a free moment, you can pray in peace. It is not just an unused space, but a house of God. Jesus himself is present here (SEE TWEET 3.20 AND 3.21).

Font

The baptismal font is where new life in Christ begins (SEE TWEET 3.36). This is where the water for Baptism is stored. Sometimes the font is located in a separate baptistery, decorated with biblical references to water and Baptism.

The traditional place for the font is the left rear of the church (from the congregation's point of view). When churches were built facing east, this location would be at the cold and dark north side of the building. The movement from the font to the altar symbolizes the route the baptized person follows: he leaves the darkness of a life without God and goes

with him into the light. Similarly, the paschal candle symbolizes the new life made possible by Jesus' Resurrection (SEE TWEET 1.50). This candle is lit solemnly at the beginning of the Easter Vigil (SEE TWEET 3.32). During the Easter Season it stands near the altar; for the rest of the year it is stationed at the baptismal font. At every Baptism the paschal candle is lit as a sign of the new life of the baptized in Christ, and his baptismal candle is lit from it.

Images and statues

Paintings, statues, and other images in a church are not idols. Just as photos in your home remind you of certain people, images are a way of remembering Jesus and the saints. We do not worship images but God alone. When we are kneeling before a statue or an icon of a saint, we are not worshipping the image or the saint it depicts. Rather, we are asking the saint to pray to God with us and for us, just as we ask our friends and relatives to pray for us (SEE TWEET 3.9). When we go before an image to pray, often there is a place to

Stations of the Cross

1. Jesus is condemned to death (Lk. 23:24).
2. Jesus takes the cross on his shoulders (Jn. 19:17).
3. Jesus falls the first time under the weight of the cross.
4. Jesus meets his mother, Mary (Jn. 19:25).
5. Simon of Cyrene helps Jesus to carry the cross (Mt. 27:32).
6. Veronica wipes the face of Jesus.
7. Jesus falls for the second time under the weight of the cross.
8. Jesus comforts the weeping women (Lk. 23: 27–31).
9. Jesus falls the third time under the weight of the cross.
10. Jesus is stripped of his clothes (Jn. 19:23).
11. Jesus is nailed to the cross (Mk. 15:24).
12. Jesus dies on the cross (Mk. 15:37).
13. The body of Jesus is taken from the cross (Lk. 23:53).
14. Jesus is laid in the tomb from which he shall rise in glory (Mt. 27:60).

....

pay a small fee for a candle. By paying for the candle, lighting it, and placing it before the image, we are adding a small sacrifice of our time and money to our prayers. When we return to our busy lives, we have the consolation that the candle continues to burn as a sign that our intentions continue to be made by the saint who is interceding for us (SEE TWEET 4.15).

Calvary

In almost every Catholic church you will see the 14 Stations of the Cross hanging on the wall. These images depict the Passion and death of Jesus in 14 steps (SEE BOX). Sometimes his Resurrection is added as a fifteenth station. By passing from station to station, from the sentencing of Jesus to his burial, we can pray and reflect on Jesus' great love for us. Thus, we are able in thought and prayer to experience his suffering and death with him. At each station, you can pray a short prayer: "We adore thee, O Christ, and bless thee. Because by thy holy cross thou hast redeemed the world."

The font is where a person is baptized & becomes a Christian. Statues & images help us to ask the saints to pray with us & for us.

Read more

Images: CCC 2129–2132, 2141; CCCC 446; YOUCAT 358.

Inside the church building

3.23 Where did different kinds of church architecture come from?

The church building is intended as a place where Christians, either as individuals or as a community, can worship God (SEE TWEET 3.24). The first Christians went to the synagogue, the Jewish house of prayer (SEE TWEET 1.16), to read from the Scriptures. Then they celebrated the Eucharist at someone's home (ACTS 2:46). Soon, a room in such a house was reserved for both reading the Scriptures and celebrating the Eucharist (SEE TWEET 3.20), and Christians no longer went to the synagogue.

Architectural styles

The oldest remains of a house church, whose ruins were found in modern Syria, date from approximately 235. In the fourth century the first large churches (Roman basilicas) were built by Emperor Constantine, of which St. John Lateran in Rome is a beautiful example (SEE TWEET 2.20). In the sixth century the Byzantine Hagia Sophia (Holy Wisdom) was built in Constantinople. The Romanesque style, with its round arches, emerged around the eighth century; you could say that it

is based on both Roman and Byzantine architecture. The famous Gothic cathedrals, which were built from the thirteenth century onward, allowed more light inside by adding more and larger windows (SEE TWEET 2.29), most of which were made of stained glass. The tall Gothic towers and pointed arches soared toward heaven. Chartres and Notre Dame in France and Salisbury Cathedral in England are wonderful examples. Renaissance architecture, which drew inspiration from classical antiquity, was followed by the sumptuously decorated Baroque: the Church of the Gesù in Rome is an example of this style (SEE TWEET 2.40).

Toward the third millennium

In the nineteenth century there was a return to architectural styles that had been successful in earlier ages. Renaissance architecture led the way to neoclassical churches (SEE TWEET 2.42). Gothic Revival was especially popular in lands where many new churches were needed, for example in England and the Netherlands, where Catholic bishops were again allowed crowds that it attracts. Other modern churches have been less warmly received by the faithful.

Places in the church

The most important place in the church is the sanctuary (SEE TWEET 3.21), which is sometimes separated by a rail, where the faithful may kneel to receive Communion. The largest part of the church, the nave, is the place where the faithful gather. Its name comes from the Latin word for ship, *navis*, because the Church is like the ark that saved Noah and his family from the flood (I PT. 3:20; SEE TWEET 1.22). When we enter the Church, our movement from the baptismal font toward the altar symbolizes the route of the baptized person: he leaves the darkness of a life without God and goes with him into the light. Confessionals are usually situated in the back or along the sides of the church. Some churches have special reconciliation rooms. As with the baptismal font (SEE TWEET 3.22), the placement is symbolic: from a place at the back of the church as a sinner, after receiving the Sacrament of Reconciliation (SEE TWEET 3.39), a Catholic approaches the sanctuary, ready to meet God.

to be appointed, and in the United States, which saw a rapid increase in the number of Catholic immigrants (SEE TWEET 2.44 AND 2.45). Architects such as the Englishman Augustus Pugin (†1852) had a great influence on the churches of this period. In the United States, the Romanesque Revival was another popular style in the nineteenth century. Modern church building uses the various shapes and styles that are now available to us, with varying results. The modern Divine Mercy Sanctuary in Krakow, Poland, is known to generate a sense of the sacred despite its large size and the vast

Although church architecture changed over time, the basic form of a church remained the same.

Read more

House churches: CCC 1179–1181, 1186, 1197–1199; CCCC 244–245; YOUCAT 190.

3.24 What is the liturgy?

Liturgy

We use not only our words but also our bodies to communicate. When we meet someone, we do not merely say hello but also extend a hand. When someone is down, we might give him a pat on the back or a hug along with a word of encouragement. Our body language expresses a great deal of what we mean.

God's hands

Knowing our nature (SEE TWEET 1.2), God has given us ways to worship that involve our whole bodies. You could say that the gestures we make during the liturgy are the body language we use to speak to God. *Liturgy* refers to the Church's public prayers. Through these, we join together with other Catholics to come into contact with God. There is a liturgy for each of the seven sacraments (SEE TWEET 3.35), for burial, for Eucharistic adoration (SEE TWEET 3.14), and for the daily prayer of the Church (SEE TWEET 3.13), for example. The word *liturgy* comes from the Greek word for "public service". Anyone can see and experience the liturgy of the Church. The ceremonies and the words are based in Scripture and Tradition (SEE TWEET 1.11). In the liturgy, all our senses are involved through singing, hearing music, smelling incense, kneeling, etc. Therefore, it is said that the liturgy is "the entirety of symbols, hymns, and actions by which the Church manifests and expresses its worship of God" (DOM GUÉRANGER). In the liturgy we express what we believe, and we receive God's grace (SEE TWEET 4.12).

A solid script

You may have noticed that the liturgy of the Roman Catholic Church is basically the same everywhere. For example, you can attend the Holy Mass in Africa or China and still understand what's happening without knowing the language. Everywhere the same liturgical books are used

Why all that fire and water?

In the liturgy there are all sorts of symbols filled with meaning. Jesus said that he is the light of the world (Jn. 8:12). The burning candles in the liturgy are signs that he is also the light of our lives. As incense is burnt, its fragrant smoke rises and fills the church with a sweet aroma. The smoke is a sign of our prayers ascending to God; the burning coals represent the offering of lives consecrated to him; and the pleasant odor expresses the sweetness of life with God.

At the Easter Vigil a fire is kindled, with which the paschal candle, representing the Risen Christ, is solemnly lit (SEE TWEET 3.32). With this candle, water is blessed for the Baptisms of those about to enter the Church (SEE TWEET 3.36). Especially during the Easter Season believers are sprinkled with holy water during Mass, and whenever you enter a Catholic church you bless yourself with holy water, making the Sign of the Cross (SEE TWEET 3.15). By these gestures we remember our own Baptisms.

(SEE BOX). Only the language differs: all the gestures and actions remain the same. By this uniformity throughout the world you can see very clearly that we all belong to the same Church. By everyone following the same script, so to speak, we show that there is something in the liturgy that is greater than ourselves. It is not the priest or the congregation who makes something happen. No, it is God who does it. The liturgy is not ours. Therefore, we should not change the actions or the words of the liturgy to suit ourselves.

Action!

The liturgy calls for action. First there is the action of celebrating the mysteries of our faith as a community. Then there is the action of expressing these mysteries in the way we live (SEE TWEET 3.50). Service to God (liturgy) and service to our fellow man (charity) are strongly linked. We are not Christians only for an hour on Sunday, but 24 hours a day, 7 days a week! Beggars know this, and that is why in large cities they are often standing outside church doors or joining in the coffee and the donuts after Mass.

> Liturgy is public prayer according to the rites of the Church. By this we express our faith in God and meet him in person.

Read more

Liturgy: CCC 1077–1112; CCCC 221–223; YOUCAT 167, 170–171.

3.25 What do these gestures, signs, and colors mean?

In the liturgy we take on many different postures, all of which express something of what we want to say (SEE TWEET 3.24).

Standing, bowing, and sitting

- Standing has been a posture for prayer since the early Christians, as a symbolic sign of resurrection. Therefore, we stand during some of the most important prayers of the liturgy. Out of respect for the Gospel, we stand when it is proclaimed.
- Bowing is another way to express reverence. We make a small bow of the head at the name of Jesus (and of Mary or a particular saint). If we do not kneel as we receive Communion, we make a profound bow (or genuflect) beforehand. The priest and those assisting him bow before the altar each time they pass before it. We too bow before the altar if when we enter a church the tabernacle is not centrally located (SEE TWEET 3.20).

- Sitting is a posture that expresses peace. Quietly and attentively we listen to the readings. We can pray while sitting, as we can in any position.
- Kneeling is a classic position for personal prayer and worship of God. Like the three wise men who adored the baby Jesus in Bethlehem, you too can humble yourself for Jesus (MT. 2:11). During important moments at Mass, we kneel before his presence in the Eucharist.
- Lying face-down, or prostration, is a sign of complete surrender to God. On Good Friday, the priest lies flat on the ground before the altar (SEE TWEET 3.31). And in the liturgy of ordination (SEE TWEET 3.41) candidates lie flat on the ground while the faithful call upon all the saints to pray for them.

Hands

We also can express a lot with our hands. When we pray, we join our hands: we use them for nothing else and focus completely on God. The early Christians often prayed

Liturgy

What are liturgical colors?

In various ecclesiastical feasts and celebrations, different colors are used for the vestments of the clergy and the liturgical space. These liturgical colors are linked to the reasons why we are together at that time (SEE TWEET 3.26).

- **White** is the color of light, purity, and glory. It is used for feast days (Christmas, Easter, and some saints' days). Sometimes gold or silver, representing triumph and joy, is used instead of or with white.
- **Red** represents the fire of the Holy Spirit (Pentecost), blood (Good Friday), and God's love. Red is also worn on the feasts of martyrs who were killed because of their faith in Christ.
- **Purple** is the color of penance and preparation in Advent and Lent (SEE TWEET 3.28–3.29). (On the Sundays halfway through these seasons rose, a mixture of white and purple, can be used.) Purple is also often used in funerals and on All Souls' Day.
- **Black**, for mourning, can be worn at funerals and on All Souls' Day (SEE TWEET 3.27).
- **Green**, for life and growth in the Lord, is used during all other celebrations throughout the year (SEE TWEET 3.27).

standing with their hands wide open, as a sign that they were ready to receive the grace (SEE TWEET 4.12) of God and that they themselves were empty-handed before him. This is the posture of the priest as he prays on behalf of the community. When the priest extends his hands over a person or an object, it is a sign of calling upon the Holy Spirit (SEE TWEET 1.31) as he implores God's blessing.

Gestures

At the beginning and the end of prayer we make the Sign of the Cross: we ask the Holy Trinity (SEE TWEET 1.33) to be with us and to help us. When the Gospel is read, we make a cross with the thumb on our forehead, on our lips, and then over our heart. Without words we ask to understand God's Word, to speak his Word, and to store it in our hearts. The liturgical kiss is a sign of respect. The priest kisses the altar, because it symbolizes Jesus himself. For the same reason he kisses the text of the Gospel after reading it aloud. We kiss relics at certain times to honor the saints and the feet of the Lord Jesus upon the crucifix on Good Friday (SEE TWEET 3.31).

> Standing is a Christian posture of prayer; bowing & kneeling express reverence. Sitting quietly & folded hands are also signs of prayer.

Read more

Signs and symbols: CCC 1145–1152, 1189; CCCC 236–237; YOUCAT 181. *Postures*: YOUCAT 486.

3.26 Does the Church have her own calendar?

The Church liturgical year does not start on January 1, but in late November or early December, four Sundays before we celebrate the birth of Jesus on Christmas. This feast is so important that we take four weeks (Advent) to prepare for it (SEE TWEET 3.28).

The preparation for the Resurrection of Jesus, which we celebrate at Easter, takes even longer, 40 days (Lent) (SEE TWEET 3.29). The Church gives us the liturgical year so that we can celebrate the most important moments in the life of Jesus. Attention is also paid to the feasts of Mary and other saints.

Feast days and Sundays
Liturgical feasts are not all equally important. Solemnities are the most important, then feasts, and then memorials. One day we may celebrate the memorial of a saint and the next day celebrate a feast of the Virgin Mary, for example. Sunday, also known as the Lord's Day, is the most important day of the week because Jesus rose from the dead on a Sunday.

Liturgically Sunday begins on Saturday evening. We have that custom from the Jews, for whom the next day begins at sunset of the previous day. Sundays and some solemnities are so important to us that on those days attendance at Mass is obligatory for Catholics (SEE TWEET 4.10). Hopefully, you do not go to church merely because you must, but because Mass is the opportunity to meet Jesus in a concrete way in the Eucharist (SEE TWEET 3.44).

Past, present, and future
During the liturgical year, we are simultaneously connected through Jesus with the past, the present, and the future. We can learn so much by looking back on salvation history, especially Jesus' life, death, and Resurrection (SEE TWEET 1.27). Now is the right time to say yes to God, to take his outstretched hand, and to be a follower of Jesus (SEE TWEET 4.50). As Christians, we also look forward not so much to the end of the world, but to the beginning of the new world, where we will be with God forever (SEE TWEET 1.50).

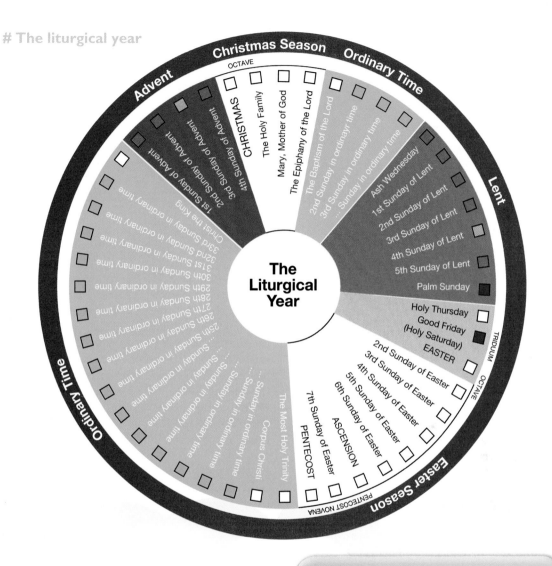

The Liturgical Year

Advent
- 1st Sunday of Advent
- 2nd Sunday of Advent
- 3rd Sunday of Advent
- 4th Sunday of Advent

Christmas Season
- OCTAVE
- CHRISTMAS
- The Holy Family
- Mary, Mother of God
- The Epiphany of the Lord

Ordinary Time
- The Baptism of the Lord
- 2nd Sunday in ordinary time
- 3rd Sunday in ordinary time
- ... Sunday in ordinary time

Lent
- Ash Wednesday
- 1st Sunday of Lent
- 2nd Sunday of Lent
- 3rd Sunday of Lent
- 4th Sunday of Lent
- 5th Sunday of Lent
- Palm Sunday
- Holy Thursday
- Good Friday
- (Holy Saturday)
- TRIDUUM
- EASTER
- OCTAVE

Easter Season
- 2nd Sunday of Easter
- 3rd Sunday of Easter
- 4th Sunday of Easter
- 5th Sunday of Easter
- 6th Sunday of Easter
- ASCENSION
- 7th Sunday of Easter
- PENTECOST
- PENTECOST NOVENA

Ordinary Time
- The Most Holy Trinity
- Corpus Christi
- Sunday in ordinary time
- Sunday in ordinary time
- Sunday in ordinary time
- ... Sunday in ordinary time
- 25th Sunday in ordinary time
- 27th Sunday in ordinary time
- 28th Sunday in ordinary time
- 29th Sunday in ordinary time
- 30th Sunday in ordinary time
- 31st Sunday in ordinary time
- 32nd Sunday in ordinary time
- 33rd Sunday in ordinary time
- Christ the King

The liturgical year begins four Sundays before Christmas. Holidays include important solemnities, feasts & memorials.

Read more

Liturgical year: CCC 1168–1171, 1194; CCCC 242; YOUCAT 186.
Liturgical time: CCC 1163–1167, 1193; CCCC 241; YOUCAT 187.

271

3.27 What kinds of feasts are there throughout the year?

Liturgy

Outside the seasons of Advent, Christmas, Lent, and Easter (SEE TWEET 3.26) is Ordinary Time. During Ordinary Time, the liturgical color is green, and the readings for Mass tell of the daily lives of Jesus and his disciples. In these verses we see and hear what Jesus did and said in order to teach us how we should live. The big events we celebrate on Christmas, Easter, and Pentecost have their proper effect only if we learn to walk daily with Jesus.

Baptism and light

The Solemnity of the Baptism of the Lord marks the transition from the Christmas Season to Ordinary Time. At the moment when Jesus was baptized by John in the Jordan, a voice came from heaven saying: "This is my beloved Son, with whom I am well pleased" (MT. 3:17). God also says that of everyone who is baptized. During Ordinary Time we are asked to learn step-by-step to live better as his children in our daily, or ordinary, lives. That is the time to apply what we celebrated during Advent and Christmas. After a first stretch of Ordinary

Time, the seasons of Lent and Easter follow. On the Monday after Pentecost, Ordinary Time resumes again. During the liturgical year we celebrate a number of important feasts of Mary (SEE TWEET 1.38), other saints (SEE TWEET 4.15), and angels (SEE TWEET 1.41). Unless otherwise indicated, the liturgical color for these feasts is white. On February 2, for example, we celebrate the Presentation, when Jesus was dedicated to God in the Temple according to Jewish custom, namely, 40 days after his birth. At that moment, Simeon recognized Jesus as the Savior and the light of all people (LK. 2:25–32; SEE TWEET 3.13). On this day the candles for the coming year are blessed and there is a procession with lighted candles. An old name for this feast is Candlemas.

Blessed Sacrament and Sacred Heart

On the first Sunday after Pentecost (SEE TWEET 3.34) we celebrate the Solemnity of the Holy Trinity (SEE TWEET 1.33). On the following Thursday or Sunday we celebrate the Solemnity of the Most Holy Body and Blood of Christ (or, Corpus

Gloria

Glory to God in the highest,
and on earth peace to people of good will.
We praise you,
we bless you,
we adore you,
we glorify you,
we give you thanks for your great glory,
Lord God, heavenly King,
O God, almighty Father.
Lord Jesus Christ, Only Begotten Son,
Lord God, Lamb of God, Son of the Father,
you take away the sins of the world,
   have mercy on us;
you take away the sins of the world,
   receive our prayer;
you are seated at the right hand of the
      Father,
   have mercy on us.
For you alone are the Holy One,
you alone are the Lord,
you alone are the Most High, Jesus Christ,
with the Holy Spirit, in the glory of God the
      Father. Amen.

we celebrate the Sacred Heart of Jesus. This solemnity recognizes the great goodness of his heart, both human and divine, overflowing with love for us, especially when he gave his life on the cross (SEE TWEET 1.26).

All Saints' and All Souls'

The saints have their own feast days. For example, on October 4 we celebrate St. Francis of Assisi. He was so full of the good news of Christ that he preached even to the birds! In many places pets are blessed on his feast day. On All Saints' Day, November 1, we remember all holy men and women, both known and unknown, who are in heaven. We ask them to pray for us because they are with God. November 2 is All Souls' Day, when we pray for all the deceased. The liturgical color is purple (or black). On the last Sunday of the liturgical year we celebrate Christ the King. Our God is the King of Kings, who not only rules the universe with laws but especially with love. He even calls us, his faithful subjects, his friends. He reigns on earth and also in heaven. He is so worthy of adoration that we again and again praise him by singing the Gloria (SEE BOX).

Christi). This day is dedicated to the great gift of the Eucharist (SEE TWEET 3.14). Often a procession is held, in which the displayed Host, Jesus' Body, is visible to everyone, and we walk with him through the streets (SEE TWEET 3.17). Twelve days after Holy Trinity, on a Friday,

There are many feasts that celebrate Jesus, the angels, Mary, and the other saints. These help us to bring glory to God by our lives.

Read more

Liturgical year: CCC 1168–1171, 1194; CCCC 242; YOUCAT 186. *Remembrance of saints*: CCC 1172–1173, 1195; CCCC 242.

SCAN

3.28 Is Christmas the greatest feast or holiday of the year?

The liturgical year begins with Advent, which consists of four weeks of preparation and reflection, of hope and expectation. The readings focus attention on God's promises of the Messiah (SEE TWEET 1.26) in the Old Testament, which the birth of Jesus finally fulfilled. The liturgical color of Advent is purple (SEE TWEET 3.25). The Gloria (SEE TWEET 3.27) is not sung until Christmas Eve. On the third Sunday (the joyful Gaudete Sunday) we are halfway to Christmas, and therefore rose, the color halfway between purple and white, can be used (SEE TWEET 3.25). During Advent we are expecting the birth of our Savior, Jesus Christ, at Christmas, but also anticipating his Second Coming at the end of time (SEE TWEET 1.50).

Christmas

The angel of the Lord announced on Christmas: "To you is born this day in the city of David a Savior, who is Christ the Lord" (LK. 2:11). After Easter and Pentecost, Christmas is the biggest feast or solemnity of the Christian year. In the *Roman Missal*, a total of four different Christmas Masses are available, with proper (particular) readings and prayers for the Vigil Mass, the Midnight Mass, the Mass at Dawn and Christmas Day Mass. In practice, the Midnight and Christmas Day Masses are the ones said most often. At Christmas, the Gloria that has not sounded during all of Advent is again joyfully sung to honor God (LK. 2:14, SEE TWEET 3:27). During the Creed we kneel at the words: "For us men and for our salvation he came down from heaven, and by the Holy Spirit was incarnate of the Virgin Mary, and became man" (SEE TWEET 1.31) or "who was conceived by the Holy Spirit, born of the Virgin Mary" (SEE TWEET 1.33).

Octave of Christmas

So that what we celebrate can really penetrate our being, there are eight liturgical days of Christmas. We call this the Christmas Octave, which lasts from December 25 through January 1. The day after Christmas we honor St. Stephen, the first martyr who died for Christ (ACTS 7:54–60). On December 27

with the Solemnity of Mary, the Mother of God (JAN. 1).

Epiphany

January 6 (or the Sunday near it) is the Epiphany of the Lord, when we celebrate how Jesus was revealed as the Messiah to the three magi. These wise men from the East read in the stars that a great king was to be born to the Jews and then followed a star that led them to the Christ Child in Bethlehem. They knelt before Jesus and honored him. Their gifts say a lot about Jesus: gold for a king, frankincense for a priest, and myrrh for embalming the dead (MT. 2:11). In many countries, Epiphany cake, or king cake, is baked with a bean or a charm inside. The person who finds it in his piece of cake is crowned king for the day. On the doors of houses that are blessed on Epiphany, you often see written "C+M+B" with two numbers representing the year on either side. This is an acronym not only for the traditional names of the three wise men – Caspar, Melchior, and Balthasar – but also for the Latin words *Christus Mansionem Benedicat*: "May Christ bless the house."

we celebrate St. John the Evangelist, and on December 28 we remember the Holy Innocents, the boys in Bethlehem of less than two years old who were killed by order of Herod (MT. 2:16). On the Sunday after Christmas we celebrate the Holy Family of Jesus, Mary, and Joseph. The new calendar year begins

> After Easter and Pentecost, Christmas is the greatest feast day in the Catholic Church.

Read more

Christmas: CCC 525–526, 563; CCCC 103.

3.29 Why do we fast for 40 days during Lent?

The 40 days before Easter (Lent) is a time of repentance. Aware that we are sinners in need of God's forgiveness and grace (SEE TWEET 4.12), we confess our sins (SEE TWEET 3.39), fast (SEE TWEET 3.19), pray, and do works of mercy (SEE TWEET 3.50) in order to undo the harm we have done. We fast in imitation of Jesus, who fasted in the wilderness for 40 days (MT. 4:1–2; SEE BOX).

Just as during Advent, the atmosphere of the liturgy during Lent is subdued: the festive Alleluia and Gloria are not sung (SEE TWEET 3.27); there are no flowers; and the music is less exuberant. The liturgical color is purple. Halfway through Lent, on the fourth Sunday (the joyful Laetare Sunday), rose can be used (SEE TWEET 3.25).

According to ancient custom, on the fifth Sunday of Lent (formerly Passion Sunday), the images and statues in the church are often covered as a sign of repentance and mourning.

Ash Wednesday

Lent begins on Ash Wednesday. There is a bit of partying in many Catholic places beforehand – exuberant eating and drinking during Carnival (from two Latin words meaning so much as "good-bye meat") or on Mardi Gras (French for "Fat Tuesday"). The blessed ashes used in the celebration of Ash Wednesday are made by burning palm branches (SEE TWEET 3.15) from the previous year's Palm Sunday. With the ashes crosses are made on the foreheads of the faithful with the words: "Remember that you are dust, and to dust you shall return" (GEN. 3:19) or "Repent, and believe in the gospel" (MK. 1:15). In brief, these expressions tell us: "Life is short; use it well."

Preparation

On Ash Wednesday we firmly resolve to join in the penitence of Lent by praying more, fasting, and doing good works for other people (MAT. 6, 2–18). Through all this, we desire to repent of our sins and to prepare for Easter. It is the perfect time to receive the Sacrament of Reconciliation (SEE TWEET 3.38). The 40 days before Easter is the final period of preparation for the catechumens, those who are going to be baptized at Easter. During Lent there are special prayers for them, and they are formally given copies of the Gospels, the Creed, and the Our Father.

Palm Sunday, or Passion Sunday

Palm Sunday Mass begins with the Gospel about the entry of Jesus into Jerusalem, where he was given a royal welcome. We then accompany him, like the inhabitants of Jerusalem, in a procession with palm branches, singing "Hosanna" (MT. 21:8–9).

After the procession, the atmosphere changes, and we hear the Passion of Jesus, beginning with the Last Supper and ending with his death on the cross. During his trial before Pilate, the crowd that had cheered him as he entered the city turned against him and called for his execution: "Crucify him!" (SEE MT. 27:22). Jesus was then scourged, mocked, forced to carry his own cross, and crucified (SEE TWEET 1.28). Because of his sufferings, the liturgical color is red, and this day is also called Passion Sunday. The Church congregation takes their palm branches home with them, to place behind a crucifix or other image (SEE TWEET 3.15).

After the Palm Sunday Mass, in certain countries children visit the elderly and sick. They give them a palm branch formed into a cross and decorated with sweets and a bun in the shape of a rooster.

> We fast during Lent because Jesus fasted in the wilderness. We can also set aside other things we like to do in order to grow closer to him.

Read more

Lent: CCC 538–540, 566; CCCC 106; YOUCAT 88. *Palm Sunday*: CCC 560.

SCAN

 ## 3.30 What is the Easter Triduum, which starts on Holy Thursday?

The last week of Lent, Holy Week, begins with Palm Sunday and ends with Holy Saturday. This week is holy because it recalls when Jesus suffered and died for our salvation (SEE TWEET 1.28).

The Easter, or Paschal, Triduum is the three-day observance of the Passion, death, and Resurrection of Jesus, which begins the evening of Holy Thursday and ends on Easter Sunday. During the Triduum we celebrate the core of our faith. The high point is the Easter Vigil, which begins Holy Saturday night and is the celebration of Christ's Resurrection from the dead. During these days we celebrate the essence of our Christian faith.

Chrism Mass

On Holy Thursday the Church celebrates Jesus' institution of both the Eucharist and the priesthood. On the morning of Holy Thursday (or earlier in Holy Week) the priests of the diocese gather together with their bishop for a solemn Mass in order to renew their priestly vows. In this Chrism Mass the three oils needed for the sacraments in the coming year are blessed (SEE BOX).

Eucharist

On the evening of Holy Thursday we celebrate the feast of three great gifts that Jesus has given to the Church: the Eucharist (SEE TWEET 3.44), the priesthood (SEE TWEET 3.41), and the love of God that overcomes death (SEE TWEET 1.26). As a sign of celebration, the liturgical color is white.

We remember how Jesus instituted the Eucharist at the Last Supper with his friends, as described by the Evangelists Matthew, Mark, and Luke. It is striking that John said nothing in his Gospel about the important moment when Jesus changed the bread and wine into his Body and Blood, but he mentioned other things Jesus did that night. When Jesus washed the Apostles' feet, he did the work of a humble servant (JN. 13:2–17). Then, calling them his friends, he commanded them

Holy oils

In the Chrism Mass, three vessels with pure olive oil are blessed by the bishop. These oils are used during the year to administer the sacraments. Each parish is given small amounts of the oils, which are kept in a special place in the church.

- **Oil of the catechumens** is used to anoint those preparing to be baptized. We pray that they may be protected from evil by the power of Christ (SEE TWEET 3.36).
- **Oil of the sick** is used in the Sacrament of the Anointing of the Sick. We pray for the spiritual strength the sick person may need to endure his suffering in union with Christ and for healing (SEE TWEET 3.40).
- **Holy chrism** includes balsam, a fragrant resinous substance produced by various plants. The bishop breathes over it to signify Jesus giving the Holy Spirit to the Church. Chrism is used in the Sacraments of Baptism, Confirmation, and Ordination (SEE TWEET 3.36, 3.37 AND 3.41).

so, during the liturgy of Holy Thursday, after the homily, the priest lays aside his vestment and washes the feet of 12 people. Jesus' love thus becomes very visible, and we are inspired anew to follow his example (JN. 13:15). Would you be willing to have your feet washed by Jesus? It may seem very strange and difficult to accept. In that, you are not alone: St. Peter also struggled to accept the love of Christ in this way (JN. 13:6–10).

Jesus' prayer

Toward the end of the liturgy, the vessel containing the Hosts is placed on the altar and incensed. Leaving the tabernacle empty and open (SEE TWEET 3.21), the priest processes with the Blessed Sacrament to a temporary altar, where it will stay until Easter. This altar of repose, nicely decorated with candles and flowers, is to remind us of the Garden of Gethsemane, where in agony Jesus awaited his arrest. He asked his Apostles to stay awake and to pray with him, and he invites us to do this too: "Watch and pray that you may not enter into temptation; the spirit indeed is willing, but the flesh is weak" (MT. 26:41).

> Jesus suffered, died, and rose again in three days (Triduum). On Holy Thursday we commemorate the institution of Eucharist & priesthood.

to do the same. Thus, Jesus showed that the Eucharist is directly connected to loving and to serving one's neighbor (SEE TWEET 3.50). And

Read more

Last Supper: CCC 610–611, 621; CCCC 120; YOUCAT 99.

3.31 Do I really have to go to church on Good Friday?

At three o'clock in the afternoon on the first Good Friday, hanging from the cross, Jesus cried out: "Father, into your hands I commit my spirit" (Lk. 23:44–46). After these words, he died to give us life. Since then, three o'clock in the afternoon is seen as the "hour of mercy", of love in the extreme. That is the "good" in Good Friday (SEE TWEET 1.26).

Solemn liturgy
On Good Friday we celebrate an essential part of our faith in Jesus: had he not suffered and died for us, his Resurrection on Easter Sunday would not have been possible (SEE TWEET 3.33). It is very important for our relationship with Jesus that on this day, the most difficult in his life, we take some time to go to church. If you have to work or go to school on Good Friday, you may still use your lunch break to pray the Stations of the Cross. Even more important is to attend the solemn liturgy of Good Friday.

Looked at superficially, the Good Friday liturgy may appear long and gloomy, but when we grasp the love Jesus poured out for us on the cross, the service is particularly beautiful and moving. When we enter the church on Good Friday, we notice that the holy water fonts are empty and the statues are covered. There are no candles burning, and the organ is silent. The altar is empty and bare; there are no decorations. The empty and open tabernacle mournfully confirms: Jesus has died.

The Passion and intercession
The Good Friday liturgy begins when the priest and his assistants arrive in silence, dressed in red vestments, and lie down flat on the ground before the altar (complete prostration) (SEE TWEET 3.25). All others kneel. After the first reading (Isa. 52:13—53:12) and the second reading (Heb. 4:14—16; 5:7–9), the account of the Passion and death of Christ from the Gospel of John is read (Jn. 18:1—19:42). When we hear that Jesus has died, all kneel. Next is a series of solemn intercessions for the Church, those preparing for Baptism, the unity of Christians, the Jewish people, those who do

Holy Saturday

The day after Good Friday is Holy Saturday. This day is often forgotten, but it is not just a day for the final preparing and shopping before Easter. It is most of all a day to be with Jesus, who truly died. Through his death, he conquered death and defeated the devil, "him who has the power of death" (CCC 635). Jesus "went down into the depths of death", not only for Christians but also for those who lived before Christ (JN. 5:25; SEE TWEET 1.45). Jesus saved all men of all times and all places who desire reconciliation with God (CCC 634). On Holy Saturday, we can reflect on the Passion and death of Christ. On this day, there is no celebration of the Eucharist, and the altar remains empty until the solemn celebration of the Easter Vigil. We continue our Lenten fasting until the Easter Vigil (SEE TWEET 3.29). Until about 1955, the Easter Vigil was celebrated in the morning of Holy Saturday, and fasting was over at noon, when church bells were rung. Just like the first Christians, we now celebrate the Easter Vigil after sundown (SEE TWEET 3.32).

not believe in God, those in public office, and all those in special need.

Adoration of the cross and Communion

Adoration of the cross follows. A crucifix is solemnly carried between two burning candles. The priest displays the cross to all as a sign of the superhuman sacrifice that Jesus took upon himself for us (SEE TWEET 1.28). Up to three times, the following prayer is sung: "Behold the wood of the cross, on which hung the salvation of the world." All answer: "Come, let us adore." All kneel for a while in silent adoration. Then, as a sign of our love for Jesus, we go forward to kiss the cross. It is good to be aware that Jesus asks everyone to take up his cross and follow him (MK. 8:34). Jesus' sacrifice on the cross and the sacrifice of the Mass are one and the same (SEE TWEET 1.26). Because of that, even on this day of remembrance of his death, we can receive the Eucharist, which was stored on a temporary altar on Holy Thursday (SEE TWEET 3.30). After the final prayer, the priest leaves in silence. The cross remains behind in an empty, dark church, lit only by two candles, as a subtle sign that the light of God will overcome even the darkest evil.

On Good Friday Jesus died for you. Do you need a better reason to take some time to go to church on this day?

Read more

Paschal sacrifice: CCC 613–617, 622–623; CCCC 122; YOUCAT 101. *Taking up our cross*: CCC 618; CCCC 123; YOUCAT 102.
Christ opens the doors of heaven for us: CCC 634–635; CCCC 125.

SCAN

3.32 What happens during the Easter Vigil?

Christians have long had the tradition of gathering during the night Jesus rose from the dead. They spent this night praying, singing, and reading from the Scriptures. The Eucharist was celebrated at dawn because Jesus rose just before sunrise. It was still dark when the women went to his grave and heard: "He is not here; for he has risen, as he said" (Mt. 28:5–6). The Easter Vigil is the most important feast of the liturgical calendar. Only through his Resurrection does all that Jesus said and did make sense (SEE TWEET 1.50). Through his Resurrection, he promises eternal life to us, too!

The liturgy of light

We begin the Easter Vigil liturgy by gathering together in the darkness of night. A fire is made outside or inside the church and is blessed. This is used to light the paschal candle, which symbolizes Christ, our Light (SEE BOX). A deacon or priest carries the candle through the otherwise dark church, singing three times, "The Light of Christ." Then everyone responds, "Thanks be to God." The little candles of the people assembled are then lit from that one flame of the paschal candle, and all of a sudden, the dark church is filled with light.

The Liturgy of the Word

During the Easter Vigil, seven texts from the Old Testament are read, showing how God's plan for the salvation for mankind unfolded over time (SEE TWEET 1.27). Each reading is followed by a psalm and a prayer. The readings include the story of Creation (GEN. 1:1–2:2; SEE TWEET 1.3), the sacrifice of Abraham (GEN. 22:1–18; SEE TWEET 1.23), and the escape from slavery in Egypt (Ex. 14:15–15:1; SEE TWEET 1.24). Also read are passages from the prophets about the New Jerusalem (ISA. 54:5–14; SEE TWEET 1.45), the salvation of all peoples (ISA. 55:1–11; SEE TWEET 1.26), the source of wisdom (BAR. 3:9–15;32; 4:4), and the new heart and the new soul that God wants to give us (EZ. 36:16–17A; 18–28). Then, the Gloria is sung (SEE TWEET 3.27). Like the Alleluia, it has not been sung since the start of Lent. All the lamps are lit, along with the

Baptism and the Eucharist

Easter is the prime moment for Christian
initiation (SEE TWEET 3.35). When those who are
to be baptized stand with the priest before the
baptismal font, we ask for God's blessing over
the baptismal water. With the Litany of the
Saints, we ask the saints one by one to pray for
those to be baptized and for all of us. During
the prayer by which the priest blesses the
water, we hear the story of the history of our
salvation (SEE TWEET 1.27). After the catechumens
(candidates for Baptism) have renounced evil
and the devil, and have professed Jesus as their
Savior, they are baptized and confirmed (SEE
TWEET 3.36–37). Then all the faithful renew their
baptismal vows. As a sign of the new life that
began with Baptism, everyone is sprinkled
with the new baptismal water. During the night
Jesus was brought to life again by God, and he
promised that we, too, will be resurrected. In a
manner of speaking, through Baptism we die
and are resurrected with Christ and start a new
life with him (SEE TWEET 3.36). The Easter Vigil
is then completed with a joyful and solemn
celebration of the Eucharist.

candles on the altar, and the church bells are
rung. This is the greatest celebration of the
year, for during this night, Jesus truly rose
from the dead! Then we hear St. Paul's words
that Christ, once risen, will not die again (ROM.
6:3–11). Before the Gospel is read, the Alleluia is
sung triumphantly: "Alleluia! Christ is risen!"

> The Easter Vigil celebrates Jesus'
> resurrection with candles, readings
> about God's plan of salvation,
> Baptism & Eucharist.

Read more

Baptismal water: CCC 1217. *Paschal Mystery*: CCC 1085; CCCC 222; YOUCAT 171.
Resurrection: CCC 639–647, 656–657; CCCC 127–128; YOUCAT 105–106.

3.33 How important is Easter? What is the "Urbi et Orbi"?

Great Church feasts

Easter is the most important feast of the liturgical year. On this day, we celebrate the foundation of our faith. Because Jesus rose on a Sunday, every Sunday is somewhat like Easter: a day we remember and celebrate his Resurrection. St. Paul wrote: "If Christ has not been raised, your faith is futile and you are still in your sins" (I Cor. 15:17). But Jesus has risen: that is the great joy of Easter. Eastertide lasts for 50 days, and its liturgical color is white.

Resurrection

The festive celebration of the Eucharist on Easter morning is aimed at a joyful, exuberant remembrance of the Resurrection of Jesus, the Lord. We are sprinkled with water that was blessed during the Easter Vigil, as a reminder of our own Baptism (see Tweet 3.32). Through Baptism, our sins are forgiven and we become children of God (see Tweet 3.36). On Easter morning (as on the first day of Christmas) the pope appears on the balcony of St. Peter's Basilica in Rome to bless the city and the world (in Latin: *urbi et orbi*) (see box).

Easter Lamb

With Easter, as with Christmas, one day of celebration is not enough for us to internalize the enormity of God's gift to us. Therefore the Church gives us eight days, an octave, to celebrate Easter. During the liturgy on these days, before the Alleluia and the Gospel, a festive sequence is sung or recited in honor of Jesus, our Paschal Lamb (see box). The Latin word *pascha* means "Passover", which is the Jewish celebration of their Exodus from Egypt (see Tweet 1.24). Jesus is the lamb that was slain to save us from death like the lambs that were sacrificed to save the Jewish people with their blood (see Tweet 1.26).

But Easter is more than a continuation of the Jewish Passover. It is also something entirely new: instead of delivering us from slavery to Pharaoh, the death of Jesus frees us from slavery to sin. Instead of leading us out of Egypt and into the Promised Land, the Resurrection of Jesus leads us to eternal life with God.

Easter Sequence (Victimae Paschali)

Christians, to the Paschal Victim
Offer your thankful praises!
A Lamb the sheep redeems;
Christ, who only is sinless,
Reconciles sinners to the Father.
Death and life have contended in that combat stupendous:
The Prince of life, who died, reigns immortal.
Speak, Mary, declaring
What you saw, wayfaring.
"The tomb of Christ, who is living,
The glory of Jesus' resurrection;
bright angels attesting,
The shroud and napkin resting.
Yes, Christ my hope is arisen;
to Galilee he goes before you."
Christ indeed from death is risen, our new life obtaining.
Have mercy, victor King, ever reigning!
Amen. Alleluia.

Divine Mercy Sunday

The Easter Octave is concluded on the Sunday after Easter. Pope John Paul II has dedicated this day to Divine Mercy. The mercy and love of God, who gave us his only Son, become fully apparent at Easter (Jn. 3:16). The Polish sister St. Faustina Kowalska (†1938) learned from Jesus himself how everyone can rely on God's mercy through faith and prayer. For that faith to be real, it should always be joined by acts of charity (see Tweet 4.7).

Jesus' death & Resurrection are the center of our faith & salvation. On Easter, the pope blesses the city of Rome and the world.

Read more

Baptismal water: ccc 1217. *Paschal Mystery*: ccc 1085; cccc 222; youcat 171.
Resurrection: ccc 639–647, 656–657; cccc 127–128; youcat 105–106.

3.34 When do we celebrate Ascension and Pentecost?

After his Resurrection, Jesus appeared to his disciples for a period of 40 days, speaking to them about the Kingdom of God (Acts 1.3). For those who were baptized at Easter, and for all Catholics, these days are a period of continued reflection on the new life in Christ offered by the Church, as can be seen in the readings at Mass.

Ascension

On the fortieth day of Easter (40 days after Easter Sunday), we commemorate Jesus' Ascension into heaven. On that day, Jesus led his disciples to a place outside of the city: "While he blessed them, he parted from them, and was carried up into heaven" (Lk. 24:51). From that moment Jesus could be present to anyone, anywhere, anytime. The Church celebrates the solemnity of the Ascension on Thursday, nine days before Pentecost. Sometimes Ascension is transferred to the next Sunday. The liturgical color during this festive celebration is white.

Novena

After Jesus ascended into heaven (Acts 1:14), the disciples returned to Jerusalem, where they prayed and waited for the coming of the Helper, the Holy Spirit Jesus had promised them (Jn. 16:7; Acts 1:8). For us too, the days between Ascension and Pentecost are an important time of preparation and prayer. Having already received the Holy Spirit through Baptism and Confirmation, we pray for a greater share of his gifts. These nine days of prayer are the Novena of Pentecost. You can pray novenas anytime. To do that, you pray a certain prayer for nine days, usually with a special request in mind. You may start a novena nine days before an important event (an exam, an operation, etc.) or before the feast day of the saint to whom you are praying.

Pentecost

On the fiftieth day of Easter, we celebrate when the Holy Spirit descended upon the Apostles and the Virgin Mary on Pentecost. Filled by the Holy Spirit, the Apostles could

Sequence for Pentecost
(Veni, Sancte Spiritus)

Come, Holy Spirit, come!
And from your celestial home
Shed a ray of light divine!

Come, Father of the poor!
Come, source of all our store!
Come, within our bosoms shine.

You, of comforters the best;
You, the soul's most welcome guest;
Sweet refreshment here below;

In our labor, rest most sweet;
Grateful coolness in the heat;
Solace in the midst of woe.

O most blessed Light divine,
Shine within these hearts of yours,
And our inmost being fill!

Where you are not, we have naught,
Nothing good in deed or thought,
Nothing free from taint of ill.

Heal our wounds, our strength renew;
On our dryness pour your dew;
Wash the stains of guilt away:

Bend the stubborn heart and will;
Melt the frozen, warm the chill;
Guide the steps that go astray.

On the faithful, who adore
And confess you, evermore
In your sevenfold gift descend;

Give them virtue's sure reward;
Give them your salvation, Lord;
Give them joys that never end. Amen.

....

no longer remain silent about the love of God for all people (Acts 2:4). They simply had to spread the good news about Jesus. Everyone who asked to be baptized after hearing their words was accepted into the community of the Church: "And they held steadfastly to the apostles' teaching and fellowship, to the breaking of the bread and to the prayers" (Acts 2:42).

Today, the Holy Spirit is still assisting the Church and helping the faithful to believe in Christ and to do good works in his name (see Tweet 1.32 and 4.8). He helps us to spread the good news about Jesus (see Tweet 4.50) and to do the Will of God on earth. After Easter, Pentecost is the most important feast of the year for the Church. The liturgical color is red, the color of fire, love, and the power of the Holy Spirit (see Tweet 3.25). Before the Alleluia and the Gospel, the Sequence for Pentecost is sung (see box). At the end of Mass, just as during the Easter Octave (see Tweet 3.33), we hear once more: "Go in the peace of Christ. Alleluia, alleluia!" With Pentecost, the Easter Season has ended. Afterward, the paschal candle no longer burns during the liturgy.

Jesus ascended to heaven 40 days after Easter; 9 days later the Apostles received the Holy Spirit at Pentecost.

Read more
Ascension: ccc 659–662; cccc 132; youcat 109. *Pentecost*: ccc 731–732, 2623; cccc 144; youcat 118.

3.35 What are the sacraments?

God knows that we cannot get close to him without his help. That's why Jesus instituted the sacraments. Through a sacrament, God is with us in a very concrete way and gives us his grace, which is a share in his own life (SEE TWEET 4.12). Sacraments are a kind of doorway through which God gives us access to himself.

Outside and inside
In a way, every sacrament has an outside and an inside: the outside is what you see and hear the priest or deacon do. The inside of the sacrament is the grace that God gives you at the moment the sacrament is administered. You cannot see the inside, but it is there. It is therefore said of the sacraments that they are a visible sign of an invisible reality. For example, during a Baptism you can see that water is poured over a person's head (the visible sign), but you cannot see that he thereby becomes a child of God (the invisible reality) (SEE TWEET 3.36).

Different sacraments?
Our Church has seven sacraments, which can be divided into three groups (SEE BOX).
- Sacraments of *initiation* bring you into the life of God: Baptism, Confirmation, and Eucharist. These three sacraments form the foundation of life in Christ.
- Sacraments of *healing* help when we are struggling in our relationship with God or when we need extra strength. In the Sacrament of Reconciliation, God himself forgives our sins. In the Anointing of the Sick, God heals the sick person or gives him strength to bear his suffering.
- Sacraments at the *service of communion* are Marriage, through which a man and a woman dedicate themselves to each other in Christ, and Holy Orders, whereby a man dedicates himself completely to God in order to continue the ministry of Jesus, by preaching and administering the sacraments.

Some sacraments can be received only once: Baptism, Confirmation, and Holy Orders.

The seven sacraments

For all Catholics			
	BAPTISM	**We are born:** we start a new life with Jesus, freed from sin, as members of the Church.	Initiation
	CONFIRMATION	**We grow up:** the Holy Spirit binds us to the Church in a special way and makes us adult Christians.	Initiation
	EUCHARIST	**We are fed:** Jesus offers us his own life, Body and Blood, as food.	
	RECONCILIATION	**We are forgiven:** God forgives us our sins, for which we ask pardon.	Healing
	ANOINTING OF THE SICK	**We are healed:** we are given strength, hope, and comfort from God when faced with disease or even death.	Healing

Particular callings			
	MARRIAGE	**We form a family:** a man and a woman form an intimate union of love and life before God, and welcome children as gifts of God.	Service of communion
	HOLY ORDERS	**We are given leaders:** God gives us men whom he himself has called to administer the sacraments in his name.	Service of communion

Marriage can be received again only by a person whose spouse has died. The other sacraments – Eucharist, Reconciliation, and Anointing of the sick – can be received again and again, whenever you need the grace of God.

The Church

Jesus entrusted administering the sacraments to the Apostles and their successors, the bishops, who are assisted by priests and deacons (SEE TWEET 2.15). In that way the Church was given the responsibility to ensure that the faithful have access to God's grace. Thankfully, Jesus did not make himself completely dependent on human weakness. It is so important to God that we can receive his grace, that he himself ensures the sacraments are efficacious if performed with the correct words, matter, and intention. The grace of the sacraments is not dependent on the virtue or holiness of the priest administering them (SEE TWEET 2.13). The effectiveness of the sacrament, however, does depend on whether you are receptive to it.

> The 7 sacraments are doors through which we enter into the life of God. He entrusted their administration to the Church.

Read more

The Sacraments: CCC 1210–1212, 1275, 1420–1421, 1533–1535; CCCC 251, 259, 321; YOUCAT 193, 224, 248.

3.36 What is the effect of Baptism?

The sacraments

Jesus entrusted the Church with the task of making all people his followers, by teaching and baptizing them (Mt. 28:19–20). Baptism is very important: "Unless one is born of water and the Spirit," said Jesus, "he cannot enter the kingdom of God" (Jn. 3:5).

Baptism is the beginning of a new, personal relationship with God, of a new life in Christ that demands a new lifestyle. To help the baptismal candidate overcome his attraction to evil, he is anointed with the oil of the catechumens (see Tweet 3.30). After the Baptism he is anointed with chrism as a sign that through the Holy Spirit he shares in the ministry of Jesus as king, prophet, and priest (see Tweet 3.30). The baptismal candle shows that like Jesus he is to be a light to the world (Mt. 5:14).

A child of God

Through Baptism, we are adopted as God's own children. From that moment on, we form part of his Church, the extended family of Christians (see Tweet 2.1). This sacrament washes away original sin, the separation from God that was caused by the first sin of Adam (ccc 405; see Tweet 1.4). Baptism also washes away and forgives personal sins, that is, those that are voluntarily committed. With Baptism, a new, supernatural life with Christ starts. We die to our old way of life in order to rise to a new life in him (Rom. 6:3–6). From that moment on, the Holy Spirit helps us to live as good Christians

....

Child or adult?

The first Christians were adults who consciously decided to follow Jesus. If they had children, they also were baptized and reborn in Christ. Good parents love their children and give them everything they need. Because a relationship with God through Baptism is so important for salvation, Catholics want to give that gift to their children.

After Baptism, children are educated in the faith so that they can eventually choose for themselves to follow Jesus in the Catholic Church. The greatest gift parents can give their child is a personal relationship with God.

Sacrament of Baptism					
Repeatable:	no		*Materials:*	water	
Minister:	bishop, priest, deacon (in case of an emergency, anyone can baptize)		*Action:*	pouring or sprinkling water, or immersion into water, three times	
Effect:	person becomes a child of God and a member of the Church; original sin is washed away; personal sins are forgiven; and the Holy Spirit is received		*Words:*	"N., I BAPTIZE YOU IN THE NAME OF THE FATHER, AND OF THE SON, AND OF THE HOLY SPIRIT."	

(I COR. 12:13). For sins we commit after Baptism, we can ask forgiveness through the Sacrament of Reconciliation (SEE TWEET 3.38).

Sooner or later?

If personal sins are forgiven through Baptism, why not wait until the end of life to be baptized? That way, one could go on sinning as long as possible and still go straight to heaven, right? One problem with this idea is that nobody knows when he will die. Another is that God does not forgive our sins unless we are sorry for them: how sorry is a person who deliberately sins for as long as possible? Sly calculations or self-interest can have no place in a good relationship, especially a relationship with God.

If you consciously and for no good reason postpone Baptism, you cannot really love God! You do not have to be perfect to be baptized: what matters most is that you long for friendship with God.

Too late?

Still, it is never too late in life to reconcile with God: someone who is sorry for his sins can receive Baptism even just before he dies. If he dies before being baptized, this can sometimes be considered a baptism of desire, with the same results as the actual sacrament. The Church believes that an unbaptized person who dies for his faith in Jesus receives a baptism of blood, as did the children killed by Herod, who was trying to kill Jesus (MT. 2:16).

 Through Baptism, we become a child of God and a member of the Church. Original sin and personal sins are washed away.

Read more

Baptism: 1213–1284; CCCC 252–264; YOUCAT 194–202.

Necessity of baptism: CCC 1257–1261, 1281, 1283; CCCC 261–262; YOUCAT 199.

3.37 With Confirmation, does the Holy Spirit descend on us for a second time?

SCAN

At his Baptism, Jesus received the Holy Spirit (Mt. 3:16), which gave him the strength to resist the temptations of the devil in the desert (Mt. 4:1–11). Jesus promised his disciples that after his Ascension they would receive the Holy Spirit too (Jn. 15:26). This happened on Pentecost, when the Apostles were given the courage and the power to spread the good news about Jesus to the entire world (Acts 2:1–4; see Tweet 3.34). Confirmation completes the Sacrament of Baptism, as when, for example, the Apostles Peter and John prayed over some people who had previously been baptized, that they might receive the Holy Spirit (Acts 8:15–17). Eventually, the Church began baptizing and confirming new converts during the Easter Vigil.

A new beginning

Before being confirmed, someone who was baptized as a child renews the vows his parents and godparents made on his behalf during his Baptism. Someone entering the Church as an adult receives Confirmation directly after Baptism. As a sign of new life, a (new) name

Armor

St. Paul urged us to find our strength in God and to arm ourselves against evil by putting on the armor of God, which can be seen as a description of the gifts of Confirmation: "Stand therefore, having fastened the belt of truth around your waist, and having put on the breastplate of righteousness, and having shod your feet with the equipment of the gospel of peace; besides all these, taking the shield of faith, with which you can quench all the flaming darts of the Evil One. And take the helmet of salvation, and the sword of the Spirit, which is the word of God" (Eph. 6:14–18). We can do anything God asks of us through the help of the Holy Spirit, whose gifts we receive in a special way through the Sacrament of Confirmation.

St. Paul did not mean that we ought to go to war literally, but that a true follower of Christ would sooner or later meet with opposition and adversity. A Christian must be ready to fight temptation and evil and to dedicate himself to doing the Will of God (see Tweet 4.43). To discern what is good and evil, we need the gifts of the Holy Spirit (see Tweet 1.32). For these reasons the Sacrament of Confirmation is very important.

The sacraments

Sacrament of Confirmation

Repeatable:	no	Materials:	chrism (oil)
Minister:	bishop (priest if given permission)	Action:	laying on of hands, and anointing the forehead with chrism
Effect:	binds the baptized more closely to the Church and strengthens him in the gifts of the Holy Spirit	Words:	"N., BE SEALED WITH THE GIFT OF THE HOLY SPIRIT."

is given to a person as he is baptized. When he is later confirmed, he might add another name to reflect his decision to follow Christ as an adult. This Confirmation name is usually that of a saint he admires (SEE TWEET 4.16). The task of godparents is to help the parents of the baptized to raise their child as a Christian. Confirmation sponsors help the person being confirmed to be a mature disciple of Jesus.

Giving strength

When we were born again as Christians through Baptism, we received the Holy Spirit. Through Confirmation, the presence of the Spirit is confirmed, or strengthened, in us. (In Latin, *firmare* means "to strengthen".) Through this sacrament, we receive the special power and help of the Holy Spirit and are bound closer to the Church (CCC 1285). Confirmation leaves an invisible and indelible mark on the person. This seal, or sign, of the Holy Spirit indicates that we now belong fully to Christ.

Spreading the faith

Together with the other sacraments of initiation – Baptism and the Eucharist (SEE TWEET 3.35) – Confirmation makes us adult Christians, called to witness our faith and to defend it if necessary. In doing so, we are the "salt of the earth" and the "light of the world", as Jesus asked all Christians to be (MT. 5:13–14). With the Holy Spirit, we are capable of doing great things for God, of going beyond our human weaknesses, just as the saints did. To do that, the gifts of the Holy Spirit are a great help (SEE TWEET 1.32).

Confirmation strengthens the gift of the Holy Spirit received at Baptism. Close to the Church, the confirmed Catholic witnesses God's love.

Read more

Confirmation: CCC 1285–1321; CCCC 265–270; YOUCAT 203–207.

3.38 Why confess to a priest, instead of just to God?

The sacraments

God does not want to punish us for our sins. He wants us to be sorry for them and to resolve not to do them again so that we can live life to the full. Jesus welcomed people known to be sinners. He forgave them and told them to change their lives: "Your sins are forgiven" (Mk. 2:5); "Go, and do not sin again" (Jn. 8:11). He wants nothing more than to take away the sins of the world (SEE TWEET 4.14). That is why he instituted the Sacrament of Reconciliation, also called confession.

Through a priest

Jesus gave his Apostles the power to forgive sins on behalf of God (Jn. 20:21–23). So that this ministry of forgiveness would continue until the end of time, the authority passed from the Apostles to their successors, the bishops and their priests. If we prayed on our own to be forgiven, we might easily doubt whether we really were pardoned. But we can be full of confidence and joy whenever we confess our sins to a priest and hear him say: "I absolve you from your sins."

Sincere confession

Everybody sins (SEE TWEET 4.13). Everybody needs God's forgiveness. Thus the Sacrament of Reconciliation is a tremendous gift of

....

Penance

In the Sacrament of Reconciliation God forgives your sins and restores your relationship with him, but the damage your sins have caused remains. When you drop a vase (even by accident), you should not only say you are sorry but also try to replace or repair it (SEE TWEET 2.35). Similarly, we should not only tell God that we are sorry for our sins, but also try to undo the harm they have done. To help you do so, the priest gives you a penance during confession. Justice demands that you repair any harm you have done to your neighbor (return stolen goods, correct a false report, etc.). You also need to repair the harm done to yourself and your relationship with God. You cannot do this on your own, but with the grace of God such practices as praying, fasting, and doing works of mercy can heal what was broken. For souls still needing repair at the time of death, there is purgatory in the afterlife (SEE TWEET 1.47).

Sacrament of Reconciliation				
Repeatable:	yes		*Materials:*	
Minister:	bishop, priest		*Action:*	after the penitent confesses his sins and expresses contrition, the minister stretches out his hand
Effect:	reconciliation with God, forgiveness of all sins confessed with true remorse, restoration of the state of grace when this has been lost by mortal sin		*Words:*	"*I ABSOLVE YOU FROM YOUR SINS IN THE NAME OF THE FATHER, AND OF THE SON, AND OF THE HOLY SPIRIT.*"

the Church. The moment a priest absolves you of your sins (absolution), you really are forgiven by God. Forgiveness is not automatic, however. There are three conditions: that you honestly tell the priest your sins (confession), that you are truly sorry for what you have done and firmly resolve not to commit these sins again (contrition), and that you do the penance the priest gives you (satisfaction).

Contrition

When St. Peter realized that he had denied Christ three times, he "wept bitterly" (LK. 22:62). He knew that he had committed a serious sin and repented of what he had done. You also can repent of what you have done wrong. The Church distinguishes between perfect and imperfect repentance, or contrition.

With *perfect contrition*, you are sorry for what you have done wrong because you know you have offended God, whom you love; you also intend to avoid this sin in the future.

With *imperfect contrition*, you are sorry about what you have done because you fear punishment. Whatever the reason for your repentance, God wants to forgive you. Imperfect contrition is sufficient, but perfect contrition is better: if you take your relationship with Jesus seriously, hopefully you are sorry most of all because you hurt him! Every time you repent and go to confession, God gladly forgives you. He does not count the times you have received the sacrament: he willingly forgives you again and again (MT. 18:22).

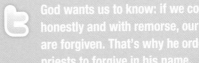
God wants us to know: if we confess honestly and with remorse, our sins are forgiven. That's why he ordered priests to forgive in his name.

Read more

Confession: CCC 1422–1498; CCCC 296–312; YOUCAT 224–239.

 ## 3.39 How can I confess properly?

The sacraments

Everybody needs God's forgiveness. St. John wrote: "If we say we have no sin, we deceive ourselves, and the truth is not in us. If we confess our sins, he is faithful and just, and will forgive our sins and cleanse us from all unrighteousness" (I Jn. 1:8–9). Smaller (venial) sins can be forgiven through the Penitential Rite at Mass, for example (SEE TWEET 3.46). Still, it is very good for your relationship with God to bring all your faults before him in the Sacrament of Reconciliation (SEE TWEET 3.38). For more serious (mortal) sins (SEE TWEET 2.35 AND 4.13), the Penitential Rite at Mass is not sufficient: you need to confess them in the Sacrament of Reconciliation.

Confession

Regular sacramental confession of your sins is very helpful for your relationship with Jesus. Many Catholics confess every month, and some more often than that. Regular confession helps us to recognize our sins more easily and to overcome our weaknesses more quickly, with the help of the Holy Spirit.

Act of contrition and absolution

PENITENT: O my God, I am heartily sorry for having offended you, and I detest all my sins, because of your just punishments, but most of all because they offend you, my God, who are all good and deserving of all my love. I firmly resolve, with the help of your grace, to confess my sins, to do penance, and to amend my life.

PRIEST: God, the Father of mercies, through the death and resurrection of his Son has reconciled the world to himself and sent the Holy Spirit among us for the forgiveness of sins; through the ministry of the Church, may God give you pardon and peace, and I absolve you from your sins in the name of the Father, and of the Son, and of the Holy Spirit.
PENITENT: Amen.

How to confess?

You can prepare for the Sacrament of Reconciliation by asking for God's help to know your sins. Then you can look at what you did wrong and at what you failed to do. Thus you examine your conscience, for example by considering each of the Ten Commandments. Once you know your sins you can follow these next steps:

- Go to a priest and say: "Bless me, Father, for I have sinned. My last confession was (number of weeks, months, or years) ago."
- Tell the priest all of the sins you have committed since your last confession. Be brief but complete and clear as to what you have done wrong and how often.
- Answer possible questions and listen as the priest gives you advice and a penance (SEE TWEET 3.38).
- When asked by the priest, say an act of contrition to show that you really repent of your sins. You can use a standard prayer (SEE BOX) or tell Jesus in your own words that you are sorry for your sins, intend not to do them again, and seek his grace to improve your life.
- The priest will stretch out his hands and give you absolution (SEE BOX). Thereby God forgives you all the sins you confessed. After that, your sins no longer stand in the way of you and Jesus, who tells you: "Go, and do not sin again" (JN. 8:11).
- Take a moment to pray, thanking God for his mercy. Do your penance as soon as possible.

....

Pipeline

You can imagine your relationship with God to be like a kind of pipeline between you and him. Every time you sin, dirt gets into the pipeline between the two of you. Thus, communication with God becomes increasingly difficult. In the Sacrament of Reconciliation, the pipe is cleaned, and you are better able to receive God's grace again.

Seal of confession

Most parishes have regular times for confession, and also at other times you can ask any priest to hear your confession. It is ideal to have one regular confessor, who can help you to grow in your relationship with Jesus. But God's forgiveness is more important than the priest who hears your confession. So do not wait until you find the perfect priest. Priests are obliged to keep everything they hear during confession completely secret. This seal of confession goes further than the confidentiality of doctors and lawyers, because for a priest there are no exceptions. Even if it would cost him his life to withhold the information, he still may not disclose anything you have confessed. Therefore, you can be completely honest and open during confession. The priest is interested not so much in your sins as in the forgiveness he can offer you on God's behalf! He knows that he also needs God's forgiveness. Only God is perfect.

> To confess well, pray to know your sins and be honest with the priest. God truly forgives you through the priest's absolution.

Read more

Confession: CCC 1422–1498; CCCC 296–312; YOUCAT 224–239.

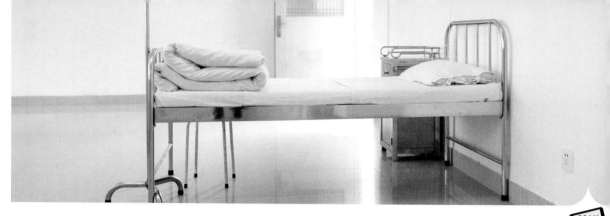

 ## 3.40 Is the Anointing of the Sick the same as extreme unction?

Jesus visited the sick and healed them (Lk. 4:38–40). His disciples were commissioned to do the same (Mk. 16:17–18). The first Christians called on a presbyter, or elder, (SEE TWEET 3.41) when somebody was sick to "pray over him, anointing him with oil in the name of the Lord" (Jas. 5:14–15).

Hope or despair?

When people are ill or seriously injured, they experience pain, both physical and mental, and a feeling of being powerless and restricted. Their lives change, and they are dependent on the help of others. Because all of this is difficult to accept and to bear, a sick or injured person can easily become sad, afraid, or hopeless. Even a believer can be tempted to self-pity, anger with God, or despair. On the other hand, illness or injury can bring a person closer to God as it reveals the true purpose of life: communion with him. To help with the challenges of being ill or injured, the Church offers the Anointing of the Sick, which is meant for all who have serious diseases,

Last sacrament?

The Anointing of the Sick is sometimes called extreme unction if administered to people who are about to die.

However, if a person is still capable of it, the last sacrament he receives before dying includes Holy Communion (SEE TWEET 3.44–3.50). This last Communion is also called viaticum (from the Latin words for "provision for the journey"), because Jesus' Body gives the dying person the strength to undertake the last leg of his journey toward God.

Some people postpone the Anointing of the Sick until they are at the point of death. That is a pity for several reasons. They deny themselves the strength and healing that God wants to give during illness, and maybe the grace needed to prepare for death. In addition, if the person waits too long to call for a priest, he might be unconscious when the priest arrives and unable to receive Communion. Another reason not to postpone the Anointing of the Sick is that a person can receive it more than once.

Sacrament of the Anointing of the Sick

Repeatable:	yes		Materials:	oil of the sick
Minister:	bishop, priest		Action:	anointing with oil of the sick on the forehead and hands
Effect:	spiritual strength, connection to the suffering of Christ, forgiveness of sins, healing of the soul and possibly healing of the body		Words:	*"Through this holy anointing may the Lord in his love and mercy help you with the grace of the Holy Spirit. [Amen.] May the Lord who frees you from sin save you and raise you up."* [Amen.]

injuries, or disabilities; whose life is in danger; who are suffering the frailty of old age; or who have to undergo an important operation.

Strength, peace, and courage
Through the Sacrament of the Anointing of the Sick, God gives us strength, peace, and courage to bear our sufferings. The sacrament also helps to cure us physically, if that is granted by God. If not, the sacrament helps the faithful to prepare for death or to deal with an ongoing disease or disability. If at all possible, it is good for the sick person to receive the Sacrament of Reconciliation (SEE TWEET 3.38) beforehand. If that's not possible, he will receive forgiveness for his sins through the Sacrament of the Anointing of the Sick.

Community
St. Paul wrote: "None of us lives to himself, and none of us dies to himself. If we live, we live to the Lord, and if we die, we die to the Lord; so then, whether we live or whether we die, we are the Lord's" (ROM. 14:7–8). Suffering can be seen as a purely negative thing or as something that can unite us with Jesus and make us more like him (SEE TWEET 1.37). Having faith is not something you do by yourself, and being sick shouldn't be endured alone. It is one of the corporal works of mercy to visit the sick and to pray for them (SEE TWEET 4.7). It can give a person great comfort to receive the Sacrament of Anointing of the Sick in the presence of family, friends, and caregivers. They act as the representatives of all Christians, the Church, who are praying for the sick.

Don't wait too long to call a priest: Anointing of the Sick is for the sick and the dying. It gives strength and sometimes physical healing.

Read more
Anointing of the Sick: CCC 1499–1532; CCCC 313–320; YOUCAT 240–247.

 ## 3.41 Why can't women and married men become priests?

The sacraments

The Apostles passed on their ministry to their successors, the bishops and their priests. St. Paul ordered Titus to appoint priests (elders) in each city (Ti. 1:5).

Three ordinations

There are three degrees, or grades, of ordination (SEE TWEET 2.21).

- The *diaconate* is the first degree. Deacons assist the bishop in their attention to the poor and needy. They administer the Sacraments of Baptism and Marriage and assist the priest with the Eucharist. Permanent deacons, who will never be ordained priests, can be married. Candidates for the priesthood serve for at least half a year as a deacon before being ordained a priest.
- The second degree is the *priesthood*. Priests administer God's sacraments, explain the faith, and help the bishop in the governance of the Church.
- The third degree is the *episcopate*. As successors of the Apostles, bishops receive the fullness of the Sacrament of Ordination (CCC 1557). They govern their diocese (Mt. 18:18; SEE TWEET 2.2), administer the sacraments (Mt. 28:19), and teach the faith (Mt. 28:20).

Just as in the time of the Apostles, every ordination involves a bishop laying hands on the candidate and praying over him (I Tim. 4:14). Priests and bishops are anointed with chrism (SEE TWEET 3.30).

....

Pope Francis on the role of women

"The Church acknowledges the indispensable contribution which women make to society.... We need to create still broader opportunities for a more incisive female presence in the Church.... The presence of women must also be guaranteed ... in settings where important decisions are made, both in the Church and in social structures.... In the Church, functions 'do not favor the superiority of some vis-à-vis the others'. Indeed, a woman, Mary, is more important than the bishops" (EVANGELII GAUDIUM, 103–104).

Sacrament of Ordination

Repeatable:	no	Materials:	chrism
Minister:	bishop	Action:	laying on of hands and prayer
Effect:	permanent change and spiritual power to act and speak in the name of Christ	Words:	(FOR A PRIEST) "GRANT, WE PRAY, ALMIGHTY FATHER, TO THIS YOUR SERVANT THE DIGNITY OF THE PRIESTHOOD; RENEW DEEP WITHIN HIM THE SPIRIT OF HOLINESS; MAY HE HENCEFORTH POSSESS THIS OFFICE, WHICH COMES FROM YOU, O GOD, AND IS NEXT IN RANK TO THE OFFICE OF BISHOP; AND BY THE EXAMPLE OF HIS MANNER OF LIFE, MAY HE INSTILL RIGHT CONDUCT."

Married priests?

St. Peter was married, for he had a mother-in-law (Lk. 4:38). It is therefore not impossible for a priest to be married. Eastern Catholic priests (SEE TWEET 2.30) are often married, but their bishops remain unmarried. In our Western Catholic Church, priests and bishops are in principle unmarried. They choose freely to be totally consecrated to God in celibacy (SEE TWEET 4.21) as Jesus was. Thus, they are completely free to go where they are sent and to dedicate themselves totally to the people they serve.

Female priests?

Some say that Jesus chose no women Apostles because he was bound by the social norms of his day. But Jesus, who in many cases went against the customs of his time, deliberately chose only men as Apostles. His female disciples received other important roles (SEE TWEET 2.16). Man and woman are equal, but not the same. This is demonstrated in fatherhood and motherhood, which are equally important yet different (SEE TWEET 2.1). St. Paul called himself a "father" in Christ (I COR. 4:15). A priest is a spiritual father who acts in the name of God. When he offers the Mass, he is acting in the person of Jesus, who is the Bridegroom of the Church. Pope Francis said: "The reservation of the priesthood to males, as a sign of Christ the spouse who gives himself in the Eucharist, is not a question open to discussion" (EVANGELII GAUDIUM, 104).

> Jesus chose only men to act in his name & in his person as Apostles. By celibacy priests are completely available for Jesus and the Church.

Read more

Sacrament of Ordination: CCC 1536–1600; CCCC 322–336; YOUCAT 249–259.
Ordination of men only: CCC 1577; CCCC 333; YOUCAT 256–257.

3.42 What is the common priesthood of all believers?

In the Bible Jesus is called our "high priest" (HEB. 5:5–10). Anyone who is baptized shares in the priesthood of Jesus. This is the common priesthood of the people of God. Every Christian is part of that people, which together forms the Church (SEE TWEET 2.1).

It is the vocation of all Christians to present Jesus to the world through doing good deeds and preaching the good news about Jesus (SEE TWEET 4.50). That is what St. Peter meant when he said to believers: "You are a chosen race, a royal priesthood, a holy nation, God's own people, that you may declare the wonderful deeds of him who called you out of darkness into his marvelous light" (I PT. 2:9).

Many vocations

The vast majority of our Church is composed of the lay faithful, who share in the common priesthood (SEE TWEET 2.1). They are called to share the good news of salvation wherever they find themselves. Each of them has a personal calling (SEE TWEET 4.4). Most are called to marry and to practice the common priesthood from within the family. This is clear, for example, when parents teach their children the faith, pray with them, and bless them before they go to sleep or to school (SEE TWEET 3.15 AND 4.7). Other lay people are called to consecrate themselves to God in celibacy (SEE TWEET 4.21). This could be as a brother or a sister in a religious community or as a single person dedicated to service for the love of God. For both the married and the unmarried, there are many ways they can bring Jesus into the world: as a missionary who proclaims the faith in a foreign land, as a baker who cares for his customers, as a catechist who explains the faith to those preparing for the sacraments, as a business manager who is an example of Christian leadership (SEE BOX), or as a parishioner who serves as an acolyte or takes Communion to the homebound.

Ministerial priesthood

Just as only 12 disciples were chosen to be Apostles, so too are a limited number of

Christian leadership?

A Christian leader is first and foremost a servant. Jesus gave the best example of this when he washed the feet of his Apostles at the Last Supper (SEE TWEET 3.30). Then he said: "You also should do as I have done to you" (JN. 13:15). When James and John asked Jesus to give them authority over others, Jesus said: "Whoever would be great among you must be your servant" (MK. 10:43–44).

Every Christian in a leadership position is obliged to follow the humble example of Jesus, whether he is the chancellor of a diocese, a corporate executive, a choir director, or a congressman.

This is especially true for the bishops and priests who lead the Church, who have received the Sacrament of Ordination, which authorizes them to act in the name of Jesus himself. Pope Francis told them that "being free from ambitions or personal goals is important.... Careerism is a form of leprosy" (JUNE 6, 2013).

Christians called to the ministerial priesthood as bishops and priests of our Church (SEE TWEET 3.41). St. Paul said he could speak boldly about God because of the grace given him by God "to be a minister of Christ Jesus ... in the priestly service of the gospel of God" (ROM. 15:15–16). Because of the ministerial priesthood, Jesus can be concretely present through the sacraments in the lives of believers (SEE TWEET 3.35). In this way, Jesus continues redeeming the world. Therefore, it is fundamental to our Church that there are priests. Jesus' disciples were told to pray for helpers for the Apostles (MT. 9:37–38). He thus called on all believers to pray regularly for vocations to the priesthood.

Everyone has his own job

The ministerial priesthood is essential for the whole Church, and so are other roles of service. All believers have been given gifts for building up the great edifice that is the Church. Each of these contributions is essential.

Therefore, it does not matter what your task is, but only that you do it with love. No Christian is more important than any other. All the different roles are necessary within the Church and all share in the common priesthood. All share in the responsibility to live and to proclaim the good news of Jesus.

> Every believer is called to present Jesus to the world through his own particular calling.

Read more

Common priesthood: CCC 1546–1547, 1592; CCCC 336.

 ## 3.43 Why is marriage so important for Christians?

arriage has been around since the Creation: from the beginning "a man leaves his father and his mother and clings to his wife, and they become one flesh" (GEN. 2:24). The specific feature of a marriage between a man and a woman who are both baptized is that Jesus has a very special place in their relationship: for them, marriage is a sacrament (CCC 1601). The Church compares the union between a man and a woman in marriage with the loving bond between Christ and his Church: "Husbands, love your wives, as Christ loved the Church and gave himself up for her" (EPH. 5:25).

Three essential elements

The Sacrament of Marriage has three essential elements or characteristics: unity, indissolubility, and openness to children (CCC 1664). It is a bond between one man and one woman, who together are called to a faithful and exclusive union. Once a marriage is concluded, it is indissoluble until the death of one of the two spouses. As Jesus said: "What therefore God has joined together, let

Mixed marriage

There are examples of very happy mixed marriages, enriched by the mutual differences. Still, marriage with a non-Catholic Christian, someone of another religion, or an atheist can place difficult choices before you: situations in which you are tempted to act against who you are and what you deeply believe.

In a mixed marriage it can seem simple at the outset to live and let live on matters of religion. But the danger is that at some point one spouse or the other will feel forced to choose between love for God and love for one's husband or wife. That is an inhumane choice! This danger often becomes concrete when children are born. In which tradition or faith are they going to be raised? At the moment of their marriage, Catholics promise to bring their children up in the Catholic faith. How do Mom and Dad explain that they do not agree about something as essential as their faith? How do they teach their children to enter into a personal relationship with God? These are questions you'll have to take seriously before you consciously enter into a mixed marriage. The basis for such a decision should always be prayer.

Sacrament of Marriage

Repeatable:	only after the death of spouse or annulment	*Materials:*	
Minister:	bride and groom (in the presence of a representative of the Church)	*Action:*	the consent of the spouses: the mutual gift of self and acceptance of the other
Effect:	unity of the spouses as Christ is one with the Church; between baptized spouses, a sacramental bond	*Words:*	*"I, N., TAKE YOU, N., FOR MY LAWFUL WIFE/HUSBAND, TO HAVE AND TO HOLD FROM THIS DAY FORWARD, FOR BETTER, FOR WORSE, FOR RICHER, FOR POORER, IN SICKNESS AND IN HEALTH, UNTIL DEATH DO US PART."*

not man put asunder" (MK. 10:9; SEE TWEET 4.19). A Christian marriage is open to children (SEE TWEET 4.19 AND 4.20), but if one or both of the spouses are infertile for reasons beyond their control, children are not necessary for a complete marriage (SEE TWEET 4.32).

The family as a church

The bride and the groom administer each other the Sacrament of Marriage. They enter into an intimate and lasting relationship with each other before God and a representative of the Church, usually a priest or a deacon, who then blesses the couple. By beginning his public life at a wedding in Cana, Jesus showed the importance of married life. In the family, children learn about and practice their faith for the first time; thus the family is a domestic church. Pope John Paul II called the family the "first school of love", because here children learn the most important skill of all: how to give of themselves to others. The family is "a community of grace and prayer, a school of human virtues and Christian charity" (CCC 1666; SEE TWEET 4.19).

Your whole life?

Marriage is supposed to last for the rest of your life. But how can you be sure that your love for your spouse will last until death? First, you can trust that God will help you (SEE TWEET 4.3) because he is the origin of love. Second, loving another person is a choice, not just a feeling. Feelings alone do not make a marriage last. Rather, the commitment to love each other no matter what causes love not only to last but to grow through the years.

> By its very nature, Christian marriage is one, indissoluble, and open to children. It is a sacrament between the baptized.

Read more

Marriage: CCC 1601–1666; CCCC 337–350; YOUCAT 260–271.

3.44 Why is Mass so boring?

The Eucharist is the most important of the seven sacraments, because Jesus is present in his own Body and Blood, offered to us as food and drink. In the Eucharist, or Holy Mass (SEE BOX), he is truly present, but recognizable only to those who want to believe in him. Therefore, during the Mass the priest says the Eucharist is the "Mystery of Faith" (I Tim. 3:9; SEE TWEET 3.48).

Boring?

Some people complain that the Mass is boring. But Jesus himself said that without the Eucharist there is no life in us: "He who eats my flesh and drinks my blood has eternal life, and I will raise him up at the last day. For my flesh is food indeed, and my blood is drink indeed. He who eats my flesh and drinks my blood abides in me, and I in him" (Jn. 6:54–56).

If you believe that Jesus himself comes to you in the Eucharist, how can that be boring? Especially if you consciously and actively participate at Mass?

Be prepared

Jesus is truly present in the tabernacle – that's why a candle is always burning nearby (SEE TWEET 3.21). You can greet Jesus by genuflecting in the aisle before you sit down. It is a good custom to be quiet in the church. This is out of reverence for the divine presence and to leave room for those who want to pray in silence, including yourself.

Before the liturgy begins, you can make good use of your time by taking a few minutes

....

Many names

Eucharist comes from the Greek word *eucharistia*, which means "thanksgiving". We also speak of the Blessed Sacrament (SEE TWEET 3.14). The Eucharist is in fact the most sacred of all the sacraments. Another name for this sacrament is the Holy Mass, because the liturgy in Latin ends with the sending out of the faithful: "Ite, missa est" (SEE TWEET 3.50). That word *missa* has in the course of the centuries evolved into the word *Mass*.

Sacrament of the Eucharist

Repeatable:	yes	Materials:	Unleavened bread, wine, and a little water (and Scripture)
Minister:	bishop, priest	Action:	holding the bread and chalice, respectively
Effect:	the real presence of Jesus, Body, Blood, Soul and Divinity, which he sacrificed on the cross and which he gives to us as spiritual food	Words:	"TAKE THIS, ALL OF YOU, AND EAT OF IT, FOR THIS IS MY BODY, WHICH WILL BE GIVEN UP FOR YOU." "TAKE THIS, ALL OF YOU, AND DRINK FROM IT, FOR THIS IS THE CHALICE OF MY BLOOD, THE BLOOD OF THE NEW AND ETERNAL COVENANT, WHICH WILL BE POURED OUT FOR YOU AND FOR MANY FOR THE FORGIVENESS OF SINS. DO THIS IN MEMORY OF ME."

to prepare yourself to meet Jesus. Your busy schedule is a lot less important than meeting Jesus in the Eucharist. But you do not have to leave your daily life outside the church. On the contrary, during the Mass you can offer your whole self to God: your gratitude, praise, and love, as well as your sorrows, fears, and needs. You can tell Jesus everything (SEE TWEET 3.1).

Actively participate

In the Mass, you are invited to be active by listening, responding, praying, singing, and reflecting on what is happening. The Eucharist is so important that it deserves all your attention. If you consciously participate in this way you are less likely to become bored. If there are things you do not understand, do not be afraid to ask questions (afterward). Receiving Communion is the most important action you can perform in your life because you are receiving Jesus, your Lord and God! After Communion, take a moment to pray in silence, so that you can thank God for the grace you have received. When the Mass has ended, the time has come to share Jesus with others (SEE TWEET 3.50).

> In the Mass, Jesus comes very close to you. Can Mass be boring if you are wholeheartedly participating in this?

Read more

Eucharist: CCC 1322–1419; CCCC 271–294; YOUCAT 208–223.
Structure of the Mass: CCC 1345–1355, 1408; CCCC 277; YOUCAT 213–215.

3.45 How is the Holy Mass arranged?

At every Mass we come together as Christians to meet Jesus in his Word and in the Eucharist (SEE TWEET 3.44). The liturgy consists of four major parts.

The introductory rites

The priest opens the Mass with the Sign of the Cross and greets the people with these or similar words of St. Paul: "The grace of our Lord Jesus Christ, and the love of God, and the communion of the Holy Spirit be with you all" (II COR. 13:14). We ask God for forgiveness for our sins and may sing or recite the Kyrie ("Lord, have mercy") (SEE TWEET 3.46).

On most Sundays God is glorified and praised as we sing the Gloria, a very old hymn (SEE TWEET 3.27). The priest then closes this first section of the Mass by saying the opening prayer for the day, the Collect.

The Liturgy of the Word

There then follow some readings from the Old or New Testament of the Holy Scriptures (SEE TWEET 3.47). After the first Scripture reading, a psalm is read or sung. On Sundays and major feasts a second reading follows. In either case, the Gospel comes next. To show how important this is to us, we stand as the Alleluia is sung and as the Gospel is read by a deacon or a priest, who then explains the Scriptures in a homily (sermon). On Sundays and solemnities, the Creed is confessed, meaning it is recited aloud together (SEE TWEET 1.31 AND 1.33). Then we bring our collective prayers to God in the general intercessions (SEE BOX).

General intercessions

The general intercessions begin with an invitation to prayer by the priest, followed by a series of petitions. Customarily, the first prayers are for the Church and her leaders; the next are for grave situations in society and throughout the world. There are usually prayers for the sick and lastly ones for the dead. The priest closes the intercessions by offering them all to God.

Communion service outside Mass

In times and places where a priest cannot be present for Sunday Mass, Catholics can still come together for prayer and Communion. After the readings from Scripture and prayers by the community, the Body of Christ (which was consecrated on an earlier occasion during Mass) (SEE TWEET 3.48) is distributed. Such a Communion service is not a Mass, nor could it ever replace the celebration of the Eucharist. Only when access to Mass is impossible is the Communion service an appropriate substitute.

The Liturgy of the Eucharist

Bread and wine are brought to the altar, where the priest offers them to God on behalf of everyone present. The faithful join themselves to this sacrifice by offering their lives, which are symbolically represented by their financial contributions. The priest says the prayer over the offerings, and after the Preface, which is essentially a prayer of thanksgiving, we sing the Sanctus ("Holy, Holy, Holy"). In the name of all, the priest prays the Eucharistic Prayer. He speaks the words that Jesus spoke at the Last Supper, as he takes first the bread and then the wine. When the priest pronounces the words of Consecration, the bread and the wine are changed into the Body and the Blood of Jesus (SEE TWEET 3.48). Through their "Amen" at the end of the Eucharistic Prayer, the congregation affirms its participation in the whole prayer (SEE TWEET 3.50).

After the Our Father, at the invitation of the priest or the deacon, each person offers an appropriate sign of peace to his neighbors. The Host is broken during the singing or reciting of the Agnus Dei ("Lamb of God"). The priest elevates the Lamb of God, who has come among us under the appearances of bread and wine, and all pray: "Lord, I am not worthy ..." As the Body of Christ is distributed, non-Catholics and others who do not receive Communion remain in their seats (SEE TWEET 3.49). Sometimes they are invited forward – hands across their chests – to receive a blessing.

The concluding rites

After the Prayer after Communion, the priest gives the final blessing to all present, who then are sent into the world (SEE TWEET 3.50), where we live proclaiming the Word of God in our own way.

> Jesus speaks to us through Scripture, his Word, and offers himself to us in the Eucharist. We are then sent to bring Jesus into the world.

Read more

Structure of the Mass: CCC 1345–1355, 1408; CCCC 277; YOUCAT 213–215.

3.46 Why all this emphasis on sin instead of hope?

The Eucharist

At the beginning of every Mass is the Penitential Rite (SEE BOX). We confess openly to God and all present that we have sinned. Then the Kyrie is prayed: like a beggar in the Bible, we ask Christ our Lord to have mercy on us (LK. 18:38). On some Sundays, especially during the Easter Season, the Penitential Rite and the Kyrie are replaced by a sprinkling of holy water (SEE TWEET 3.32 AND 3.33). This recalls the forgiveness of sins in Baptism.

Jesus wants to forgive

Some people think that the Church emphasizes too strongly what people do wrong, rather than the good that they do. Should we not look hopefully toward heaven instead of focusing on our sins (SEE TWEET 1.45 AND 1.46)? Yes, surely! Jesus came to bring life, abundant life (JN. 10:10). Yet, everyone is aware of the fact that he falls short of the person he is meant to be (SEE TWEET 4.13). Fortunately, Jesus gladly forgives us and gives us the strength to do better (SEE TWEET 4.14). Time after time he gives us the chance to start anew.

In the celebration of the Eucharist, our whole faith comes together. It is precisely because of our sins that Jesus died on the cross. In every Mass we are connected to the time when he died (SEE TWEET 3.31). By his death and Resurrection, he obtained for each of us forgiveness for our sins and new life in God

....

Penitential Rite

All: I confess to almighty God and to you, my brothers and sisters, that I have greatly sinned, in my thoughts and in my words, in what I have done and in what I have failed to do, (ALL STRIKE THEIR BREAST) through my fault, through my fault, through my most grievous fault; therefore I ask blessed Mary ever Virgin, all the Angels and Saints, and you, my brothers and sisters, to pray for me to the Lord our God.

Priest: May almighty God have mercy on us, forgive us our sins, and bring us to everlasting life.

All: Amen.

Eucharist in canon law

"The most August Sacrament is the most Holy Eucharist in which Christ the Lord himself is contained, offered, and received and by which the Church continually lives and grows.

"The eucharistic sacrifice, the memorial of the death and resurrection of the Lord, in which the sacrifice of the cross is perpetuated through the ages, is the summit and source of all worship and Christian life, which signifies and effects the unity of the People of God and brings about the building up of the body of Christ.

"Indeed, the other sacraments and all the ecclesiastical works of the apostolate are closely connected with the Most Holy Eucharist and ordered to it." (CIC 897)

the source because in the Eucharist we receive the presence and the power of Jesus so that we can live as good Christians. It is the summit, or culmination, because nowhere else on earth except in the Eucharist, where Jesus is really and truly present, can we come closer to God (SEE TWEET 3.48). In the Eucharist Jesus gives us his own life.

Removing obstacles

To prepare for that meeting with Jesus, it is good for us to remove as many obstacles as possible between him and us. These obstacles are caused by our sins and are removed when we ask for forgiveness (SEE TWEET 3.39).

The Church helps us to prepare ourselves for that encounter with Jesus through the Penitential Rite in the Mass (SEE BOX). Remember, though, that you obtain forgiveness only for small sins by the Penitential Rite (SEE TWEET 4.13). For mortal sins, we need to ask for forgiveness in the Sacrament of Reconciliation before receiving Communion.

(SEE TWEET 1.26). He doesn't want us to brush our sins under the carpet, but to bring them out into the open so that we can overcome them.

The main sacrament

The Eucharist is the most important sacrament (SEE BOX). It is both the source and the summit of our Christian life (CCC 1324). It is

> Our sin is a reality, and so is the forgiveness of God in which we hope. Without forgiveness we cannot move forward in our faith.

Read more

Eucharist as the culmination of your life: CCC 1324; CCCC 274; YOUCAT 208.
Communion in the state of grace: CCC 1389; CCCC 291; YOUCAT 220.

3.47 Who chooses the readings? Am I allowed to sleep during the homily?

During the celebration of the Eucharist, readings from the Gospels and other books of the Bible are proclaimed. The Scriptures contain the Word of God and are often self-explanatory. But sometimes they are not easy to understand because they were written poetically or within a particular historical context. Furthermore, we can never fully understand God because he is always greater than our concepts of him (SEE TWEET 1.9).

Still, the Word of God has a lot to say to you today, and there are several ways to understand the Bible better (SEE TWEET 1.10).

Readings

On weekdays there are two readings from the Bible at Mass, and on Sundays and solemnities, three. Often these texts shed light on each other (SEE BOX). The first and second readings come from the Old or New Testament. Often the second reading comes from the letters of St. Paul. The psalm between the readings can be seen as a prayerful response to the readings. In every Holy Mass, a text is then read from one of the four Gospels, with the Alleluia preceding it (SEE TWEET 3.45).

Cycles

The Church has drawn up a schedule for the Bible readings, so that during a year of daily Holy Masses as many different Bible texts as possible can be heard. The whole Bible is the Word of God and is ultimately, therefore, worthy to be read.

A three-year cycle has been established for the Gospel readings on Sundays. In year A we read texts especially from the Gospel of Matthew, in years B and C we read from Mark and Luke, respectively. During the Triduum and the Easter Season the Gospel of John is widely read, as it is on Christmas morning. For the weekdays, a two-year cycle of readings has been established, for even and odd years.

The Bible explains itself

A good example of Scriptures that shed light on each other are the readings for the Feast of the Exaltation of the Holy Cross, which is celebrated annually on September 14. The first reading on this day tells how the Israelites complaining in the wilderness were attacked by poisonous snakes. To heal the people, God told Moses to hold up a bronze serpent. Anyone who was bitten continued to live if he looked at the bronze serpent (Num. 21:4–9). If this feast day happens to be celebrated on Sunday, there is also a second reading, wherein St. Paul says that God has exalted Jesus on high to redeem us (Phil. 2:6–11).

In the Gospel we hear Jesus say the same about himself: "As Moses lifted up the serpent in the wilderness, so must the Son of man be lifted up, that whoever believes in him may have eternal life" (Jn. 3:14–16). Jesus was lifted up on the cross on which he died out of love for us.

Jesus is set before us like the bronze serpent. However, those who looked at the bronze serpent and lived still had to die one day. We who look upon Jesus in faith ultimately live forever with him (see Tweet 1.26).

Importance of the homily

In the homily, or sermon, the Word of God that we have heard in the readings is explained and explored. Often a link is made to our daily life. The homily may well help you to understand the words of the Bible better. But the priest in your parish probably does not preach as extensively as St. Paul, who once spoke so long that a boy fell asleep and tumbled out of the window. After St. Paul had brought him back to life, he still continued his sermon (Acts 20:7–12).

Some people say they would rather not go to church because they do not like the homilies. That's a bad reason to stay home. The homily is only one part of the Mass. One time the homily might strike you more than at another time, but either way you can still receive Jesus in the Word of God and at Communion, and obtain the grace that can help you on your journey of faith.

> The readings at Mass have been carefully chosen by the Church. The homily explains the Word of God to us, which makes it important.

Read more

Readings & sermon: CCC 1346–1349, 1408; CCCC 277; YOUCAT 213–214.

3.48 Is Jesus really present in the Eucharist? What is the Consecration?

At the Last Supper Jesus took bread, gave thanks, broke it and said: "Take this, all of you, and eat of it, for this is my Body, which will be given up for you." (SEE Lk. 22:19.) He also took a cup of wine and said: "Take this, all of you, and drink from it, for this is the Chalice of my Blood, the Blood of the new and eternal covenant, which will be poured out for you and for many for the forgiveness of sins. Do this in memory of me." (SEE MT. 26:27–28; Lk. 22:19.) With these words and gestures, Jesus instituted the Eucharist. These words, repeated at every Holy Mass, are the words of Consecration.

This is my Body

The disciples fulfilled their commission quite literally. Every time an Apostle or any of their successors visited the first Christians, he celebrated the Eucharist with them by doing what Jesus did at the Last Supper (I Cor. 11:23–25). Jesus did not say "This is a sign of my body", but "This is my body" (Lk. 22:19). Earlier he had said: "My flesh is food indeed, and my blood is drink indeed. He who eats my flesh and drinks my blood abides in me, and I in him" (Jn. 6:55–56). Jesus literally offered himself as food to the Apostles and gave them the commission to continue to celebrate the Eucharist. In every Holy Mass, we are very specifically related to the sacrifice that brought Jesus to the cross. Our simple offering of bread and wine, which the priest sacrifices to God on our behalf (SEE TWEET 3.45), is changed into the great sacrifice of Jesus, who offers himself with us and for us.

Although we see and taste bread, the consecrated Host is in reality Jesus. The essence or substance of the bread has been changed (transformed) into him. This change is called transubstantiation, and the moment when that happens is called the Consecration. Most Protestants do not believe this (SEE TWEET 3.49).

Why only the Host?

From the moment of Consecration, Jesus is wholly present with his Body and Blood,

The Eucharist

Bread and wine

Because the Eucharist is something very sacred, the bread (the hosts) is specially baked from pure wheat flour. The hosts used for the Roman rite contain no yeast in keeping with the Gospel accounts of the Last Supper occurring during the Passover, when Jews are forbidden to eat leavened bread. Consecrated Hosts that remain after Mass are reserved in the tabernacle (SEE TWEET 3.21) in a ciborium, a beautiful golden vessel with a lid. The wine used in the Eucharist must be pure and natural, made from the juice of grapes. Because wine spoils quickly when exposed to air, the Precious Blood contained in the chalice is not reserved but is always consumed entirely during Mass. To show how important we find the Body and Blood of Jesus, the paten (plate) and the chalice are often beautifully decorated.

together with his Soul and Divinity (CCC 1374). He is fully present in what looks like wine. He is also fully present in what looks like bread, in the consecrated Host (SEE BOX). Therefore, it is enough to receive only the Host. Similarly, one can receive Communion by partaking only of the chalice. Because Jesus is present in every particle and drop, we are extremely careful with the consecrated bread and wine. Certainly, one may receive Communion under both kinds, but it is not necessary to do so in order to receive Jesus fully.

The Mystery of Faith

Just before the Consecration, the priest extends his hands over the gifts of bread and wine and calls upon the Holy Spirit (the epiclesis). If you listen carefully you will hear how, after the Consecration, during the Eucharistic Prayer, the Holy Spirit is invoked again, this time to make the whole community holy (second epiclesis). That is, after all, the purpose of Jesus' presence in the Eucharist – to make us one with God. How ordinary bread and wine become the Body and Blood of Jesus, we cannot explain. It is something supernatural that only God can do through the Holy Spirit (SEE TWEET 4.18). Therefore, immediately after the Consecration, the priest says: "The Mystery of Faith." And we reply to this with the words of St. Paul: "When we eat this Bread and drink this Cup, we proclaim your Death, O Lord, until you come again." (SEE I COR. 11:26.)

> Through the words of Consecration, the bread and the wine are changed into the Body and Blood of Christ, who thus is really present.

Read more

Christ present in the Eucharist: CCC 1362–1367, 1373–1377, 1413; CCCC 280, 282–283; YOUCAT 216.

 SCAN

3.49 Can anyone receive Communion?

In the Church, the word *Communion* means being united with Jesus. When we receive Communion at Mass, Jesus is literally within us and we are in a very special way united with him. Because of that connection with Jesus, we are also connected to others who receive Communion. Everyone is invited to join in the celebration of the Eucharist. Jesus gave his life so that all men may be saved. But one should not come forward to receive Communion unless he is properly prepared and disposed.

First Holy Communion

The first time a Catholic receives Communion is a big event, because a person cannot be closer to Jesus on earth than when he receives Communion. An adult will usually receive First Communion immediately after Baptism and Confirmation. Someone baptized as an infant will have to wait until he is the age of reason, usually around seven years old. If a person does not receive First Communion directly after Baptism, he needs to receive the

Sacrament of Reconciliation to remove any sins committed after Baptism. He should also receive instruction in the Catholic faith so that he understands what the Eucharist is and what it brings about, namely, a union not only with Christ but with the whole Catholic Church. After his First Communion, a Catholic may receive Communion again and again. Were he to commit a serious sin, he should confess it to a priest before presenting himself for Communion again, in order to be reconciled with Jesus before receiving him (SEE BOX).

Protestants

Many Protestants (SEE TWEET 2.37) believe their communion services merely symbolize what Jesus did at the Last Supper. They do not believe that during the Mass the elements of bread and wine literally and permanently change into Jesus himself (SEE TWEET 3.48). St. Paul emphasized the importance of believing that Jesus is truly present in the Eucharist (I COR. 11:27–29). Because Catholics and Protestants differ on this important point,

How can I receive Communion worthily?

None of us is worthy to receive Jesus, and we acknowledge this right before we receive Communion when we pray: "Lord, I am not worthy that you should enter under my roof, but only say the word and my soul shall be healed" (Mt. 8:8). The fact is, we need Jesus to make us worthy of friendship with God, which is what he does for us through the sacraments. The great gift of the Eucharist and the other sacraments can only be fully effective if we are living in friendship with God, in a state of grace (SEE TWEET 4.12). We are asked to receive Communion only after having received forgiveness for all our grave sins in the Sacrament of Reconciliation (SEE TWEET 3.38). Lesser sins are forgiven during the Penitential Rite at the beginning of Mass (SEE TWEET 3.46). Those who are unable or refuse to confess their serious sins may not receive Communion because they do not live in union with Jesus and the Church.

St. Paul warned us not to receive Communion flippantly: "Whoever … eats the bread or drinks the cup of the Lord in an unworthy manner will be guilty of profaning the body and blood of the Lord. Let a man examine himself, and so eat of the bread and drink of the cup. For any one who eats and drinks without discerning the body eats and drinks judgment upon himself" (I Cor. 11:27–29). We must, therefore, approach Communion seriously. As a sign of this, the Church asks that we not eat or drink at least an hour before we receive Communion, with the exception of water and medicine. Active sharing in the experience of the Mass (SEE TWEET 3.44) is a very good preparation for receiving Communion. We may, optionally, receive Communion a second time during the same day, as long as it is during Mass.

....

the Catholic Church asks Catholics not to participate in Protestant communion services, and Protestants not to receive Communion at a Catholic Mass.

Orthodox

Eastern Orthodox Christians (SEE TWEET 2.30) believe in the real presence of Jesus in the Eucharist under the species of bread and wine. All of their sacraments are valid because their priests are validly ordained (by means of apostolic succession). Therefore, Orthodox Christians may receive Communion and other sacraments with us if they are not able to get to an Orthodox priest. Conversely, Catholics may

also, in a similar case, rightly go to an Orthodox priest. However, it is not certain that this priest will permit Catholics to receive Communion, because the Orthodox see the Eucharist as the sacrament of unity, just as we do.

As long as Christians are divided, only Catholics may receive Communion at Mass, and they must be in a state of grace.

Read more

Preparation for the Eucharist: CCC 1385–1389, 1415; CCCC 291; YOUCAT 220.
Receiving the Eucharist: CCC 1398–1401; CCCC 293; YOUCAT 222.

3.50 Why are we sent away at the end of Mass?

The Eucharist

At the end of the celebration of the Eucharist the deacon or priest says: "Go forth, the Mass is ended." In Latin it is "Ite, missa est", from which the word *Mass* (from *missa*) is derived (SEE TWEET 3.44). This one last sentence is what our whole life as Christians is about.

Go forth

After we have met Jesus himself during the Holy Mass, in his Word and in his Body and Blood (SEE TWEET 3.45–3.49), we are sent out with him into the world. Jesus sent out his disciples in the same way, saying: "Go into all the world and preach the gospel to the whole creation" (MK. 16:15).

In our daily life we are to live what we have received; we are to be Jesus for everyone we meet. We begin by wanting to serve Christ at every moment of our lives, opening ourselves to the needs of those around us and desiring to share what we have with them. We call such service to others charity (SEE TWEET 4.7).

Around-the-clock Christians

Receiving Jesus' Body and Blood makes sense only if it can transform us, that is, if it can make us more like Christ. We are not Christians for an hour on Sunday, but 24 hours a day, 7 days a week. When we bring Christ into our lives, we bring him into our homes, neighborhoods, classrooms, and places of work. Experiencing the merciful and transformative love of God in their own lives, Christians are signs of hope for others, especially as they reach out to those who are poor, sad, hungry, sick, or oppressed. It is the vocation of every Christian to entrust his whole being to Jesus (SEE TWEET 4.4) in order to witness to the truth of God's love not only for him, but for every person. Down to our own day, Christians through the ages have risked their lives in order to remain faithful to this calling (SEE BOX).

Amen

Just as the last book of the Bible, the Eucharistic Prayer ends with "Amen" (REV.

318

Standing up against injustice

The Dutch Carmelite priest Titus Brandsma (†1942) was a professor at the University of Nijmegen. In the years before World War II he warned clearly against the dangers of the National Socialism of the Nazis and against racial hatred. As a counterpart, he talked about the "unknown heroism" of a man who honors Christ in other people by his prayer and help: "Do not ask. Do not look back. Do not judge. Just help." He would stand very resolutely by these words a few years later. In response to the German occupation of the Netherlands, the Dutch bishops condemned Nazism and forbade Catholics to be members of organizations that had ties to the Nazis.

In 1942, as an advisor to Catholic journalists, Father Titus addressed a letter to the directors and editors of the Catholic press. It stated that no Catholic publication should take Nazi-affiliated articles or advertisements. Supported by the bishops, Father Titus distributed the letter personally and explained it to the addressees. Despite warnings that he was being watched by the occupiers, he continued his effort because he knew how important this resistance against the Nazis was. On January 19, Titus was arrested and sent to the prison in Scheveningen, Netherlands. In June of the same year, he was sent to the Dachau concentration camp, where he had a special influence on his fellow prisoners because he remained faithful to his vocation as a priest. Many of them were comforted and supported by his words and example. Blessed Titus Brandsma was killed on July 26, 1942, as a martyr for the faith.

22:21). By this word, we join with all believers in the prayer that the priest, on behalf of the whole community, directs to God. The Hebrew root of this word means "fixed" or "sure". The acclamation in Greek means "so be it" or "truly". Thus at the end of prayer we say "Amen" to mean "Yes, so be it, to the glory of God" (II Cor. 1:20; ccc 1065). A good example is the "Amen" at the end of the Creed, which refers back to the first two words, "I believe" (ccc 1064).

If we truly believe in the words, promises, and commandments of God, we want also to affirm them wholeheartedly. Therefore, our whole life must be an "Amen" in response to the love and faithfulness of God. After the Eucharist we go in the peace of Christ, to offer help to those who need it and to proclaim the gospel.

> "Go in peace" means that we must follow Jesus and proclaim him to the world. We are to be Christ for others.

Read more

Amen: ccc 1061–1065; cccc 217; youcat 165. *Evangelization*: ccc 425–429; cccc 80.

Part 4

Tweets about Christian life: Faith & Ethics

Introduction

When a young man asked Jesus what he must do to have eternal life, Jesus answered: "If you would enter into life, keep the commandments." And the young man asked: "Which?" (Mt. 19:17–18). Which indeed? In a world of increasingly complex ethical questions, it's hard to know sometimes what the right thing to do is.

For those who follow Christ, his Church offers sure guidance in making moral judgments. Not only is she, in the words of Blessed Paul VI, an "expert in humanity", but she is guided by the Holy Spirit in matters of faith and morals. And yet, the Church's moral teachings contradict what many today say we should or should not do. That is why it is essential for every Catholic to know not only *what* the Church teaches, but *why*. This section of *Tweeting with GOD* provides a sound, concise summary of this teaching, with helpful suggestions for further information.

You can be sure that if you strive to follow Christ and to live as his Church teaches, you will meet with incredulity and even hostility. Our moral principles are based on reason and revelation – on natural law, the Ten Commandments, and the teaching of Christ – and these sources are rejected by many people today. The popular culture insists that the Church's moral doctrines are "out of date" and at variance with science, and yet so often it is science which, albeit with the noble purpose of improving life, rejects its own first principles. How else to explain the denial of the sexual complementarity of man and woman in marriage or the human identity of an unborn child? The Church also affirms the dignity of every human being regardless of circumstances, and for centuries her sons and daughters have selflessly devoted their lives to alleviating hunger, caring for the sick, teaching, and working for peace and justice in the world.

That last point suggests another: not only must we educate ourselves about right and wrong—what everyone should or should not do— but each of us must also ask: "What is God's Will for *me*? How does he want me to glorify him?" When the young man assured Jesus that he had indeed kept all the commandments (ah, the confidence of youth!), Jesus looked at him with love and told him to sell everything he owned, give the proceeds to the poor, and follow him. Jesus did not tell everyone to do that; this was God's will for this particular person.

The young man went away in sorrow, for he had many possessions. Did he return later? We don't know. But we can be sure that Jesus continued looking on him with love as he walked away, and welcomed him back with great joy if he returned. As you ponder the challenging moral issues presented in this section, do not lose sight of that more personal question we should each put to the Lord: "What must *I* do to have eternal life?" And pray for the generosity to accept the answer!

✠ Salvatore Cordileone
Archbishop of San Francisco

 ## 4.1 Why are we here on earth?

An old book about the faith answered the question "Why am I here?" in the following way: "God made me to know him, to love him, and to serve him in this world, and to be happy with him forever in the next" (BALTIMORE CATECHISM).

All of us are called to recognize God as the one who created us (SEE TWEET 1.2). As our Creator, he is our Father. It may be difficult to imagine, but he loves every human being (JN. 3:16). God also loves you (SEE TWEET 4.2). That's why he deserves our love and also our reverence. To serve God we do not submit to him like slaves. Rather, we choose out of love to obey God as our Lord and Father. To do this we need to discover what it is that he asks of us (SEE TWEET 4.3).

Wanted: your happiness

Our final purpose is to be perfectly and eternally happy with God in heaven (SEE TWEET 1.45). Although it's sometimes hard to believe, we can already be happy here on earth. As

Jesus said: "Behold, the kingdom of God is in your midst" (LK. 17:21).

God is present everywhere people love each other, care for each other, and pray together. Because of sin, and its consequences of suffering and death, life on earth is far from perfect (SEE TWEET 1.34). But you can still have a meaningful and happy life on earth by living consciously with God and caring for others. By living like that, you are directed toward your destination in heaven, where you will be perfectly happy forever.

Only God

To be happy, we must learn to trust and to confide in God, who alone can make us completely happy. All of us desire many things: love, health, success, and comfort. These are good things, but our desires for them can be so strong that we are sometimes tempted to break the commandments of God in order to obtain them. In doing so, we make these things into idols that we serve and adore instead of God.

How can I live well?

The Bible tells us that some basic rules have been written into our hearts (ROM. 2:15). These rules form the natural law, so-called because people from different times and places have seen that it fits with our human nature and therefore helps us to live well. Conscience is the inner voice that tells us which of our actions conform to the natural law and which do not (ROM. 9:1; SEE BOX).

Thus, we must always listen to our conscience. But we also must form our conscience by a sincere search for the truth. Sometimes we think a particular action is good only because we have a very strong desire to do it. To prevent us from deceiving ourselves, God gave us the Ten Commandments (SEE TWEET 4.9). He also gave us Jesus and the Church to help us to tell the difference between right and wrong (SEE TWEET 1.20).

We are here to know, to love, and to serve God. This will make us as happy as we can be now & perfectly happy forever in heaven.

Read more

Reason for the creation: CCC 358; CCCC 67; YOUCAT 59. *Natural law:* CCC 1954–1960, 1978–1979; CCCC 416–417; YOUCAT 333.

 ## 4.2 What should I do with my life?

Vocation

Everyone in the world has to find an answer to that question. Maybe you still don't know the answer. Or, maybe you feel that you are (still) not really doing what you were meant to do. Actually, the answer to what you have to do is quite simple: you have to be happy! But that may be more easily said than done. You can be sure that God has a plan for every person, including you (SEE BOX). It is his Will for you to be profoundly happy (SEE TWEET 4.1).

God wants you to be happy

Roughly translated, in the Bible God says to you: "My child, I understand you and know you completely. I know when you sit down and when you rise up. I know your every thought. I know everything you do" (Ps. 139:1–3). "I created you in my own image" (GEN. 1:27). "I formed you in your mother's womb" (Ps. 139:13). "Every hair on your head is numbered" (MT. 10:30). "I know the journey of your life, and you will be blessed if you follow my path (Ps.139:16; JAS. 1:25). "You are my child, and I am

the Father who loves you" (I JN. 3:1–2). "I have always loved you, and my love will always be with you" (ISA. 31:3).

You sometimes hear somebody say about a great new job: "I have found my calling." What this person usually means is that he has found a job that matches his talents and training. Our happiness is related to our doing things that match our abilities. When we do a particular thing well, we often say that we "love" doing it. Thus, our happiness has something to do with love. Most of us have experienced that our greatest happiness comes not simply from doing things we love but from doing things for someone we love.

One day Jesus asked Peter three times: "Do you love me?" To which Peter responded: "You know that I love you" (JN. 21:15–17). In just such a way, God asks us whether we love him. We may muse, together with Pope Francis: "I ask myself: 'What have I done for Christ? What am I doing for Christ? What

God knows you better than you know yourself and knows what you are like. He made you! (GEN. 1:27; SEE TWEET 1.2).

What now?

"Okay," you might think, "God loves me for who I am. But I can't sit around doing nothing all day!" You are right. That is why the next step is to walk together with God to find your path in life. This can be difficult, as you usually have to find it while attending to the many things you must deal with every day (SEE TWEET 4.6), but discovering what will make you truly happy is worth the effort as it will change all your life for the better.

To find an answer to the question of what you are called to do in life, it is important first to work on your relationship with God. The answer can be found only with him. By praying (SEE TWEET 3.1), by learning more about yourself and your faith, and by caring for others (SEE TWEET 4.7), you can become better at listening to God.

should I do for Christ?'" (INTERVIEW WITH FR. A. SPADARO, S.J., AUG. 19, 2013)

Loving yourself

But how can you love God if you have trouble believing that other people really love you? Or when you cannot really love yourself? These are good questions, to which everybody has to find an answer. For starters, you may be sure that God loves you the way you are. People often appreciate us for what we do, or for what we have. But you don't need to do anything for God to love you: he really does love you exactly the way you are, with your less than perfect exterior appearance and personality, with both your talents and your shortcomings.

Trust that God loves you and wants you to be happy, then share that love with others. The rest will follow.

Read more

Longing for happiness: CCC 1718–1719, 1725; CCCC 361; YOUCAT 281.
Freely choosing God: CCC 1730–1733, 1743–1744; CCCC 363; YOUCAT 286.

4.3 What does God ask of me?

Do you ever wonder: What should I do? Or more specifically: What does God ask of me? What is God's Will for my life? These questions mean that you are trying to discover your calling in life, your vocation (SEE BOX). Once you find your calling and fulfill it, you are doing the Will of God. The good thing is that this is the best, and even the only, way to be really happy!

Is Jesus still calling?

During his life on earth Jesus invited people to follow him. Those who did so became his disciples. Jesus called men and women, young and old, poor and rich, healthy and sick. Some he asked to be his Apostles, and the rest to fulfill other tasks in service of the Church (SEE TWEET 2.15 AND 2.16). Jesus loved them all without exception, just as he loves you.

Jesus still calls people to follow him. We can't see or hear Jesus in the same way his first disciples did, but we can encounter him within ourselves by hearing the Word of God in the Bible and in the Church, by receiving the sacraments, and by sharing our lives with other believers. Listening to what Jesus asks of you begins by being close to him and by following him as his first followers did.

Everyone has a calling in life

For some people their calling is clear straightaway; they know from an early age God's plan for their lives. For others, it can be difficult to discover (SEE TWEET 4.6). The most important thing during this search is to follow your heart. What may surprise you most of all, is that your vocation is hidden deep within yourself, there where your deepest desire can be found. God asks you to be true to yourself, to live the life that is just right for you. By doing this you will find inner peace (SEE TWEET 3.4). Following your heart does not mean being led by superficial feelings; this could never fulfill you completely or bring you total happiness. Rather, it means being guided by your deepest longing, which God himself has placed within you. Every choice you make in life requires

What do I need to know about vocation?

- It is a calling from God, not your own initiative.
- A calling can come into your life at any given moment. It could come gradually or suddenly.
- Your basic calling is to be married in the Lord or single for the Lord.
- You can freely say yes or no. If you say yes, it won't always be easy, but it will bring you great happiness.
- Don't be impatient: God will give you the time you need to find your true calling.
- The Bible and the history of the Church show you that whoever says yes to God can do great things (SEE TWEET 4.5).
- You will only find your calling by growing in your relationship with Jesus. It is all about your journey with him. Prayer is essential in this respect (SEE TWEET 3.1).
- You don't need to do the searching all by yourself; regularly speak with a spiritual director (SEE TWEET 3.4 AND 4.6).

of mind. Whatever you had to give up won't seem so important anymore.

What is my vocation

There are many different ways to serve God. St. Paul said: "There are varieties of gifts, but the same Spirit; and there are varieties of service, but the same Lord; and there are varieties of working, but it is the same God who inspires them all in every one. To each is given the manifestation of the Spirit for the common good" (I COR. 12:4–7). Amid the variety of gifts are two basic Christian vocations: to be married in the Lord or to remain single for the Lord. Each of these vocations requires a total commitment, and one of them fits you perfectly. Whatever your calling is, it demands a fundamental choice in your life: the choice to find and to do the Will of God. To figure out your vocation, first put God at the center of your life and dedicate yourself to him. The next step is to discern whether your calling is to marry and start a family (SEE TWEET 4.19), or to remain unmarried in order to serve the Church with your undivided attention, just as Jesus did (SEE TWEET 4.21).

you to give up something. Choosing to do one thing means you cannot do another thing. We just cannot do everything at the same time. To follow your calling you will need to give up something. However, you will get much in return—contentment, fulfillment, and peace

God asks you to do what he wants for you. Everybody has his own calling: by choosing it you will become truly happy!

Read more

God calls you too!: CCC 1877; CCCC 401.

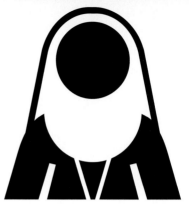

4.4 How can I follow Jesus, and what is my calling?

Vocation

The first question Jesus asks of you is "Do you love me?" (Jn. 21:15–17). If your answer to that question is a heartfelt yes, and you are willing to give up everything for Jesus, then you can ask him: "Lord, what should I do?" (SEE Mt. 19:16).

The answer to that question lies deep within your heart. You are free, of course, to say no. But God knows you better than you know yourself; he knows what will make you truly happy. Although most people are called to be married, and although it may seem as if marriage is the most obvious choice, take some time to pray about whether Jesus is calling you to follow him more closely by remaining unmarried like him.

Not to marry?

Every Catholic should seriously consider whether it may be God's Will for him to remain unmarried in order to serve God and his Church without the responsibilities of a family (SEE Tweet 4.21). The choice is not as strange as it

may seem: if God calls you to serve him in this way, you can be sure to find fulfillment and happiness (SEE BOX). Even if you are in a romantic relationship now, celibacy may still be your vocation. If you suspect God is calling you to live a celibate life, the next question is "How?" There are as many different ways to serve God in the unmarried state as there are individuals. Here are some examples.

Religious, priest, or deacon

Maybe God is asking you to join a religious community of sisters or brothers. Living in such a community is called religious life. There are so many different religious communities and orders (SEE Tweet 2.9) that it can be difficult to choose one of them. But don't make things too hard on yourself: you can never visit all of them before making a decision. If God calls you to the religious life, he will also help you to find the right place for you. Start therefore with the communities that you already know: do you feel that God is calling you to join one of these?

Career or calling?

For many people, their career comes first. They are convinced that their work is the greatest source of their happiness. But how does that relate to the calling that God has in mind for each of us?

- If you believe in God, you know that your career is not the most important thing in your life. What matters most is loving God and your fellow man (SEE TWEET 4.7).
- Priests, deacons, and religious men and women place their gifts and talents at the disposal of God to serve his people wherever they are sent without considerations for their careers (SEE TWEET 3.42).
- Married men and women need to work in order to provide for their families and to contribute to society, and their jobs provide them with opportunities to share the love of Christ with others. In every trade and profession we need people who are honest and respectful of the rights and dignity of others.
- Everyone wants to be successful, but a Christian must not try to advance himself by doing things that are unethical, such as lying, cheating, or taking bribes. A Christian doctor will not perform euthanasia (SEE TWEET 4.38), and a Christian soldier will refuse to fire upon nonthreatening and unarmed civilians (SEE TWEET 4.44).

God calls some men to be priests (SEE TWEET 3.41 AND 3.42). Priests have the important job of mediating between men and God. They present their people to God, intercede for them, and then pass on to them the grace they receive from God, particularly through the sacraments. Celibacy allows priests to be completely available to God and the people they serve. It allows them to be a father to not just a few people but many. Albeit in different ways, priests and deacons share in the same Sacrament of Orders (SEE TWEET 3.41). Deacons are the successors of the seven men chosen by the Apostles to look after the poor (ACTS 6:1–6). Some deacons are later ordained priests. Permanent deacons can be either married or unmarried.

Marriage

Marriage is a true calling, where a man and a woman vow to dedicate themselves to each other in lifelong love and fidelity (SEE TWEET 3.43). The crowning glory of a Christian marriage is their children who grow into responsible Christian adults and have children of their own (SEE TWEET 4.19).

> Jesus asks you: "Do you love me?" Maybe your calling is to marry, or maybe it is to be a priest, brother, or sister.

Read more

The religious life: CCC 873, 914–933, 934, 944–945; CCCC 178, 192–193; YOUCAT 138, 145.

Bishops, priests and deacons: CCC 1554, 1593; CCCC 325; YOUCAT 251. *Matrimony:* CCC 1601–1605; CCCC 337; YOUCAT 260.

4.5 What are examples of real vocations?

SCAN

In the Old Testament God called Abraham (GEN. 12:1–9), Gideon (JUDG. 6:11–24), Samuel (I SAM. 3:1–21), Isaiah (ISA. 6:1–13), Jeremiah (JER. 1:4–19), and Ezekiel (EZ. 2:1–3:14). In the New Testament God called Mary, and Jesus called the Apostles such as Matthew (MT. 9:9) and Paul (ACTS 9:1–19; SEE TWEET 1.11).

The calling of Moses

According to the book of Exodus, Moses was grazing his sheep on Mount Horeb when he saw a burning bush that was not being consumed by the flames. He heard the voice of God calling his name: "'Moses, Moses!' And he said, 'Here am I.'... Then the Lord said, 'I have seen the affliction of my people who are in Egypt.... Come, I will send you to Pharaoh that you may bring forth my people, the sons of Israel, out of Egypt" (EX. 3:1–10). The calling of Moses led to the liberation of the entire people of Israel from their bondage in Egypt. This is because Moses – not, in fact, without any protests – did what God asked of him (SEE TWEET 1.24).

Mary's calling

Another very important calling is that of Mary, the Mother of God (SEE TWEET 1.39). Mary was at home in Nazareth when suddenly an angel appeared and told her: "Do not be afraid, Mary, for you have found favor with God. And behold, you will conceive in your womb and bear a son, and you shall call his name Jesus" (LK. 1:30–31). Mary did not protest but trusted God completely, even though she could not understand or foresee exactly how God's Will would be accomplished. She replied: "I am the handmaid of the Lord; let it be to me according to your word" (LK. 1:38). This humble and affirmative response by Mary began a chain of events that led to the salvation of all of us (SEE TWEET 1.38).

Other callings

The Apostles Peter and Andrew were also specially called by God. Jesus was walking by the Sea of Galilee when he saw the brothers casting a net in the sea; for they

The story of St. Ignatius

Ignatius was a young Spanish nobleman who loved to fight. He joined an army at seventeen and fought in many campaigns without injury. But one day he was unlucky: soon after the start of the battle, a cannonball shattered one of his legs and wounded the other. For months, he had to stay in bed. Out of boredom, he read and reread books about Jesus and the saints, and he started thinking about the purpose of his life. Sometimes he thought how beautiful it would be to be a "Knight of Faith", just like the saints, and dedicate his life to God. At other moments he dreamt of courting beautiful ladies and gaining honor and renown on the battlefield.

To his surprise, he discovered that when he thought of attractive women or warfare, he felt happy for a little while, but then that feeling disappeared the moment he stopped thinking about it. It was as if that dream was not really his. On the other hand, whenever he thought of the great deeds he would accomplish for God, the feeling of happiness and inner peace stayed with him (SEE TWEET 3.4). And so he found out that he was called to serve God as a priest. Following Jesus was more important to him than his old life of courting, fighting, and luxury.

He promised God that he would always put him first, instead of doing as he pleased. As soon as he was healed from his wounds, Ignatius started to prepare to become a priest. That gave him a deep, lasting inner peace. Eventually Ignatius founded an important order in the Church: the Society of Jesus, also known as the Jesuits (SEE TWEET 2.40). He wrote a book of spiritual exercises, which is still used by people seeking the Will of God for their lives (SEE TWEET 3.8).

were fishermen. "And Jesus said to them, 'Follow me and I will make you become fishers of men.' And immediately they left their nets and followed him" (MK. 1:16–18). In a similar manner, Jesus called the other Apostles. For instance, Jesus told Matthew, whom he saw sitting in a tax office: "Follow me" (MT. 9:9). And Matthew left everything and followed Jesus.

Jesus also calls each of us. His words to you are also "Follow me" (LK. 9:59). And he tells you, just like he told the one who wanted to go home first to say good-bye: "No one who puts his hand to the plough and looks back is fit for the kingdom of God" (LK. 9:62). To follow your vocation means that you decide resolutely to put Jesus in the very first place at every moment of your life. The people who preceded you in taking that step demonstrate how such dedication leads to true happiness in life.

> Moses did what God asked him & freed his people from bondage. Mary also said yes to God, and thereby made our salvation by Jesus possible.

Read more

Mary's obedience: CCC 494; CCCC 97; YOUCAT 84.

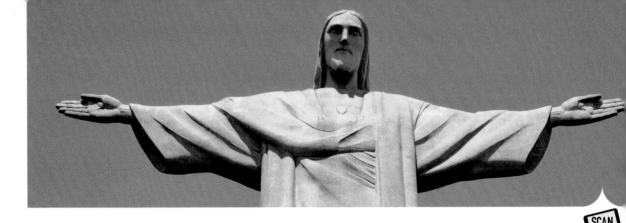

SCAN

4.6 How can I know the Will of God?

There is one thing you must realize: the only way to be truly happy in your life is to discover and to do the Will of God. You may be sure that if he calls you to make a certain life-decision, he's not doing that because he needs you to do something for him. God calls you in order to give your life purpose and meaning (SEE TWEET 4.4). God has a good plan in mind for you.

What does God want from me?

The answer to the question "What does God want from me?" can be found deep within yourself. After all, God created you! (SEE TWEET 1.2.) But it can take a little bit of effort to find this answer (SEE TWEET 3.4).

To listen to what you feel deep inside can be difficult (SEE BOX). So much has already happened in your life, so many large and small decisions have already been made. You are busy. A lot is expected of you. Maybe you act as a different person in different circumstances, to fit in.

Listening

All those things can make it hard to become truly yourself. Becoming your true self requires listening, to yourself and to God. The first step in listening to God is to accept that you cannot accomplish much all by yourself. You need God. Recognizing that you need him can be scary. But God loves you! Why then be scared of what he may ask of you? The next step in listening is to make room in your life for prayer. In prayer you can ask God for his guidance and the strength to do whatever he might ask.

How can I pray?

Prayer is not just talking to God (SEE TWEET 3.2). It is working on your relationship with Jesus. That starts with setting aside some time to be with him in prayer (SEE TWEET 3.7). Your relationship with Jesus is similar to your relationships with friends and family: from time to time, you meet them, phone them, send them a text message, or contact them

332

How can I listen to God's Will?

1. Accept that God loves you and place your trust in him! Put your relationship with Jesus first in your life. This is the basis for finding out the Will of God for you.
2. Pray each day (SEE TWEET 3.3). Talk to God freely from your heart, asking for his guidance and listening for what he might say. Thus you can grow in your relationship with Jesus.
3. Receive the Eucharist often (SEE TWEET 3.49) and confess your sins regularly (SEE TWEET 3.38). Here you can find the grace (SEE TWEET 4.12) and inspiration to continue the search for God's Will.
4. Seek examples of Christian virtue – in the Bible (SEE TWEET 4.5), the lives of the saints (SEE TWEET 4.16), and the people around you – who can inspire you to be your better self.
5. Lead a full Christian life: build friendships with other people who share your faith, join into the life of your parish or community, and look for ways to be of service to others (SEE TWEET 3.50).
6. Find a spiritual director, a priest or a religious, who can advise you well. He can walk with you and help you to recognize the signs from God. Be cautious of others who seem to know what you should do: this is about your calling, not theirs.
7. Be open! Know that the way to true happiness in your life can be different from what you initially think. Are you brave enough to do God's Will and not yours? Are you ready for that challenge? Because Jesus is calling you!

through social media. If you don't make the effort to communicate, your relationships will suffer. And the same is true about your relationship with Jesus. When you pray, try to listen to what God wants to tell you. The Bible, the Word of God, can play an important role in that respect (SEE TWEET 1.10 AND 3.8).

Try also to get to know yourself and your own feelings. In your deepest aspirations, you can discover God, and discover what he asks of you (SEE TWEET 3.4 AND 4.3). In his presence, you can be totally yourself. That way you can find out what you are called to do (SEE TWEET 4.8). It is very important to pray each day. You can do so in many different ways (SEE TWEET 3.3). The most important thing is to pray regularly.

 You can discover God's Will for you only if you have a personal relationship with him. Learn how to pray and be loyal to him.

Read more

Prayer: CCC 2558–2565, 2590; CCCC 534; YOUCAT 469.

4.7 Do Christians live differently from everybody else?

Many non-Christians are basically good people. But basic goodness is not the only thing God wants for us. His plan goes further than that (SEE TWEET 1.27). He desires to be part of our lives and wants us to become saints. That sounds like a tall order, but with Jesus we are capable of amazing things.

Love or rules?

The most important thing Jesus tells you is that God loves you. To help you to return that love, he gave us two commandments: "You shall love the Lord your God with all your heart, and with all your soul, and with all your mind.... You shall love your neighbor as yourself. On these two commandments depend all the law and the prophets" (MT. 22:37). So, our central task is to love both God and our neighbor. In everything Jesus said and did, he explained these two commandments. He gave his followers the task of living accordingly. That means you too! If you love God, you want to live according to what he wants. The Ten Commandments further explain his

purpose. But Jesus asks us to do more than follow the Ten Commandments. He also gave us the Beatitudes (MT. 5:1–12; SEE TWEET 4.14) and a sermon about the Last Judgment (SEE TWEET 1.44), when he will say to us: "What you did or refused to do for others, you did or refused to do for me" (SEE MT. 25:31–46). The Church has summed up the charity asked of us by Jesus in the Works of Mercy (SEE BOX).

The two commandments of love work two ways: we live better lives by helping others to live better lives. Giving food to a homeless person, visiting a lonely old person, helping your handicapped neighbor – these are just a few examples. True Christian charity and care for others (SEE TWEET 3.50) should always be accompanied by evangelization, telling people about Jesus (SEE TWEET 4.50).

With good reason, the most important spiritual work of mercy is to instruct. That means that every Christian is called to explain the good news of Jesus to others. The thing we want a truly deep statement, since, if you really do everything with love, what can go wrong? True love is concern for another. To learn how to be truly concerned about the well-being of others, we can ask God for his grace (SEE TWEET 4.12). That way, we can grow step-by-step in our lives, and behave more and more like true Christians. As St. Paul put it: "As many of you as were baptized into Christ have put on Christ" (GAL. 3:27). From our Baptism onward, we are named Christians, because we belong to Christ. We ought to show that we belong to him in the way we love others.

Friendship and God's commandments

God's commandments show how much he loves us. He knows much better than we do what we need to find true happiness. The commandments are an aid to living well with God and others. St. Thomas Aquinas explained it as follows: Whoever grows in his friendship to God will have a greater desire to keep his commandments, because if someone really loves God, he also loves the things that God loves.

to share with others most of all is our faith in Jesus. After all, it's the most beautiful thing we have, and we want everybody to be able to believe!

Love, and do what you will

The great St. Augustine once said: "Love, and do what you will" (SERMON ON I JN.). That is

As Christians, we belong to Jesus forever through Baptism. Hopefully, that shows in the way we love God and others.

Read more

Works of Mercy: CCC 2447; CCCC APPENDIX B; YOUCAT 450–451. *Double commandment of love:* CCCC APPENDIX B.

4.8 What is the relationship between faith and actions?

The Apostle James summarized it well: "Faith apart from works is dead" (Jas. 2:26). If you really believe in Jesus, you also want to do what he asks you: to love God and your neighbor by following his commandments (see Tweet 4.7). If we say we have faith in God, but don't try to obey him, what is our faith worth? The choice to have faith in Jesus must be visible in your life. Otherwise you do not really believe!

More than a good life?

A young man who really wanted to believe what Jesus was telling him, asked: "Teacher, what good deed must I do, to have eternal life?" (Mt. 19:16). Jesus answered that he must obey the Ten Commandments (see Tweet 4.9). Above all, he had to love God and his neighbor. That way he could cooperate, in a way, with the good that God would give him (see Tweet 4.12). The same applies to us, because as Christians both our faith in Jesus and our actions are important. When the young man declared that he obeyed the commandments,

he asked: "What do I still lack?" Jesus replied: "You lack one thing; go, sell what you have, and give to the poor, and you will have treasure in heaven; and come, follow me" (Mk. 10:21).

The young man wanted Jesus to challenge him, and so Jesus did: he asked him to put his trust in God alone, without having the security of wealth, and to follow him as one of his disciples. But such a course of action was clearly very difficult for him, because he quietly slipped away. Jesus is challenging you in the same way. Are you prepared to leave everything behind to follow Jesus, by living according to your calling? (See Tweet 4.4.)

What would Jesus do?

To live as Christians means that we base what we will and will not do on our relationship with Jesus. We ask ourselves: "In this situation, what would Jesus do?" That question can help us to take a step back and to look at our lives and ourselves from the outside. "Not my will, but yours, be done", you can pray (Lk. 22:42). The Bible does not give you concrete advice on what to do in all situations. For example, there were no social media and Internet when Jesus lived (SEE TWEET 4.47). But the Bible still gives us all the basic principles we need to lead a good Christian life in our modern technological age. What matters is that our attitude toward life is infused with the love of God and neighbor.

I can't help everybody who needs help!

As Christians, we have the task to care for our fellow men. We may not reject people who need our help (Mt. 25:34–40). Jesus did not give us the Works of Mercy for nothing (SEE TWEET 4.7). But of course, it is impossible to help everybody in need. Since we are not obliged to do the impossible, God is more concerned about the love we give, than about how many people we help (Mk. 12:41–44). Luckily, we are part of a larger whole, the Church, where everyone has his own job to do (SEE TWEET 2.1).

We don't have to worry about not being able to do everything or to help everybody. Each of us has to fulfill his own calling within the Church as a whole (I Cor. 12:27–30). Thus, everyone contributes to the magnificent structure of all the people who make up the Church of Jesus. Together, we dedicate ourselves to him, through our faith and through our works.

Praying in a monastery or helping people?

If all Christians have the duty to care for their neighbor, how can you serve God by staying locked up in a monastery? Wouldn't it be better to use that time and effort to help people? That is a question you sometimes hear.

The best service you can offer to your fellow man is to help him go to heaven. And for that you need prayer. Monks and nuns in monasteries and convents pray for people inside and outside the Church (SEE TWEET 2.9). When trying to help people in need, it is comforting to know that there are always some people praying for you, your work, and the whole Church. We all really need those prayers!

Without good works our faith is dead. Our task is to work with the grace we receive from God and thereby testify to our faith.

Read more

Love of the poor: CCC 2443–2449, 2462–2463; CCCC 520; YOUCAT 449.

4.9 Are the Ten Commandments still important?

God gave Moses the Ten Commandments on Mount Sinai (Ex. 20:2–17; Deut. 5:6–21). They were destined for all people. The Ten Commandments are also called the Decalogue, which is Greek for "ten words" (of God). With these words, God wants to help us to lead good lives.

Acceptable for everybody?

The first three of the Ten Commandments are about your relationship with God. The fourth through the tenth commandments are about your relationships with other people. These seven commandments are acceptable to most people, even those who do not believe in God. This is because they can also be known and understood through our reason or conscience, since they are part of the natural law (see Tweet 4.1).

God's help remains necessary

Many of the commandments have a reasonable basis, which makes sense to most people in society. However, we still need God's help to know and to do what is right (see Tweet 4.12). Because of original sin, our minds and our wills are weakened (see Tweet 1.4). We cannot reach God on our own accord, and we continuously need his wisdom and strength.

Selfishness

If you choose to disobey one of the Ten Commandments, unconsciously, or maybe even consciously, you choose to consider yourself to be more important than God or another person. The thing is, nobody can really become happy by making selfish, egoistical choices. Although we are told to "do our own thing", if we base our actions only on this shallow advice we will find ourselves sad and lonely. Only by considering the Will of God and the good of others can we find true happiness, even when we sometimes have to sacrifice something for our choices. The Ten Commandments can help you to do this and at the same time to be truly yourself. In that sense they are a kind of recipe for happiness.

God's gift: Ten Commandments

1. *I am the Lord your God: you shall have no other gods before me*. God has to come first in your life. Nothing is more important. That also means you try to make time for daily prayer, however brief (SEE TWEET 3.7).

2. *You shall not take the name of the Lord your God in vain*. The name of the Lord is holy (SEE TWEET 3.15). We should avoid saying it disrespectfully or calling upon God to witness promises we have no intention of keeping. Also everything dedicated to him must be treated with care (SEE TWEET 3.44).

3. *Remember the sabbath day, to keep it holy*. Sunday, the day of Jesus' Resurrection, is when we take the time to rest from work and to worship God. Catholics are obliged to go to Mass on this day (SEE TWEET 3.44). It is a day to spend time with family and friends.

4. *Honor your father and your mother*. Children must obey their parents (EPH. 6:1). When their parents are sick or old, children have the duty to care for them (SIR. 3:12). In principle, citizens should cooperate with civil authority for the just ordering of society.

5. *You shall not kill*. Human life is a great gift from God and must be respected from conception to natural death (SEE TWEET 4.26 AND 4.37). This commandment forbids all intentional and unjust killing: murder, abortion, suicide, and euthanasia (SEE TWEET 4.28, 4.41 AND 4.38). It also forbids the anger or hatred that causes bullying, picking fights, and starting wars (SEE TWEET 4.43 AND 4.44).

6. *You shall not commit adultery*. Outside of marriage (SEE TWEET 3.43), all sexual acts are wrong. Fornication, adultery, pornography, prostitution, and masturbation do not bring happiness, because they substitute for or disrupt marital love (SEE TWEET 4.22).

7. *You shall not steal*. Theft and vandalism destroy or deprive people of their personal property. Cheating on tests and taxes and pirating copyrighted materials are also examples of stealing.

8. *You shall not bear false witness against your neighbor*. Lying, fraud, slander, and gossip are wrong because they do harm to other people. Withholding information from someone who does not have a right to it is not telling a lie (SEE TWEET 4.47).

9. *You shall not covet your neighbor's wife*. To long for those things forbidden by the sixth commandment is to objectify other people. When we indulge in impure entertainments and thoughts, we become less respectful of others and more prone to lustful actions (SEE TWEET 4.22).

10. *You shall not covet your neighbor's goods*. It is also wrong to lust for someone else's possessions. Envy and greed make us ugly and selfish as well as more prone to deceit, theft, and even murder.

The 10 Commandments teach how to love God & neighbor, by willingly offering something of yourself to another.

Read more

Ten Commandments: CCC SECTION 2; CCCC PART 3, SECTION 2; YOUCAT 349.
Applying the Ten Commandments: CCC 2052–2557; CCCC 434–533; YOUCAT 348–468.

 4.10 Why are some Christians hypocritical?

God has given us clear commandments, but no one obeys them perfectly. Surely you know how hard it is to do absolutely everything right! Because the first people sinned and turned against God, we are born damaged (SEE TWEET 1.4). Our minds are darkened and our wills are weakened, so that we are easily tempted to do what is wrong. We have a wounded nature that cannot return to God on its own accord. Therefore, we need God's grace, which Jesus gives to anyone who asks (SEE TWEET 4.12).

The fact that Christians sin does not automatically mean they are hypocritical. It does mean they are not perfect. A hypocrite is someone who pretends to believe something but really doesn't and acts accordingly. Some Christians are hypocrites indeed, but most of us are simply ordinary sinners.

Vices

After Baptism, in spite of the grace received in this sacrament, certain bad inclinations remain present in everybody (SEE TWEET 1.4).

When we follow these repeatedly, we develop bad habits, or vices, the opposite of virtues. Vices are often perverted forms of a good habit: caring for others, for example, is very good, but you must not become a busybody or neglect your other responsibilities in the name of helping someone else. We develop bad habits by repeatedly committing a harmful act. Although certain vices may seem interesting and adventurous from a certain point of

....

The five precepts of the Church

1. You shall attend Mass on Sundays and on holy days of obligation and avoid work or activity that could impede the sanctification of such days.
2. You shall confess your sins at least once a year (SEE TWEET 3.39).
3. You shall receive the Sacrament of the Eucharist at least during the Easter Season (SEE TWEET 3.49).
4. You shall observe the days of fasting and abstinence established by the Church (SEE TWEET 3.29).
5. You shall help to provide for the needs of the Church.

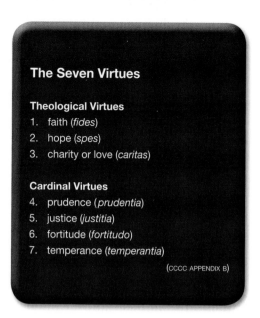

The Seven Virtues

Theological Virtues
1. faith (*fides*)
2. hope (*spes*)
3. charity or love (*caritas*)

Cardinal Virtues
4. prudence (*prudentia*)
5. justice (*justitia*)
6. fortitude (*fortitudo*)
7. temperance (*temperantia*)

(CCCC APPENDIX B)

Christian, someone burning with love for God, transmits that love to others and thus transforms the world. It is impossible not to be touched if you are in the presence of somebody like that. Think of Blessed Mother Teresa and St. John Paul II. They were not born saints. They became people of extraordinary goodness by practicing virtues with the help of God's grace.

Sin

Growing in virtue is not without difficulties, because again and again we sin. It is easy to become discouraged. But in the end, our sins are not the most important thing. The most important thing is our recognition that we need the grace of God and to be forgiven by him! The Church on earth is not a community of perfect people. As Pope Francis described the Church, it is a field hospital for the wounded on the battlefield of life. Though we are sinners, if we love God we want to be saints! But we need the grace of God and the help of the Church (SEE BOX) for that. You can become a saint only by taking small steps at a time.

view, they will never lead us to true, lasting happiness. They may make us feel good, but only for a very short time. The more we give in to our bad habits, or vices, the more they control us. The more we become enslaved to our bad habits, the more empty, dull, and dark our lives become.

Virtues

Virtues are good habits, or stable dispositions, that help us do what is right and good (SEE BOX). Through practicing the virtues, we can live fulfilling lives. In our times the word *virtue* has almost become synonymous with all things boring and dull. Not true! A virtuous

Apart from Jesus and Mary, nobody is without sin. But we can try our best to live virtuous lives with the help of God's grace.

Read more

The five commandments of the Church: CCC 2041–2043, 2048; CCCC 431–432; YOUCAT 345–346.
The Seven Virtues: CCC 1804–1829, 1833–1844; CCCC 378–388; YOUCAT 300–309.

 ## 4.11 Why does the Church have its own laws?

Whenever people work or live together, rules are needed. Etiquette helps to foster mutual respect and to protect one's privacy. Company rules of civility and behavior help people to work harmoniously together. Even within a family, house rules help all members to live peacefully together. This is no different in the Church, where people also want to live as one big family, constantly growing in love and faith.

Nations, states, and cities have civil laws, and, as good citizens, Catholics need to be law-abiding. However, if a civil law goes against the laws of God, nature, or the Church, then a Catholic is obliged to oppose it (ccc 1903). Should there be, for instance, a law that interferes with or contradicts our freedom of religion, we must protest. After all, freedom of religion is a basic right for everybody in the world! We must also, for example, try to change laws that do not protect the right to life (SEE TWEET 4.30 AND 4.43).

Canon law

The Church has her own system of laws called canon law. The Greek word *canon* means "rule". The rules, or canons, of the Church are written down in the Code of Canon Law, the *Codex Iuris Canonici* (CIC). Those rules are not fixed for all times: from time to time, the Code of Canon Law must be revised. The purpose of canon law is to help us to live as good Christians and to govern the Church. The CIC contains an application of the principles of divine and natural law (SEE BOX): the specific laws are suited to each time, but the principles themselves are eternally valid.

There are many canons and laws in the Code of Canon Law, but they share the same underlying principles. The last canon says that the salvation of the soul (*salus animarum*) must always remain the highest principle in the Church (ccc 1752). That indicates the purpose of the canon law: helping people to live in such a way, as to make it possible for Christ to redeem them!

Three kinds of law

We can distinguish three kinds of law, which are ultimately based on God's plan for mankind (SEE TWEET 1.27). Here they are, in order of importance:

1. **Divine law:** these laws we find in the Holy Scripture, for example, the Ten Commandments (SEE TWEET 4.9).

2. **Natural law:** these are the laws that God has implanted in creation itself (SEE TWEET 4.11).

3. **Human law:** these laws must be based on the above, but can change from time to time. Within these, we can distinguish
   a) canon law and
   b) civil law.

of a proper way to evangelize and to teach the faith. After that, the sacraments and the liturgy are covered in book 4, and the remaining books 5 through 8 are about the Church's criminal law, and what the right procedures are in situations where the law is violated.

Applicable to everyone

The Code of Canon Law is applicable for all faithful! For example, it says: "All the Christian faithful must direct their efforts to lead a holy life and to promote the growth of the Church and her continual sanctification, according to their own condition" (CIC 210). The duty to spread the gospel everywhere is also mentioned, and not just for priests and bishops (SEE TWEET 3.42 AND 4.50): "All the Christian faithful have the duty and right to work, so that the divine message of salvation more and more reaches all people in every age and in every land" (CIC 211).

#The books of canon law

The Code of Canon Law is divided into different parts, or books, covering all aspects of Church life. Book 1 explains where the rules come from. Book 2 explains the different rights and obligations of all the faithful, including priests, bishops, and religious. Book 3 underlines the importance

Canon law is there to help all Catholics to live in accordance with what Jesus teaches us through the Bible and the Church.

Read more

Authority of Law: CCC 1903–1904, 1921; CCCC 406; YOUCAT 326.

 ## 4.12 What is grace?

Grace is the gift of God's own supernatural life; it is Jesus' great gift to us (Jn. 1:17). Grace makes us children of God (through Baptism). It gives us the faith, hope, and love we need to be friends of God. We cannot do what God asks of us without grace. The effect of grace becomes apparent in many different ways. Look at the lives of the saints (SEE TWEET 4.16; SEE BOX). All the good they have done is the result of God's grace. St. Luke told of the young Jesus: "The child grew and became strong, filled with wisdom; and the favor of God was upon him" (Lk. 2:40). That is what God wants for everybody.

A different attitude

We are unable to come to know God without the help of his grace. That is the result of the fall into sin, which has corrupted our human nature (SEE TWEET 1.4). Through God's grace, our eyes are opened to his presence in our lives. Our attitude toward others changes as we see that they are children of God and therefore, our brothers and sisters. Our attitude toward the world also changes: many things that seemed so important, such as money, possessions, careers, and power, become far less so, while other things, such as giving loving attention to God and neighbor, grow more important. All of that is the result of God's grace. St. Paul wrote: "I give thanks to God always for you because of the grace of God which was given you in Christ Jesus" (I Cor. 1:4).

Your relationship with God

The most important thing that grace can give us is our relationship with God himself. We fully depend on God for that. By looking at nature and thinking rationally, we can discover that God must necessarily exist (SEE TWEET 1.6). But by reasoning alone we cannot advance much further than that. Only through God's grace can we get to know him and establish a loving relationship with him. It's not just the great saints who can receive the grace of God. He wants to give his grace to everybody. But not everybody is open to receive it. When we are focused only on ourselves, led by pride and vanity, we simply don't allow enough room and time for God and his grace. Remember that pride and egoism are the root of all sins.

Grace and sin

We receive God's grace especially through the sacraments (SEE TWEET 3.35). Through Baptism, we become a child of God (sanctifying grace). Afterward we try to follow God's commandments by loving him and our neighbors in daily life. For that, we also need grace (actual grace). But grace does not have a chance to operate in us if we consciously choose to disobey God, which is sin.

Why not? Because when we disobey God, we reject him and refuse his gifts. And that is devastating, because without the gift of grace, we cannot live as good Christians! Sin not only offends God and injures our fellow man, but also harms ourselves by weakening our ability to do good.

Our relationship with God and our receptivity to his grace can only be restored by being sorry for our sins and receiving God's forgiveness, for example through the Penitential Rite at Mass and especially the Sacrament of Reconciliation. God's forgiveness returns us to a state of grace, that is, to a relationship with God (SEE TWEET 3.38). Hence, the urgent call from St Paul: "We beg you on behalf of Christ, be reconciled to God" (II COR. 5:20).

Can you feel grace?

For a period of 20 years, Blessed Mother Teresa had the feeling that God was not with her. In prayer she felt dry, empty, and lonely (see Tweet 3.6). She later called this period a "dark night". She wrote: "The silence and the emptiness are so vast, that I watch and do not see, listen but do not hear."

Despite this difficult ordeal, she was able to do many good works for the poor. How? Through the grace of God. She did not feel it, but God and his grace were certainly with her!

She had experienced this grace early in life, when she was filled with a burning love for Jesus. Because of this grace, she dedicated her life totally to God, by caring for the poorest of the poor, in whom she met Jesus.

Grace is a gift from God that helps us to live as good Christians. Without grace, we cannot believe, cannot convert, cannot do good.

Read more

 ## 4.13 What is sin anyway?

Sin is deliberately disobeying God with our thoughts, our words, what we do, and what we fail to do (SEE BOX). It is to go against the Will of God for us. To be a sin a thought, a word, or an action must be knowingly and freely chosen or one that could have been avoided by making other choices. Only Jesus and Mary perfectly obeyed God (SEE TWEET 1.39). Everybody else is a sinner.

And yet, our Creator did not intend us to sin. He gave us freedom, and his greatest desire is for us to choose him with our own free will (SEE TWEET 1.4 AND 1.42). God made us in his image, after his likeness (GEN. 1:26). Every time we sin, part of God's image is blocked or hidden, and we become less like him. The more sins we commit, the less we are ourselves and the more difficult it is to draw close God. That is why committing a sin is so serious.

Mortal sin

Although it is wrong to commit any sin, some sins are worse than others.

The worst is called *mortal sin*. Three elements define a mortal sin:

- It concerns *grave matter*, in other words, it is a very serious offence, for example, a violation of one of the Ten Commandments (SEE TWEET 4.9).
- The sin is committed *knowingly*, that is, the person is fully aware of the fact that what he is doing is wrong.
- The sin is committed *willfully*, as in freely chosen, without coercion.

We speak of mortal sin, because God's grace cannot live within us if we have done something so bad: God's presence and therefore love itself die within us. As a consequence, we are no longer in a state of grace, and we cannot go to heaven unless this grace is renewed (SEE TWEET 4.12). We badly need to open our hearts to God's mercy. Only by repenting and asking for God's forgiveness will we be freed from this terrible situation (SEE TWEET 3.39).

Venial sins

All other sins (non-mortal sins) are called *venial*. This word may sound less serious, but venial sins are still real sins. They do not fully destroy God's presence within us, but we are weakened by them, and if we keep sinning, this weakness gets worse and worse. The more sins you commit, the easier it becomes to say: "Who cares, whatever, what does it matter?" But if you are honest, you know how unhappy your sins make you. And therefore it is good to ask God for forgiveness time and time again and thereby lead a happy life with him on your side.

Love, and do not judge

It is very easy to see the sins and shortcomings of other people, but it is often more difficult to be aware of your own! Jesus said: "Why do you see the speck that is in your brother's eye, but do not notice the log that is in your own eye?" (Mt. 7:3). It is therefore a good principle to be strict with yourself and regularly confess your sins (see Tweet 3.38), while not condemning others for their sins.

The Bible gives us the story of people wanting to stone a woman who had committed adultery. Jesus said to them: "Let him who is without sin among you be the first to throw a stone at her" (Jn. 8:7; see 1.19). But of course, nobody there was without sin, and so, one by one, they left Jesus alone with the woman. Jesus then said to her: "Go, and

do not sin again" (Jn. 8:11). Every time you confess your sins to a priest, Jesus will say that to you as well, again and again: "Your sins are forgiven, go in peace and do not sin again."

The seven deadly sins

These are called the seven deadly sins, because they kill the life of the soul. They are the root causes of all other sins and vices.

1. pride
2. avarice (greed)
3. envy
4. anger
5. lust
6. gluttony
7. sloth (acedia)

 To sin is to disobey God. By doing so we break our connection with him, which is restored through confession.

Read more

Christ still governs the Church: CCC 869; CCCC 174; YOUCAT 137. *Holiness of the Church:* CCC 829; CCCC 165; YOUCAT 132. *The seven deadly sins:* CCC 1866, 1876; CCCC 398; YOUCAT 318.

4.14 Jesus forgives, but how can I forgive myself and others?

Jesus tells us how important it is to forgive: "If you forgive men their trespasses, your heavenly Father also will forgive you; but if you do not forgive men their trespasses, neither will your Father forgive your trespasses" (Mt. 6:14–15).

So Jesus has a condition for the forgiveness he gives us: we must also forgive others. The Golden Rule is very appropriate here: "Whatever you wish that men would do to you, do so to them; for this is the law and the prophets" (Mt. 7:12; CCCC APPENDIX B). All of us really want God to forgive us our sins. The same goes for the people around us, who are waiting for our forgiveness!

Forgiving others

Jesus forgives our sins through the Sacrament of Reconciliation (SEE TWEET 3.38). But how can we forgive those who have caused us pain and suffering? That may seem impossible. But ask yourself this question: Does your anger or hatred effectively punish those who have hurt you? Or is it mostly a problem for you? Maybe the person who hurt you has already forgotten about it. Maybe he never even realized that he hurt you. Maybe the action that hurt you was an accident. Even if it was deliberate, mean, and really meant to hurt you, maybe the person is really sorry. What would you say if he hesitatingly came to see you to beg forgiveness? Or what if he is so shy that he doesn't dare to ask for it? No matter what, you need to forgive him for your own sake as well as his!

How often do we forgive?

One day Peter asked Jesus how many times he should forgive others: seven times perhaps? Jesus answered: "I do not say to you seven times, but seventy times seven" (Mt. 18:22). In other words, don't count and forgive your fellow man as often as is necessary, even if he has hurt you terribly. To forgive clears the air, and gives both you and the other person a chance to go on with your lives. Jesus does the same for you! He tells you: "Judge not, and

The Beatitudes

These eight sayings of Jesus show us what awaits those who follow Christ. Even when following Christ is difficult, the Beatitudes demonstrate what can give us true satisfaction (blessedness) now, and help us on our way to heaven (Mt. 5:3–11):

1. *Blessed are the poor in spirit, for theirs is the kingdom of heaven.* Not wealth, an important career, or possessions, but openness to God leads to happiness.
2. *Blessed are those who mourn, for they shall be comforted.* What is difficult, painful, and sad during our lives now, will not be so in the time to come.
3. *Blessed are the meek, for they shall inherit the earth.* Controlling one's anger and being patient after the example of Jesus who bore his suffering without protest bears much fruit.
4. *Blessed are those who hunger and thirst for righteousness, for they shall be satisfied.* Those who contribute to making God's love a reality find true fulfillment.
5. *Blessed are the merciful, for they shall obtain mercy.* Really forgiving others brings mercy upon oneself.
6. *Blessed are the pure in heart, for they shall see God.* As Jesus said, those who seek God, find him.
7. *Blessed are the peacemakers, for they shall be called sons of God.* Bringing peace means helping family members, friends, and even enemies to be reconciled with one another.
8. *Blessed are those who are persecuted for righteousness' sake, for theirs is the kingdom of heaven.* If you are persecuted because of your loyalty to the truth, you resemble Jesus!

you will not be judged; condemn not, and you will not be condemned; forgive, and you will be forgiven" (Lk. 6:37). Pope Francis said: "God never ever tires of forgiving us, but at times *we* get tired of asking for forgiveness. Let us never tire, let us never tire! He is the loving Father who always pardons, who has that heart of mercy for us all. And let us too learn to be merciful to everyone" (Angelus, Mar. 17, 2013).

Forgiving yourself

Forgiving yourself can be even more difficult than forgiving others. But it is not impossible. God wants to give you the grace (see Tweet 4.12) you need to forgive yourself. What may help, if after receiving the Sacrament of Reconciliation you still feel unable to forgive yourself for something you have done, is to take a moment in prayer to reflect on your sins. After that, you may realize that God has already forgiven you. And that he knows far better than you what you did wrong! Then, you can ask God for the strength to forgive yourself. Don't just plan to do so, but resolutely decide it. Then, go on with the life that God has given you.

 Fully accept Jesus' forgiveness. He knows everything: when he forgives, you truly are forgiven. Now forgive yourself & others.

Read more

Beatitudes: CCC 1716–1717, 1725–1726; CCCC 359–360; YOUCAT 282–284. *The Golden Rule*: CCC 1789; CCCC 375.

SCAN

4.15 What is a saint?

God created all of us in his own image (GEN. 1:27). That is why we all are called to become holy, just like him. Saints are not weird or unusual people; we all should strive to love God and our neighbors the way they do, not so much because we should, but because it's the best way to find happiness in this life and the next. Only saints go to heaven! (SEE TWEET 1.45.)

All of us can be saints

St. Paul often addressed his letters to the "saints" of a certain community (EPH. 1:1, II COR. 1:1), meaning all the people in that particular church. Pope Francis said that the communion of saints "reminds us that we are not alone but that there is a communion of life among all those who belong to Christ. It is a communion that is born of faith; indeed, the term 'saints' refers to those who believe in the Lord Jesus and are incorporated by him into the Church through Baptism" (AUDIENCE, OCT. 30, 2013). The Church is full of saints and sinners, goes an old saying, and they are the same people!

Being baptized changes us into children of God (SEE TWEET 3.36), through the gift of grace (SEE TWEET 4.12), but we are still a work in progress, still on the way to full friendship with God. Jesus calls each of us to "be perfect, as your heavenly Father is perfect" (MT. 5:48), and we do this by following him one step at a time.

As Christians, we must strive to imitate Christ. Unfortunately, not all Christians embrace their calling to be saints (SEE TWEET 4.10). That should not discourage us; as long as we keep trying to lead better lives, God will help us. We need his grace (SEE TWEET 4.12), and everyone who is truly open to receiving that grace can become a saint!

Connected with Jesus

Some Christians live such exemplary lives, that whoever meets them meets Jesus himself. Their heroism lies not so much in particular extraordinary acts but in their whole way of life. They are constantly connected with Jesus (SEE TWEET 4.8), and in this way they allow the Holy Spirit to help them to excel in the practice of

Do we worship the saints?

The saints, who are very close to Jesus in heaven, can pray for us there. That is why we can ask them to be our intercessors with God. That does not mean we worship the saints! We worship only God and no one else. We ask saints to pray for us. That is something very different from worship. Still, we can honor the saints for the good they have done. And we can venerate their relics as a sign that we want to follow Jesus closely, as they did (SEE TWEET 3.16).

But why don't we just pray directly to Jesus? In the Bible, many people approach Jesus to ask for something on behalf of someone else. Think of the woman who asks that her daughter be healed (MT. 15:22), or the soldier who asks that his servant be healed (LK. 7:2–10). Jesus did not say: "Let them come to me themselves." Rather, he did what these believers asked and cured those who were sick.

Similarly, we can ask the saints to pray for us (SEE TWEET 3.9). Of course, you can also pray directly to Jesus. The advantage of praying to the saints is that you can develop a relationship to them and learn to follow their example. Also, when we have to stop praying in order to do something else, they will continue praying in heaven.

faith, hope, and charity. After such a person dies, the Church sometimes declares him a saint, meaning that surely the person is in heaven.

Living for God

A saint is somebody who does not live for himself, but for God. A saint is not the opposite of a sinner. On the contrary, a saint knows full well that he is a sinner, that he needs God's grace to live a good and happy life. Stories of the saints show that such a way of life does not come on its own accord. Think about St. Peter, who spoke before thinking and denied Jesus three times (JN. 18:17, 25, 27). Like all Christians, saints struggle against evil. Again and again, they ask God's forgiveness, particularly through the Sacrament of Reconciliation (SEE TWEET 3.38). A saint can say, with St. Paul: "I can do all things in him who strengthens me" (PHIL. 4:13). The only reason he can say that is because he consistently puts God first in his life. It is a comforting thought that we are in one Body of Christ with the saints. They were ordinary people who made it into heaven through Jesus. So can you!

> A saint is someone who lives as a true friend of God. With God's grace you can also become a saint.

Read more

Saints: CCC 946–962; CCCC 194–195; YOUCAT 146. *Call to holiness:* CCC 2012–2016, 2028–2029; CCCC 428; YOUCAT 342.

4.16 Which saint shall I pray to? There are so many!

All saints reflect God's love, but they also have their own personalities and backgrounds. God's love is not reduced to one image: the many different saints show the richness of God's creative love. They all are with God in heaven, yet each has his own specialty. For example, we can pray to St. Anthony of Padua when we have lost something and to St. Rita when we are faced with an impossible task.

Lost and found

You might be wondering why we pray to St. Anthony when we have lost something. Here is a little background. Anthony was born in Lisbon, Portugal, where he became a priest. When in 1220 he heard about five Franciscan missionaries who were killed in Morocco for their faith, he decided to continue their work. Anthony became a Franciscan, and despite the great danger he departed for Morocco. To his great disappointment, Anthony ended up in Padua, Italy, because of an illness. He made the best of the situation by preaching the gospel there, and he quickly became widely known in the area for his great, passionate sermons. One day a novice ran away with a valuable book Anthony had been using. He prayed for the young man to return with the book, and he did. This incident is the reason we ask St. Anthony to help us when something is missing.

With God everything is possible

And what about St. Rita? As a young girl Rita wanted to dedicate herself completely to God. But at a young age, she was forced by her parents to marry. Her husband turned out to be a brute, but by her prayers, patience, and good example, Rita helped him to become a better man during the 18 years of their marriage. When he ended up being murdered, her two sons swore to avenge their father. Rita tried to persuade them not to do this, but they would not listen to her. She therefore begged God to let them die a natural death rather than letting them become murderers. Making this prayer was no doubt one of the most difficult things she ever did, and within one year, both her sons died of illness after making their peace with God. Despite her immense grief, Rita was very grateful to God and withdrew to a monastery in Cascia, where she became famous for her holiness. Soon after her death she became known as the saint for impossible causes.

Role models

You may ask whether there are any modern-day saints. Blessed Pier Giorgio Frassati is a twentieth-century Christian role model. He was handsome, athletic, and from a prominent family. He had everything going for him, we might say. Yet he dedicated himself to Jesus in service to the poor and advocacy for the less-fortunate. Thus he helped many people, and they lined the streets for his funeral procession after he died of illness at the age of 24. We may not know their names, but many people living today place their love for Jesus and others above everything else.

How are people capable of such immense self-sacrifice? How can you choose to risk your life to preach the gospel in a hostile land? How can you put up with a horrible husband and pray that your own children die before they can commit a terrible crime? How can you give up so much of your time and talent for the poor? Anthony, Rita, and Pier Giorgio did these remarkable things with the help of God. They knew deep inside that God loved them, and they trusted him completely. That is why they were capable of such self-denial. You too can choose to be a saint! You can achieve great things for God if you place your trust in him!

Some saints are the patrons of specific causes or situations. Follow their example & become a saint too!

Read more

Saints: CCC 946–962; CCCC 194–195; YOUCAT 146. *Baptismal name:* CCC 2156–2159; 2165–5167; YOUCAT 201, 202.

 ## 4.17 How does one become a saint?

In all ages there have been Christians with a particular openness to the grace of God. From the very beginning, the Church has declared such Christians to be an example to others and declared them to be saints. Over the centuries, a special procedure developed to make sure that people considered saints really were holy.

When the Church officially declares somebody a saint, we can be sure that person is in heaven. And that can be very useful to know, because it means we can ask the saint to pray for us (SEE TWEET 4.15). After all, the saints in heaven are far closer to God than we here on earth!

Canonization

Someone is declared a saint through the process of canonization (SEE BOX). Part of this process includes gathering objective evidence that somebody has lived a truly good and virtuous life. In addition, the future saint needs to have performed a miracle after death, as proof that he is interceding with God for us (SEE TWEET 4.18). Such a miracle is often the recovery of a person from a serious sickness, without there being any possible medical explanation for it. A commission of doctors and scientists critically examines such cases, because there must be no room for any doubt: the healing must be impossible to explain scientifically. On the basis of such evidence, the pope can decide to declare somebody a blessed or a saint.

....

Everybody must become holy!

"To ask catechumens: 'Do you wish to receive Baptism?' means at the same time to ask them: 'Do you wish to become holy?' It means to set before them the radical nature of the Sermon on the Mount: 'Be perfect as your heavenly Father is perfect' (Mt. 5:48).... [T]his ideal of perfection must not be misunderstood as if it involved some kind of extraordinary existence, possible only for a few 'uncommon heroes' of holiness. The ways of holiness are many, according to the vocation of each individual."

(JOHN PAUL II, NOVO MILLENNIO INNEUNTE, 31)

Steps toward sainthood

There are several steps to be taken in the process of being declared a saint:

- First, a diocese or religious order puts together a file of evidence about the person proposed for canonization. As soon as the file is accepted for an inquiry by the Congregation for the Causes of Saints, which is the official Vatican organization tasked with these matters, the person under investigation becomes a *servant of God* (SEE TWEET 2.5).
- If the evidence confirms that the person in question tried to live as a good Christian and led a life of heroic virtue, he is declared *venerable*.
- If a miracle happens through the intercession of the person declared venerable, the pope can decide to declare him *blessed*, through an official liturgical celebration. On October 19, 2003, for example, Mother Teresa was beatified. For martyrs, who died because of their faith, a miracle is not required.
- If yet another miracle happens, the case is put before the pope again, and he can then decide to declare the blessed person to be a saint, an example and an intercessor for all the Church.

A miracle!

A recent miracle is the cure of the French nurse Marie Simon-Pierre, who had a serious form of Parkinson's disease. Because of this sickness, she could no longer work, and doctors couldn't do anything for her. But in 2005, her illness suddenly disappeared completely, after she had prayed to John Paul II (SEE TWEET 2.50) to be cured. Doctors and scientists could not find any possible explanation.

After an exhaustive inquiry, Pope Benedict XVI recognized this healing as a miracle, and as evidence that John Paul II is truly in heaven. He beatified, or declared blessed, John Paul II on May 2, 2011. Pope Francis canonized John Paul II, or declared him a saint, on April 27, 2014.

Anyone can become a saint!

Everyone in heaven is a saint. Your grandparents or others you love who have died may not have been canonized, but they still can be saints in heaven! (SEE TWEET 3.27.) With the grace of God, you too can become a saint, through prayer, sacraments, and works of mercy.

> With the grace of God, anyone can become a saint. Only the pope can officially declare somebody to be a saint.

Read more

Saints: CCC 946–962; CCCC 194–195; YOUCAT 146. *Canonization:* CCC 828.

Call to holiness: CCC 2012–2016, 2028–2029; CCCC 428; YOUCAT 342.

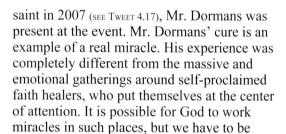

4.18 What's the deal with miracles, magic, and the occult?

When God does something that surpasses the powers of nature, we call that a miracle (SEE TWEET 4.17). God created the laws that govern the physical universe and does not revoke them, but he does, in the case of a miracle, cause things that would not happen without his intervention. Science therefore cannot explain miracles. Because they are from God, miracles are supernatural. A good example is when Jesus raised Lazarus from the dead a few days after he died (JN. 11:38–44).

Miracles continue to happen

God alone is the all-powerful Creator, and only he can perform true miracles. Although we cannot make a miracle happen, we can pray for one (CCC 2734–2741). For example, in 1999 Adolf Dormans prayed to the nineteenth-century priest Charles of Mount Argus to be healed of a lethal disease. Any hope of recovery had been abandoned by his doctors, who expected him to die shortly, but he was cured! The doctors could not explain what had happened. When Fr. Charles was declared a

saint in 2007 (SEE TWEET 4.17), Mr. Dormans was present at the event. Mr. Dormans' cure is an example of a real miracle. His experience was completely different from the massive and emotional gatherings around self-proclaimed faith healers, who put themselves at the center of attention. It is possible for God to work miracles in such places, but we have to be careful not to be fooled by showmanship.

Paranormal

Miracles are also very different from so-called paranormal activities such as UFOs and poltergeists, the reports of which may be sensational but are hardly credible. Tarot cards, Ouija boards, palm reading, astrology, and other practices that aim at obtaining knowledge of the future are also doubtful, but worse than that, they contradict our faith and hope in God. The Church is very clear about these things: we must stay away from anything that weakens our relationship with God. The most important thing in the life of a Christian is to trust God completely. Unhealthy curiosity

What about magic?

The use of magic is the attempt to exercise power over nature (including human beings) through special formulas (spells and incantations) or gestures (waving magic wands, burning certain objects, etc.). Magic is opposed to God because it ascribes to the natural world, or even evil spirits, power that belongs only to God. People usually turn to magic when human know-how or God has failed to give them what they want. Black magic is especially evil because it seeks power from the devil. But evil spirits can never achieve anything good; only God's love can do that. Hence black magic is often used to do terrible things. The Church opposes recourse to magic of any kind (ccc 2117). Even things that seem innocent, such as white magic potions intended to cure a disease (as opposed to actual medicines), are dangerous because they weaken both our reason and our faith in God.

about the unknown future (ccc 2115) weakens this trust. God has sometimes shown prophets and other saints what was going to happen in the future. But these were exceptional cases, concerning people who were specifically called by God to receive this grace.

Messages from God always fit with the whole of Christian faith, and God's true messengers always humbly allow themselves to be evaluated by the authority of the Church. Professional soothsayers, on the other hand, answer to no one and are often after money or fame. They prey upon people who are suffering and afraid, luring them with false hope. That is completely contrary to the hope God wants us to have in him.

Warning

The Bible warns us against following false messengers: "Do not believe every spirit, but test the spirits to see whether they are of God; for many false prophets have gone out into the world" (I Jn. 4:1). Pope John Paul II said: "If we want to give good direction to our life, we must learn to discern its plan, by reading the mysterious 'road signs' God puts in our daily history. For this purpose neither horoscopes nor fortune-telling is useful. What is needed is prayer, authentic prayer, which should always accompany a life decision made in conformity with God's law" (Angelus, Sept. 6, 1998; see Tweet 3.4).

God can perform miracles to help us to grow in our love for him, so who needs magic? Magic of any kind leads us away from God.

Read more

Praying for a miracle: ccc 2734–2741, 2756; cccc 575; youcat 507. *Trusting divine providence*: ccc 2115; cccc 445; youcat 355. *Occult matters*: ccc 2116; cccc 445; youcat 355–356. *Magic*: ccc 2117; cccc 445; youcat 355–356.

4.19 Why all this emphasis on marriage and the family?

God created human beings in his own image out of his great love. "Male and female he created them" (GEN. 1:27) so that they could share in God's love and his creation of life. He therefore commanded them to "be fruitful and multiply" (GEN. 1:28). As Christians we can give form to this vocation to love in one of two ways: the Sacrament of Marriage or celibacy dedicated to God (SEE TWEET 4.21). John Paul II said about these two states: "Either one is, in its own proper form, an actuation of the most profound truth of man, of his being 'created in the image of God'" (FAMILIARIS CONSORTIO, 11).

God is there

A man and a woman affirm their choice for each other in a definitive manner in the Sacrament of Marriage (SEE TWEET 3.43). They let God become part of their relationship and agree to seek him out together from that day forward. By their marriage vows, they give themselves unreservedly and exclusively to each other, agreeing to care for one another for the rest of their lives and to welcome children as gifts from God. This loving and life-giving union is what God intended from the beginning: "Therefore a man leaves his father and his mother and clings to his wife, and they become one flesh" (GEN. 2:24).

Love and investment

God intends every child to be conceived through the love that his mother and his father share together in marriage. Sometimes parents fall short of this ideal, but it is hard to imagine a better beginning for a child!

Sadly, there are many broken marriages (SEE BOX). But luckily there are also many examples of marriages that stay together with the assistance of an invisible bond of love, the source of which is God. A successful marriage requires the continual investment of both spouses: they live not only for themselves, but just as much for the other. When things are not going so well in a marriage, it is usually because the spouses have lost sight

What is the problem with divorce?

On their wedding day, the bride and the groom promise to love and to honor each other as husband and wife for the rest of their lives. But what if later they feel as if they cannot go on together? In our society divorce is commonly accepted. Why is it not accepted in the Church?

Jesus said emphatically that before God the marriage bond is unbreakable: "What therefore God has joined together, let not man put asunder" (Mk. 10:9). He set these words against the common practice of divorce in his own society. The Church cannot alter the words of Jesus.

On the day of their marriage, two persons are joined together, and this unity cannot be broken until the death of either spouse. When a Church investigation shows that a true Christian marriage never took place, the Church grants an annulment. That is not the same thing as a divorce, which dissolves a civil marriage contract.

It is very painful when a married couple realizes they have difficulty in living together. It brings great sorrow to both spouses, and sometimes even greater sadness to their children. Still, divorce is no solution to marital problems. Divorce simultaneously "disrupts the family and society" (ccc 2385). Even if a couple temporarily or permanently separates, if they made valid, solemn promises to each other, they remain married for the rest of their lives in the eyes of God and the Church.

of this principle. Yet, it is precisely when love is being tested that even more love, even more consideration of the other, is needed. Christian couples who persevere through tough times together, forbearing and forgiving each other, find that their love grows stronger with time. They learn that the key to marital happiness is, in the words of St. Paul, to "be subject to one another out of reverence for Christ" (Eph. 5:21).

Cornerstone of society

Studies show that it is best for a child to grow up in a family with a father and a mother who are committed to each other in love. Alas, because of illness, accidents, or divorce, this is not always possible. Family life makes people more sociable, generous, and resilient, which is why it is a good preparation for responsible adulthood. Families are "the foundations for freedom, security, and fraternity within society" (ccc 2207). For these reasons the family is spoken of as the cornerstone of society.

> Marriage is a bond for life between a man and a woman. Children that come from their parents' married love are raised in the family.

Read more

The family: ccc 2207–2208; cccc 457; youcat 369. Divorce: ccc 2382–2386, 2400; cccc 502; youcat 424.

 4.20 Is "no sex before marriage" old-fashioned?

SCAN

Sexuality

Sex fulfills the twin aims of marriage: the growth in mutual love of husband and wife (unity), and the continuation of life (procreation). The Church also recognizes that "sexuality is a source of joy and pleasure" (CCC 2362).

Husband and wife do not wish to keep their love to themselves, but want to share it with the children that may be born of their union. This is part of the natural order of creation, and the plan that God has for human happiness (SEE TWEET 1.2 AND 1.27).

True love

There is much to say about love. You can understand that God himself is love only if you yourself know what true love is: "He who does not love does not know God; for God is love" (1 JN. 4:8). True love is loyal and, once given, always lives up to its promise to be faithful "in good times and in bad" (SEE TWEET 3.43 AND 4.19). True love is based on a free choice: you cannot love based on a command.

True love means you are always ready to surrender yourself to the other and are also ready to receive the other as a gift in turn. True love sets no conditions and accepts the shortcomings of the loved one with patience and understanding. True love is open to new life and fruitful.

No sex before marriage

It is not a good idea to have sex before you are married. A sexual relationship means that you give yourself fully to the other person (SEE BOX). Only when you have promised to remain loyal and true to one another for the rest of your lives, and have received God's blessing in marriage, can your surrender to each other be complete and unconditional. By its very nature, the sexual act has the potential to conceive a child. That too makes sex outside marriage problematic, because a child needs a stable family (SEE TWEET 4.19). St. Paul considered the temptation to sex outside of marriage (fornication) to be a real problem. His solution was that marriage should be held in honor (HEB.

Truly human sexuality

"Sexuality, by means of which man and woman give themselves to one another through the acts which are proper and exclusive to spouses, is by no means something purely biological, but concerns the innermost being of the human person. It is realized in a truly human way only if it is an integral part of the love in which a man and a woman commit themselves totally to one another until death. The complete physical self-giving would be a lie if it were not the sign and fruit of a total personal self-giving, in which the whole person, including the temporal dimension, is present: if the person were to withhold something or reserve the possibility of deciding otherwise in the future, by this very fact he or she would not be giving totally." (Pope John Paul II, Familiaris Consortio, 11)

13:4) and that "each man should have his own wife and each woman her own husband" (I Cor. 7:2). The Church has always said that sex belongs within the context of marriage.
If the most personal and intimate expression of your love for another person is to be found in a sexual relationship, doesn't it make a lot of sense to save yourself for your one true love, the person you want to spend the rest of your life with? How could such a beautiful understanding of sexuality be old-fashioned?

Is sex bad?

Sexuality is something far more than just pleasure-seeking, but without the unconditional surrender of marriage, the other person easily becomes an instrument to seek personal satisfaction. This is clearly the case in prostitution and pornography, where people are treated as mere objects (see Tweet 4.22). That is unworthy of the human person. Under such circumstances, sex is indeed something bad.

Unfortunately, there are many examples of selfishly sought sexuality leading to terrible abuse. Even when two people agree to have sex just for pleasure, they are still using each other. For the reasons mentioned above, they are not giving themselves fully to each other in love, which is what makes the sexual union between two married people so beautiful and so deeply human in the first place (see box). As St. Paul said: "[If I] have not love, I am nothing" (I Cor. 13:2).

Only within marriage can sex be a full surrender in love to the other person & a source of joy, while remaining open to life (children).

READ MORE

Love, faith and fertility: ccc 2360–2367, 2397–2398; cccc 495–496; youcat 416–417.
Prostitution and pornography: ccc 2354–2355, 2396; cccc 492; youcat 411–412.

4.21 Why choose celibacy if people are made for marriage?

From the very beginning of the Church there were men and women who chose to remain unmarried for the love of Christ (SEE TWEET 2.25). Even though the whole earth is available to man for the taking, some promise to live in relative poverty. Although man is created free and may make his own choices, some choose to obey someone else. And in spite of the many nice men and women that they could marry, some promise to live their lives without having sexual relations. They choose to remain celibate.

Jesus

Why? Because, just as the first disciples, they heard Jesus say to them: "Follow me" (MK. 1:17; SEE TWEET 4.4). Their relationship with Jesus is stronger than that with anyone else. They desire with their heart, soul, and body to belong to him exclusively (SEE BOX). Jesus promised a good future to those who would lay everything aside – even a possible spouse – in order to follow him: "Truly, I say to you, there is no man who has left house or wife or

brothers or parents or children, for the sake of the kingdom of God, who will not receive manifold more in this time, and in the age to come eternal life" (LK. 18:29–30).

Celibacy

Priests, brothers, sisters, and others who feel called by God to follow the example of Jesus as closely as possible take the vow of celibacy (also called the vow of chastity). That means they will never marry and will live for the rest of their lives without sexual relationships (SEE TWEET 4.22).

God said: "It is not good that the man should be alone" (GEN. 2:18). And in celibacy consecrated to God, a man or a woman is not alone but rather extremely close to God. There are many examples of priests, brothers and sisters, and other celibates who are perfectly happy in their vocation and who have lives full of friends, relatives, and the people they serve. Precisely because they are not married, and so do not have to care for a family of their own,

they are free to be of service wherever God calls them to proclaim the gospel.

Calling

Celibacy is a wonderful vocation that fundamentally fits with how we were created by God. It frees a man or a woman to follow Jesus more closely than they otherwise could. Of course, just like married people, those who choose celibacy sometimes experience difficulties in fulfilling their vocation. But that is no reason not to begin! Christians can always count on the help of God's grace (SEE TWEET 4.12). Hopefully they can also count on the support of their brothers and sisters in Christ. No Christian, whether married or celibate, can thrive without that.

Is God calling you to dedicate your whole self to him in celibacy, or is he calling you to marriage? Both are noble vocations, but there is only one calling that fits you best (SEE TWEET 4.4). Search for it, if you have not yet found it. Ask God himself, and speak about your relationship with him to a good priest, brother, or sister (SEE TWEET 4.6). And above all, as Jesus said: "Be not afraid." Jesus promised to help you to live out your vocation when he said: "I am with you always, to the close of the age" (Mτ. 28:20).

> Jesus was unmarried. Choosing not to marry for his sake is the closest way to follow his example.

READ MORE

The consecrated life: CCC 873, 914–933, 934, 944–945; CCCC 178, 192–193; YOUCAT 138, 145.

Celibacy: CCC 1579–1580, 1599; CCCC 334; YOUCAT 258, P. 147.

 ## 4.22 Is it bad that I struggle with chastity?

Sexuality

Chastity helps us to control our sexual desires in a positive way. Christian chastity is not some bizarre protest against sexuality, but a testimony that human sexuality is for more than momentary physical pleasure (SEE TWEET 4.20). In many areas of our life, it can sometimes be difficult to practice self-control. Yet, there are many reasons to keep striving. Chastity and self-control help us to lead very happy lives – full of friendship, love, and self-giving. These are not exclusive to sexual relationships!

Chastity for all

Everyone needs the virtue of chastity. For someone who is not married, chastity means refraining from sexual relations (SEE TWEET 4.20). For those who are married, chastity means being faithful to one's spouse and accepting that the other is not always available or equally interested in sex. Chastity concerns your whole being. In order to live happily and harmoniously with your own body and to be your best self, all of your desires – whether

for food, drink, sex, or other pleasures – need to be under your control. You also need self-control to avoid harming yourself and others by overindulgence of any kind. Everyone has sexual desires. And everyone must learn how to give those desires the proper place in his life.

Sexuality

God gave us our sexuality. He made us male or female with certain natural desires, or instincts.

....

Why no masturbation or porn?

Maybe it does not seem bad, but masturbation is wrong (CCC 2352). Sexual pleasure is meant to be shared with another person in marriage (SEE TWEET 4.20), not to be secretly enjoyed alone. Masturbation cannot make you really happy, because it is never fully satisfying. And masturbation can become a bad habit, which can make sexual intimacy with the one you love difficult. In pornography and prostitution people are being used as mere objects for pleasure (CCC 2354; SEE TWEET 4.31). Even with consenting adults, they are forms of exploitation that degrade everyone involved.

How can I think less about sex?

The solution is not to suppress our sexual feelings and desires, but to decide how to handle them. Sins against chastity include masturbation, fornication, adultery, pornography, and prostitution (CCC 2352–2356). We should avoid these, and ask for forgiveness whenever necessary. But, do not become too fixated on sexual sins, because otherwise your thoughts always revolve around sex. Also, understand that when our freedom is weakened by a bad habit, we are not as guilty as we would be if we were freely choosing to do something we know is wrong (SEE TWEET 4.13). A good way to break loose from sexual obsessions is to serve others. The satisfaction remains with you longer than short-lived sexual excitement. And this helps you to overcome the loneliness and sadness that make you vulnerable to bad habits.

He also gave us free will so that we would not become the slaves of our desires. We are different from animals in that we can choose rationally how to deal with our instincts and passions (CCC 2339; SEE BOX). We can choose how to deal with our sexual desires. Especially in the media, sex sometimes seems as if it were the most important thing in life. At the same time it often is presented as if it were merely about personal pleasure. There is something boring about this portrayal of sex. Most of us want more than just to satisfy our sexual urges; we want love (SEE TWEET 4.20; SEE BOX).

Choosing love

Ask yourself this question: Would you rather sacrifice some immediate pleasures in order to have a lasting and loving relationship with someone; or would you rather sacrifice that kind of relationship for some moments of pleasure? If you want a true relationship, you need chastity; however, it is not that simple. Sexual urges can be very strong, and many people struggle with them. Do not be afraid to speak about this with your confessor (SEE TWEET 3.39). The battle for chastity is worth fighting, because you need this virtue in order to find true love and to be truly free and happy. Chastity will also help you to follow Jesus more closely. He has chosen us to be his friends and has given himself totally to us, even by his chastity (CCC 2347).

 Sexual desire is part of being human. Chastity helps us to choose well how to handle it. Real love, not lust, makes us happy.

Read more

Self-control: CCC 2339–2342; CCCC 489; YOUCAT 405. *Self-giving:* CCC 2346–2347; CCCC 490; YOUCAT 402.
Sins against chastity: CCC 2351–2356, 2396; CCCC 492; YOUCAT 409–413.

4.23 If the Church wants to protect life, why is it against distributing condoms in Africa?

A few years ago, Pope Benedict XVI was on a plane to Cameroon when he told the media that distributing condoms was not the solution to the AIDS epidemic in Africa, that it even makes the problem worse. This caused an immense uproar of criticism, and most media completely ignored the rest of his seven-day visit to Africa. The pope later explained that "the sheer fixation on the condom implies a banalization of sexuality, which, after all, is precisely the dangerous source of the attitude of no longer seeing sexuality as the expression of love (SEE TWEET 4.20), but only a sort of drug that people administer to themselves" (SEEWALD, LIGHT OF THE WORLD, P. 118). The focus should be on love – not the condom!

Condoms are no solution

It is often said that the best solution for Africa's AIDS problem is to distribute condoms. There are scientific studies, however, that cast doubt on the results of such a policy. Therefore, many official help organizations encourage the ABC method: Abstinence, Be Faithful, Condom Use. Abstinence before marriage and faithfulness in marriage remain the ideal way to avoid sexually transmitted diseases, which is a deeply Christian approach. Increasingly, the use of condoms is seen even by secular experts as a last resort. It will not solve the underlying cause of AIDS, in which a distorted vision of human sexuality plays an important role.

The beauty of sexuality

The use of condoms, to prevent either the spread of disease or pregnancy, goes against what God intended for human sexuality (SEE BOX). The Church works hard to fight AIDS all over the world. In many countries, Catholic hospitals are the ones treating patients and helping them to prevent further spread of HIV, the virus that causes AIDS. But the best way to fight AIDS is to rediscover the beautiful meaning and purpose of human sexuality (SEE TWEET 4.20). In this sense, the C of the ABC method could stand for "chastity" (SEE TWEET 4.22).

Is there also a good way to avoid pregnancy?

Artificial birth control methods such as the pill and condoms prevent the conception or the implantation of a new human being (SEE TWEET 4.26). By suppressing fertility during the sexual act, these artificial means prevent a couple not only from being open to the possibility of life but also from giving and receiving each other totally. Both are in contradiction with the Christian view of sexuality.

Natural Family Planning (NFP) (SEE TWEET 4.25), on the other hand, is very different. As a method of fertility awareness, it helps couples to know when to have sex based on whether they want to avoid or to achieve pregnancy. NFP does not suppress a person's fertility. Women who use NFP report that they are healthier than they would be if they were using chemical contraceptives.

preventing pregnancy or the spread of terrible diseases. Given the facts about sex, the Church reasonably concludes that sexual intimacy ought to be a profound expression of both committed love and openness to the possibility of new human life.

As John Paul II wrote: "When couples, by means of recourse to contraception separate these two meanings that God the Creator has inscribed in the being of man and woman ... they 'manipulate' and degrade human sexuality – and with it themselves" (FAMILIARIS CONSORTIO, 32).

Avoiding conception

Nevertheless, there could be times when it would be responsible for a couple to avoid having a child. For example, when one of the spouses is ill, when the spouses are struggling to make ends meet or to raise the children they already have, when the family is fleeing war or oppression. But you do not need contraceptives to avoid pregnancy for a period of time. Married people can choose not to have sex for a while or at least not during times of fertility (SEE BOX).

The big problem with condoms, and with all artificial methods of birth control, is the trivialization of sex their use presupposes. They also give a false sense of safety, that is, that by using condoms we can completely prevent the natural consequences of our sexual behavior. Condoms don't always succeed in

 Condoms don't solve the problem of sexually transmitted diseases. What would help is a different understanding of sexuality!

Read more

Birth control: CCC 2370, 2391; CCCC 498; YOUCAT 421. *Condoms and HIV:* YOUCAT 414.

4.24 Why is the Church against "same-sex marriage"?

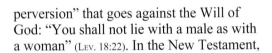

When asked in a provocative manner about a known homosexual, Pope Francis replied: "Tell me: When God looks at a gay person, does he endorse the existence of this person with love, or reject and condemn this person?" (Interview, Aug. 19, 2013). The pope was reminding us that everyone, no matter what his struggles are, is loved by God.
To have homosexual feelings is not in itself a sin. It is simply a fact that some men and women sometimes feel attracted to people of their own sex. While not everyone experiences these particular feelings, all of us struggle with sexual desires that, for our own good, we must not act upon.

Sin

The Church teaches that all sexual relations outside of marriage are sinful. This goes also for sexual relations with a person of the same sex, because a marriage is only possible between a man and a woman. The Old Testament calls sodomy (homosexual acts) an "abomination" (Lev. 20:13) or a "grave perversion" that goes against the Will of God: "You shall not lie with a male as with a woman" (Lev. 18:22). In the New Testament,

Compassion does not change the truth

"Unfortunately ... the mass media put forth initiatives that are essentially 'anti-family'. These are initiatives that give priority to what diminishes the value of the family and the human person.... Here we can think of ... a resolution of the European Parliament. There not only are people with homosexual inclinations defended, rejecting their unjustified discrimination. In this the Church could not agree more, and supports it completely, because every human person is worthy of respect. What is morally unacceptable is the legal condoning of homosexual practice. Showing understanding for the sinner who is unable to free himself of this tendency, does not mean that the moral standard changes. Christ forgave the adulteress and saved her from death by stoning (Jn. 8:1–11), but at the same time said: 'Go and sin no more'" (John Paul II, Angelus, feb. 20, 1994).

St. Paul described those who engaged in same-sex relations: "They exchanged the truth about God for a lie and worshiped and served the creature rather than the Creator.... Their women exchanged natural relations for unnatural, and the men likewise gave up natural relations with women and were consumed with passion for one another, men committing shameless acts with men" (Rom. 1:25–27). Other New Testament texts also plainly reject homosexual acts (I Cor. 6:9–10; I Tim. 1:10).

Male and female, he created them

The Church teaches that homosexual feelings are disordered, meaning they do not correspond to the meaning and purpose of our sexuality. Homosexual relations are opposed to natural law (see Tweet 4.1). Male and female reproductive organs are designed to fit together and to create new life, but in a homosexual relationship neither is possible (see Tweet 4.20). A homosexual act is therefore very different from the potentially procreative union of a man and a woman in marriage. For these reasons, a same-sex union can never be considered as a marriage, which always is a bond between a man and a woman.

God created male and female for a reason (Gen. 1:27; Gen. 5:2). The sexes have different qualities that are designed to complement each other. You often see a husband and a wife become a strong team precisely because they are different from each other in important ways. They are both equal, but not the same (see Tweet 2.16). They need each other to form one family. Mothers and fathers bring different qualities to the task of raising children. That is what the Creator of the world meant for us. In line with this, the Church is against adoption by homosexual couples. The best way for a child to grow up is in a family with a father and a mother, preferably his biological parents who are committed to love one another for life (see Tweet 4.19). It is not the same with two fathers or two mothers.

Chastity

Everybody is called to love and to be loved, but for this a person does not need a sex-life; there is so much more to life than sex (see Tweet 4.22). All of us need the virtue of chastity in order to love others in the proper way. Being chaste can be a real struggle, especially since our society does not help those trying to live a pure life. For this reason, the Church offers us the sacraments. Reconciliation (see Tweet 3.38) and Eucharist (see Tweet 3.45) give us the grace (see Tweet 4.12) we need to keep our sexual desires in perspective and to decide rationally how to handle them.

Homosexual feelings are contrary to the meaning and purpose of sexuality. The Church clearly states that same-sex marriage is impossible.

Read more

Homosexuality: ccc 2357–2359, 2396; cccc 492; youcat 65, 415.

 ## 4.25 How does Natural Family Planning work?

SCAN

The menstrual cycle goes through different phases: a woman is fertile for part of the cycle and cannot get pregnant the rest of the time. These periods coincide with certain changes in the body, which indicate whether a woman is in the fertile phase or not. Natural methods of family planning involve observing these signs, which can help couples either to avoid or to achieve pregnancy. Thus they live their sexual relationship in accordance with the way in which God has created us.

Living with awareness

As opposed to the pill and other chemical contraceptives, fertility awareness does not interfere with a woman's biology to make her infertile. Rather, it teaches a woman when she is fertile and when she is not. Knowing this, she and her husband can decide when to have sexual relations. If they are ready to welcome a child, they can choose to make love during the fertile phase of the woman. But if they have serious reasons for avoiding pregnancy, they can choose to make love only during the

phase when she cannot get pregnant. There are several ways to recognize these phases.

Natural Family Planning

One of these methods is called Natural Family Planning (NFP) or Natural Fertility Awareness. This method is very reliable,

The effectiveness of birth control

TYPE	Perfect use	In practice
Male sterilization	<0.1 %	0.1 %
Female sterilization	0.2 to 3 %	0.2 to 3 %
The pill	0.5 %	0.5 to 10 %
NFP (temp. & mucus)	0.4 %	2 %
Temperature only	1 %	2.5 to 7 %
Billings (mucus only)	1 to 3 %	3 to 35 %
Rhythm	3 to 5 %	12 %
Condom	2 to 5 %	10 to 12 %
Nothing	85 %	85 %

PEARL INDEX: MEAN CHANCE OF CONCEPTION WHEN APPLIED DURING 1 YEAR

Sexuality

What natural methods are there to measure the fertile phase of a woman?

A woman can calculate when her infertile phase occurs based on the **rhythm** of her previous cycles, but because the human body does not exactly follow the same pattern every cycle, this method is very imprecise.

A 0.5-degree rise in basal body **temperature**, which is measured when a woman wakes up in the morning, indicates that ovulation has taken place. Within a few days of this, the infertile phase begins. Because there can be other causes for the body temperature to rise, other signs of fertility are also sometimes observed. The start and end of the fertile period can be recognized through the changes in the cervical mucus, which is needed for sperm cells to survive in the woman's body. The **Billings** method observes mucus. **NFP** observes mucus and temperature.

Another method is to test the hormonal level of morning urine, to see whether the fertile phase has begun.

When women struggling with infertility first seek medical help for this problem, they often are taught to observe the physical signs that indicate when they are capable of conceiving a child. Given all its benefits, you would think that more couples would practice fertility awareness.

because it keeps track of more than one sign of fertility (SEE BOX). Once that has become a habit, it is hard not to recognize the bodily signs of the fertile cycle. Many couples use contraceptives because they don't know any better or lack confidence in natural methods, but surprisingly, Natural Family Planning is as reliable as the pill and five times more reliable than condoms (SEE BOX).

Suitable for marriage

In principle, the sexual relationship between husband and wife should always be open to new life (SEE TWEET 4.20). Because NFP does not suppress the natural ability to conceive, couples using it are always open to the possibility of a child. This is the main difference between artificial and natural birth control: one chemically or mechanically suppresses fertility while the other respects and cooperates with it. Practicing NFP fosters body-awareness, communication, consideration, and self-discipline. As a result, marriages in which couples use these natural methods have a high success rate.

> NFP **works by checking for certain bodily signs that tell the couple whether the woman is in a fertile phase.**

Read more
Birth control: CCC 2368–2372, 2399; CCCC 497–498; YOUCAT 420, 421.

4.26 When does human life begin?

Science can explain a great deal about the origins of human life. The moment of conception is when a man's sperm cell and a woman's egg cell join. At that moment, a new human organism is formed, consisting of one single cell, which is either a boy or a girl. That is the start of human life.

When do you become human?

When a baby is born after nine months of pregnancy, it's clear that he is a little human person. But what was he before birth? Was he at some point merely an unorganized lump of cells? If he were, we would have to be able to point to a specific moment when those cells turned into a tiny human being.

But when would that occur? The moment the heart starts to beat, after 18 days? The moment when the baby can live outside the womb, at about 23 weeks? Is there an exact moment when the group of multiplying human cells suddenly changes into a human being? Or must this organized, living, and growing group of human cells be a human being from the very beginning?

Budding children

Modern science has demonstrated that everything needed for a human being is present in the DNA from the moment of conception.

Perhaps a comparison can help. If you are given flowers, you don't throw away the buds because they do not look like flowers. You know very well that the buds are indeed flowers at an earlier stage of development

A continuous process

The science of biology has given many names to the different phases of a human life growing in a mother's womb. Immediately after conception the new human being is called a zygote. The zygote quickly starts to divide and is then called a morula. Four days after conception, the morula migrates through the mother's fallopian tube and develops into a blastula before nestling into the uterus. The blastula then grows into an embryo. After growing a little more, the embryo is called a fetus, before finally being called a baby.

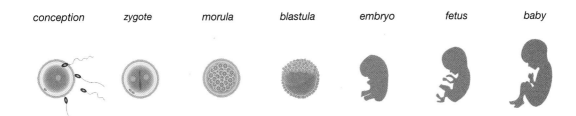

| conception | zygote | morula | blastula | embryo | fetus | baby |

Don't be distracted by all these different names: what happens is one continuous process of growth. Biologically speaking, from the moment of conception to the moment of birth, the same living human organism is developing and growing.

and that they will quickly blossom if you put the stems in a vase with water. In the same way, the zygote, the embryo, the fetus, etc. are all phases of early human development (SEE BOX). The human being is already there and needs only time and nourishment to mature and blossom.

Conception

A human being has not only a human body but also a human soul. Since human life starts with conception, both the human body and the human soul must be present from that moment. A father and a mother conceive new life, which is given to them by God. From the very beginning, we must cherish and protect every human being at every stage of his life!

> Human life starts when a woman's egg cell and a man's sperm cell fuse together to become a new and unique human being.

Read more

A human embryo is a human being: CCC 2273, 2323; CCCC 472; YOUCAT 385.

SCAN

4.27 What is wrong with prenatal testing?

Prenatal testing is done before birth. Its purpose is to determine whether an unborn child has certain diseases or disabilities. That helps to be fully prepared to start necessary medical treatment as soon as possible, including while the child is still developing in the womb.

Methods

Recent preliminary research shows that a mere eight weeks after conception, the DNA of the fetus can be found in the mother's blood, which might allow doctors to check for problems. Currently, however, the following methods are predominantly used:

- Echography uses ultrasound. The echo of the sounds waves provides an image of the embryo. It is the method most often used, because a few echoes during the pregnancy cannot harm the embryo. But the echo cannot reveal all the possible problems because it shows only the outside of the fetus.

- Chorionic villus sampling (from week 10) involves a surgical procedure to take a sample from the placenta, which transfers oxygen and food from the mother to the child. This sample of tissue is used to test for possible genetic disorders. The procedure does slightly increase the risk of birth defects or miscarriage, which is the spontaneous ending of a pregnancy.

- Amniocentesis (from week 16) is performed by using a hollow needle to puncture the amniotic sac, which holds the baby, to extract a small quantity of amniotic fluid. Tests are then carried out on the fluid. This method carries a small risk of blood loss, infection, or miscarriage.

Death sentence

It is great when prenatal tests can contribute to the health and well-being of the unborn child or if they help to prepare for necessary medical procedures after or sometimes even before birth. But the purpose of such tests must always be to treat the child. In each individual case, the doctor and the parents of the child must carefully determine whether the possible benefits of testing outweigh the chances of harming the baby.

To use prenatal testing to determine whether to have an abortion, for example because the child may have serious disabilities, is wrong (SEE TWEET 4.28; YOUCAT 384). A human being, even a very tiny one, must not be killed because he is sick, deformed, or disabled. The right to life either applies to everyone or is meaningless.

Therefore, the results of a medical test must never be a death sentence!

Selection

Does a child with Down syndrome have less right to be born than other children? Sadly, prenatal diagnosis is sometimes used to prevent certain children from being born. Some children are even being aborted simply because they are girls. As Christians we utterly reject these practices. Even a child with disabilities can give great joy and happiness to his parents. But because children with special needs can also be a heavy burden, society should offer assistance to their parents. To do so is the Christian duty to love and to care for our neighbors (SEE BOX). Pope Francis said: "A widespread mentality of the useful, the 'culture of waste' that today enslaves the hearts and minds of so many, comes at a very high cost: it asks for the elimination of human beings, especially if they are physically or socially weaker. Our response to this mentality is a decisive and unreserved 'yes' to life" (TO CATHOLIC DOCTORS, SEPT. 20, 2013).

Prenatal tests are good if their purpose is to help the child; the purpose must never be to determine whether to have an abortion.

Read more

Prenatal care: CCC 2274; YOUCAT 384–385.

 ## 4.28 Is abortion wrong?

SCAN

Whenever the media reports on an abusive mother who has beaten her own child to death, everyone agrees that, whatever the exact circumstances may have been, this is a terrible crime. But when a pregnant mother has an abortion, because she did not want her child for financial or other reasons, many people shrug their shoulders.

In both cases, whether the child was 10 years old or had been growing in his mother's womb for 3 months, an innocent child was put to death. A human life starts with conception, when his mother's egg cell is fertilized by his father's sperm cell (SEE TWEET 4.26). When parents deliberately do something that interferes with the growth of their child and causes him to die, no matter how soon after conception, they are killing their child. That is completely contrary to what a child deserves from his parents: to be cherished, protected, and nurtured.

Abortion
Sometimes a pregnancy spontaneously discontinues, without that being anyone's fault. The mother's body then expels the embryo in a miscarriage. Sad as it is, a miscarriage occurs naturally when something is going seriously wrong with the pregnancy (SEE TWEET 1.34). That is very different from an elective abortion, which is deliberately caused (SEE BOX). When you see the grief that parents, and especially mothers, can feel about a miscarriage, you can understand a little better the inhumanity of an abortion. Jesus said: "Whoever receives one such child in my name receives me" (MK. 9:37). We have to take that statement seriously. Our God is the God of life. The fifth commandment is "You shall not kill" (SEE TWEET 4.9). Every person, no matter how young, has the right to life. That is why the Church condemns abortion under all circumstances (SEE TWEET 4.30).

U.S. abortion laws vary from state to state, but since the 1973 *Roe v. Wade* case, the Supreme

The stain of an abortion

"The one eliminated [in an abortion] is a human being at the very beginning of life. No one more absolutely innocent could be imagined. In no way could this human being ever be considered an aggressor, much less an unjust aggressor! He or she is weak, defenseless, even to the point of lacking that minimal form of defense consisting in the poignant power of a newborn baby's cries and tears.

"The unborn child is totally entrusted to the protection and care of the woman carrying him or her in the womb. And yet sometimes it is precisely the mother herself who makes the decision and asks for the child to be eliminated, and who then goes about having it done." (Pope John Paul II, Evangelium Vitae, 58)

Terms such as "terminating the pregnancy" and "products of conception" are common (SEE TWEET 4.29). These are not technically incorrect, but they are misleading when they replace the ordinary language we use to describe unborn children and thereby dehumanize them. Blessed Mother Teresa once said that abortion is a double murder: it kills not only the child, but also the conscience of the mother. The decision to have an abortion is sometimes made quite quickly and coolly. But more often, this decision, with its grave and irreversible consequences, is a harrowing experience. Many women who have undergone an abortion suffer from guilt, grief, and depression (SEE TWEET 4.29). Sometimes the first feeling after an abortion is relief that a problem has been solved, but later, sometimes even years later, regrets can arise. And nothing can be done to bring back the life of the child. That pain can be almost unbearable. Thankfully, God always forgives those who repent what they have done (SEE TWEET 3.38). Many women have received mercy and healing after an abortion in the Sacrament of Reconciliation.

Court has upheld the principle that a woman's right to privacy includes the decision to have an abortion. Abortions can be legally restricted when the baby is deemed to be viable, that is, capable of living outside the womb, but such restrictions are rare.

Shameful cover-up

In the abortion industry and the popular culture, the words used disguise that an abortion kills an innocent human being.

> Abortion is the deliberate killing of a human being in the womb. That is a great wrong & must be condemned under all circumstances.

Read more

Abortion: CCC 2270–2274, 2322; CCCC 470; YOUCAT 383.

 ## 4.29 How is an abortion performed?

What actually happens during an abortion is often downplayed in abortion clinics, where the procedure is not described for what it really is: taking the life of a human being (SEE TWEET 4.28). An early abortion may seem like a simple procedure, but as with all operations, it poses certain physical risks. It can also cause emotional pain and psychological problems, which sometimes don't arise until years later (SEE BOX).

Abortion pill

Up to 7 weeks after menstruation, there is the option to take abortion-causing drugs. In the seventh week, the first signs of the child's arms and legs are already recognizable. The embryo is still very small but already has a beating heart. A first pill slows the production of pregnancy hormones and loosens the embryo from the wall of the uterus. A second pill produces contractions, which expel the embryo. Common side effects of these drugs include severe cramping, nausea, vomiting, blood loss, and diarrhea.

Suction-aspiration or vacuum aspiration

If pregnancy has advanced between 7 and 12 weeks, two commonly used procedures are suction-aspiration and vacuum aspiration. At this point, the child has grown larger and his arms and legs have formed. As a result, the child cannot easily be removed from the womb. First, the cervix is widened and then a powerful syringe or vacuum is inserted into the uterus to suck the child out. This procedure can injure the cervix or the uterus. An incomplete abortion can result in hemorrhage or infection.

Evacuation

By week 12, the important organs of the child are functioning and his nose, mouth, and eyes are clearly visible. At this point the fetus measures about 4 inches from head to rump. From this age onward, evacuation requires that the child is taken from the uterus bit by bit. It is crucial that no parts of the fetus remain behind, because they can lead to a serious

Human life

378

Sarah chose to have an abortion

Sarah (28) accidentally got pregnant. She found it very difficult to make the decision, but did not dare to keep the child. Immediately after the abortion, she regretted it. The following weeks she felt sad, anxious, and afraid of being punished. To overcome these negative feelings, she then decided that she wanted to be pregnant. But the moment she became pregnant again, she felt very confused. She said: "I was playing with life: I had one child killed, and then got pregnant again.... The abortion was a huge mistake." After giving birth, she really enjoyed her newborn son, but her sorrow and regret remained. She had sleepless nights, and kept wondering what would have happened if she had allowed her first child to live. "This is what it now feels like for me: I have lost a child" (VIVA MAGAZINE, MAY 2001).

Morning-after: contraception or abortion?

The morning-after pill is often described as a contraceptive, but depending on when it is taken it can cause an abortion. On average the menstruation cycle lasts 28 days. The most fertile time lasts about 4 to 5 days, surrounding ovulation. If the morning-after pill is taken a few days before ovulation (period A), the ovulation is sometimes blocked. Under these circumstances, the morning-after pill functions like a contraceptive (SEE TWEET 4.23). But if this pill is taken later on (period B), it can stop an actual embryo from nestling in the uterus, and then it is functionally an abortion. Some chemical contraceptives act in a similar way. Thus some women on regular birth control pills could be having abortions without even realizing it.

menstruation cycle (28 days)

	ovulation	
1	12 16	28
A	B	

infection. Methods used at later stages of pregnancy may involve inducing labor after poison is injected into the child or the sac he is in. If the baby is born alive he is killed directly or left to die. In another late-term procedure, the living child is partially pulled from the womb by his legs. His brains are then sucked out to cause his head, which is the largest part of his body, to collapse.

Abortion is a drastic and violent procedure carried out through drugs or various surgical procedures.

Read more
Abortion: CCC 2270–2274, 2322; CCCC 470; YOUCAT 383.

SCAN

4.30 What if a woman has been raped, doesn't want to have a child, or is ill?

The right to life is the first and most important right. Most people agree that a child has rights, even before being born. But in some cases, it can seem almost inhuman to protect the rights of the unborn child when that would cause pain, sorrow, and suffering to the mother. Thankfully, the situations discussed in the next paragraphs are uncommon.

Rape

Many people believe a woman who has been raped should not be stopped from having an abortion. Rape is truly a dreadful crime. A rapist violently abuses another person to rob something that can only be freely given with love (SEE TWEET 4.20). It is therefore understandable when a woman who becomes pregnant after being raped considers an abortion. Something terrible has happened to her, and the child growing inside her keeps reminding her of it. But an abortion is also a violent act (SEE TWEET 4.29). We must not think only about the horrors of the rape but also those of the abortion. The child carries no blame. How does killing him punish the crime of the rapist? Both mother and child are innocent. They both deserve care and support. And should the mother decide to give the child up for adoption, she should be given the help that she needs to do that.

Regret

Somebody can voluntarily have sexual relations with another person and then regret it later. If such an encounter results in pregnancy, the father and the mother may not want to bring their child into the world. Maybe they are both very young, maybe for other reasons neither of them is able to care properly for their child, or maybe the woman has been left to face this situation alone. But here, too, we must consider that the child already exists, and, as every human being, has a right to live. For everyone's sake society should help the parents not to kill their child. The mother needs support so that she can give birth and then perhaps give the child to adoptive parents if that is the best option.

Human life

Human rights

From the moment a man's sperm cell and a woman's egg cell have fused, a new human life has come into being (SEE TWEET 4.26). It would never be human if it were not so from the very beginning. Ultimately, the new life comes from God: "You formed my inward parts, you knitted me together in my mother's womb" (Ps. 139:13).

A human embryo is a human being from the earliest moment of his existence. Therefore, no matter how small and vulnerable, a human embryo has the same right to life as everyone else has. That is why an embryo has the right not to be destroyed, frozen, cloned, interfered with, stored, or archived. A human being must never be regarded as a thing: it is a person who is going through an early phase of his development!

The mother's life is at risk

A very difficult situation arises when the life of the mother is endangered by her pregnancy. The starting point for any decision in this situation is respect for both the mother and the child. Efforts must be made to save both lives and not to sacrifice one for the other. Neither mother nor child may be deliberately and directly killed for the benefit of the other. But if, for example, removing an afflicted uterus could save the mother, that procedure would be moral, even if the baby died in the process, so long as the death of the child was not intended. There are mothers who, at the cost of their own lives, voluntarily and heroically chose to forego medical treatments during pregnancy in order to save their unborn children.

When it comes to these terrible decisions, we really need God's help. Any decision needs to be always based on his love for every person.

Thankfully, there are many organizations, some related to the Church, that can help young mothers in these circumstances. Abortion is never necessary! An unplanned and initially unwanted child is still an important member of the human family.

> Rape is a terrible crime. Sometimes, pregnancy can come at a bad time. But the unborn child has a right to live, just as the mother does!

Read more

Morality of human acts: CCC 1755–1756, 1759–1761; CCCC 368–369; YOUCAT 292.

4.31 Do I have to accept my body the way it is?

The Bible tells us: "Your body is a temple of the Holy Spirit within you, which you have from God. You are not your own.... So glorify God in your body" (I Cor. 6:19–20). God has created your body as a place in which he himself wants to live. Our loving God wants us to be happy with ourselves in a relationship with him (see Tweet 4.1).

Self-mutilation and sterilization

We can be willing to bear a small amount of physical discomfort for the sake of our relationship with God (see Tweet 1.37). That is the basis for fasting and other acts of penance (see Tweet 3.19), which are noble expressions of our longing to be as close to Jesus as possible, even in his suffering. Causing ourselves pain for health reasons, for example dieting to treat diabetes or pulling a decayed tooth, is also acceptable. Apart from this kind of reason, however, deliberately causing ourselves physical suffering or mutilating our bodies is contrary to God's Will for us. God has given us our bodies and commands that we care for

and not abuse them. Only surgical procedures that are necessary for health reasons are allowed (ccc 2297). That is why sterilization, for example, is wrong. Sterilization is an operation that deliberately damages a person's healthy reproductive organs. It not only mutilates the body, it also makes somebody incapable of having children, which goes against the Christian view of marriage (see Tweet 4.19). Removal of cancerous ovaries, on the other hand, even though it results in sterilization, is permissible in order to save a woman's life.

Plastic surgery

A plastic surgeon can do many things to repair a damaged body. Replacing seriously burned skin or reattaching separated limbs is aimed at restoring bodily integrity. So are surgeries that fix cleft palates or other physical deformities. The matter is more complicated if the surgery is a facelift, a breast enlargement, or a liposuction. Are these procedures done for reasons of health or vanity? Many people

A transsexual is a man who identifies himself as a woman or a woman who identifies herself as a man. This is not the same as a transvestite, which is a person who likes to wear the clothes worn by the other sex. Some transsexuals have operations to make their bodies look like those of the opposite sex. The Church opposes these operations because sex is a physical, biological reality that cannot be changed by surgery. Such an operation mutilates the body, causes infertility, and makes marriage impossible. Transsexuality is a serious psychological problem that can cause great suffering, but surgery cannot remedy this. Rather the transsexual needs psychological help so that he can learn to accept himself and to find meaningful relationships the way he is. We may be sure that the God who made us loves us the way we are, and that whenever somebody is suffering, Christ is suffering with him (SEE TWEET 1.37).

Bodies as instruments

Our value does not lie in our physical appearances! Our lives have value because we were created by God in his own image, and that resemblance is found chiefly in our souls, where true beauty lies. God gave us our bodies, so when we reject our bodies as they are, wishing we looked like someone else, we are rejecting God's gifts. We must take care not to use our bodies as if they were mere instruments, for example to obtain an artificial beauty which does not fit us. As part of this fallen world, our bodies are not perfect, and they are subject to illness, aging, and death. While we are to take care of our physical health, we must accept that we cannot be young and physically beautiful forever. Another problem arises with medical experiments on people in return for payment. Your body is not something that can be sold. Of course, you may choose to undergo certain experiments that can contribute to finding ways to cure others, if that is your motive, provided that you do not do undue harm to yourself. It is important that you care for the body that God has given you (SEE TWEET 4.40) and not treat it recklessly.

feel insecure about the way they look. Some people who think they are fat or ugly when objectively they are not, are suffering from a mental disorder. The inability to accept and to love oneself is a psychological, or spiritual, problem that cannot be solved with surgery.

> We are not owners but custodians of our bodies. We may not unnecessarily harm or mutilate the bodies God gave us.

Read more

Respect for the body: CCC 2297; CCCC 477; YOUCAT 387, 392. *Experimenting on people:* CCC 2292–2295; CCCC 475; YOUCAT 390.

4.32 What if people cannot have children?

SCAN

Married couples often suffer greatly when they discover that they physically cannot have children. After all, procreation is one of the aims of their loving union that is expressed in their sexual relationship (SEE TWEET 4.19). Understandably, some people turn to medicine to have the children they so desire, and modern medicine can achieve many wonderful things. But not everything that is medically possible is good. An infertility treatment is ethical only if it respects both human sexuality and the life of the unborn child. When weighing such matters, three things are important to the Church.

A child is a gift

First, every human being is a gift and deserves to be treated as a person, no matter how small he may be. Parents do not have a right to a child, and they should never treat a child as a product or a thing. A person should never be produced (in a fertility clinic), but must always be received as a gift and as a result of the love between both parents.

Unity and procreation

Second, a married couple unites intimately through their sexual union, which is of itself open to new life. Those two elements, unity and procreation, must not be separated from the sexual act (SEE TWEET 4.20). The only infertility treatments acceptable to the Church are those that do not break that connection. Thus, conception must take place within the physical union of husband and wife, and not outside of it in a laboratory.

Childless but fruitful?

It can be very difficult for a couple to accept that, despite their heartfelt desire for children, they cannot have them. But even in their grief, they can be fruitful in many other ways. There are beautiful examples of childless couples who generously serve others. They can, for example, help relatives, friends, and others in ways that would not be possible with children. Childless against their will, such couples can still find fulfillment by being mothers and fathers in other ways.

The family

Third, the unity of a family must always be defended (SEE TWEET 4.19). A child deserves to be conceived within the marital embrace of his own father and mother and to be raised by them. When children are conceived in such a way as to be deliberately cut off from their own biological parents, they may become confused about themselves, their parentage, and their connection to the people they live with.

A marriage can be fruitful without biological children, and the couple can contribute significantly to the lives of others (SEE BOX). Adoption is one possibility. This has two benefits: a parentless child can be given a family, and a childless couple can receive a child. In this case too, however, couples do not have a right to demand adoption; the best interests of the child must always come first. In principle, a child deserves to be raised by his own father and mother, who love each other and their child. Unfortunately, that is not always possible, for example, if one of the parents dies. But that is no reason to abandon the important basic principle of family life. As Pope Francis said: "If God's love is lacking, the family loses its harmony, self-centeredness prevails, and joy fades. But the family which experiences the joy of faith communicates it naturally. That family is the salt of the earth and the light of the world, it is the leaven of society" (HOMILY ON FAMILY DAY, OCT. 27, 2013).

Infertility can be very sad. In some cases it can be cured. But a child is not a right & must never be demanded or treated as a product.

Read more

Infertility: CCC 2375, 2379; CCCC 501; YOUCAT 422.

4.33 What about artificial insemination and surrogate mothers?

SCAN

With a natural conception, sperm cells swim through the fallopian tube toward the egg cell, where conception takes place (SEE TWEET 4.26). However, something could go wrong, stopping the sperm cells from reaching the egg cell. Medical science can do much, but it is important also to consider what is moral from a Christian point of view.

Artificial insemination

Couples struggling to conceive a child sometimes try artificial insemination. In this procedure sperm is collected and inserted into the woman by a doctor. Another method of artificial insemination is gamete intrafallopian tube transfer (GIFT). Before this procedure, the woman is given hormonal treatments to ripen some of her ova, which are then surgically removed. These egg cells and the man's sperm cells are inserted into the fallopian tube at the same time so that conception can then take place.

Unity and procreation

The Church disapproves of artificial insemination because the child is conceived outside the sexual act of a married couple (SEE TWEET 4.20). Furthermore, all of the people involved are treated as objects in a manufacturing process (SEE TWEET 4.34), and the actions the man must do to collect the sperm are immoral (SEE TWEET 4.22). Medical assistance in reproduction is acceptable only if the loving sexual union of a married couple remains directly linked to conception. That could be the case if the married couple's egg cells and sperm cells are inserted in the fallopian tube immediately after their sexual union so that conception can then take place in a natural way inside the body. This exception is an altered form of GIFT.

Donor sperm

If the man's sperm is found to be inadequate, or if a woman is trying to conceive without direct involvement with a man, donor sperm is sometimes used for artificial insemination.

What is the problem with surrogate mothers?

If a woman cannot have children, she sometimes asks or hires another woman to be a surrogate mother. The surrogate agrees beforehand that, after the baby is born, she will give the baby to the other woman, who then legally adopts the child. In most of these cases artificial insemination or in vitro fertilization (SEE TWEET 4.34) is used to impregnate the surrogate mother. Sometimes she is a family member or a friend who volunteers to carry the child; often she is a hired stranger, sometimes a poor woman living in another country.

Surrogate arrangements have led to a number of different problems. Pregnancy and giving birth has sometimes caused health problems for the surrogate, without the outweighing benefit of being able to continue as the mother. Some surrogate mothers have refused to give away the baby because they, quite naturally, formed an attachment to the child. Some have refused to abort the child when it was discovered through prenatal testing that he had a medical problem or was otherwise "unsuitable for the hiring party". Some have been left with a child without the means to provide for it, after its rejection by the hiring party. In all of these cases, the child became the object of a legal battle.

Surrogacy diverges from the ideal, built into nature, that the child be born from the loving sexual union of a man and a woman who are married to each other. To rely on surrogate mothers can lead to unnatural and inhuman situations and must therefore always be rejected. It would be even less humane to place the embryo in an animal such as a goat or a sheep, or even an artificial womb, as some scientists claim will soon be possible.

....

In this case, not only is the child conceived outside of the marital embrace, but the child is deliberately separated from his biological father from the very beginning of his life. The man who raises the child can sometimes feel estranged from him, while the biological father can sometimes regret that he has an unknown number of children who are strangers to him. The child can feel hurt and angry when he later understands the implications of his origin. More and more such grown children are tracking down their natural fathers and any brothers and sisters who also were conceived with his sperm, in some cases because they fear committing incest by unknowingly becoming romantically involved with a sibling.

> The Church rejects artificial insemination & surrogacy for these break the bond between marital love & children and treat people as objects.

Read more

Artificial insemination and surrogate mothers: CCC 2376–2377; CCCC 499; YOUCAT 423.

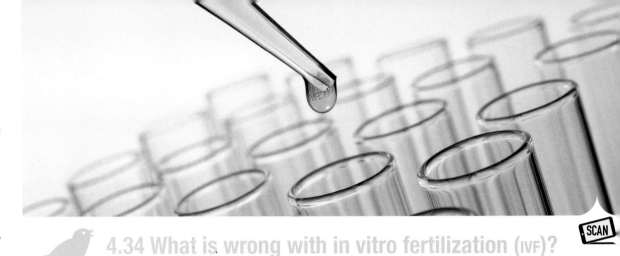

SCAN

4.34 What is wrong with in vitro fertilization (IVF)?

With in vitro fertilization (IVF), egg cells are fertilized in a laboratory. First a woman is given hormone treatments to ripen unnaturally a large number of her eggs. These cells are surgically removed and placed together with sperm cells in glass petri dishes ("in vitro"). Alternatively, sperm cells are injected directly into egg cells. After fertilization, the cells begin to divide and the embryo begins to grow (SEE TWEET 4.26). Within days after conception, one or more of the developing embryos are transferred to a woman's uterus or fallopian tube. If an embryo successfully nestles in the womb, the child can continue to grow until birth. The first such "test tube baby" was Louise Brown, who was born in England in 1978.

Problems

The biggest problem with IVF is that multiple egg cells are fertilized in the lab, but only a few of the embryos are transferred to a uterus. Embryos with a higher risk of serious defects or disorders or with other characteristics not wanted by the eventual parents are rejected. Embryos are also rejected at this stage by parents who want only a boy or a girl. The rejected embryos are destroyed or used for research; they sometimes are

....

Your brother in a freezer

There are embryo banks with millions of frozen human beings. This presents us with an unsolvable dilemma. These are embryos that could not be transferred to the mother after IVF or that were produced specifically for the purpose of research.

What can we do with freezers full of human beings? It would be wrong to kill them directly. Yet it seems wrong to let them die. But to have them adopted and born would also cause some immense problems (SEE TWEET 4.33). This is a dead end: every solution is wrong here. The origin of this evil is the separation of reproduction from the sexual union of husband and wife, which has resulted in human embryos being produced as if they were mere objects for our use (SEE TWEET 4.26 AND 4.32).

temporarily frozen (although about half of those do not survive the thawing process [SEE BOX]).

Here, human embryos, human beings, are used as objects or raw material, which cannot be right. Another objection against IVF is that there is a certain health risk to the woman whose egg cells are ripened and harvested. In addition, with IVF, procreation and sexual union are completely separated from each other (SEE TWEET 4.20). Even though the wish to have children is completely understandable and legitimate, a child must never be treated as a mere means, which the parents can demand for their own happiness: a child is a person and a freely given gift from God.

Complicated relationship

With IVF, all sorts of problems can arise. Sometimes parents regret having chosen which children in the lab would live and which would die. Sometimes they anguish over what to do about their offspring who are in a frozen state. Australian research has shown that with IVF, the chance of genetic disabilities is higher than with natural conception. With the use of donor cells (SEE TWEET 4.33), the relationships between parents and their children can become very complicated. In the most extreme case, a child can have three mothers (a biological mother, a surrogate mother, and an adoptive mother) and two fathers (a biological father and an adoptive father). Children are being produced by multiple building blocks coming from multiple people: sperm cell, egg cell, and uterus, which can be combined in different ways. There are even experiments in which genetic material from yet another person is being added to the mix. The Church cannot accept this playing with human life.

Human dignity

In 2010 the Nobel Prize for Physiology or Medicine was awarded to Robert Edwards for his research on IVF. A large group of Catholic doctors protested. They declared: "Although IVF has brought happiness to the many couples who have conceived through this process, it has done so at an enormous cost.... Many millions of embryos have been created and discarded during the IVF process.... This has led to a culture where they are regarded as commodities, rather than the precious human individuals which they are.... We can only be fully human when we live in accordance with the will of God, respecting the special dignity which is accorded to all human beings."

> With IVF multiple human embryos are conceived, of which only one or two are used. The others are killed or frozen for later use.

Read more

Artificial insemination: CCC 2376–2377; CCCC 499; YOUCAT 428.

4.35 What is cloning?

Cloning replicates a living organism – a plant, an animal, or a human being. Cloning procedures create a genetically identical copy of the original organism. If a human being were ever cloned and allowed to mature, however, there would be other factors that would make the clone a unique individual. Identical twins have the same DNA and are also two different people! There are two ways to clone:

- An embryo can be split in a laboratory (as happens spontaneously and naturally with identical twins).
- With somatic cell nuclear transfer (SEE PICTURE), the nucleus of an egg cell is replaced with the nucleus of a cell from the organism being cloned (the "parent"). After certain treatments, the new cell will behave like a fertilized cell and start to grow accordingly.

Reproductive cloning

The purpose of reproductive cloning is to make a copy of an animal or a human being. In 1996, the sheep Dolly was cloned by somatic cell nuclear transfer. Soon other animals were also cloned.

These animals often had deformities, disabilities, and severe health problems, and they typically died prematurely. That shows that this kind of procedure is not as straightforward as it may seem. After somatic cell nuclear transfer, the embryonic clone is transferred to the uterus of a surrogate mother, where it continues to develop until birth. So far attempts at human reproductive cloning have not been successful, and the procedure has been made illegal in many countries.

....

Who has eight parents?

With reproductive human cloning, all DNA is from one single person, while a normal embryo is a mix of the two sets of DNA from his parents. This raises all sorts of questions. For starters, the person whose DNA is being cloned is not really a father or a mother, but rather a brother or a sister. In fact, eight people could claim the title of parent, or even owner, of the clone: the source of the DNA, the father or the mother of the source, the source of the egg cell, the surrogate mother, the adoptive mother or father of the clone, and the person who fathered the process in the laboratory.

Cloning by somatic cell nuclear transfer

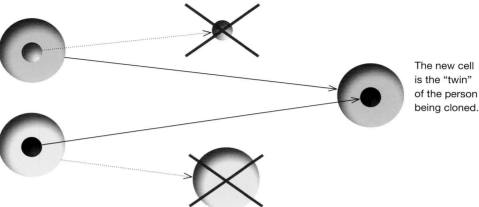

The egg cell of a woman is taken, and its nucleus removed.

The nucleus of the cell from the person being cloned is taken, and placed inside the egg cell.

The new cell is the "twin" of the person being cloned.

Therapeutic cloning

The purpose of therapeutic cloning is to produce human cells that might repair damaged tissue or cure certain diseases. First a human being is cloned as described above. Once the human embryo has grown to about 100 cells, its stem cells are removed, which of course kills the embryo. These stem cells are then transferred to the patient or used to grow tissues needed for treating the patient (SEE TWEET 4.36).

Better not to

Cloning animals could be acceptable as long as it is done to help human beings and does not do unnecessary harm to the animals involved (SEE TWEET 4.48). Cloning humans, however, is absolutely wrong. A human clone is a full human being and deserves to

be treated as such and not as a means to cure someone else (SEE TWEET 4.19). In addition, in the case of reproductive cloning, the normal relationship between human sexuality and reproduction is entirely absent (SEE TWEET 4.20). There is also the danger that cloning could be used to produce a specific kind, type, or race of humans. In short, the Church emphatically rejects all kinds of human cloning.

> Cloning makes a genetically identical copy. Human cloning makes some human beings the tools of others.

Read more
Production of embryos: CCC 2275.

4.36 What about stem cells and genetically modified crops?

Stem cells are special cells that have a crucial part to play in the development and repair of the human body. They are cells that can develop into different kinds of cells, such as skin, blood, etc.

Different kinds of stem cells
There are three kinds of stem cells.

- Between conception and the formation of the blastula (SEE TWEET 4.26) stem cells can grow into all kinds of different cells. These are called *totipotent* stem cells. Identical twins result when the organism splits at this stage of development (SEE TWEET 4.35).

- At a later stage of development, stem cells can no longer develop into every kind of cell. But they can still develop into a number of different cells the body needs. These are *pluripotent* stem cells. These are also present in a child's umbilical cord, the placenta that connects a mother and her unborn child, and the bone marrow of children and adults.

- Blood stem cells and skin stem cells are examples of stem cells that exist in the human body and can develop to repair damaged tissue. These are *multipotent* stem cells.

Medicinal cells
Pluripotent stem cells can be used to grow tissues that can help to treat certain diseases. That is a noble goal. But whether it is ethically acceptable depends on where the stem cells come from. There are no objections against using stem cells from the umbilical cord or the placenta donated by a mother after her child has been born. There is also nothing wrong with using stem cells from the bone marrow of a consenting donor. The problem is that the supply of cells from these sources is very limited, and stem cells from adults are difficult to match with the patient and do not divide as well. For this reason, many people want to clone human beings in order to harvest their embryonic stem cells.

Genetic manipulation

By manipulating the DNA in the nucleus of cells, certain traits of plants, animals, and people can be altered in laboratories. It is acceptable to try to cure a defect in human DNA and thereby cure a genetic disorder so long as no artificial methods of reproduction, such as in vitro fertilization (SEE TWEET 4.34) or cloning (SEE TWEET 4.35), are involved and no one is deliberately harmed or killed in the process. Another crucial condition is that the risks to the patient must not outweigh the likely benefits.

We have been manipulating genes for a very long time. After all, crossbreeding plants and animals has been going on for many centuries. Crops that have been genetically modified can have improved yields or be resistant to certain pests or diseases. Animals that have been genetically modified can produce more meat, milk, or wool, or they can be more resistant to disease.

The opponents of genetic manipulation argue that it interferes with nature and goes against the Creator. God has created plants to yield seeds "according to their own kinds" (GEN. 1:11–12), and because of that, we ought not to change them and "play God". But the issue is not that simple. God has made us the stewards of the earth and put us in charge of the plants and animals (GEN. 1:29). He has given us the ability to reason so that we can make use of the things of the earth for the benefit of all. We must, however, use them wisely (CCC 2293).

We make wise use of nature if our actions help to "make accessible to each what is needed to lead a truly human life" (CCC 1908). So, in principle, there are no objections against eating or using genetically modified plants or animals. Of course, we have to monitor carefully whether any damage is being done to human health or to the environment.

Pope John Paul II condemned "man's attempt to control the sources of life through experiments in human cloning" which is sometimes "arrogantly seen as better even than the plan of the Creator" (AUG. 6, 2004).

Embryo cells

It is never acceptable to obtain stem cells from human embryos, not even if they are produced through therapeutic cloning (SEE TWEET 4.35), because human beings are used as objects and killed in the process. Every human embryo is a human person and has the right to live! The purpose of medical science is to cure people and to save their lives. But you cannot do that by deliberately killing another person!

> Stem cells can be used for cures, but never at the cost of another human life. We can use, with caution, genetically modified crops.

Read more

The common good: CCC 1905–1912, 1924–1927; CCCC 407–409. *Humans and Science*: CCC 2292–2294; CCCC 475; YOUCAT 390.

4.37 When is somebody dead?

Death is not something we like to talk about. We usually experience the death of someone we know as something grievous, a great loss. At the same time, death also fascinates us. Think about the success of murder mysteries and horror films. Every person must die, but there is much we do not yet know about death. The Second Vatican Council (SEE TWEET 2.48) said: "It is in the face of death that the riddle of human existence grows most acute" (GAUDIUM ET SPES, 18). Death is part of nature as we know it, but is also "the wages of sin" (ROM. 6:23). Death came into the world through the Fall. Since that moment, all human beings have to die (SEE TWEET 1.4).

Looking forward to death?

Christians look forward to death because they hope to meet God. Because of Jesus, death can be seen as a positive thing. St. Paul said: "To me to live is Christ, and to die is gain" (PHIL. 1:21). He actually longed for death: "My desire is to depart and be with Christ, for that is far better" (PHIL. 1:23). But it is not up to us

A vegetative state?

People who are in a coma are sometimes said to be in a "vegetative state", as if their lives are like that of vegetables. This term is misleading because usually people in a coma are breathing, have beating hearts, and register some brain activity. Those are all signs of life.

Somebody in a coma has a right to proportional medical attention, which includes the artificial administration of oxygen, hydration, and nutrition (SEE TWEET 4.39). We cannot judge the value of a person in a coma: human life can never be considered really vegetative. However, when further medical intervention is of no benefit to the patient, we can discontinue extraordinary means of care (SEE TWEET 4.39).

to decide when we will die (SEE TWEET 4.38). For this reason, St. Paul added: "But to remain in the flesh is more necessary on your account. Convinced of this, I know that I shall remain and continue with you all" (PHIL. 1:24–25).

When does a person die?

We have paid close attention to the questions that surround the origins of human life (SEE TWEET 4.26). It is good to think carefully about the end of our life on earth as well. To determine the exact moment of death is very important – especially when the person who is dying is an organ donor (SEE TWEET 4.40). If you were to remove organs too quickly and cause the person's death, that would be murder, but if you wait too long, the organs may already have started to decay and could no longer be used. On a congress about organ donation, Pope John Paul II reiterated the Church's belief that death is the moment the soul leaves the body (AUG. 29, 2000). It is clear, however, that this moment cannot exactly be determined by scientific means. That is why, according to the pope, scientists should not try to find the exact moment of death, but rather, to find biological signs that ensure that somebody is truly dead.

Determining death

Usually, it's enough to determine that breathing has stopped, and that the heart has stopped beating. For a person on a respirator, however, is breathing necessarily a sign of life? The current medical consensus is that somebody is certainly dead when all brain activity has stopped completely and irreversibly (in the cerebrum, the cerebellum, and the brain stem). If rigorously applied, these criteria can lead a doctor to the moral certainty that a person is truly dead (POPE JOHN PAUL II, AUG. 29, 2000).

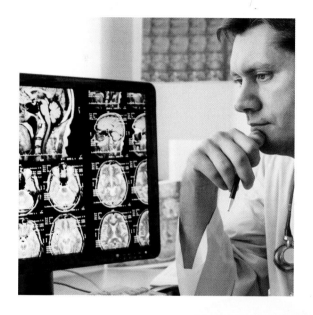

Somebody dies when his soul leaves the body. Legally and medically, death is determined to have occurred when the brain has stopped working.

Read more

Death is not the end: CCC 1005–1014, 1016, 1019; CCCC 206; YOUCAT 155.
Separation of body and soul: CCC 997–1004, 1016–1018; CCCC 205; YOUCAT 154.

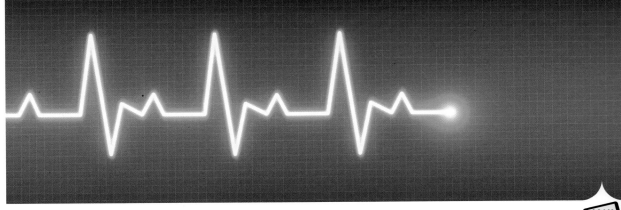

4.38 Is euthanasia always wrong?

The end of life

The word *euthanasia* is from ancient Greek and literally means "good death". Originally, the word was used for the medical treatment of people at the end of their lives, to ensure that they could die peacefully and naturally. During the Second World War, the term was abused by the Nazis to murder thousands of disabled people and others they considered to be undesirable. But, more recently, euthanasia has become synonymous with *assisted suicide*, that is, killing somebody who no longer wants to live and requests to die.

Pope John Paul II defined euthanasia as "an action or omission which of itself and by intention causes death, with the purpose of eliminating all suffering" (EVANGELIUM VITAE, 65). The pope also said that euthanasia is a grave violation of God's laws: deliberately killing an innocent person is always wrong. Committing euthanasia is morally similar to helping a person to commit suicide (SEE TWEET 4.41): instead of helping somebody to respect his God-given life, you help him to end it.

Contradicting the doctor's oath

Performing euthanasia is contrary to the ancient oath of the Greek doctor Hippocrates: "I will give no deadly medicine to any one if asked, nor suggest any such counsel" (HIPPOCRATIC OATH).

When does life become unbearable?

One day, an elderly patient called Mary was so seriously ill that the doctors advised euthanasia. The family thought about it, but decided against it. It wasn't just religious considerations that they weighed. It is very hard to decide about a person's life! This was just as well, because against all odds Mary was cured and continued to live happily, with a minor handicap, for another 20 years. Of course, it doesn't always go that way. But it does show that we cannot control everything. How can we ever be certain that a life has become unlivable? Pope Benedict XVI called euthanasia a "false solution to the drama of suffering, a solution unworthy of man. Indeed, the true response cannot be to put someone to death, however 'kindly', but rather to witness to the love that helps people to face their pain and agony in a human way" (ANGELUS, FEB. 1, 2009).

It is remarkable that many nursing homes in the Netherlands, where euthanasia is legal, give doctors a few days off after they have euthanized someone. Time to recover emotionally is not given to doctors after any other procedure. Even if someone dies, after everything has been tried to save the life, a doctor can calmly reflect on what he did. Apparently, that's not the case with euthanasia.

Needing attention

A person needs special attention when the quality of his life starts to decline (ccc 2276). People suffering from old age, debilitating illnesses, or disabilities must be helped to lead a life that is as normal as possible. Some people say unbearable suffering and the incurability of an illness or a disability are arguments for euthanasia.

It is terrible to see a loved one suffer (see Tweet 4.40). But who decides what constitutes unbearable suffering? Patients often learn to bear greater suffering step-by-step. They may even find that suffering is serving a purpose in their lives, giving them an opportunity for reflection and spiritual growth. Sometimes the suffering does not last, even though doctors thought otherwise (see box). Human life can be stronger than we think. You may be confident that we will not be asked to suffer more than we can handle: "God is faithful, and he will not let you be tempted beyond your strength" (I Cor. 10:13).

But at the same time, we should do what we can to ease our own pain and suffering and that of others (see Tweet 4.39).

Who is in charge?

The more human beings can do, the more they want to control every aspect of life, including death (see Tweet 4.36). That tendency is clearly visible in our time. But who is really in charge of his life? We were given our lives without having asked for them. And they will also end without us having to do anything to bring that end about. We are not the owners of our lives, we are their stewards. St. Paul says that when someone destroys his body, "God will destroy him" (1 Cor. 3:17). Thus suicide is not an option (see Tweet 4.41). Furthermore, you never know when you might receive a very special grace from God. Look at the Good Thief on the cross: only when he was in great suffering, just before he died, did he encounter Jesus (Lk. 23:40–43). With euthanasia, we turn against God, by rejecting his gift of life; therefore, euthanasia is always wrong.

> Euthanasia is the intentional killing of someone, requested by himself or those caring for him. It's a rejection of God & his gift of life.

Read more

Euthanasia: ccc 2276–2279, 2324; cccc 470–471; youcat 382.

4.39 Do you have to keep people alive at all costs?

The end of life

There is a huge difference between a natural death and a death that is directly caused by other people (euthanasia [SEE TWEET 4.38]). The latter is always wrong. However, the Church does not take the position that you have to keep people alive at all costs. In this context, it is important to think carefully about the kinds of treatment available. An important distinction has to be made between ordinary, or proportional, care and extraordinary care.

(Dis)proportional care

Ordinary, or proportional, care consists of administering food, drink, and standard medicines; binding wounds; and perhaps even giving oxygen. This kind of care is essential to life: if you don't eat or drink; if you can't stop bleeding or fight an infection; or if you cannot breathe, you will quickly die. That's why refusing this kind of care is tantamount to active euthanasia. Even if death seems imminent, you may not deny a patient ordinary care unless it is no longer beneficial, or even harmful, to him.

The expected effects of medical care, however, must be proportional to the costs and difficulties born by the patient. Some treatments are extremely expensive, dangerous, burdensome, or damaging to other parts of the body. Such extraordinary, or disproportionate, treatments do not always have to be given, and may be discontinued if they offer no proportional benefit to the patient, even if it leads to the death of the patient. Doctors and their patients, or those making decisions on their behalf, need to weigh all the factors in deciding whether to discontinue care: "Here one does not will to cause death; one's inability to impede it is merely accepted" (ccc 2278).

An example

The difference between proportional and disproportional care may be clarified with the following story. A young woman sees her rich grandmother knock her head while bathing and slip under the water in the tub. Although she only needs to lift her grandmother's head above the water to save her life, she

398

does not interfere – perhaps thinking of the inheritance. Everyone will agree that this young woman must be blamed for the death of her grandmother. The way she acted can be compared to refusing to give patients ordinary treatment. Things would be very different, however, if her grandmother had fallen overboard in a wild river filled with hungry crocodiles. The young woman might still have been thinking of her inheritance, but people would not blame her for not jumping into the river. The risk of losing her own life in the attempt to save her grandmother is disproportionate to the chances of success in this case. Similarly, it can be acceptable not to offer or to discontinue certain disproportional medical treatments.

Resuscitation

In the hospital, patients are often asked whether they want to be resuscitated, should the need arise. But is it morally acceptable to refuse a treatment that could save your life? (SEE TWEET 4.40). Resuscitation is usually not an expensive or complicated form of treatment, and therefore not disproportional in that sense. On the other hand, some elderly, injured, or sick patients can be permanently damaged by attempts at resuscitation while receiving no benefit, as in no hope of improvement, from being prevented from dying naturally. Doctors have to decide per individual case what the chances of survival and recovery of health really are so that patients or those making decisions for them can make moral choices.

Care for the dying

Caring for people who are dying (palliative care) is aimed at easing their suffering and improving their comfort. Such care is extremely important. With incurable diseases, the emphasis is not so much on curing the patient, but on relieving his pain and helping him to prepare for death. Such care should go beyond physical and medical care: attention to spiritual and psychological matters is just as important.

It is sometimes said that palliative care does not add days to life, but life to days. It is remarkable that the number of requests for euthanasia in the Netherlands, one of the first countries where it was legalized, declined substantially after the palliative care was improved. Proper, humane care can enormously improve the quality of life of patients, even if they will soon die.

> Not at any cost: disproportionally expensive or burdensome treatments are not mandatory, but ordinary care must continue until death.

Read more

Euthanasia: CCC 2276–2279, 2324; CCCC 470–471; YOUCAT 382. *Discontinuing medical treatment:* CCC 2278; CCCC 471; YOUCAT 382.

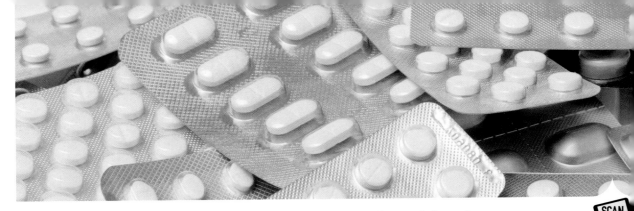

4.40 What about organ donation, blood transfusions, and heavy medication?

Medical dilemmas that touch on matters of life and death raise all sorts of questions that cannot simply be answered with a yes or a no. It is very important to think carefully about these things, about our duties toward our fellow man and the way we treat each other.

Organ donations and blood transfusions

Giving up one or more of your organs to help others, is a concrete act of Christian charity, according to Pope Benedict XVI (Nov. 7, 2008). The same applies to donating blood.

It is important to emphasize that this must be a gift: nobody should be forced to make such a donation. Human organs and blood may not be bought or sold. A donation may not lead to unacceptable risks to somebody's life; vital organs can be removed only after death. That is why it is very important to know whether somebody is really dead (SEE TWEET 4.37). In addition, you can donate your body to

medical research for the benefit of students or scientists. Such research must always respect the dignity of the human body, and human remains must be properly laid to rest. Sometimes, the tissues and organs of animals are transplanted into humans. This is called xenotransplantation. That calls for a careful approach: what effect does it have, if the heart of a pig is transplanted into a human being? But it could be a good solution, if it helps people to live. The dignity of the human person must always be respected. We must also be respectful toward the animal that is being used for our sake (SEE TWEET 4.48).

What if medicines don't prolong but shorten life

It is terrible to watch a person suffer, especially a loved one! Thankfully, there are different ways to lessen pain, such as morphine (SEE BOX). The problem is that morphine and other pain-relieving drugs can hasten death. That means we have to be

Morphine or full consciousness?

Pain relief can cause patients to lose consciousness, partially or fully. For a Christian the need to relieve pain should be balanced with the need to be conscious enough to prepare for death, which, after all, is the great moment of meeting God (SEE TWEET 1.43). That is why it is very good to try to be as alert as possible at the moment of death. That is also why we ask a priest to pray by the bedside of a seriously ill person and to administer the sacraments, if possible, while he is still conscious (SEE TWEET 3.40). Physical pain is an evil, and evil must be fought (SEE TWEET 1.34). But as Christians, we can choose to bear some pain and, thereby, to share in the suffering of Christ, especially if that means we can die while conscious. But only the dying person himself can make this choice to decrease or to stop his pain relief: nobody can make that decision for him.

May I refuse treatment?

Sometimes a certain treatment can cause a lot of pain and suffering. It is understandable that someone dreads taking medication that will make him feel absolutely terrible. People who can prolong their lives through chemotherapy or radiation, for example, sometimes refuse to be treated for that reason. It is not true that we are obliged to stay alive at any cost (SEE TWEET 4.39). But it is not right to refuse a treatment that actually has a good chance of helping just because it causes some suffering. For Christians, suffering can be a way to grow closer to God through Christ (SEE TWEET 1.37).

Some people refuse medical treatment because they think they should simply accept whatever happens to them. But created by God in his image (SEE TWEET 1.2), we were given the power of reason, and therefore, we should try to find ways to preserve our lives and our health. Therefore, we must do what we can to improve our lives, so long as we remain within reasonable, ethical, and moral boundaries.

careful. If the purpose of a medicine is pain relief, even if it shortens a person's life as an unintended side effect, it can be given to him. Providing pain relief is a form of loving attention and care for the patient (SEE TWEET 4.39). Although not all kinds of pain can be relieved, euthanasia is never an acceptable solution (SEE TWEET 4.38).

> Blood and organ donations have great merit. But to endanger your life or health unnecessarily is wrong: your body was given to you by God.

Read more

Organ donation: CCC 2296; CCCC 476; YOUCAT 391. *Pain relief:* CCC 2279; CCCC 471; YOUCAT 382.
Refusing treatment: CCC 2278; CCCC 471; YOUCAT 382.

4.41 Will you go to hell if you kill yourself?

Killing yourself, or committing suicide, is an extremely serious and desperate act. When somebody feels completely stuck in endless darkness and sees no way out, to go on living may appear pointless. Nevertheless, suicide is always wrong. We have received our life from God, and it is not up to us to decide when to end it (SEE TWEET 4.38).

No way out?

Suicide goes directly against our natural tendency to protect and to preserve our lives (CCC 2281), but somebody who ends his life is often so entangled in his problems that he can't see them in the right perspective anymore. He has forgotten that there is always hope and has lost sight of God. He can no longer listen to the inspiration from the Holy Spirit. But those are the times, precisely when life doesn't seem to be going so well, when we most need that inspiration! That's why St. Paul prayed: "May the God of hope fill you with all joy and peace in believing, so that by the power of the Holy Spirit you may abound in hope" (ROM. 15:13).

Sin

Our lives are not our own, but were given to us by God (CCC 2280). Suicide is a sin against the gratitude and the love God deserves. The life that he has created with such love should not be destroyed in a moment of desperation. That is completely opposed to the Will of God.

....

What if you sacrifice your life for another?

In 1941 the Polish priest St. Maximilian Kolbe was sent to the Auschwitz death camp. When a father of two children was condemned to death by the Nazis, Fr. Kolbe volunteered to take his place. He thereby saved the life of the father by sacrificing his own life. That is very different from killing himself: following the example of Jesus, Fr. Kolbe offered himself on behalf of another out of love. He did not die at his own hands, but was murdered by the camp guards. Fr. Kolbe was eventually declared a saint (SEE TWEET 4.17).

Burial or cremation?

It has long been a Christian tradition to bury the dead. That way, we show respect to the body that was created by God, which during our lives served as a "temple of the Holy Spirit" (I Cor. 6:19). We believe that, at the end of time, the bodies of all the dead will resurrect from the grave (see Tweet 1.50). They will then be reunited with their souls. It is not true that if you were buried instead of cremated you have a better chance of being resurrected. Everyone who dies will be resurrected. That is why the Church leaves open the option of cremation. After the cremation, the ashes must not be stored in the house or scattered someplace, but should be buried with honor or placed in a columbarium. Still, burial is the preferred option. In Scripture, people are always buried (Deut. 21:23; Jn. 11:38–39; 19:40). This signifies that the deceased are "at rest" or "asleep in the Lord", awaiting their resurrection in sacred ground.

Suicide goes against the self-love, in the right sense, that we need so as to care for the gift of life God gave us. Suicide also goes against love of neighbor because it harms the people around you and society as a whole (Lev. 19:18). Parents, family, and friends are left behind with terrible grief and regrets.

It is very clear that nobody may assist a person to commit suicide (ccc 2282; see Tweet 4.38). When somebody is depressed, he cannot make an informed and well-considered decision, particularly if he is contemplating suicide. Depression usually lasts a limited period of time, but death is permanent! We have to be extra vigilant if people around us appear depressed: we must be careful that they are and remain open to receiving help.

Do not judge

Still, we must not judge a person who kills himself, and we must not assume that he will not go to heaven. Often people who kill themselves are not fully accountable for what they are doing because they are suffering from serious psychological problems. Only God can judge the soul of a person after death. Only he knows the reasons that drove a person to this desperate act (Heb. 4:13). That means we may hope and pray that a person who commits suicide will still go to heaven.

> Suicide is a very serious sin. Those who kill themselves are often not fully accountable: we may hope & pray that they go to heaven.

Read more
Suicide: ccc 2280–2283, 2325; cccc 470; youcat 379.

4.42 Should Christians be opposed to the death penalty?

The end of life

Some crimes are so terrible that the death penalty seems to be the most just form of punishment for them. In the Old Testament, the death penalty was given for murder (Ex. 21:12), kidnapping (Ex. 21:16), adultery (Lev. 20:10), homosexual relations (Lev. 20:13), rape (Deut. 22:25), and bestiality (Ex. 22:19). Clearly these are serious matters. Still, the death penalty was not always carried out: God forgave David his adultery, for example, and he did not have to die (II Sam. 12:13).

Forgiveness as the highest norm

Jesus definitely and definitively brought us a new approach, whose foundations are love and forgiveness. The Ten Commandments remained in place, but Jesus preached love and forgiveness instead of "eye for eye, tooth for tooth" (SEE TWEET 1.19). A woman, for example, had committed adultery. The law prescribed that she be put to death by stoning. But Jesus told the bystanders, who stood ready to carry out the sentence with stones in their hands: "Let him who is without sin among you be the first

to throw a stone at her" (Jn. 8:7). It is a bitter irony that Jesus was condemned to death himself.

Punishment or self-defense?

Of course, someone who has committed a crime must be punished by society for his actions. Punishment has different purposes:

- punishing the offender justly, that is, in proportion to his crime
- defending the community and protecting people's safety
- encouraging the offender not to commit crimes again, and to improve himself.

In some cases, the death penalty can be the only way "of effectively defending human lives against the unjust aggressor" (ccc 2267). But thankfully, that is no longer the case in most Western societies (SEE BOX). There are now other ways to punish and to prevent crime. The Church insists that the death penalty be used only as a last resort, as justice can be done in other ways that better respect the gift of human life. The state has the duty and the right to administer justice and to protect its citizens. However, whenever possible it should not end a criminal's life, but put a stop to his actions. If a murderer can be safely locked up in prison, where he can't harm anyone, society can protect itself without having to kill a human being.

No way back

Another argument against the death penalty is that it is final. People make mistakes. And in spite of precautions and rules, innocent people have been mistakenly executed. These actions can never be revoked; these lives can never be restored. The death penalty is also abused, by dictators, for example, to kill their political opponents. And in some countries the death penalty falls disproportionately upon the poor. Clearly there are a lot of arguments against the death penalty.

Abolish the death penalty?

Pope St. John Paul II wanted to foster respect for the life and the dignity of each human person. That is why he, just as his successors Pope Benedict XVI and Pope Francis, urged on several occasions for an international agreement to abolish the death penalty. He argued that "the nature and extent of the punishment must be carefully evaluated and decided upon and ought not go to the extreme of executing the offender, except in cases of absolute necessity: in other words, when it would not be possible otherwise to defend society. Today, however, as a result of steady improvements in the organization of the penal system, such cases are very rare, if not practically non-existent" (EVANGELIUM VITAE, 56; CCC 2267).

Forgiveness as the highest norm

Jesus taught his followers to forgive each other again and again (MT. 18:22). Every day, we pray the Our Father: "Forgive us our trespasses as we forgive those who trespass against us" (MT. 6:12). Every criminal should have the chance to reconcile himself with God and to ask for forgiveness.

It is very difficult for the victims of a crime to be forgiving – for example, by showing understanding for the psychological problems that the culprit may suffer from or for his terrible childhood that set him on the road to violence. Yet for the victims, forgiveness is often the only way that they can continue with their lives. This is confirmed by Jesus' call to keep forgiving each other (MT 6:14–15; SEE TWEET 4.14). Forgiveness is one of the noblest norms that Christians must live by.

 The death penalty can be just, but it should be a last resort for defending society. Forgiveness is the greatest norm for Christians.

Read more

Death penalty: CCC 2266–2267; CCCC 469; YOUCAT 381.

4.43 Are you allowed to use force to defend yourself?

Society and community

God has created every person with great care and attention. Everybody carries the image of God within himself (Gen. 1:26). Our human body is not our own, it is God's (I Cor. 6:19). Therefore, the right to life is an essential right, and murder is a grave sin.

You shall not kill

The fifth commandment is often translated as "You shall not kill" (Ex. 20:13), but the Hebrew word *ratsach* literally means "murder". That difference is important. Murder, deliberately killing an innocent person, is always wrong. But killing somebody out of self-defense is not murder, even though it is terrible that a person dies. Therefore, even in emergencies, deadly force may be used only as a last resort.

Self-defense as a choice

Because life is precious, we have the right to defend ourselves against attackers: "Someone who defends his life is not guilty of murder even if he is forced to deal his aggressor a lethal blow" (ccc 2264). But the violence used must be proportional. For example, clubbing to death a thief who broke into your home but did not threaten to use violence against you would be a disproportionate response (Ex. 22:2). But if we are attacked, we can defend ourselves. Think of David who defended himself against Goliath (I Sam. 17:40–50).

Before he was arrested, Jesus ordered his disciples to buy a sword, so that they could defend themselves (Lk. 22:36). Still, Jesus did not defend himself but sacrificed his life for others, for us, and even for his attackers. He could have resisted when the soldiers came to arrest him in Gethsemane. The Apostles were certainly prepared to fight for Jesus. Peter even hacked off the ear of one of the men arresting Jesus (Jn. 18:10). But Jesus did not want there to be violence, and healed the man's ear (Lk 22: 51). Thus, he did as he had told his followers: "I say to you, Do not resist one who is evil. But if anyone strikes you on the right cheek, turn to him the other also" (Mt. 5:39). Like Jesus, we too can choose to answer violence with love and self-sacrifice.

Defending others as a duty

Although we have the right to defend our lives, we can decide to follow Jesus and sacrifice our lives to save another person (SEE TWEET 4.41). However, that decision can never be taken on someone else's behalf. Quite the contrary, every Christian has the duty to protect those who are threatened (Ps. 82:4; Prov. 24:11). That includes the duty to warn people who are in danger: if you neglect to do so, you commit a grave sin (Ez. 33:6).

The weak and those who cannot stand up for themselves have a particular right to be defended. The duty to protect others is especially strong if you are directly responsible for them. For example, a father must protect his family. But even then, he may not use more force than necessary. Sometimes, an attacker can only be stopped by killing him. That's why policemen and soldiers may carry weapons. They have a moral duty to use force to protect the community.

In certain countries citizens have the right to bear arms to be able to defend themselves. In the United States this right is even laid down in the Constitution. But it is with good reason that this right is questioned from time to time by politicians and action groups. Be aware that owning a gun or any weapon gives you a very great responsibility. Storing or using it carelessly is a grave sin. Using your weapon to kill someone who is attacking you should always be a last resort.

> You have the right to defend yourself and others, using force only when necessary. For yourself, you can choose non-violence and sacrifice.

Read more

'You shall not kill': ccc 2258–2262, 2318–2320; cccc 466; YOUCAT 378. *Murder*: ccc 2268–2269; cccc 470; YOUCAT 379. *Self-defense*: ccc 2263–2265, 2321; cccc 467; YOUCAT 380.

4.44 May Christians enlist in the army or wage wars?

When a few soldiers came to John the Baptist, asking "What shall we do?", he did not tell them to leave the army. Rather he said they should not abuse their power or extort money (Lk. 3:14). Some early Christians served nobly as soldiers, but others left or refused mulitary service. St. Paul called for peace: "Repay no one evil for evil, but take thought for what is noble in the sight of all. If possible, so far as it depends upon you, live peaceably with all" (Rom. 12:17–18).

War and peace

As you read this, wars are being waged in many parts of the world. We pray that they may swiftly be over. But is it ever justified to wage war? Are not death, destruction, and violence completely the opposite of Jesus' message of love and peace? Everyone has to cooperate to spread peace. But "as long as the danger of war remains and there is no competent and sufficiently powerful authority at the international level, governments cannot be denied the right to legitimate defense once

every means of peaceful settlement has been exhausted" (Gaudium et Spes, 79). Thus, under very strict conditions, war can be justified (see box). But can Christians take part in the fighting?

Honest soldiers

A soldier who fights for peace and justice has an honorable profession. Soldiers are "servants of the security and freedom of nations. If they carry out their duty honorably, they truly contribute to the common good of the nation and the maintenance of peace" (ccc 2310).

That praise supposes that the commanders lead in accordance with the moral law and their conscience. Nobody can excuse himself by claiming blind obedience. Every soldier should listen to his conscience before any action. Nobody can commit mass murder, for instance, without having to answer for it. Quite the contrary, every soldier given such an order has a moral duty to resist it.

Can war ever be justified?

Based on the principle of self-defense (SEE TWEET 4.43), war sometimes can be justified to avoid a greater evil and when certain important conditions are met:

- **A just cause:** there must be a real and immediate danger (for example, a country is under attack).

- **A last resort:** all other means of addressing the problem need to have been considered and tried.

- **Proportional:** there has to be a reasonable balance between the evil (of the war) caused and the result (peace).

- **Expectation of success:** there must be a serious and reasonable prospect of success.

Based on these principles, the government should take a considered decision. The moral laws are still in force during a war: "It is one thing to undertake military action for the just defense of the people, and something else again to seek the subjugation of other nations. Nor, by the same token, does the mere fact that war has unhappily begun mean that all is fair between the warring parties" (GAUDIUM ET SPES, 79).

Defense of others

A soldier is prepared to kill and to risk his own life for the sake of others (SEE TWEET 4.43). A Christian who joins the army must do so only to contribute to peace and safety. It is a sad reality that the means to achieve this, war, is barbaric and terrible. But sometimes war is the only way to protect the innocent and to secure the peace, which are very Christian purposes: "Blessed are the peacemakers, for they shall be called sons of God" (MT. 5:9; SEE BOX).

War, like other uses of force, should be used only as a last resort. Pope Benedict XVI said: "The search for peace, justice and understanding among all must be priority targets" (DEC. 14, 2006). Pope St. John Paul II told diplomats from all over the world: "No to war! War is not always inevitable. It is always a defeat for humanity" (JAN. 13, 2003). Pope Francis repeated this, and at the same time quoted Pope Paul VI: "Peace expresses itself only in peace, a peace which is not separate from the demands of justice but which is fostered by personal sacrifice, clemency, mercy and love" (SEPT. 7, 2013).

> Working toward peace and justice is very Christian. War is sometimes unavoidable, but it is always a defeat for mankind.

Read more

War and Peace: CCC 2302–2317, 2327–2330; CCCC 480–486; YOUCAT 395–399.

4.45 Is Catholic social teaching about caring for the poor?

Jesus came to "preach good news to the poor", to "proclaim release to the captives", and to restore "sight to the blind" (Lk. 4:18). He said that he himself was one with "the least" of them, the poor (Mt. 25:40). That identity is the basis for the charitable works of the Church. Christians have always taken special care for those who are poor, weak, sick, and lonely, as well as others needing help. Jesus also urges us to care for our fellow man (SEE TWEET 3.50). If we look at the world through his eyes, we can see that each person has a special dignity.

Social teaching

God himself is a social being, because he is a bond between three Persons (SEE TWEET 1.33). They do not want to keep their love for themselves; they want to share it with us. We too are asked to share our love with others. That is what the social teaching of the Church is based on, with human dignity at its core. Every person was created by God with love and deserves our love and help. With that principle, you can say a lot about wealth and poverty, economic and social conditions, and the role of the state, which Pope Benedict XVI wrote about in his encyclicals (letters) *Deus Caritas Est* (God Is Love) and *Caritas in Veritate* (Charity in Truth). These highlighted Catholic social teaching, which is as old as Jesus. Every age needs a different application of the same principles of charity. For example, in 1891, in his encyclical *Rerum Novarum*, Pope Leo XIII wrote about the housing and working conditions of laborers (SEE TWEET 2.45). They must receive a just wage, and they have a right to work and to personal property. Capitalism without justice for those who work is not Christian (SEE TWEET 4.48).

Solidarity and subsidiarity

Solidarity is an important principle of Catholic social teaching. It involves uniting your concerns with those of others. We shouldn't only share what we possess, but also make sure that others can share in the resources of the earth and participate in the dignity of work (SEE TWEET 4.48). Another important principle of

The Gospel of Life!

Pope St. John Paul II wrote that the protection of human life often receives less attention than social questions. On a global level, he found that "there is a growing moral sensitivity, more alert to acknowledging the value and dignity of every individual as a human being, without any distinction of race, nationality, religion, political opinion or social class." But at the same time, the pope saw "the continual increase and widespread justification of attacks on human life ... and refusal to accept those who are weak and needy, or elderly, or those who have just been conceived" (SEE TWEET 4.26).

His observations correspond with the social teaching of the Church. The pope saw attacks on human life as direct threats to human rights, which is a danger for democracy: "Rather than societies of 'people living together', our cities risk becoming societies of people who are rejected, marginalized, uprooted and oppressed." Thus, he said: "Should we not question the very economic models often adopted by states which, also as a result of international pressures and forms of conditioning, cause and aggravate situations of injustice and violence in which the life of whole peoples is degraded and trampled upon?" (EVANGELIUM VITAE, 18).

Catholic social teaching is subsidiarity, which Pope Pius XI discussed in his 1931 encyclical *Quadragesimo Anno*. To put it briefly, the principle of subsidiarity is that whatever people can do themselves should not be done by the government: "Just as it is gravely wrong to take from individuals what they can accomplish by their own initiative and industry and give it to the community, so also it is an injustice and at the same time a grave evil and disturbance of right order to assign to a greater and higher association what lesser and subordinate organizations can do" (NO. 79). Thus, individuals, organizations, and governments should each do only what is proper to them.

Three cornerstones

Pope St. John Paul II said that Catholic social teaching "rests on the threefold cornerstone of human dignity, solidarity and subsidiarity" (ECCLESIA IN AMERICA, 55). Everything that goes against this cornerstone must be rejected. That is why the Church opposes socialism, communism, fascism, and Nazism, as well as unlimited liberalism (or, individualism) and capitalism. Again and again, we need to emphasize the importance of human dignity and the fair division of property and opportunity.

> Brotherly love becomes concrete through the Church's social teaching. It is founded on human dignity, solidarity, and subsidiarity.

Read more

Social teaching of the Church: CCC 2419–2423; CCCC 509; YOUCAT 438.

4.46 Are gambling, drugs, alcohol, or excessive wealth sinful?

Money and power cannot make a person truly happy, but they can be used to do good; for example, by supporting charitable works and efforts to spread the gospel (SEE TWEET 4.50). Money itself is not evil, but greed is. Greed is the selfish desire to have more money than one needs, and its antidote is generosity. The words St. Paul spoke to the wealthy actually apply to everyone, rich or poor: "They are to do good, to be rich in good deeds, liberal and generous, thus laying up for themselves a good foundation for the future, so that they may take hold of the life which is life indeed" (I TIM 6:18–19).

Our true life in heaven is our only real future, the one that will last forever. With heaven in mind, earthly riches seem very relative. Other things are vastly more important. An important principle for each Christian is that "the virtue of temperance disposes us to avoid every kind of excess" (CCC 2290). Almost anything in excess is bad. That applies most of all if you endanger yourself or others with

Is it a sin to be rich?

It is not a sin to be rich. Jesus had rich friends such as Lazarus, whom he resurrected from the dead (JN. 11:38–44). Another wealthy follower of Jesus, Joseph of Arimathea, is described in the Gospels in a very positive light (MT. 27: 57–60 AND LK. 23:50). Jesus did warn against the dangers of wealth when he said that it is difficult for a rich man to enter the Kingdom of heaven (MT. 19:23). He urged his followers not to worry about money. It is not our earthly but our heavenly life that matters most: "Do not lay up for yourselves treasures on earth, where moth and rust consume and where thieves break in and steal, but lay up for yourselves treasures in heaven" (MT. 6:19–20). If you have money, you must use your wealth wisely and generously, "[f]or the love of money is the root of all evils" (I TIM. 6:10).

your behavior. Such recklessness causes you to incur grave guilt (ccc 2290).

Do I have to be against gambling?
Gambling is putting money or other things of value at stake in a game of chance. That in itself is not a sin (ccc 2413). Thank goodness, because otherwise we wouldn't even be allowed to organize a lottery to raise money for repairing the church roof! But it is very important that the player only bets something he owns and can afford to lose. The danger of gambling is in the fact that it can be so alluring: it is easy to get carried away by your passion for the game or by your greed. You can then lose the ability to make rational decisions. If somebody has become addicted to gambling, he needs help: because of his addiction, he is no longer free to make choices for himself. Even in the game, the normal moral rules apply. You are allowed to put on a poker face, but real fraud, for example by marking cards, is not allowed. Deceiving and cheating are serious matters (ccc 2413).

Is it a sin to drink alcohol?
Jesus himself drank wine (Mk. 14:23). He changed water into wine when he was at a wedding feast (Jn. 2:3–10). His enemies even falsely accused him of being a drunkard (Mat 11:19). Drinking alcohol is not a sin, but drinking too much is (Rom. 13:13), which can be very bad for your health, for the body you received from God. If you are drunk, you can no longer control yourself, which hampers your ability to do what you need to do. Even worse is endangering yourself or others while under the influence (ccc 2290). There is also the danger of becoming an alcoholic. "Enjoy your drink, but drink with moderation" is a good slogan for Catholics who choose to drink.

Is the Church against drugs?
Using drugs to obtain an altered state of mind is a grave sin, because it can seriously damage your health and endanger your life (ccc 2291). Abusing drugs makes you less aware, less able to think, and less able to respond to your surroundings. For this reason driving or operating machinery under the influence of mind-altering drugs is a crime. Abusing drugs is also selfish: instead of sharing in the lives of the people around you, you turn inward. Abusing drugs is also addictive, and in becoming an addict a person loses his freedom. It is even worse to make drugs or to sell them, because doing so helps other people to harm or to endanger themselves and others. Taking drugs prescribed by a doctor for particular therapeutic reasons is okay, but abusing or selling them is always wrong.

> Temperance is an important virtue. Gambling for fun, wealth without greed, and alcohol in moderation are not sinful. Abusing drugs is.

Read more

Gambling: ccc 2413 youcat 434. *Temperance*: ccc 2290. *Drugs*: ccc 2290–2291; cccc 474; youcat 389.

4.47 How can you use social media in the right way?

We live in an age with lots of different media, where you can find huge amounts of information about almost everything. But how do you know what is true and what isn't? (SEE TWEET 1.8). In the competition between websites, newspapers, and TV programs, it is very tempting for journalists to opt for sensationalism. That's what sells and draws visitors, readers, or viewers. You have to keep that in mind, for example, when you see news about a suspected criminal; he is innocent until proven guilty. You shouldn't condemn people just based on the news.

The right to information

You sometimes hear people say: "The public has a right to know." But the right to information is not absolute (CCC 2488). There are things that should remain a secret (SEE BOX). The same applies to your social network webpages: you cannot just post anything you know or think you know – not about yourself and not about others. In every situation, you have to consider whether it is wise or charitable

to make certain things known. Such caution has to do with love, the love of our neighbor. Everyone has the right to a private life, even famous people, politicians, and priests. Therefore, it is very important to think carefully about the way you write about someone. How will other people read and understand it? It is good to realize that keeping things a secret is impossible on the Internet, which is a public, not a private, place.

Stress? Go offline!

Social media make it very easy to make friends quickly and to stay in touch with friends and relations. At the same time, it can cause a lot of stress, because in addition to all your other work, you have to respond to messages. All those e-mails, Tweets, text messages, posts, and other communications keep calling for our attention. The stress that this can unconsciously cause can make it more difficult to make time for more important things, such as prayer, for example (SEE TWEET 3.7). How can you listen to God when you keep hearing the beeps and

Can I lie in order to save someone?

If you lie, you are breaking the commandments of God (Ex. 20:16). Lying, gossiping, and slandering: these are all ways in which you abuse the truth and can hurt others. Of course, you can make jokes and use sayings or tell stories that are not really true, as long as the person you're speaking to knows that they are examples you are using to explain something. Not telling the whole truth is not the same as lying: for example, you don't tell a person you think he's ugly because you would hurt him.

Sometimes, you must hide the truth. Think about a war, where innocent people are being killed. If you have people hiding in your house and their lives depend on your answers, in rare cases, you can make a mental reservation, that is you deliberately withhold part of the truth from someone with evil intent. The purpose must be to protect the safety of yourself or others. Priests who are confessors, and up to a certain point people with a professional duty to keep private things secret, may also exercise mental reservation. But even in these exceptional cases, one should try to avoid deliberately lying.

noises of incoming messages? How can you really take the time for him if just before praying you quickly read a few e-mails that are awaiting your reply? The same goes for your relationships with friends and relatives. It seems obvious, but it is still important to realize that you'll live if you switch off your mobile phone or computer for a while. Dare to go offline so that you can be online with God and the others whom you love!

Abuse

Social media are a fun way to stay in touch, but they can also be abused. It may seem very cool to have lots of "friends" on your social network, but it's easy to "de-friend" someone; it's also easy to pester, persecute, or bully people. Deliberately hurting others in this way is a grave sin. Everybody has the right to be respected; everybody has dignity. Jesus asks his followers to love everybody! That appeal also applies to the way we treat people on the Internet, even to the extent that Jesus asks you to "love your enemies and pray for those who persecute you" (Mt. 5:44).

> When online you're still a Christian! Don't just post or type anything. Go offline for God and others; give them your loving attention.

Read more

Right to information: CCC 2488–2489; CCCC 524; YOUCAT 457. *Media:* CCC 2493–2499, 2512; CCCC 525; YOUCAT 459.
Confessional secret and professional secret: CCC 2490–2491, 2511; CCCC 524; YOUCAT 457–458.

SCAN

4.48 What about politics, economics, and the environment?

An important duty for the faithful is to participate in public life. Our society comprises both Christians and non-Christians, who must live together peacefully. Politics is an important aspect of that challenge. Catholics working in politics ought to work toward peace and justice for all (ccc 2442). The Gospels and the teachings of the Church must always be the starting point.

If you are going to vote, it is often difficult to find candidates whose political stances fully match Catholic teaching. But voting is still important in order to have your say about the way the country is run. Your prayers and your conscience along with perspectives on the issues from your bishop or Bishops Conference can help you to make the best choices.

Economics

Politics and economics are closely tied. Just like the political system, the economic system should take everyone into account. Often that is not the case. Capitalism stimulates private ownership and free trade (the market economy). Those principles have brought great prosperity to Western societies. But they also present a danger: the poorest and the weakest can become marginalized. If politicians do not intervene, the wealthy can grow richer, while the poor grow poorer. This can also happen on a global scale: wealthy countries, with their ability to

Vatican City and the environment

In his first public Mass, Pope Francis called for defending the environment (Mar. 19, 2013). Under Pope Benedict XVI, on the roof of the large audience hall in the Vatican, solar panels were installed, which produce so much energy that the Vatican is now the greenest state on earth, producing up to 200 watts of power per inhabitant, compared to 80 watts in Germany and 4 watts in Italy. The police on St. Peter's square use electric cars, as do the tourists in the Vatican gardens. In addition, the Vatican is the only carbon-neutral state in the world, where all carbon dioxide emissions are offset by planting trees; a forest was acquired for this purpose in Hungary in 2007.

Test animals

When he created the world, God entrusted the care for animals to mankind (Gen. 2:19–20). There is a large difference between humans and animals (see Tweet 1.3). Animals do not have the same rights as humans do. We can use animals to eat and to dress, for example.

Because God entrusted animals to us for our well-being, we can also use them for scientific testing. But "it is contrary to human dignity to cause animals to suffer or die needlessly" (ccc 2418). Experiments on animals are therefore allowable only if they are the only way to contribute to the quality and the preservation of human life.

management of the available natural resources. It is therefore very important to respect God's creation. It is also important to make sure that we share the resources we have at our disposal in a fair manner. Not only must the present generation have access to the riches of the earth, but also the generations who come after us. At the same time, our concern for the environment must not stop the economic development of poor countries. These questions of human solidarity, world peace, and care for the environment are closely connected. A frugal lifestyle can help enormously to give everyone access to the natural resources of the earth (see Tweet 3.19).

Papal care for the environment

Maybe the pope is not the first person you think about when it comes to finding partners in protecting the environment (see box). But Christians are entrusted by God to care for the natural world. God has made animals, plants, and the entire creation for the well-being of mankind (ccc 2415; see box). Pope Benedict xvi emphatically said that everyone is responsible for the protection of creation (Jan. 1, 2010).

get resources, can grow richer at the expense of poorer countries. It is therefore necessary for national governments to cooperate with each other in such a way that everyone benefits from the goods of the earth. In one of his encyclicals, Pope Benedict xvi called for politics and economics to be guided by Christian charity (see Tweet 2.3).

Stewardship

Man was ordained by God to be the steward, or caretaker, of nature (Gen. 1:28; see box). We are responsible for a proper and sustainable

> Politics & economics need the gospel: sharing resources and protecting the environment are only possible with true charity.

Read more

Politics: ccc 2442; cccc 519; youcat 440. *Capitalism and the market economy:* ccc 2426, 2459; cccc 511; youcat 442. *Globalization:* youcat 446. *Care for the environment:* ccc 2407–2418, 2450–2457; cccc 506–508; youcat 436–437.

4.49 What is the New Evangelization?

Just before his Ascension into heaven, Jesus told his disciples: "Go into all the world and preach the gospel to the whole creation" (Mk. 16:15). This task still applies to all the followers of Jesus – that is, to all Christians. Our faith in the love of God is the most important thing that we have received. Therefore our faith is the first thing we should share with others.

Passionate testimony

Jesus said of his own mission: "I came to cast fire upon the earth; and would that it were already kindled!" (Lk. 12:49). His first followers found that they simply had to speak about Jesus; they couldn't help it (I Cor. 9:16). A prophet of God had already said: "If I say, 'I will not mention him, or speak any more in his name,' there is in my heart as it were a burning fire shut up in my bones, and I am weary with holding it in, and I cannot" (Jer. 20:9). People of all ages have had this experience. They had to speak of the enormous love of God for all people. Since its beginnings, the

Church has sent people to spread the gospel, the Word of God, everywhere in the world. These missionaries do not work alone: they work together with the Holy Spirit. Missionaries are needed today; you are one of them (see Tweet 4.50).

Reevangelization

In 1983, Pope John Paul II called for the New Evangelization. He wanted the gospel to be spread "new in ardor, new in methods and new in expressions" (Mar. 9, 1983). He explained that the New Evangelization is aimed at people who have never heard of Jesus before, but also at the large number of baptized people who no longer live their faith (Redemptoris Missio, 33). Some no longer consider themselves members of the Church. In this way, they lead their lives far from Christ and his message of salvation (see Tweet 1.27).

The pope emphasized that in this new situation, which he found in many places, a New Evangelization, or reevangelization is desperately needed. Pope Benedict XVI also

New Evangelization

At the beginning of this millennium Pope John Paul II wrote:

"To nourish ourselves with the word in order to be 'servants of the word' in the work of evangelization: this is surely a priority for the Church at the dawn of the new millennium.

"Even in countries evangelized many centuries ago, the reality of a 'Christian society' which, amid all the frailties which have always marked human life, measured itself explicitly on Gospel values, is now gone. Today we must courageously face a situation which is becoming increasingly diversified and demanding, in the context of 'globalization' and of the consequent new and uncertain mingling of peoples and cultures.

"Over the years, I have often repeated the summons to the New Evangelization. I do so again now, especially in order to insist that we must rekindle in ourselves the impetus of the beginnings and allow ourselves to be filled with the ardor of the apostolic preaching which followed Pentecost. We must revive in ourselves the burning conviction of Paul, who cried out: 'Woe to me if I do not preach the gospel!' (1 Cor 9:16).

"This passion ... must involve the responsibility of all the members of the People of God. Those who have come into genuine contact with Christ cannot keep him for themselves, they must proclaim him."

(Novo Milennio Inneunte, 40)

....

frequently called for the New Evangelization. Pope Francis spoke about the gentle manner in which we need to undertake this task: "The New Evangelization, while it calls us to have the courage to swim against the tide and to be converted from idols to the true God, cannot but use a language of mercy which is expressed in gestures and attitudes even before words" (Address, Oct. 14, 2013).

All aboard!

In principle, every Christian is called to the New Evangelization (see Tweet 3.50). All baptized Christians have been tasked by Jesus to spread the gospel to all who will hear (Mk. 16:15). It is up to all of us to make sure that the message we have received from him is spread (see Tweet 4.50). Jesus also tells you: "Go therefore and make disciples of all nations, baptizing them in the name of the Father and of the Son and of the Holy Spirit, teaching them to observe all that I have commanded you; and behold, I am with you always, to the close of the age" (Mt. 28:19–20).

> The New Evangelization seeks to spread the faith to all who are far from Christ, in particular to the baptized who no longer believe.

Read more

Evangelization: ccc 425–429; cccc 80.

4.50 How can I help to spread the gospel?

The gospel of Jesus is so important – everyone should have the chance to hear it! To make that happen requires all the faithful. Experience is not mandatory, and you do not have to be a perfect Christian to spread the gospel. Your enthusiasm and love of Jesus are all it takes. Are you in?

You can do it!

If you have faith in Jesus, then he also calls you to help spread the gospel of God's love. With good reason St. Peter said: "In your hearts reverence Christ as Lord. Always be prepared to make a defense to anyone who calls you to account for the hope that is in you, yet do it with gentleness and reverence; and keep your conscience clear" (I Pt. 3:15–16). That last thing is a crucially important addition. Every person has great worth in the eyes of God, who created us. Nobody can be forced to believe in God's love: it is always a free choice. We must always try to treat people gently and with respect. We can testify and spread the Word, but we cannot change a

person's heart. Only the Holy Spirit of God can do that. But what we can do is give testimony and speak of our bond with Jesus and the Church. The most important thing we do for another person is to give him an example of a personal relationship with Jesus.

Go, do not be afraid, and serve

With this in mind, you too can help with the New Evangelization! (SEE TWEET 4.49). Go and talk to people. Speak to them about your faith, about your experience of Christ. And pray for them. You will not only grow in your own faith, but increasingly discover how logical our faith actually is. There are no valid arguments against the Catholic faith, because it only brings one crucial message, the truth that Jesus came to give us: "God so loved the world that he gave his only-begotten Son, that whoever believes in him should not perish but have eternal life" (Jn. 3:16). As Pope Francis said: "Go, do not be afraid, and serve. If you follow these three ideas, you will experience that the one who evangelizes is evangelized, the one who

How can I contribute to the proclamation of the gospel?

- For starters, you will have to work on **your own relationship with Jesus**. You do this primarily through prayer, in which you make time for Jesus (SEE TWEET 3.1). Prayer is the first way of evangelization. Jesus wants to give you the strength to grow in your faith and your ability to speak about him. He does this in a very special way through the sacraments (SEE TWEET 3.35). You received the Holy Spirit through Baptism and Confirmation. Jesus will forgive you again and again in Reconciliation, and you can receive his love through the Eucharist.

- Secondly, of course you do have to **know what you are talking about**. Keep learning about your faith, about Jesus and his Church, about prayer and life as a Christian. Check out the "read more" entries in this book, the app, and the website. But, most of all, try to read the Bible frequently, and pray with it. That is the Word that he wants to speak to you at this very moment (SEE TWEET 1.10). In this way you can learn about the meaning of your faith and recognize how logical it is and how much sense it makes.

- Thirdly, dare to **speak from the heart**. Dare to speak of your experiences with Jesus. Don't say: "Christians believe that …", but say instead: "With all my heart, I believe that God loves you." You can put it in your own words. People pay more attention to how you say something than to the exact words you use. Show how much you care about Jesus! Do not be afraid: Jesus has promised the help of the Holy Spirit to all those who honestly want to speak of him (MK. 13:11).

transmits the joy of faith receives more joy.... Jesus Christ is counting on you! The Church is counting on you! The pope is counting on you! May Mary, mother of Jesus and our mother, always accompany you with her tenderness: 'Go and make disciples of all nations'" (MT. 28:19) (HOMILY, JULY 28, 2013).

> You can evangelize by growing in your love of Jesus, by praying, by learning more about him, and by speaking of him from your heart.

Read more

Evangelization: CCC 425–429; CCCC 80.

Appendix 1: The Books of the Bible

Old Testament

Gen.	Genesis	Song.	Song of Solomon
Ex.	Exodus	Wis.	Wisdom
Lev.	Leviticus	Sir.	Sirach
Num.	Numbers	Isa.	Isaiah
Deut.	Deuteronomy	Jer.	Jeremiah
Josh.	Joshua	Lam.	Lamentations
Judg.	Judges	Bar.	Baruch
Ruth	Ruth	Ez.	Ezekiel
I Sam.	1 Samuel	Dan.	Daniel
II Sam.	2 Samuel	Hos.	Hosea
I Kgs.	1 Kings	Joel	Joel
II Kgs.	2 Kings	Am.	Amos
I Chr.	1 Chronicles	Ob.	Obadiah
II Chr.	2 Chronicles	Jon.	Jonah
Ezra	Ezra	Mic.	Micah
Neh.	Nehemiah	Nah.	Nahum
Tob.	Tobit	Hab.	Habakkuk
Jdt.	Judith	Zeph.	Zephaniah
Esth.	Esther	Hag.	Haggai
Job	Job	Zech.	Zechariah
Ps.	Psalms	Mal.	Malachi
Prov.	Proverbs	I Mc.	1 Maccabees
Eccl.	Ecclesiastes	II Mc.	2 Maccabees

New Testament

Mt.	Matthew	I Tim.	1 Timothy
Mk.	Mark	II Tim.	2 Timothy
Lk.	Luke	Ti.	Titus
Jn.	John	Phlm.	Philemon
Acts	Acts of the Apostles	Heb.	Hebrews
Rom.	Romans	Jas.	James
I Cor.	1 Corinthians	I Pt.	1 Peter
II Cor.	2 Corinthians	II Pt.	2 Peter
Gal.	Galatians	I Jn.	1 John
Eph.	Ephesians	II Jn.	2 John
Phil.	Philippians	III Jn.	3 John
Col.	Colossians	Jude	Jude
I Thes.	1 Thessalonians	Rev.	Revelation (Apocalypse)
II Thes.	2 Thessalonians		

Appendix 2: Ecclesiastical titles

A pope is, of course, not addressed by his first name but with "Holy Father". If you write a letter to the pope, the salutation is not "Dear Francis", but "Most Holy Father" or "Your Holiness". On the envelope you write "His Holiness Pope Francis". In addition, below you will find the main terms of address, with introduction and address titles for envelopes, with *N.N.* where you enter the name of the person. If you are familiar with a priest, you can of course also write "Dear Fr *N.N.*", but it's good to know that he is actually a "Reverend".

	Title	Addressing	Salutation	Address on the envelope
Clergy	Pope	Holy Father	Most Holy Father (UK: Your Holiness)	His Holiness Pope *N.N.*
	Cardinal	Your Eminence	Your Eminence (My Lord Cardinal)	His Eminence *(FIRST NAME)* Cardinal *N.N.*
	Patriarch	Your Beatitude	Your Beatitude	His Beatitude Patriarch *N.N.*
	Nuncio	Your Excellency	Your Excellency (UK: Your Grace)	The Most Reverend *N.N.*
	Archbishop	Your Excellency	Your Excellency (UK: Your Grace)	The Most Reverend *N.N.*
	Bishop	Your Excellency	Your Excellency (UK: My Lord)	The Most Reverend *N.N.* (UK: The Right Reverend *N.N.*)
	Protonotario Apostolic	Monsignor	Dear Monsignor	The Right Reverend Mgr *N.N.*
	Prelate of Honour	Monsignor	Dear Monsignor	The Reverend Mgr *N.N.*
	Chaplain to His Holiness	Monsignor	Dear Monsignor	The Reverend Mgr *N.N.*
Functions	Vicar General, Dean, Episcopal/Judicial	Father	Dear Reverend Father	The Very Reverend *N.N.*
	Vicar	Father	Dear Reverend Father	The Reverend *N.N.*
	Priest	Father	Dear Reverend Father	The Reverend *N.N.*
	Deacon	Deacon (Reverend)	Dear Deacon *N.N.*	The Reverend Mr *N.N.*
	Seminarian	*OWN NAME*	Dear Mr *N.N.*	Mr *N.N.*
Religious	Abbot	Father Abbot	Right Reverend Father	The Right Reverend *N.N.*
	Prior	Father Prior	Dear Reverend Father	The Very Reverend *N.N.*
	Religious (male)	Father	Dear Reverend Father	The Reverend *N.N.*
	Abbess / Superior	Mother	Reverend Mother	The Very Reverend Mother *N.N.*
	Brother	Brother	Dear Brother	Brother *N.N.*
	Sister	Sister	Dear Sister	Sister *N.N.*

Name (duration pontificate)

1 **St Peter** (33–64/67)
2 **St Linus** (68–79)
3 **St Anacletus** (80–92)
4 **St Clement I** (92–99)
5 **St Evaristus** (96/99–108)
6 **St Alexander I** (108/109–116/119)
7 **St Sixtus I** (117/119–126/128)
8 **St Telesphorus I** (127/128–138)
9 **St Hyginus I** (138–142/149)
10 **St Pius I** (142/146–157/161)
11 **St Anicetus** (150/157–153/168)
12 **St Soter** (162/168–170/177)
13 **St Eleuterus** (171/177–185/193)
14 **St Victor I** (186/189–197/201)
15 **St Zephyrinus** (198–217/218)
16 **St Callixtus I** (218–222)
17 **St Urban I** (222–230)
18 **St Pontian** (230–235)
19 **St Anterus** (235–236)
20 **St Fabian** (236–250)
21 **St Cornelius** (251–253)
22 **St Lucius I** (253–254)
23 **St Stephen I** (254–257)
24 **St Sixtus II** (257–258)
25 **St Dionysius** (259–268)
26 **St Felix I** (269–274)
27 **St Eutychian** (275–283)
28 **St Caius** (283–296)
29 **St Marcellinus** (296–304)
30 **St Marcellus I** (306–309)
31 **St Eusebius** (309–309)
32 **St Miltiades** (311–314)
33 **St Sylvester I** (314–335)
34 **St Mark** (336–336)
35 **St Julius I** (337–352)
36 **Liberius** (352–366)
37 **St Damasus I** (366–384)
38 **St Siricius** (384–399)
39 **St Anastasius I** (399–401)
40 **St Innocent I** (401–417)

41 **St Zosimus** (417–418)
42 **St Boniface I** (418–422)
43 **St Celestine I** (422–432)
44 **St Sixtus III** (432–440)
45 **St Leo I the Great** (440–461)
46 **St Hilarius** (461–468)
47 **St Simplicius** (468–483)
48 **St Felix III (II)** (483–492)
49 **St Gelasius I** (492–496)
50 **Anastasius II** (496–498)
51 **St Symmachus** (498–514)
52 **St Hormisdas** (514–523)
53 **St John I** (523–526)
54 **St Felix IV (III)** (526–530)
55 **Boniface II** (530–532)
56 **John II** (532, 533–535)
57 **St Agapetus I** (535–536)
58 **St Silverius** (536–537)
59 **Vigilius** (537–555)
60 **Pelagius I** (556–561)
61 **John III** (561–574)
62 **Benedict I** (575–579)
63 **Pelagius II** (579–590)
64 **St Gregory I the Great** (590–604)
65 **Sabinian** (604–606)
66 **Boniface III** (607–607)
67 **St Boniface IV** (608–615)
68 **St Deusdedit** (615–618)
69 **Boniface V** (619–625)
70 **Honorius I** (625–638)
71 **Severinus** (638, 640–640)
72 **John IV** (640–642)
73 **Theodore I** (642–649)
74 **St Martin I** (649–655)
75 **St Eugene I** (654–657)
76 **St Vitalian** (657–672)
77 **Adeodatus II** (672–676)
78 **Donus** (676–678)
79 **St Agatho** (678–681)
80 **St Leo II** (681, 682–683)
81 **St Benedict II** (684–685)

82 **John V** (685–686)
83 **Conon** (686–687)
84 **St Sergius I** (687–701)
85 **John VI** (701–705)
86 **John VII** (705–707)
87 **Sisinnius** (708–708)
88 **Constantine** (708–715)
89 **St Gregory II** (715–731)
90 **St Gregory III** (731–741)
91 **St Zachary** (741–752)
92 **Stephen II (III)** (752–757)
93 **St Paul I** (757–767)
94 **Stephen III (IV)** (768–772)
95 **Adrian I** (772–795)
96 **St Leo III** (795–816)
97 **Stephen IV (V)** (816–817)
98 **St Paschal I** (817–824)
99 **Eugene II** (824–827)
100 **Valentine** (827–827)
101 **Gregory IV** (827, 828–844)
102 **Sergius II** (844–847)
103 **St Leo IV** (847–855)
104 **Benedict III** (855–858)
105 **St Nicholas I the Great** (858–867)
106 **Adrian II** (867–872)
107 **John VIII** (872–882)
108 **Marinus I** (882–884)
109 **St Adrian III** (884–885)
110 **Stephen V (VI)** (885–891)
111 **Formosus** (891–896)
112 **Boniface VI** (896–896)
113 **Stephen VI (VII)** (896–897)
114 **Romanus** (897–897)
115 **Theodore II** (897–897/898)
116 **John IX** (879/898–900)
117 **Benedict IV** (900–903)
118 **Leo V** (903–903)
119 **Sergius III** (904–911)
120 **Anastasius III** (911–913)

(See Tweet 2.46 for the most recent popes)

Appendix 4: Praying with a text from the Bible

According to the method of St. Ignatius of Loyola (SEE TWEET 4.5).

1) Preparing to pray

- Decide which text you will use (SEE TWEET 3.4) and how long you will pray.
- Choose a place and a body posture – sitting, standing, or kneeling – and read the text.
- Focus on a few passages and imagine what is happening. What do you see and what do you hear? How would you show that in a film? Use your other senses too: What do you feel, smell, or taste?
- Ask for the grace (SEE TWEET 4.12) you desire to receive from God at that particular moment.

2) Beginning to pray

- Start your prayer by making the Sign of the Cross. Tell God: "Lord, I am here; I seek you."
- Thank God for the gift of your life and offer it back as your gift to him. Say that you want to listen to him and to be changed by him.
- This opening of your prayer may be the same every day, using your own words or an existing prayer.

3) Listening to God

- Now pray with the text you have chosen. Receive with joy what happens in your prayer, as a gift from God, knowing that you cannot really determine what happens to you during prayer.
- Meditate on the passages that move you. Try to understand what they mean for your life.
- You are not the one talking at this point. Try to be quiet with God. This is the longest part of your prayer.

4) Speaking with God

- While before you tried to listen, now it is your chance to talk. You can talk to Jesus about anything, as if you're talking to a friend. Sometimes you can ask for mercy, sometimes you can accuse yourself of something you did wrong, sometimes you entrust him with your problems and ask for his help.
- Finish with a vocal prayer, such as the Our Father, followed by the Sign of the Cross.
- Be loyal and stick to the time you had reserved for prayer, even if it's hard. After all, you seek God for who he is and not for what he can give you.

5) Looking back

- Take a few minutes to look back on your prayer and to write down, if possible, any possible conclusions you can draw from what you experienced during your prayer. By making a prayer diary, or journal, you can learn to recognize the thread of your life with God. Ask yourself about two things:
  a) *That which depends on you*: the form of your prayer. Did the place where you chose to pray and your chosen body posture help you to pray? Were you fully dedicated to your prayers? How did you deal with distractions and dry periods? How long did you pray?
  b) *That which happened during your prayer*: What were your feelings? Did you experience joy or sadness after reading passages from the Bible? Did a thought or an image come to you? Do not be afraid to listen to your feelings, reactions, and desires, because it is precisely through your deepest longings that God's Will for your life is manifested.

Appendix 5: Reflecting on your day through prayer

1) Remind yourself that you are in the presence of God

- Wherever you are, you were created by God, who is with you and knows you. Ask the Holy Spirit for help to look at your own life and all that surrounds you with love.

2) Be grateful for what you were given today

- Try to remember one or more special moments of the day. Maybe the smell of your first cup of coffee, the smile you received in return for a friendly word, something you learned, etc. Thank God for his good gifts.
- Reflect on the gifts and talents that helped you today. Remember where you found the strength and the hope when things got difficult. Thank God for your sound mind, your health, your family and your friends. You can thank him for the fact that, despite your shortcomings, you were given another day to live. God gave all of this to you, and you may thank him for it.

3) Ask for help from the Holy Spirit

- The Holy Spirit helps you to grow spiritually, by reflecting on your own life with growing freedom, without condemnation or rejection.
- Ask the Holy Spirit for the ability to learn from what happened as you reflect on the day. Ask him to help you to grow in your self-knowledge and in your relationship with God.

4) Reflect on the day

- This is the longest part of your prayer. Try to remember what happened during the day. Reflect on what you did, and how you did it. Recognize the moments you felt torn between helping and ignoring, between hoping and doubting, speaking and remaining silent, blaming and forgiving. This is not about punishing yourself for what went wrong, but about thinking about how you dealt with what God gave you.
- Recognize what helped you to be free and more of the human being God created you to be. Try to see at what point Jesus played a part in your decisions and where you may have pushed him away for a moment.
- The purpose is to continuously improve your ability to understand what is going on inside you, and how the Spirit of God is pointing you in the right direction. See how God is speaking to you during the day, and how Jesus, with the Holy Spirit, is always with you to help you and give you strength.

5) Speak to Jesus heart-to-heart

- By this time, you have seen what happened during the day. Now you can talk to Jesus about what you did or failed to do, your feelings and your attitude. Sometimes, you will ask for forgiveness for what you did wrong, sometimes you will want to ask for help and strength, and sometimes you will thank him.
- After going through the day with God, think about yourself with charity, just like as does, and recognize how much you need his love and help. You may also recognize where God showed you the way, a correct course of action, and realize how much you need his guidance.
- You can finish with a vocal prayer – the Our Father, for example.

Index

The author would like to thank
E. Peters for her enthusiastic and ongoing commitment to the project *Tweeting with GOD*, the members of the #TwGOD team, as well as S. van Aarle, K. Beenakker, R. Blesgraaf, Rev. Mgr. Duarte da Cunha, J. van Halem, Rev. Fr. H.W.M. ten Have, S. Huig, S. Jansen, B. Lexmond, R. Mozes, E. Oudshoorn, M. Pots, A.M. Rijsdijk, Rev. Fr. J.H. Smith, E. Severijnen, J.W. and P.A.M. Severijnen-Van Buuren, J. Stuurman, L. Tax, P. Tax-Lexmond, N. Versteeg, B. Voskuil, H. and M. van Zutven-Van Kampen. The youth of the JP2 Group, in particular Alexandra, Anne, Annemieke, Annemarij, Anne-Marijn, Ashley, Barbara, Bart, Bas, Bastiaan, Ben, David, Eline, Eveline, Gerard, Jamie, Lidwine, Liesbeth, Linda, Lodewijk, Maartje, Margreet, Marijke, Merel, Miranda, Myrna, Patrick, Pauline and Rowy. Thanks to His Eminence W.J. Cardinal Eijk, H.E. Abp. A. Dupuy, the Rt. Rev. J.H.J. van den Hende, the Rt. Rev. G. De Korte and the Rev. Mgr. Duarte da Cunha, for their support, and to Rev. Fr. L.J.M. Hendriks, Lecturer in moral theology at Rolduc Major Seminary, Rev. Fr. M. Lindeijer S.J., Doctor of Church history, Rev. Fr. A. Pinsent, Research Director at the Ian Ramsey Centre for Science and Religion of the University of Oxford, Rev. Fr. H.M.H. Quaedvlieg, Lecturer in dogmatic theology at Rolduc Major Seminary, the Rt. Rev. H.W. Woorts, episcopal vicar for liturgy, for reviewing the manuscript. Many thanks to J. Price for his great help in translating the text into English, and to Rev. Fr. N. Brett for all his corrections.